WORK – QUO VADIS?

Work – Quo Vadis?

Re-thinking the Question of Work

Edited by
JAN HOLMER
JAN CH. KARLSSON

Routledge
Taylor & Francis Group
LONDON AND NEW YORK

First published 1997 by Ashgate Publishing

Reissued 2018 by Routledge
2 Park Square, Milton Park, Abingdon, Oxon, OX14 4RN
52 Vanderbilt Avenue, New York, NY 10017

Routledge is an imprint of the Taylor & Francis Group, an informa business

A Library of Congress record exists under LC control number: 97061060

ISBN 13: 978-1-138-37048-7 (hbk)
ISBN 13: 978-0-429-42798-5 (ebk)

Contents

Foreword

In 1996 an international symposium on working life in the future, entitled 'Work – Quo Vadis?', was held in Karlstad, Sweden. This was the third symposium on work arranged by the University of Karlstad in collaboration with Göteborg University. The first, 'Work in 1984 – Emancipation or Derogation' took place in 1984 and the second 'Work and Welfare' six years later.

The aim of this third Karlstad symposium was to bring together and reflect current empirical trends and theoretical discussions on the questions: What exactly is happening to work and, as a consequence; What should happen to work?

A number of leading scientists were invited to take part in the symposium to present their answers to these questions. Their contributions provided a fruitful and interesting illustration of what is happening to work in the time of transition that we currently seem to be passing through. The purpose of this book is to disseminate these contributions by seventeen scientists from eleven countries to a wider circle than those who took part in the symposium.

We are convinced that the book will prove stimulating to postgraduates, researchers, policy-makers and others, and thereby encourage further research on work as well as actions to improve conditions both at work and on the labour market.

We would especially like to thank Madelene Fryklind and Lena Hansson for making this book possible by dealing with all the practical and administrative details. Further, we want to thank Ingrid Lindqvist for all her efforts in the extensive task of transcribing the text. Finally, special thanks to Michael Cooper who translated some parts and scrutinised all parts of the book.

Last, but not least, we also would like to thank the Swedish Council for Work Life Research for their financial contribution to the symposium.

Karlstad, April 1997

Jan Holmer and Jan Ch. Karlsson

Acknowledgements

The original English version of Louise Waldén's chapter has previously appeared in the book *Swedish Folk Art: All Traditions is Change*, published in 1994 by Harry N. Abrams Inc., New York.

Johanna Esseveld's chapter is a revised version of an article that was originally published in *The Sociological Review* 1989.

The OECD Jobs Study: Evidence and Explanations, Part I and II, 1994, is reproduced in Adrian Sinfield's chapter by permission of the OECD.

We are grateful for permission to include them in this book.

1 Introduction

Jan Holmer and Jan Ch. Karlsson

A questionnaire survey at comparable workplaces in Spain and Sweden (Grinups et al., 1996) included a question which listed a number of tendencies in society. The respondents were asked to indicate the tendency that concerned them most. Crime/lawlessness and unemployment proved to be the most worrying tendencies.

Worry about unemployment may be seen as a reflection of what in recent years has become one of the most debated issues at all levels in society: What is happening to work?

Today, unemployment in Europe is at an alarming double-figure percentage. And unemployment has brought with it economic and social problems, diminishing welfare, social divisions, a lack of standards, drug addiction, xenophobia and an increase in crime.

However, it is worth remembering that the population of the industrialised world is only a small proportion of the total population – about 1.2 of 5.5 billion people; the United Nations (1996) estimates that, in the year 2000, it will be 1.2 of 6.1 billion. The remainder, i.e. the great majority, live in the developing countries. And even here growing unemployment is one of many serious social problems. One billion people, or about 30% of the world population of working age, are unemployed or underemployed.

So what is really happening to work – and what should be done about it? In this introductory chapter we shall attempt to suggest some answers to these questions with the help of the conclusions which the other authors in the book have reached. Thereafter, we shall provide a short description of each of the authors' texts. But first we shall consider a number of important concepts and points of departure.

Concepts and points of departure

The question: What is work? has been posed in hundreds of articles and books during the last century – and the answers have been very diverse. We cannot discuss this in any great detail but can only propose a definition and indicate the reasoning behind it (the arguments are based on Karlsson, 1983 and 1995). The definition we propose is: Work is activities performed within the social relations which structure the sphere of necessity.

The advantages of this definition of work, as we see it, include the following. Firstly, it is delimiting, i.e. it distinguishes a relatively specific category of phenomena as work, something which many other suggested definitions, in fact, fail to do. Here it is a matter of what people must do in order to survive. Secondly, this sphere is delimited more specifically through its social relations. This means that an activity which is work during a given historical period or in connection with a specific social category, may be non-work during another period or in connection with another social category; it all depends on the social relations. There has been an intense critique of the (mostly implicit, but dominant) definition, 'work is wage labour', and this critique has been extremely important. All too often, however, it has been followed by the addition of a number of activities per se to wage labour, for instance 'domestic activities'. Thereby the critique has missed the crucial theoretical point in the formulation, the fact that it indicates a specific *work form,* a specific internal social relation: that between capitalists and wage labourers; neither of them would be what they are without the relationship between them. Instead of adding a number of activities to wage work, our definition makes it possible to delimit *other such relations,* as well, thus developing a terminology that covers a whole set of work forms – i.e. internal social relations structuring the sphere of necessity. We may include among them (different forms of) household work, which is also structured by patriarchal relations. This is a step on the way to remedying the deficiencies of work research and taking women's unpaid work into account – a shortcoming that several of the authors (for example, Allen, Björnberg and Kollind, and Esseveld) have clearly indicated.

Thirdly, the delimitation is made 'objectively', i.e. independently of what the agents define as work or the ways in which they experience an activity. If we did not apply such a principle, we would exclude whole 'subjective' fields from being researched. When, for example, an agent's experience of an activity as arduous is made part of the definition of work, as is often the case, it is impossible to investigate whether different kinds of work are experienced as arduous.

The formulation also has greater potential for clarifying the relationship between what is commonly called formal and informal work. There are two forms of work that are unequivocally classified as formal work: wage labour and self-employment – and the knowledge we have of them is extensive. In contrast, informal work appears to be an extremely heterogeneous phenomenon, whose work forms are not so well conceptualised, and knowledge about which is less systematic. This also means that the relation between formal and informal work is insufficiently understood. One of the authors (Pahl) also points to the romanticisation that informal work is often exposed to. To modify this picture, he argues that informal work is not always an alternative to formal; the individual who has a strong position in the latter also tends to have a strong position in the former. Further, he mentions the Mafia economy as an example that informal work is not always built on trust; in this case, it is rather a question of fear. Another author (Valiente) emphasises the fact that there is strong gender and age segregation in the informal economy.

Underpinning the arguments in the book we also find a certain scepticism of much of the rhetoric in the ongoing debate on the development of working life: what, for instance, are the real consequences of technical innovations (Schmutzer)? This also includes what may be termed 'hype' (Sayer), which may mean that a limited phenomenon is presented as a generally applicable standard for a completely new form of working life. Another form of hype is the failure to maintain the distinction between prescriptive, predictive and descriptive statements.

A good many rhetorical arguments are deservedly criticised in the book, among them the idea of the death of Taylorism, and the post-Fordian society (Sayer), the thesis that unemployment benefits contribute to greater unemployment (Sinfield), the related standpoint that a work ethic has been replaced by a culture of dependency (Halvorsen) and the idea that greater flexibility in working life leads to greater democracy (Appay). Let us also mention two major surveys in Sweden (Edling and Sandberg, 1993; Karlsson, 1997) which have empirically raised major question marks against the common thesis that nowadays all work organisations are flexible, with new management principles, and that the 'new' workplaces offer better conditions for all employees.

What is happening to work?

The culmination of wage labour

To judge from the authors' contributions, the twentieth century would seem to be a transition phase in the history of work. The employments and occupations of our time, which were established in the nineteenth century, are proving to be less and less appropriate for the situation today. Wage labour, therefore, would seem to have reached a culmination. This work form, which has had a predominant position in the national economy, has become less important and with it, permanent full-time work, the man providing for his family, regular employment, and the usual employer/employee relations.

The decrease in wage labour is partially connected with the technological revolution. Technical progress increases production but reduces the number of employees, i.e. greater productivity coincides with reduced human work. This seems to be true of the production of both goods and services. Work will, then, be a diminishing component in production if this trend continues. As a highly hypothetical, but nevertheless thought-provoking example, Toulmin suggests that, in fifty years, all the cars in the world will be made at a handful of production plants, each of which will be run by half a dozen skilled workers.

More temporary employment and greater social insecurity

The economic restructuring process on the labour market would appear to result in greater social insecurity. Greater flexibility does not seem to lead so much to economic recovery and democracy as to insecurity on the labour market (Appay). In many countries there is a proportional increase in the labour force working in small and medium-sized companies. These companies, who are sub-contractors, are adaptable, which means they can also disappear rapidly. This leads to insecure jobs. The situation may be visualised in metaphorical terms, as Appay suggests, as a combination of the web and the pyramid. But it is often only the top part that is visible, that between the supplier and the first level of sub-contractors. By externalising work in this way, companies reduce both their responsibility and economic risk-taking.

The proportion of full-time permanent employees is diminishing. The time of full employment, in the sense of male work and essentially relating to the manufacturing industry, with more or less the same job all one's life, is past (Pahl). The temporary employment of the labour force is on the increase, as is unemployment.

At the same time, the ideology of full employment still prevails. It is, according to the doctrine, a matter of getting people to work (workfare) so that they do not come to rely on income support (welfare). This means that those who are working are worried about losing their jobs, whilst those who are not working are worried both about not getting a job and about losing their benefits. The workless tend to be viewed as worthless (Sinfield) and the emphasis on workfare at the expense of welfare leads to an increase in the anxious class (Sayer).

Increased polarisation

The general tendency seems to be that the labour force is becoming increasing divided with the result that part of the adult population of working age is unemployed or economically inactive and that a large proportion of those who are working are in a marginalised position (uncertain employment conditions and part-time work).

The winds of change are blowing over both private and public employees. As a result, the skilled and well-educated may well come to constitute a fortunate core and elite among employees, with more qualified work. This core, including both management and other employees, will have access to a learning organisation and skills improvement. But outside the fortunate core, the periphery of wage-earners and salaried staff in a marginalised position would seem to be increasing. Workers on the periphery tend to have worse working conditions: less responsibility and influence, combined with less security of employment (Sayer).

As regards work in the public sector, we may in fact use the term neo-Taylorism. Here the opportunity for certain groups to make use of their knowledge is diminishing through pressure of time and because quantity goes before quality in the choice of what is possible to sell at a good price and of which services should be offered (Sayer).

Thus, there is a growing polarisation both in jobs (at workplaces) and on the labour market. Further, there is a growing polarisation in households where both adults are working and in those where neither are working (Pahl). Finally, there is a polarised labour market for men and women; they are in different structures in the labour market (Allen, Valiente). We can discern a trend leading to a separation into male and female work spheres. In this polarisation lies the fact that the secure and better paid jobs are dominated by male workers, who are in an ethnic majority.

Gender differences

What distinguishes the sexes when it comes to work is, among other things, that women's work has often been unpaid, has been carried out in the home and has not been included in the statistics. As Allen points out, work has, for instance, long been defined in such a way that unpaid work and women's work have not been treated as work.

The paid work which women perform is, for the majority of them, something they do in addition to what is expected of them as unpaid domestic workers. Women's wage labour has thus led to a double burden of work, irrespective of income and professional status. Women's desire for flexible working hours and part-time work reflects their own needs less than those of the family and/or employer (Allen). They are to be found more frequently, therefore, among those employed part-time, in the worse paid jobs, and with a generally weaker position on the labour market than men. The security of employment to be found in the best companies is not infrequently matched by insecure work and poor security of employment in other companies, particularly for women (Valiente, Esseveld). To summarise, there is a division of labour according to gender which is generally accepted and which starts early, even in school.

What should happen to work?

At the same time as unemployment is increasing, we can also establish that there is a generally high degree of willingness to work and that work, like the ideology of full employment, has a predominant value in western society (Halvorsen). People, quite simply, want to have something meaningful to do – and people want to live in security.

So what should happen to work? The statements below are intended to give some idea of the proposals for renewal and new thinking put forward by the authors as a result of the tendencies they have detected.

Behind the proposals there lies a common denominator: Everybody should have the right to meaningful employment. By ensuring that people who cannot get a job on the traditional labour market are engaged in a meaningful way in socially productive undertakings, we do not only do them a service but we also make a contribution to the common good (Toulmin).

Combination of work forms

Sayer asks whether, given the increasing level of temporary employment, it is sensible to allow incomes to be based to such an overwhelming extent on wage labour, as is the case today. He suggests the possibility of a new system for the distribution of income, a combination of work forms (wage labour, domestic work, self-employment etc.) and a radically altered taxation system. This might, for instance, include economic activity with a social function, the so-called 'social economy' or 'the third sector', which has been developed, above all, in the Latin countries.

Pahl outlines how a person's way of life could be adapted to make it possible to combine work forms. This is reminiscent of the patterns of work which were described for a flexible labour force during the early days of industrialism. It would be possible, for instance, to allow people who had performed wage labour for perhaps fifteen years – say between somewhat over twenty and into the forties – to take things easier in smaller communities while maintaining the same quality of life. The course of one's life would then follow a geographical pattern, and work would be valued in other terms than money. With few wage-labourers but many working, it would be possible to return work to life.

Combination of benefits and work forms

Many people find it difficult to achieve a good balance between various forms of work. It would seem that those who most need balance in their lives are those who have the least chance of achieving it. What is needed is a wider view of what benefits are beneficial for.

According to Sinfield, we should distinguish between different labour market states and not just between employment and unemployment. It is not valid to see benefits as a hindrance to those seeking employment; that benefits deter people from seeking work or being in work. It is wrong to speak of a benefits system as a passive programme and labour market schemes as active programmes. Much of what is included in the benefits can in fact activate people whilst bad benefits can lead to longer unemployment, and to a diminished capacity to cope with the situation. With such a high rate of unemployment as we have today, it would be better to speak of the positive and negative aspects of various programmes. We should ask ourselves which combination of benefits, employment, education and other things would be best for reducing and preventing unemployment and its injurious effects on the individual/family and society.

The right to benefits or the right to an income and the duty to work?

Unemployment should be seen as a typical feature of the society in which we live and not as a typical feature of the people who become victims of it. It should be self-evident that a society should pay those who are forced to bear the burden of what for others means success. Benefits must be seen as a right and as part of an implicit social contract, says Sinfield.

Adler-Karlsson goes a step further and puts forward the following suggestion as a provisional utopia: the European Union should introduce a basic income for all European citizens. This basic income should be low and, in general, only cover the basic necessities. To earn the right to a basic income, each citizen should have the legal obligation to work for the state for a short period in their life. After that, they should have the right to live in freedom for a considerably longer period. Everyone can then, for instance, seek employment in the private market to earn more, if they are not satisfied with their basic income. This would mean that there is a legal obligation to work for perhaps five years and that everyone would have their fundamental material needs guaranteed by the state through a basic income.

Change through education

One of the areas in which a change could be brought about is education. Some of the authors see in the post-modern market society an opportunity for the liberation of the individual – perhaps from the chains of wage labour to the condition of free agent. This would mean that, as a member of society, the individual would be continually forced to make choices since the old ties would no longer exist. Against this background, Illeris maintains that the general qualifications which the individual needs to succeed relate to personal development, to development into a whole individual. It will, therefore, become increasingly difficult, he says, to distinguish between a vocational and a non-vocational orientation in education and in everyday life. But the prospects of being able to take advantage of these opportunities for development and education vary from person to person. Individuals who, for various reasons, are excluded from decision-making and planning processes have limited scope for action and this, in its turn, has negative consequences for learning and seeking knowledge. And this is a problem which cannot be solved unless we make changes within the institutions and structures that establish and maintain the positions of individuals.

Women and men are affected differently by processes of change since economic and political power structures are influenced by gender (as well as by class and ethnicity) (Allen, Esseveld, Sundin etc.). The majority of part-time jobs and fixed-contract employments are characterised by low education and few opportunities for skills improvement or a career. Gender and ethnicity are linked to these conditions. Lynch speaks, therefore, of the need to upgrade the value of alternative forms of knowledge, of conditions which provide equal access to education and of the elimination of hierarchies.

According to Waldén, we must dismantle the value system which sets theoretical knowledge before practical proficiency, and male interests before female, and which does not give full recognition to all types of intelligence.

But to achieve changes of this nature, it is not sufficient for the state merely to influence education. Laws, the media, taxes, etc. must also be altered. However, those who have superior resources in these areas may well oppose any moves in this direction. It is only through organised and democratic action based on participation-oriented democracy that we can bring about change, says Lynch.

The contents of the volume

The book has three sections. In the first, work is placed in relation to social development and welfare. The second considers work, family and gender; and the third, finally, focuses on work, technology and organisation.

Stephen Toulmin begins the first section. He sees the twentieth century as a transitional phase in the history of work. Given that employments in our time have proved to be less and less adapted to the present-day situation, he asks what new directions are available for work, occupations and employments. The chapter contains a short presentation of work in the context of the history of ideas. This is followed by a section on the guidelines that should be used to evaluate different occupations. He then provides arguments for evaluating the contribution of various occupations to the good of society and concludes with some thoughts on welfare and the common good.

What are the factors that influence the decision of unemployed people to take a certain job on a certain occasion? *Adrian Sinfield* believes that one major factor might be the way in which advice, help and support is given. Seeing the benefits system as a hindrance to those seeking work is far too limited. Further, we should distinguish between several different labour market states and not just between work and unemployment. Instead of talking about active and passive programmes, we should ask ourselves what mixture of benefits, employment, education and other things would be best for reducing and preventing unemployment and its injurious effects.

Ray Pahl begins by discussing the development of wage labour, which, among other things, has meant that men – and eventually women as well – have become so used to their chains that it is difficult for them when they lose their jobs. With the demand for a higher income and a higher standard of living, it has become increasingly difficult for many people to achieve a good balance between all forms of work (wage labour, domestic work and self-employment). But there are, says Pahl, ways of living today which successfully combine various forms of work. In conclusion, he outlines the content of possible ways of living, where work could be valued in other terms than money. With few wage-labourers, but many workers, we could return work to life.

Andrew Sayer begins with a quotation from the U.S. Secretary of Labor, who says that most people will become members of what he terms the anxious class. The focus in Sayer's chapter is on the increased externalisation of work, so-called vertical disintegration, in the organisation of industry services as well as in manufacturing, which means that certain processes are performed by separate companies rather than within one integrated company. This change, like others in working life which Sayer considers, seems to entail an increase in the temporary employment of the work force (fixed-contract employments, part-time work and freelancing), a process that is taking place at the same time as welfare is diminishing. It is out of these conditions that the anxious class arises. Is it reasonable then to allow people's incomes to be based to such an extent on wage labour?

Since the 1980s, there has been an 8-12% rate of unemployment in large parts of Europe, writes *Gunnar Adler-Karlsson*. Half of it would appear to be necessary in order to make the system function in a stable and non-inflationary manner. On top of this we have the unemployment which has to do to with short-term problems and with, for instance, the rapid technical progress which makes it possible to buy cheap and competent labour from outside. Whilst the debate concerns the latter, Adler-Karlsson wishes to draw attention to the former type of unemployment. He proposes a 'provisional Utopia' which, in summary, would mean that there is a legal obligation to work for perhaps five years and that everyone would have their fundamental material needs guaranteed by the state through a basic income.

Knut Halvorsen concludes the first section with a presentation of his research on the work ethic and employment commitment. There has been fairly widespread talk of a decline in the work ethic and the emergence of a culture of dependency. However, surveys of Norway, a Scandinavian welfare state, show that commitment to wage labour is generally high. It is as high among the young as among the old, among men as among women, but it is somewhat higher among those employed than those unemployed. And, above all, it seems to be linked to work experience. It would appear, therefore, that a low commitment among those outside the labour force may change if they obtain meaningful jobs. All categories, on the whole, show a very high commitment to work.

In the first chapter of the second section on work, family and gender, *Sheila Allen* writes that established theories and methods in the field of working life have contributed to hide the fact that work is structured according to gender. The theory and methodology which does not take gender into account is incomplete. Analysis requires us not to neglect the social division in the form of class and race, for instance, and gender. Shortcomings in research concerning gender reflect the marginalisation and lack of recognition of women's work in society. Work has long been defined, for instance, in such a way that unpaid work and women's work have not been treated as work. The paid work that women perform is for the majority of them something they do in addition to what is expected of them as unpaid domestic labourers.

Ulla Björnberg and Anna-Karin Kollind present a theoretical approach to a study whose main issue is: What is the importance of family relations for young people today? They assume that families differ considerably in their views of what is right and wrong, moral and immoral, when they negotiate about time, money and care. Further, they ask whether different professions and workplaces in the labour market influence the way families think and act. Gender relations are undergoing change. Women are becoming more independent and increasingly integrated with market-economic ways of thinking. The question is what implications this will have for the way in which women reason about the division of time, money and informal work within the family.

Celia Valiente discusses the Spanish labour market and the fact that women enter a segmented labour market where they are underrepresented at the core, but overrepresented on the periphery. Unemployment is considerably higher among women than among men. Women are underrepresented in sectors where there are better working conditions and overrepresented in fixed-contract employments and in the informal economy. Public services are scarce, which prevents many women from entering the labour market. Valiente demonstrates that the subordinate position of women has hardly changed but that younger well-educated women today have an opportunity to compete with men of the same age as long as they act like men, i.e. do not have and do not take responsibility for care etc.

In her article *Johanna Esseveld* studies the patterns of employment and unemployment in Sweden, particularly those for women and immigrants. She shows that the traditional conceptualisations of employment and unemployment are insufficient for capturing the changes that are taking place. Thus, for instance, many women are increasingly finding themselves in temporary employment (employment for a trial period, substituting for others, hourly employment, youth placements, seasonal work, project employment, government-created work schemes and relief work). These developments can also be seen in other Western societies but the pattern differs as a result of differences in welfare-state policies. Through its labour-market policies, Sweden has developed a special Swedish form of temporary employment.

Liberal policies for equal opportunity have dominated public policy in, for instance, the European Union, particularly in the field of education. It is true that these policies have resulted in social mobility, but they have not affected the fundamental patterns. In her article, *Kathleen Lynch* locates liberalism within an equality studies framework, where she distinguishes various goals for our endeavours to achieve equality, from equal formal rights and opportunities, and equality of access, to equality of condition. One of the aims of the liberal tradition is to ensure that disadvantaged groups have, on average, the same rights, the same access, the same participation and even the same success as other groups. But it does not eliminate the hierarchies which exist in the form of knowledge, power and privilege. To achieve this, Lynch shows, the forces of democracy must permeate not only school but also laws, the labour market, etc.

On weekday evenings throughout the year in Sweden many people leave their home to spend three hours in a group of five to ten people with the object of learning something. They are participating in study circles organised by the adult educational organisations. Study circles are a phenomenon of which most Swedes have personal experience. The study circle culture is a finely meshed net that covers the whole country. *Louise Waldén* gives three examples of study circles devoted to handicraft. The participants were all women, they had families and worked full-time. In these circles the flow of information was transmitted from modern society to everyday knowledge and practical use.

The final section of the book, 'Work, technology, organisation', begins with a chapter by *Manfred Schmutzer*. His text is intended to serve two purposes: to bridge the deplorable gap between engineering and the social sciences, and to contribute to the development of methods for assessing and evaluating technology. To achieve these objectives, he examines the links between culture, language and technology. He concludes that the engineer needs theoretically based knowledge which enables him to understand the social consequences of a technical invention. But it is a complicated issue. The same technology has different consequences depending on the organisational context, and organisational cultures differ in the importance of the role they play for the development and acceptance of technology.

Elisabeth Sundin's article begins with a discussion of the connection between technology, organisation and democracy and then provides examples from her own research and that of others. According to the model she develops in the article, technology, organisation and economy exert mutual influence. She limits herself, in the main, to the link between technology and organisation and, in short, finds that the tendencies are contradictory. To judge from her case studies, it would seem that technology leads to organisational changes. But the differences in the results cannot be explained in technical terms, the causes must be sought in the structure of the organisation. The contradictory tendencies relate very particularly to the impact of the so-called new technology, writes Sundin in conclusion.

Economic growth is good for workers according to the World Bank. It maintains that problems such as lack of work, low wages, poor working conditions and general insecurity can be solved by means of greater flexibility and mobility on the labour market. But *Béatrice Appay* shows that economic restructuring processes on the French labour market contradict this belief. When contemporary analyses focus on deconcentration, they underline autonomy and local responsibility, the formation of networks, cooperation and partnership, a new role for the small-scale and for a more democratic world. However, they then ignore one of the main tendencies, namely that the same development entails greater social insecurity, reduced welfare and a hyper-competition which is maintained and justified by national and international policy.

During the last twenty years, the predominant feature of adult education has been the ever-increasing importance that has been attached to the significance of general qualifications. But it has not been made clear what is meant by general qualifications, nor how they are developed through education or what, in that case, they demand of the teachers. In the final chapter, *Knud Illeris* investigates these conditions. A feature of the post-modern market society which is evolving at present is that the individual is continually forced to make choices since the old ties no longer exist. General qualifications are therefore very much a matter of personal development and the development of the whole individual. It will, therefore, be more difficult to distinguish between vocational and non-vocational education.

Conclusion

One conclusion that can be drawn from the contents of the book is that, at least as concerns the countries with which the authors deal, it is a matter of restructuring not only working life but the whole of society. In other words, the unemployment figures reveal a serious social crisis. When such a large proportion of the potential work force lacks meaningful employment/a proper job, what is required is a vision not only of a different type of working life but of an alternative society.

At all events, it would seem that we are in a transitional phase on our way towards a change that is so great that jobs in the future must be sought in new solutions.

On the one hand, we can see, as Toulmin puts it, a transition from material production, hired workers and quantifiable jobs to the brave new world's employments where activities are carried out which provide self-respect for those who are no longer hired. On the other hand, we can see, also in line with Toulmin, all those who, for various reasons, will not be the fortunate free agents but insecure and disillusioned people hungering for jobs, and who will also exist unless new institutions and collective initiatives contribute to a change.

References

Edling, C. and Sandberg, Å (1993), 'Är Taylor död och pyramiderna rivna? Nya former för företagsledning och arbetsorganisation', in le Grand, C. et al. (eds), *Sveriges arbetsplatser – organisation, personalutveckling, styrning*, Stockholm: SNS.

Grinups, B., Holmer, J. and Lundberg, B. (1996), *Report from the Barcelona–Karlstad Study*. Karlstad: University of Karlstad.

Karlsson, J.C. (1983), *Begreppet arbete*, Lund: Arkiv.

Karlsson, J.C.(1994), 'The Concept of Work on a Rack – Critique and Suggestions', in Richard L. Simpson and Ida Harper Simpson (eds), *Research in the Sociology of Work: A Research Annual. Vol. 5: The Meaning of Work*. Greenwich, Conn.: JAI Press.

Karlsson, J.C. (1997), 'Flexibilitet i praktiken', in Sandberg, Å. (ed), *Ledning för alla? Om perspektivbrytningar i företagsledning*. Stockholm: SNS.

United Nations (1996), *Human Development Report*, New York: Oxford University Press.

PART I.
WORK, SOCIETY AND WELFARE

2 From feudal serfs to free agents: The future of 'employment'

Stephen Toulmin

The late 20th century is proving to be a transitional phase in the history of Work. Patterns of employment and occupation established in the 19th century, following the Industrial Revolution, have in our time proved less and less adapted to our situation; and the persistence, even in the most successful industrial countries, of unemployment – or 'joblessness' – is now raising serious questions about the future of work relations. In consequence (this paper argues) we must get clear about the new directions available in the arenas of *work*, *occupation* and *employment*. The customary relations between these three ideas are ceasing to be appropriate to social and economic life in what many people call the 'post-industrial' age. If we are to discuss policies for the next century in realistic terms, accordingly, those relations have to be rethought.

The paper is in four parts. It begins with a thumbnail history of the ideas of Work and Jobs. Next, it criticizes our ways of assessing the Value of occupations. Thirdly, it argues that we need to see all occupations as generating not just a *market price* but a *social product*; and, finally, it reconsiders some of the fundamental terms involved in the debate about Work Relations – e.g., 'welfare' (nowadays a sadly corrupted word!) and 'the common good'.

The word *job* has a curious history: well caught in the noun, *jobbery*, defined in the *Oxford English Dictionary* as 'the practice of corruptly turning a position of public trust to private gain or advantage'. Early on in Tolstoy's novel *Anna Karenina*, Anna's civil servant brother, Stiva Oblonsky, is caught in an affair with the children's nursemaid, and he dreams of obtaining additional sinecures ('jobs') that might increase his income enough to cover the cost of maintaining a mistress without – he thinks – shortchanging his family. Stiva's hoped-for sinecures are what, a hundred years ago, were known as *jobs*: positions of trust capable of being corrupted for private advantage.

Our own use of the word *job* for 'paid employment' – being someone's hired hand – is, by contrast, recent and temporary. It came into use as a result of industrialization, and it threatens to become obsolete as we move into the 'post-industrial age'. Those people who have lived in industrial countries in the last 20 years are all too well aware of one phenomenon, in particular, that has puzzled the politicians. After each periodic slowdown in the economy, production has recovered more rapidly than employment, and this has been seen as calling for prodigies of 'job creation'.

Why does this phenomenon always surprise the politicians? Ever since the rise of manufacturing industry in the early 19th century, we have pursued two incompatible goals, and our efforts on the one front frustrate those on the other. On the one hand, we strive to increase production. So long as levels of technical skill remain constant, this means hiring more hands, which is *good* for employment. On the other hand, we also strive to make production processes more efficient, and so reduce the amount of human toil required to make any unit of product. Unless the demand for those products is infinitely elastic, that is necessarily *bad* for employment: with better technology, less hands are required to produce all the saleable output. The problem of employment thus ceases to be quantitative, reflecting qualitative changes in human activity.

I say 'human toil' to remind you of one central point. As a skilled craftsman, who lived by his commitment and ingenuity, William Blake understood what burdens early 19th century factories placed on those who worked in them. Being religious, he saw those burdens as un-Godly, and denounced these Factories as 'dark, Satanic Mills'. And another writer whose moral subtlety we can safely admire since the collapse of the Soviet Union – Karl Marx – foresaw a future in which the daily hours of demeaning toil would be cut down as time went on, leaving people free to spend the afternoon fishing, playing music, or in other more rewarding activities.

The facts are worth recalling because, for a dozen years or more, we have tended to see the periodic campaigns to increase industrial efficiency as responses to competition: the ideas in Marx's early manuscripts that inspired much social thought in the 1960s are obscured by narrow arguments of economic advantage. Of course, we cannot totally ignore issues of economic advantage, but let us not deceive ourselves that 19th century factory work was 'fun' – let alone 'self-realization'.

I visited a steel rolling mill at Gary, Indiana, in the 1970s. An older, dirtier plant, with more than fifty workers, had been replaced by a newer and cleaner plant run by seven or eight more highly skilled workers. Clearly, the technicians who ran the new mill relished not just the technical merits of the new plant, but the emancipation it made possible from heavy dirty toil. So, in talking about job creation, we must keep in mind not just the *number*, but also the *quality* of the jobs involved. The human need to make factory work less demeaning is as urgent as the need to make it competitive.

Before the rise of Factories, people's work took different forms. Country workers were Servants of a Master, who accepted responsibility for them, so long as they lived on his estate, or in his village. City workers, too, learned their trades *with* – not *for* – a Master craftsman, and followed the career from Apprentice, through Journeyman, to Master in their own right. Lastly, there was a smaller group called 'Masterless Men' who were highly productive, yet open to suspicion, as operating outside the accepted system of social relations. (The most notorious examples of Masterless Men were the charcoal burners and printers. Charcoal burners lived in forests away from Authority: printers were more literate than their customers, and so difficult to censor or control.) Yet all three groups of people had a feeling for their own work: none were radically alienated, as were their successors under the early Factory system.

The relations between landowners and their labourers (it is true) sometimes became contentious: peasant uprisings were familiar, and conditions of agricultural work were in continual renegotiation. Yet, for those people who were content to live where they were born and go on working where they lived, there was no structural unemployment: their housing and feeding was the responsibility of their local lord. Those who found the life of a village oppressive had other options: they could 'go to the Greenwood' along with Robin Hood and the charcoal burners, or they could sign up for a Crusade. (Recall the remarkable film that was made on the basis of Natalie Zemon Davies' book, *The Return of Martin Guerre*.)

In the City, the Guild system – of master, journeyman, and apprentice – embodied real expectations of self-advancement, and self-realization. This is something that we academics should understand, since we are heirs of that system. Guild craftsmen did not have 'tenure' as universities know it; but they could normally continue working at a lower grade, until they were ready to launch onto the higher one. Notice: I am not romanticizing the conditions of life in medieval Europe. I am only reminding you of the reasons why the problem of the Underclass – euphemistically covered today by the phrase 'job creation' – did not arise then as acutely it does for us today.

Let us remind ourselves of the long term processes that define our present situation. The great social change associated with the move to Modernity (using the term *modern* as historians do, for the period from the early 17th century on) was the change from a society in which people's occupations were a matter of Status – the key questions being 'Who is your Master?' and 'What is your Trade?' – to one in which workers were free to move from place to place, and from trade to trade, and ceased to have any permanent or lifelong Status.

Initially, work was rationalized in the *primary* industries, through which Matter is produced and transported – mining, logging, farming and fishing. Later, the emphasis shifted to *secondary* industries that transformed Matter and Energy – factories and mills – creating new commodities, or old commodities in novel forms. As the efficacy of the machines increased, the degree of craftsmanship needed to operate them lessened, and with it the satisfaction of the work itself diminished. This change was gradual. Until the 19th century, traditional work relations were unchanged. Even in late 18th century France, when Diderot and d'Alembert's *Encyclopedia* was printed in Switzerland and smuggled into France, the animus against 'Masterless' printers was still evident.

Radical changes came only with the renewed shift of population from Country to City, as farm work was mechanized in the first half of our century. As late as 1900, even in advanced countries like Britain and Germany, more than half of the work force relied for their occupation on primary activities – mainly farming. In the fields of Work and Employment, indeed, the most striking social change in the 20th century has been the progressive drop in the agricultural fraction of the work force, from more than 50% down to 5% or less.

For a while, secondary industry expanded fast enough to take on the workers who flooded from the country into the cities. Aside from fluctuations like the Depression of the 1930s, the demand for the products of secondary industry expanded fast enough to sustain that expansion. In the process, people fell into the habit of thinking of labour as one more *commodity* – one more 'factor of production' like raw materials. As a result, they concealed from themselves the *social meaning* of Work. One distinctive mark of the late 20th century is, thus, the way in which the rationalization of secondary industry has followed that of agriculture, and the demand for *labour* has fallen, as the efficiency of secondary industry increased. That, of course, is where we came in.

A colleague in the Netherlands with a computer consultancy presses his arguments to extremes. It is possible (he argues) that, by 2045, all the automobiles that the World needs will be built in a handful of plants – in (say) Indonesia, Senegal and/or Brazil – each of them run by half a dozen skilled workers. My colleague prefers to say, '*All* the cars the World needs will be built in *one* plant, run by *one* worker', which is powerful rhetorically, even if historically implausible – you see his point. Even now, at the back of their mind, some people *blame* those people who lack the skills to succeed in today's 'market' for labour. Yet, as secondary industries approach the final stage of technical development, at which the labour factor becomes a vanishing small element in the costs of production – my colleague argues – all of us will join the ranks of the 'structurally' unemployable. And, once the shoe pinches middle class feet, problems that now affect only *Them* will be seen as problems for *Us*, too.

We are not there yet; but we are well on the way. Recall the lags between renewed production after recessions, and the recovery of employment. Let us ask, 'In this state of affairs, what are our options? And how do they bear on current attitudes?' Many of these issues were debated 30 years ago, in discussing *automation*. One option was *job sharing:* dividing the available Work by hiring more people, but for less than full time. Some academics even tried out the idea: married couples signed on for one-and-a-bit teaching loads, and shared one salary. But soon, two income families were the norm. If Samuel Butler had planned a sequel to *Erewhon*, he might dream of a country where 'gross national product' divided by 'gross national labor force' decided the paid hours of work per day any worker was entitled to. In such a country, people never took more than a fair share of this work: having a Paid Job would be, not a *duty*, but a *privilege*. Marx's half-day work load would become the Law of the Land.

These fantasies about *possible futures* are not policy proposals: rather, they focus on the issues we evade, about those who are 'structurally' unemployed. As time goes on, 'job creation' lags behind our hopes: When this happens, it is implausible to claim that people who find no full time jobs fail because they are underserving or ill trained. In Germany, the standard work week at Volkswagen is now less than 29 hours; but in America the trades unions defend the interests of fully employed against those of the fully *unemployed*. The structurally jobless have no trades union.

Conversely, to state the central point of my paper, doing what is required by the current change to ensure that those to whom existing industries can give no full-time employment are *occupied* – not left at a loose end, or dismissed as worthless – is not just *doing them a favour*. On the contrary, it is to everyone's Good, and in everyone's Interest, that they should have *rewarding occupations*.

Love and Work (said Freud) are the poles around which a fruitful Life turns. But the underlying thought is much older: 'Satan finds evil work for idle hands to do', as the traditional saying went. Either way, a Life without any worthwhile occupation is material for a Tragedy.

So much for the first part of this argument: A nutshell history of *jobs* begins with Work as *status* based; this is followed by the eclipse of status by employment, and by a 'commodification' of labour; and it is ending by a return to the concept of *Occupation, not Employment*, as the key element in any account of Work. But the present argument will stand securely on its own feet, only if we deal convincingly with two other issues:

> By what measures should different Occupations be *valued*?; and How do Occupations contribute to the *shared interests* of the Community?

How, then, are we to value different *occupations*? In particular, are occupations of value only 'in the market' – only if each worker competes for the chance of a job, and is paid a monetary 'wage' by the employer? Faced with this unvarnished question, we may reply, 'Of course not!' It seems unreasonable to measure the entire value of Work only by the monetary price it fetches in a market. Yet, digging a little further, we shall find that much in present day political debate takes this 'market' measure for granted. That is one of the unexamined presuppositions in the current debate.

Instead of 'unexamined' we might say 'too little' examined. In the last few years, policy analysts have at last begun to ask if the measures for comparing economic *value* are not misleading. Does any transaction generate value only if money changes hands? Not long ago, the Organization for Economic Cooperation and Development published a report indicating why the standard indicators need to be rethought. Suppose that I am driving my car and hit a lamp post, so that the car is a total wreck. I make work for the tow truck and my insurance company, and I may even buy a new car to replace the one that was wrecked in the crash. All these things involve cash payments, and contribute to the 'gross domestic product' – so adding to the country's prosperity. By contrast, if I drive home with care and keep my car in good shape, I shall deprive the G.D.P. of the value I would have contributed by crashing. *Does this make sense*?

Worse (as Arlene Daniels shows) all the work a wife or a couple puts into family or home is unpaid: it makes no statistical difference to the G.D.P. whether such *in-family* work is creative and productive, or slovenly and demoralized. Our systems of national accounting do not cover it, so *it doesn't count*; or, to speak precisely, *it isn't counted*. (Not counted, in part, because not *taxed*. From the start, as the Babylonian cuneiform tablets show, writing and accounting developed in part to keep track of State revenues.)

Once we recognize that these figures are miscounted, however, it follows that the statisticians have collected the wrong figures, and our comparisons lack a sound basis. Yet, for generations, we have inherited 'time series' grounded on these indices, and the calculations of economists still take them on trust. People who trust economics may be unhappy, but what else can they do? Like a man who drops a coin in the street, and searches for it close to the street lamp, because that is the only place he can *see* clearly, they rely on misleading calculations, rather than no calculations at all. Yet – one asks – *at what social cost*? I will return to that question later.

In short, our ways of thinking how people spend their time and earn a living bear the stamp of the Industrial Age, whose glory and misery alike spanned the years from (say) 1815 to 1960 – prophesied by William Blake, analyzed by the young Karl Marx, chronicled by Thomas Mayhew, and made into literature by Charles Dickens. A crucial theme in this period was *Employment*: becoming another's hired hand, and so a unit in the 'labor market' – what Marx called, derogatorily, a *wage slave*. Since then, a central concern of political debate has been the employment statistics: the fraction of workers who sell their labor for Jobs (or fail to do so) in the national Hiring Hall. Looking at the social economy in these terms, we foresee that the productive capacity of the developed countries in both primary and secondary sectors will continue to give such employment to a smaller and smaller fraction of the available work force. As my Dutch colleague insists, once both Farming and Manufacture near their terminal stage of development, labour will become a sharply diminishing component in production, and we shall all end up on the brink of being 'structurally' unemployed.

How, then, can we think of the *occupations* of the future, as sources of livelihood? What kinds of activities will people get paid for? And what kinds of relations will they have to the people who pay them? In answering these questions, we can take either of two directions. One of these retains the traditional idea of *employment*, in this sense: the other seeks to move beyond it, and explore alternative patterns of work relations

Within the existing terms of debate – about *employment* – one alternative remains: employment in so-called 'service' industries. Yet there is a widespread view that such jobs are not proper sources of self-respect. As the usual story goes, a skilled worker, laid off from the steel mill after thirty years of work, sees no prospect of employment, apart from driving a cab or serving in a fast food restaurant: this destroys the essential experience of Work as he knows it, and damages his dignity. Yet this, clearly, is only part of the story. Recently, communication, computing and information handling have created new alternatives to farming and manufacturing; and we have reason to expect that novel Technology, now as earlier, will create as many job openings as it destroys. The 'occupations' in which our grandchildren will spend lives, and earn livelihoods, include some we can barely imagine: to imagine them is already half way to inventing them. Still, those who succeed in knowledge industries are those with technical skills: for the rest of the work force – or so it seems at first glance – all that remains are such unproductive activities as serving at McDonalds.

If we are to reformulate the debate in more constructive terms, we have to move beyond the limits of the existing debate. Let me focus here on two issues: ambiguities in the term *production*, and the nature of *self-employment*. As a journalist, Karl Marx did not relish the squalor and sweat of the 19th century factory: for him, emancipating the proletariat meant liberating workers from sweat and squalor. Yet, for a century, the self-image of factory workers in the industrialized countries generated a perverse pride in the *disagreeableness* of such work. 'Where there's Muck, there's Brass!', they said: i.e. 'Dirt makes Money'. Factory workers stopped *wanting* to be liberated: they might complain about excessive Overtime, but the spectacle of material productivity still gave them feelings of special virtue.

Indeed, we still tend to see *productive* jobs, handling or transforming materials for a solid wage, in primary or secondary industry, as having not just a price in the market but a unique *social* value. This is one deeper source of the problem of 'job creation'. If we view 'finding a job' *exclusively* as hiring out your labour for material production, we lay up trouble, as opportunities for employment in such industries diminish, and we exclude ourselves from the whole field of *social* investment, which creates rewarding occupations for people who have little prospect of industrial employment.

Ironically, this prejudice for *material* production helped to undermine the U.S.S.R. Overvaluing the labor of Stakhanovites – workers who overfulfilled production quotas – Russians lost sight of the need for other occupations. Factory workers (they thought) give the products of labour not only Value, but Virtue; so Soviet bureaucrats despised Distribution as a haunt of ignoble Middlemen who took indefensible cuts of the Values created by the toil of noble factory workers. (This resentment of middlemen still infects Russian attitudes toward entrepreneurs.) Ironically, again, this attitude was foreign to Karl Marx himself. Marx would have pitied, not admired, those robust dimwits who earned honor and glory by overproducing unsaleable goods: he looked forward rather to a 'withering away of the State' that would emancipate workers from the degradation of demeaning labor.

Replace the idea of *productive employment* by that of *worthwhile occupation*, and a range of new options comes into view: not just the twin (Lo Tech and Hi Tech) poles – fast food and computer programming – but the entire spectrum of 'post industrial' occupations. Life has, in fact, already gone further along the road mapped in this paper than theory suggests. A recent issue of *Le Monde*, e.g., included a significant report. The French government was embarrassed, because many unemployed workers, having lost their jobs, banded together to set up new businesses, and applied for government grants. Fifteen years ago, this was unthinkable. In 1980, Raymond Barre suggested that laid-off workers start businesses on their own account, but he was laughed out of court. Now, the 'jobless' are creating a third of all such businesses – 75,000 in 1994 alone; and this is more than the government is prepared to support.

The crucial idea, here, is that of 'Self-Employment'. The term *self-employed* was invented by revenue authorities to tax professional physicians, artists, and others who earn income without being 'employees'. Yet, in this familiar phrase, lies a paradox. If I am *self employed*, what is the 'self' that employs *me*? Does my left hand employ my right? Does my Brain hire my Body? This is not just a question of words: basic social issues underlie it. People who are self employed work *on their own initiatives*: they choose for themselves what lines of work to pursue. If the issue is 'job creation', (that is) independent contractors *create their own jobs*.

Do not misunderstand this point. This is not *praise* independent contractors above other workers, or ignore the fact that few lines of independent work are rich enough to provide an adequate return. Still less is it to deplore the fact that many still depend for a living on being 'employees'. The point is quite different: that the current rhetoric of 'job creation' distracts attention from other possibilities. It is not that we are reaching the End of Work. But we are seeing the end of the 'employer-employee' relationship that has been used to define Work ever since the Industrial Revolution.

If the young Marx was right, we should be happy about this change. When people work for themselves, the products of their labour are not diverted to the advantage of others: those products are not 'alienated' in the economic sense. So policy makers might well redirect their attention: instead of going against the whole historical trend, seeking only to multiply jobs in the Hiring Hall, they may do better to focus on ways of making *socially productive* kinds of 'self employment' rewarding, in monetary as well as psychological terms.

Back in L.A., I have an illustration of this point on my doorstep. Let me quote a remark made to a recent conference by Juanita Tate, a leader in the local organization, *Concerned Citizens of South Central L.A.* Too few people recognize (she said) that the neighborhood would be less livable, more of a slum, but for the Homeless who go around pushing shopping baskets, collecting beverage cans, bottles and other refuse, and carrying them off for recycling. Let me confirm this. For the first few months my wife and I lived on campus, we tried, without success, to persuade the University authorities to join with the students in a thorough recycling program. The only thing it was 'economic' to recycle (they told us) was *white paper*. Needless to say, they also prefered not to have unkempt figures wandering the campus with stolen shopping carts, and made sporadic attempts to clear them out. But their attempts (I am happy to report) were half hearted, and the informal recycling programme went on. We learned our lesson: we periodically leave wine cartons full of empty bottles at the curb across the street, and the Homeless, in turn, continue with their self appointed work.

Here we see how *market price* and *social product* diverge. The things that make it more or less obnoxious to live in a world of loose refuse have little to do with the resale potential of different kinds of refuse. The resale differentials are in any case arbitrary. The low price paid for irrigation water by farmers in the Central Valley of California artificially tempts them to grow water-hungry crops in a near-desert: equally, the low deposits paid on bottles and cans distract institutions like USC from serious recycling. (In Ontario, Canada, such deposits are nearer 50 cents than 5.) In social terms, that is, the work of the Homeless is not properly rewarded: what they do for the community generates unacknowledged benefits, which other people experience as free gifts.

Is this a trivial – even sordid – example? Think again. In Cairo, Egypt, much waste disposal was, until recently, the work of a community of rag pickers and waste haulers called Zabbaleen, who lived *on top of* refuse dumps, in horrible conditions, forming – to quote a new report to the U.N. Development Programme on *Environmental Justice* by the 'Mega-Cities' project – 'a marginalized and undervalued community with little or no organization or power, [that] suffered from environmental devastation, little economic opportunity, lack of education, and a host of other problems endemic to urban slums'.

The original Zabbaleen were landless labourers displaced from Upper Egypt, who ended in the City picking up a living as they could. When the City grew to a point at which its refuse overwhelmed their efforts, a number of agencies, both local and global – ranging from the community's self-help organizations to the Ford Foundation, the World Bank I.D.A., Oxfam and Catholic Charities – put together the Zabbaleen Environmental and Development Programme, which helped them transform their manner of life: rationalizing their methods of refuse processing, building brick homes, setting up education classes, and raising their whole social and economic baseline.

In the United States, the transformation of the Zabbaleen community's environment would widely be caricatured as a *hand out*: not a prudent investment with a prospect of solid economic return, but a social outlay economically unjustified in the market terms. Still, two other things need to be added. It was not only the Zabbaleen whose lives the Programme improved. The whole City benefited: not just in pocket book terms, but in a dozen ways. In narrow economic terms, the Program transformed the *market*. The Zabbaleen became consumers. Their new style of life added social value, as well as prosperity, to the whole City. By helping them to live a decent life, it improved the quality of life for the whole Community, and this was in the interest not just of the immediate beneficiaries, but of all Cairo.

There are, in any case, more basic reasons why classic equilibrium economics finds it hard to evaluate a change like that of the Zabbaleen. Let us take three quick examples: First, economic forecasting itself rest on hidden presuppositions: the outcome of an industrial process can be forecast, only if we treat the state of Technology as being for the moment *fixed*. (Economic forecasters have no way to compute in advance the exact effect of technological changes.) In a time of rapid technological innovation, this seems a handicap, but in some ways the point is only common sense: what numerical formula could have prophesied the exact consequences of the transistor, or laser technology, or the contraceptive pill? In policy choices (as with the 'n-body' problem in physics) this theoretical limitation hides the possibility of radically unforeseeable changes – what it is fashionable nowadays to call 'chaotic' phenomena.

Second: what is true of technological changes is also true of changes in *the material infrastructure* of the economy. I arrived in Boston thirty years ago, just when someone in State government had decided to build a ring road round the City, which happened to be given the number '128'. Economists and politicians alike laughed at this decision: Route 128 (they said) was the road *from* nowhere *to* nowhere. What happened next? An ingenious development firm called Cabot,

Cabot and Forbes picked on Route 128 as the location to start the pioneer Science-Based Industry Park. Years before Silicon Valley, this was where scientists at Harvard and MIT tried out the technical applications of their discoveries – e.g., Townes' new found *lasers*. The spectacular success of this decision was thus something no economist could foresee; yet it became an unforeseen source of new prosperity for the Boston area and the whole country.

Third: what is true of the material infrastructure of the economy is also true of the moral infrastructure of a community. When the UNDP raised the level of life of the Zabbaleen in Cairo, it created sound institutions where none existed before, so creating unpredictable benefits for the economy and society of Cairo and Egypt. To underline the point. If we fail to repair our roads and bridges, we allow the country's *material* infrastructure to decay: if we fail to maintain the occupations and institutions of our people, we allow their *moral* infrastructure to rot. Sound institutions and rewarding occupations for the people – *all* the people – are the 'moral and social infrastructure' of any country; and it is no accident if the same monetarist theories that distract us from the one have disastrous effects on the other, as well.

The idea of a 'labour market' – independent of social policy and investment – is thus an economists' myth. There is in fact no such universal category as 'the free market'. Each national market has its own contours, embodying the institutional framework and essential interests of a country. The 1,000 pages of the GATT agreement were a sign, not of an international decision to free the whole global market, but of all the reciprocal horse trading that had struck balances between the contours of the national markets, so reflecting their interests. If our City streets are full of Homeless, too, we should admit that this is in *no one's* interest: programs that help people find worthwhile occupations (not just 'find jobs') are good investments for us all alike. At this point, the boundary *in our minds* between Wages and Welfare is invisibly thin.

Let me return to the suggestion that the future will be a period of *self-employment*. Consider who now make the largest incomes: sports stars, entertainers, successful musicians. In such work, the line between the 'employed' and the 'self employed' is fuzzy. Is being a baseball pitcher a *job*? Is the pitcher a *hired hand*? – That depends. One of the most argued over items in sports contracts nowadays is that of *free agency*: sports stars see an advantage in working as 'self employed' independent contractors.

Other earlier ideas are becoming equally fuzzy. If you play a guitar in a group, and share in the takings, are you working in 'the music industry'? Read the newspapers – the *Wall Street Journal*, above all – and your eye slides past such phrases without a jolt. They are by-products of historical changes that are taking us from the traditional world of material production, hired hands and quantifiable *jobs* into the Brave New World of *occupations*: activities that generate self-respect, or income, or both at once, for those who are no longer *hired hands* in the old sense. Having learned to treasure the English language, I stumble over phrases like 'the health service delivery industry': *industry* suggests to me coal mines or factories – the 'dark Satanic mills' of Blake's imagination. Factory work is one thing, medicine another, playing the guitar a third: are all of these occupations different kinds of Industry? Maybe so, given the flow of the new rhetoric. Rather than set the world of material *production* against one of non-material *occupation*, maybe we must widen the idea of 'production' to include both *non-material* products, and *social* products: modes of social organization and institutions serving our interests – personal and shared – as well as, if not better than, new models of automobile, new styles of pop music, or new kinds of computer software.

Anyone who moves to the U.S.A. from Europe is struck by the lack of attention to 'intermediate institutions' – as compared with (say) the Netherlands, where the interests and loyalties of citizens' groups find expression in political parties with such names as 'the Catholic Workers' Party'. In America, individual citizens are seen as confronting the State without the mediation of such intermediate institutions; and the weakness of popular political thought in America – as Robert Bellah argues – springs from this fact. Another sign of the same weakness is the continuing pursuit of Individual Rights, as contrasted with the Common Good.

The effective parts of Lyndon Johnson's 'War on Poverty' – like the 'Head Start' program, to improve the education of poor children – created openings for community organization that had constructive outcomes in the United States, just as the Zabbaleen project did in Cairo. Work in such organizations accelerated the movement of African-Americans into the administrative middle class, and so gave the country valuable social products. As with the Zabbaleen, what started as community rescue operations ended by creating real and general social assets.

Yet the basic situation remains. The U.S. Constitution protects individual interests, and its Industry has mastered the problems of material production. Now it faces the side effects of its very success: on the one hand a steady flow of high quality material products, on the other hand a population of disillusioned would-be workers. For now, Americans find it hard to admit that *creating new social institutions* is a legitimate mode of production. Yet, if manufacturing industry alone does not generate jobs for all who are looking for work, one public task is to find ways of rewarding collective initiatives, and investing in enterprises that are the loci of *social* improvement. When this is done, the activities we learned to hate under the name of *Welfare* are stood on their heads, and become the instruments of 'human welfare' in the *moral* sense of that term: the welfare both of the individual, and of the whole community.

Finally, a little Philosophy. – Since 1970, most politicians have been emphasizing the financial 'bottom line': meanwhile, the philosophical debate in Ethics and Law has concentrated (in Dworkin's phrase) on 'taking rights seriously'. Both concentrations encourage a style of individualism that makes it sound old fashioned – even obtuse – to theorize about the Interests of the whole Community, let alone about a *Common Good*. If ten million individuals want the same thing, if they all count the same thing as Good, how can this be anything but a coincidence, or a labile political preference?

The outcome of these philosophical arguments has – one can argue – been unhappy. One need not question that 'rights' form one central idea in moral and legal philosophy; but it is not the *only* central idea, or even a self-explanatory one. Any Right is the right to satisfy an Interest. *Rights* are individual: anyone can go to Court to have his or her individual rights protected by Law. But *Interests* are not so limited: quite the contrary. Some things are *in the interest* of many people, or a whole community. So understood, questions about the Common Good cease to be merely out-of-date or obtuse.

Nor is it helpful just to replace a theory of Rights by a theory of Responsibilities. Both ideas – *rights* and *responsibilities* – operate, by themselves, in a judicial context. Courts have the duty to protect Rights, and can enjoin us to meet our Responsibilities; but both ideas involve formal interactions between the individual Citizen and the State. The move on from *Rights* to *Interests*, by contrast, focuses our attention not on Law, but on a much broader range of Social Activities.

The crucial point can be stated in a number of different ways. To use familiar ugly but jargon, we may say, 'Social Life is not a Zero-Sum Game': when framed in economic terms, radical individualism tempts us to assume that any Good, or Benefit, accruing to one individual must do so at the expense of, or to the detriment of, others. Two people can't both spend one and the same dollar. A Gain by one is a Loss to the other, your Good is necessarily my Ill, and the moral question is, '*Who* has the Right to spend this particular dollar?'

Yet is this even a moral issue *at all*? Certainly, it can be in *one* person's interest that *another* has money to spend. Commercially, a storekeeper prefers his customers to be well off, not poverty stricken. More edifyingly, one person can take pleasure in the Good of another: even, in making the other person's Good possible. (That – Aristotle says – is the highest kind of friendship.) Morally, that is, experience of a Good is not, like ownership of a Dollar, exclusive to its legal proprietor.

At this point the shift from *Rights* to *Interests* is crucial. In our present day culture, the idea of 'rights' refers, above all, to the rights of individuals. But the institutions in which 'rights' can be claimed, and enforced, are *collective*; and these rights protect us in satisfying what are, or are seen as being, our legitimate interests. (These claims are not unlimited: our rights over our bodies, for instance, do not include selling limbs or bodily organs, whatever monetary return they may bring.) In this respect, the idea of *Interests* is fundamental, while that of *Rights* is derivative. Any account of the basis of Ethics must include the needs that define our permanent interests; but the institutional mechanisms that any particular society employes to protect the pursuit of our interests 'as of right' are a secondary matter.

In an age that emphasizes Rights, we too easily overlook the things that are in the Interest of a whole City or Community, and define its Common Good. This point will ring a bell with people in some countries more readily than others: in the Netherlands, for instance, it scarcely needs making. Without their longstanding municipal traditions, the Netherlands would barely exist: half the country would still be submerged, and the *polders* would not have been drained. Netherlanders (so to say) know that they all float in a single Ark, so their shared interests demand policies and conduct that protect them. People in Amsterdam do not need to be convinced that, after all, the idea of a Common Good makes sense: the normal flow of their rivers, six or seven metres above the farm land that surrounds them, is a daily reassurance of this fact. For them, indeed, Practice is the framework within which Moral Theory must be stated.

However used they are to the squalor of Manhattan, New Yorkers today concede that the continual need to step over the Homeless on the sidewalks can spoil their day. In philosophical terms, they cannot claim a *right* to have the sidewalks kept clear of the Homeless: the mere presence of the Homeless does not threaten any Individual Good that a Court would protect. Yet New Yorkers have *shared interests* (or common goods) that are proper objects of social policy. These social policies, however, are not merely *self-oriented*: they must be based on the shared, collective interests of all citizens alike. In short – and by way of conclusion – Individualism is not enough:

By ensuring that people to whom the traditional labor market does not provide jobs are rewardingly engaged in socially productive enterprises, rather than left at a loose end and dismissed as undeserving, we are not merely doing *them* a favor. We are also doing *ourselves* a favour, satisfying our shared interests, and serving our Common Good.

3 Bringing work to life

Ray E. Pahl

It may be that full employment, defined as mainly for men and largely in manufacturing, with people having more or less the same job for life, is gone.

(Employment in Europe, 1995)

Unemployment in the European Union as a whole remains stubbornly at about 11 per cent, hiding wide variations by age and by region. For example, in the UK about a third of unskilled men are not in employment. The decline of jobs in manufacturing industry has been dramatic. Since 1950 some five million jobs have been lost from the goods-producing industries and, whilst eight million new jobs have been created in public and private services, unemployment has continued to rise because the new jobs have more likely gone to women entering the labour market than men already in the labour market but displaced from the declining industries and occupations.

All this is well known and does not require detailed documentation. The notion of a male chief earner supporting his dependant family of wife and children with the security of life-long employment and a family wage seems now to be strangely archaic. (Machin and Waldfogel, 1994). Typically, men and women live in multiple-earner householders: women are much more likely to be in employment if they live with a man who is also employed. In the UK about 60% of women with employed husbands are also employed as against only 24%of women with non-employed husbands. A new form of polarisation has emerged between multi-earner and no-earner households. Part of the reason for the quiescence of those workers in low-paid part-time jobs with poor conditions of employment is that they may see their rewards in terms of the total household income. These component wages, particularly those paid to women, are generally inadequate on their own to support dependants and hence frequently lead to individual poverty if household partners separate.

There has been an ideological shift, reflected in the emergence of so-called post-industrial values, which has attempted to identify the experience of consumption as a central and meaningful part of life which may serve as a replacement for the previously dominant position of employment as the main central life interest of men. The consumer may now appear to experience more power than the producer in a context where employment is becoming increasingly insecure, demanding and stressful. Yet, as R.E. Lane (1991) has shown, most people's experience of the market is unsatisfactory, since their main experience of it in terms of time taken out of their lives is as employees rather than as consumers. Economically the labour market has failed to solve the problem of endemic unemployment but has also failed socially and psychologically, as Lane exhaustively demonstrates. Few people can now argue with much conviction that the labour market will be able to deliver the jobs to provide adequate wages for all the potential single-earner households not only to support dependants, whether children, parents or handicapped people, but also to provide fulfilling and satisfying bases for individual self-identity.

The European Community Labour Force Survey showed that in 1994 two thirds of all women working part-time were doing so because they did not want a full-time job: indeed, in the two countries where part-time jobs were most prevalent, the UK and the Netherlands, as many as 80%of women in such jobs did not want a full-time job. Yet these part-time jobs need to be linked with the full-time or part-time jobs of others to produce adequate household incomes.

Women, seemingly, have not become so dominated by the demands of wage labour as have men. But it was not always thus. In the early decades of the industrial revolution in Britain, men resisted and resented the imposition of the time disciplines of industrial capitalism. They had been used to the more erratic work rhythms of the agricultural year and even those in craft activities preferred to work in bursts, interspersed with drinking and gaming. Recovering from the excesses of the weekend meant that on Monday very little work took place. This continued until well into the nineteenth century. One example, provided by the nailers of Stourbridge in Worcestershire in 1874, showed that they had Sunday free, Monday for seeking orders and iron, Thursday for resting or idling and Saturday as a weighing in day. This left a three day working week, when, admittedly, the hours were long – maybe from 5 a.m. to as late as 10 p.m. The working week was flexible and there were other, longer interruptions such as the summer migrations to help with the harvest. In the mid-19th century half of the workers in Stourbridge were still engaged in a task-oriented economy with highly flexible hours.

> Those who worked in the home alternated between long periods of sustained hard work and an extended weekend, in which they could indulge, if they wished, in the traditional Black Country pastimes of pigeon-flying, dog-fighting and drinking. (Hopkins, 1974)

The development of large-scale factory production enslaved men to regular, all-encompassing wage labour. The compensation of comradely solidarity based on drinking, brass-bands or sport certainly developed in the single industry occupational communities of coal-mining, steel-making or shipbuilding. However, when these industries collapsed, the men were doubly punished: having habituated themselves to regular work routines they found it hard to provide new time structures (Kelvin and Jarrett, 1985) and the collapse of occupational communities undermined their bases for affirming their masculinities and expressing fraternal solidarities. Paradoxically, those least committed to their occupational identities were more able to avoid the social and personal costs involved in the inexorable progress of global capitalism. Those who succumbed to the disciplines of factory labour and co-operated with Taylorist and Fordist techniques and styles of management were the most vulnerable to the consequences of de-industrialisation.

Those industries, such as textiles or potteries, where women dominated in employment did not become the overwhelming determinant of identity as other industries did for men. Women's unpaid domestic, caring and self-provisioning work outside employment provided a more balanced focus for their lives. The reduction of women's work to the 'housewife' role in the early twentieth century provided the same kind of vulnerability and over dependency that male manual workers experienced. Paradoxically, many working-class women who remained at home as full-time housewives suffered from depression and a serious loss of self-esteem, which was in large measure overcome by doing the kind of factory work that those who sort to reduce work that was repetitive and meaningless deplored (Brown and Harris, 1958).

This tendency of men and women to grow accustomed to their chains and to suffer deprivation when they are freed from them should not encourage us to forge new chains. The flexibilization, which in its various forms is sometimes seen as the latest tool for oppressing the increasingly defenceless mass worker, may become a blessing in disguise.

In the nineteenth century it was the bourgeoisie who pioneered the separation of spheres between men and women, partly as a way of tying social status to developing economic power. The rising capitalist class needed a visible demonstration of its success. The well-run bourgeois house became a necessary accoutrement for leading and aspiring men of substance (Davidoff and Hall, 1987). This gendered division of labour was extended to the working class for a variety of complex reasons, including a particular form of Christian morality, a concern to get labour power and soldiers well reproduced and to reduce the domestic origins of contagious diseases. The fact that this may have also have served the interests of working class authoritarian patriarchy probably made the task easier (Humphries in Pahl 1988). A further set of reasons related to the creation of a new mass-market of domestic consumption: every little flat or house needed a busy buyer and demander of the new gadgets and appliances. Until well past the middle of the twentieth century, specialised 'home-makers' were encouraged as excellent spurs to the male family providers to make them work even longer hours and to discourage them from engaging in industrial militancy or in any way risking the flow of spending money into the little domestic units which were eulogised as 'the family', that cosy stimulant to the ever-expanding production of more or less useful consumer goods. Mid-twentieth century functionalist sociology perceived the isolated nuclear family as fitting nicely into the 'needs' of industrial capitalism in a variety of ways. But, for many and complex reasons, the period of the dominant male chief earner as head of household was short-lived. The middle-class granddaughters and great granddaughters of their paternalist forbears developed a feminist critique of housewifely dependence and encouraged their married working-class sisters back into the labour market. As George Bernard Shaw wrily remarked, women refused to be dictated to in the home and so went out and became stenographers.

The attack on the separation of spheres, much helped by women's involvement in two world wars, has been overwhelmingly successful, but has brought with it new problems. As Beck and Beck-Gernsheim put it:

> To free women from the burdens of home and housework the men are expected to fit in with 'this modern feudal existence', and take over exactly what the women reject for themselves. Historically speaking it is like trying to turn the nobility into peasants' serfs ... What remains crucial is that equality between the sexes cannot be achieved in institutions which presuppose their inequality. There is no hope of forcing the new round people into the old square holes required by the employment system, town planners, and so-called social security. (1995, p.28)

The new senior salariat now finds itself doubly burdened. Not only do men and women have to, at best, share and, at worst, argue over all work outside employment, they are also working longer and longer hours. As Gershuny has shown, 'the work time, and pace, of middle class jobs has certainly been increasing since the 1960s'. Using data from the British Household Panel Study, he has shown that those with the highest monthly incomes have the longest hours of work. Even when the effect of wage rates is controlled, the best paid 20% of men work around ten hours longer per week than the worst paid. Furthermore, those who work the longest hours are most concerned to reduce their working hours – 49% of men in the highest quintile of working hours and 53% of the women (Gershuny, 1995, 43-44).

In the same way that the nineteenth century bourgeoisie led the move towards the institutionalisation of the separation of spheres so their end of the twentieth century counterparts are becoming 'time pioneers', exploring new forms of balance between the public and the private and between all forms of work. In one of the few studies of those who have consciously reduced their working hours in order to develop and innovate new lifestyles, Hörning and his colleagues (1995) contrast what they call 'time conventionalists' with 'time pioneers'. The latter have turned flexibilisation to their own advantage. They have consciously 'downshifted' themselves to engage in what they perceive to be more rewarding and satisfying life styles.

> To the time pioneers, a situation where, with the exception of tedious rest periods, the day consists of nothing but work, in which they have a 'weekend life' or live from one holiday to the next is burdensome, monotonous and unsatisfactory, indeed, all things considered, not worth living. (p.53)

A survey by a British market research organisation of 2,143 adults over 15 in 1994 showed that in response to the statement, 'Although I enjoy my work, my private life is more important to me', 75% agreed and, similarly, 80% agreed that they tried to keep a balance between their personal and working lives (Winkfield, 1995).

The problem, as Hörning and his colleagues clearly understand, is that moving to shorter working hours inevitably implies a substantial loss of income – maybe as much as 50%, which is evidently a very dramatic reduction. This almost certainly implies both a substantial drop in standard of living and a fundamental change in ways of living. Some have already adopted a more frugal standard of living with lower material aspirations. Those who have not already habituated themselves to a more modest life-style can face serious problems. The situation can be particularly difficult if a couple decides jointly to downshift and makes careful calculations based on the combination of their two reduced salaries. If, then, the couple split, both ex-partners can fall into very straightened circumstances and, if there are children, the problem will be even more acute for one or both of the partners.

The combination of downshifting and decoupling is hard to accommodate: a decision to make a re-entry into full-time employment may not be so easily implemented. Depending on the length of the period downshifted the pace of change may have enabled later entrants to the labour market to have established a strength which effectively cuts off the returning worker from re-entering at or near the level he or she left. This scenario forces many into self-employment, an area, again, of considerable turbulence and with a high rate of failure. This is part of the reason for the dramatic increase in single person households, which are now, in the UK, the fastest growing household type. The proportion of households of one person only has remained fairly stable at 15% for those of pensionable age. For those under pensionable age, the proportion has increased by 50% from 1981 to 1994-5 – that is from 8 to 12% of all households (*Social Trends*, 1996).

To summarise so far: I have argued that men and women are now finding that the restrictive burdens imposed by the traditional separation of spheres are no longer acceptable and the enslavement of a chief earner to a life time of wage labour is collapsing. This is partly due to dramatic changes in gender relations and the emergence of debates about masculinities and femininities, part of which must be due to the development of feminism in the second half of the century. It is also partly due to broad structural changes in the labour market due to technological change, massive industrial shifts and a whole range of employers' strategies – outsourcing, down-sizing, delayering and so on – claimed to be a necessary and inevitable part of a process of flexibilisation imposed by the globalisation of capitalist production and the pressure by shareholders for better short-term returns.

There is now a growing sociological literature exploring and illustrating the dilemmas and problems affecting the salariat, for example R. Scase and R. Goffee *Reluctant Managers* (1989), K.S. Newman *Falling from Grace: the Experience of Downward Mobility in the American Middle Class* (1988), B. Ehrenreich, *Fear of Falling* (1990), R. Coward *Our Treacherous Hearts* (1993) and my own *After Success, Fin-de-siècle Anxiety and Identity* (1995). These and other studies are documenting a widespread unease about the insecurities of employment, the anxieties of competitive parenting and the recognition that the secret of success may be more in finding an elusive balance between all forms of work rather than in an obsessive compulsion to one dominating and greedy form of work, namely full-time employment. Women are, perhaps, better at devising satisfactory forms of balance between all forms of work but this may be limited to those with strong labour market positions or with the capacity to employ servants to work, clean and care whilst they do their rewarding part-time jobs. The ideal of a new type of superwoman has been described by Harriet Harman (*The Century Gap* 1993). A member of the Shadow Cabinet of the British Labour Party, Harman epitomises a shallow female triumphalism, that may well generate the dangers of hybris:

> Women know with a confidence that they have not had before that they are as good as men – as clever, as competent, as capable ... when women are able fully to participate in the world of work our economy will be revitalised ... Inside ever housewife is a career woman – and both are struggling to get out. (pp.25, 7-8, 115)

The assumptions underlying this line of thinking are based on a model of economically autonomous individuals making contracts in the labour market. Yet only a privileged minority of women are, under present circumstances, likely to earn salaries to enable them to support themselves and their dependants comfortably. It is important to recall that the majority of women working part-time prefer not to be in full-time employment.

It is with all this in mind that I now turn to work outside employment. Considerable research has been done on this topic since I began my own empirical research in this area some twenty years ago. It is perhaps useful to summarise some of the main conclusions of this research. Many researchers have emphasised the important distinction between those economic activities that appear in the national accounts, what is in the UK called the Blue Book Economy (BBE), and those activities that escape for a variety of reasons. Fraud and occupational theft may appear partially in the BBE – evasion of tax, for example, may still lead to greater personal expenditure but the balance between the various headings of the BBE is skewed. Income tax may be reduced but VAT may be increased. Evaluation of the impact of various forms of fraud on the national accounts is a highly complex exercise. Those attempting to control fraud – evasion of income, corporation or value added tax or the claiming of benefits from the social security system dishonestly – are often, seemingly, more interested in social control than in balancing the books of the BBE. In strictly economic terms certain forms of fraud, particularly amongst the poorest, may have economically benign consequences for the economy as a whole.

There are other activities which could well appear in the BBE but are undertaken 'voluntarily', such as personal child minding instead of using a professional carer or servicing one's own car instead of using a garage. These quite legitimate activities can shift in and out of the BBE as circumstances change in the labour market or through the life course. The provision of services is a very complex area to analyse as the consideration of any example in detail will illustrate. Thus, fixing a tile on the roof of the house can be done by the landlord, a builder, the houseowner or tenant, a relative of that person, a neighbour, an illicit, non-registered builder, an unemployed person in receipt of benefits who may or not get paid and so on. The bill can be paid with appropriate VAT, it can be paid in such a way that it may seem that the VAT is included but it is not, or the VAT may not be declared or the payment is made in cash, which may or may not be declared to the tax authorities and so on. It is one thing to make distinctions between the formal economy (BBE) the household economy, the communal economy and so forth, but these apparently clear-cut spheres remain dependant on the capacity to allocate given transactions unequivocally to each. Despite the apparent confidence of many researchers in this area, this remains a serious stumbling-block.

Evidently, a hugely complicating factor is the state's system of regulation, so that what may be readily allowed in one national state or period of time, is illegal in another. Admittedly the EU is attempting to standardise such regulations, but different welfare systems and types of company law still exist and there is considerable diversity, even within Europe. Work that is fraudulent or dishonest in one context may be perceived to be enterprisingly wealth creating in another.

By and large, attempts to measure the value of work outside employment have floundered, largely due to applying a BBE mentality to activity that is operating according to different principles. Again an example may make this clear. Sociologists have been interested in the expansion of Local Employment and Trading Schemes (LETS) (Offe and Heinze, 1992). Typically these have their own currency and banking system and depend on people exchanging tasks – for example, digging someone's garden might be repaid by someone else baby-sitting. A directory of skills and tasks is provided for members and payment is made by a cheque in the local 'currency'. Economists may readily show that if all the exchanged tasks were monetised a relatively small proportion of local economic activity would be covered. However, if valuation is made in terms of social cohesion, it may be that local LETS are more cost-effective than, say, increased expenditure on policing or certain forms of health promotion.

Those researching into work outside employment hitherto, may have been, perhaps, over-much concerned with problems of measurement and classification. The field is thick in vested interests: fraud squads seek to protect the interests of their work force; the voluntary sector wants to stress the need for a state-supported infrastructure; politicians seek to displace voters' dissatisfactions on to 'scroungers', free-marketeers wish to reduce the 'burdens' on entrepreneurs; employers seek to reduce labour costs by avoiding what they perceive as burdensome employment protection legislation. Most of those bureaucrats who set the research agendas are concerned either with more or less regulation or approaches to measurement. Even those sympathetic to extra-market forms of work often justify their interest by arguing that such forms provide a valuable seed bed for, as it were, trainee members of the BBE. Thus, small businesses run by ethnic minorities in an illegal manner may be justified as providing an essential dynamism in local economies and providing less-conventional routes for outsiders to penetrate the BBE. Hence, rule-bending can be seen as a functionally desirable form of making the BBE more innovative, internationally competitive or whatever.

So far little research has been done on how the BBE can provide support and help for those who wish to engage in more work outside employment. For example, there are few signs of tax incentives to encourage self-building in Britain (although maybe there are more enlightened authorities elsewhere). Power tools and computers could be provided tax free or with other inducements in order for people to do more work for themselves. Self-employed people under a certain threshold could work tax free; those on benefits could be encouraged to work cash-in-hand without having to declare it up to a certain threshold. Instead of deregulation by the state being limited to the BBE, it could be massively extended to work outside employment.

If that were done what are the possible consequences and who would benefit from such a shift? There would, of course, be a redistribution of the provision of services as self-provisioning took a market share from formal provision. Would de-regulation help downshifters from the salariat more than the low-skilled unemployed, for example? In my own research, carried out over a period of ten years on the Isle of Sheppey in Kent (*Divisions of Labour* 1984), I demonstrated that forms of work and service provision outside employment were not alternatives to employment, self-employment and formal provision by the BBE. Rather than one form of work substituting for another, I showed unequivocally that those who had high household incomes were able to engage in all other forms of work as well. They were more able to engage in self-provisioning, since those best placed had access to their own land, labour and capital. If they owned their own house or had a second holiday home, they were in a position to effect improvements which those renting properties were not in a position to do. If they had land they could grow their own produce, keep a boat or a second car on which they could work or have a shed in which they could store things. With multiple earners in the household they had access to skills and had the means to buy tools. If they wished to earn extra money by engaging in non-BBE recorded work, it is likely that their place of employment provided social contacts to find such work. Having access to a phone and being able to buy potential clients drinks in pubs all help to improve access to informal markets.

Single people living on their own, those renting property, unemployed people, elderly people and many other categories less well-endowed with property, skills and financial resources have greater difficulty in engaging in productive work outside employment. Certainly, if they have 'sleeping skills', that is skills they acquired earlier in life but cannot now use for gainful employment, they may trade these in LETS. But even here there are problems. Someone who is a skilled joiner or seamstress could be seen to be undercutting those in the local labour market who are attempting to sell these skills. An unemployed plumber who does work for a LETS partner and gets vegetables or game in return might be investigated for possible income tax evasion. This is a grey area which the British Inland Revenue Authorities have not fully clarified. Perhaps they will never be able to. Again, those engaged in unpaid voluntary work need to have a secure source of income to underpin their activities. Those arguing for more public support for the voluntary sector can claim that, if monetized, the contribution to the GDP would be colossal: even as much as £41 billion a year! (Volunteer Centre, 1995). The various categories of work I have been discussing can be schematically presented as follows:

CATEGORIES OF WORK (after Bryan Roberts)

Market Values
(Monetary)

	Irregular Tax evasion. Illegal transfers of goods and services Clandestine labour Occupational theft Periodic markets	**Regular**	
Unregulated			**State Regulated**
	Household Household Self-provisioning DIY etc.	**Commercial/Voluntary** Mutual aid (LETS) Self-Help Co-operatives Voluntary activity	

Non-market Values
(Utility, Reciprocity)

The growth of economic informalisation in the state-regulated sector has blurred the lines between formal and the informal economic activity. The decline of the real value of welfare payment has encouraged the poor to find other ways of generating money and getting by. The state is caught in a dilemma: on the one hand it wishes to encourage sturdy independence, standing on one's own two feet and so forth, yet at the same time it fears the undermining of the work ethic and the development of a culture of tax evasion and welfare scrounging. The more deregulated the economy, the more collusion is likely between employers and employees. Cash-in-hand payments benefit the employer who does not have to pay the National Insurance contribution and employee benefits such as holidays with pay, sick leave and so on. Governments are reluctant to be seen to be too heavily controlling their allies in the tasks of job and wealth creating. So Governments collude with employers but do not perceive clearly that they should also collude with the casual employees who are subsidising the growth of small firms with their lower, erratic wages and lack of benefits. The same ambivalence occurs in the financial sector where deregulation has led to greater opportunities for fraud yet global competition is put forward as an excuse to preclude over-enthusiastic surveillance of the BBE. Indeed, the growth of regulatory bodies accompanying privatisation is a good indication of the emerging low-trust society that is being created in the late twentieth century.

If the scope, range and intensity of regulation or surveillance is coming to dominate the BBE based on reduced trust, work outside employment, by contrast, is much more likely to be based on trust among kin, friends and neighbours in specific locales. Typically, there is generally higher trust between partners in exchanges in the informal than in the formal spheres of work. Of course, it is important not to romanticise the informal sphere: in Italy and the former communist world, for example, the Mafia's control of much irregular work is based on fear more than trust. A great paradox that underlies much of the discussion of work outside employment is that the same terminology is used to cover both highly exploited shadow wage labour on the one hand, and forms of self-provisioning and benign exchange systems which are perceived to be liberating on the other.

Quite rightly, sociologists and anthropologists have been chary of accepting some distinct and alternative 'economy' whether irregular, informal, underground, black, shadow, grey or any other over-simplistically general term. Rather, as I have argued elsewhere, there are not so much separate *economies* as different *forms of work* (Pahl, 1989). These forms of work depend heavily on the *meanings* people bring to the activities, which, in turn, are related to the social relations in which the work is embedded. I have enlarged on what I mean by this in detail in an Appendix to this chapter.

I have referred, somewhat sketchily, to trends in employment and I have argued that the social changes of the past were pioneered by the bourgeoisie – particularly the development of the separation of spheres and the emergence of the male breadwinner. This model has largely collapsed for a variety of reasons but new themes must be the bourgeois feminist reaction to the separation of spheres and the determination of married working women to retain their commitment, even if only part-time, to the labour market. The application of new styles of management thinking based on leaner, flatter and, arguably perhaps, more fitter organisation has created a new stress and anxiety in employment. These pressures are compounded by increased burdens in the private sphere caused by increasing divorce rates, the complexities of step-family relationships, the emergence and re-emergence of courtship as part of the psychic costs of serial monogamy, the care of dependant relatives, the anxieties involved in gaining appropriate schooling and credentials for children, the problems, in Britain, of negative equity in housing, the loss of inheritance as parents live longer and use up their savings in nursing homes, the new reluctance of unmarried children to leave home even in their 20s – the list seems endless.

Faced with these and similar worries, the salariat does not feel good: long hours at work may be as much due to insecurity and fear of losing their jobs as to the extra work produced by delayering or by responses to regulatory or quality controlling bodies, checking and double-checking. This may be particularly strong in the public sector but it is growing in the private sector too.

Let us now turn directly to the conference theme '*Work – Quo Vadis*?' My response has to be speculative and an attempt to use straws in the wind to make solid bricks can go badly wrong. The issue is this: how far are the time pioneers and downshifters the vanguard of the future or how far are they the 1990s equivalents of the commune builders and drop outs of the 1960s, who will not make any substantial difference to the main expansionistic tendencies of the BBE?

There are several important differences between the 1960s and 1990s:

- Levels of unemployment are now much higher and even optimistic forecasts do not see dramatic reductions.
- The idea of a life-long career no longer has much salience. Individuals have a kind of privatised career based on their CVs which are essentially employability tickets.
- The more pressured senior salaried style of employment is compounded for couples who are both working intensely and for long hours.
- 'Family' life is a further source of insecurity and individuation as people seek an ever elusive happiness in 'the normal chaos of love'.
- The care of dependants has been privatised on to already over-burdened putative carers.

These, and other factors suggest that something will have to give. Those who most need more balance in their lives are least able to achieve it. They are trapped by their materialistic aspirations for themselves and their children. They are also, crucially, trapped by the taxation system. As I have noted above, all informal forms of work that are not based on simple exchanges of labour, as in LETS and similar trading schemes, are based on money. Even these barter schemes require equipment such as chain saws and sewing machines that need to be maintained. At present the links between regulated and unregulated forms of work are viewed by governments with great suspicion. If people are not in the formal economy then, somehow, they are morally at fault.

There is, in fact, a way of life based on combining small state benefits with petty trading or petty commodity production. Many state pensioners dabble in 'antiques' with stalls at a market or boot fair. Many men in rural areas shift between jobs, often being paid cash in hand. They may have an old pick-up truck and can supply logs, help with milking or repoint a wall. Few farms can maintain a very large permanent workforce and so there is a need for such 'just-in-time' flexible workers. In a sense this is very similar to the pattern of work described by Malcolmson for eighteenth century England (in Pahl, 1988). Can this more flexible way of life be adapted for downshifting professionals and managers who use their computers instead of a pick-up truck?

At present most of the highly paid and overworked salariat in the UK are focused on London and other big cities. This is the case in most countries: the geographical concentration of one sort of work is highly concentrated whereas other forms of work, particularly domestic work, child care and much self-provisioning reflects the overall pattern of the distribution of the population. In my view, shifts from one form of work to another need to be approached firstly through a consideration of taxation policy, and secondly through geographical changes through the life course. At present land, labour and capital are taxed. Everyone has to pay a Council Tax based on property; all those in employment or self-employment are taxed over a given threshold and there are taxes on capital gains, capital inheritance and on most goods that are bought. There are also, of course, licenses for many things such as guns, TV sets and cars and extra excise duty is imposed on alcoholic drinks and tobacco. This complex and ever-changing system is based on conventional assumptions about earning, spending and saving which are firmly tied to fiscal years and the BBE. However, most work outside employment operates according to different rhythms. Child-care work is at one stage of the life-course and payment for residential nursing care at another. Chain saws are not much used by elderly men and women. There are ways in which a different kind of taxation system would encourage people to prepare at one stage of their life, when engaged heavily in one form of work, for a period later in life when engaged in another. Thus, at present certain expenditures such as personal pension plans get tax relief during the period of high earnings so that the individual may reap the benefits later. But why restrict these benefits to the period of retirement? Someone who is going to suffer from downsizing in his or her early 40s may have up to 30 years of active working life ahead – even if not working in employment. If such a person had been able to acquire a house in a cheaper part of the country when his or her earnings were higher, the sale of the first property could supplement the pension.

The basic idea would be that people would not expect to spend a life time in conventional employment, but would transfer the resources built up in their earlier, intense period in the labour market – about 15 years, say, between the ages of 22 and 42 – and would then live on these resources in their 'down-sized' situation in smaller communities where the quality of life could still be high. People would, of course, carry with them their CD Roms, film projectors, computers and so forth, so that they could view and hear in virtual reality the latest artistic production from anywhere in the world, and communicate in a way that was not possible for earlier generations seeking a less materialistic or more 'authentic' way of life. Rather than every dwelling having the whole range of equipment, many small communities will have IT centres where office space and equipment can be rented and various training courses provided.

All this smacks of back-to-the land romanticism, with all the negative connotations of stifling and oppressive gemeinschaft. However, it need not necessarily be so, as the French rural sociologist, Henri Mendras, so wittily illustrated in his utopian vision of France in the next century, which he published in the 1970s (Mendras, 1979). The idea that the life course follows a geographical pattern is not new. In the past, young people travelled long distances to serve their apprenticeships and returned to their home to practise their crafts. It is hard to see how low-energy using sustainable development can be easily implemented in large cities. In smaller centres, however, the idea of a local economy can make sense. In these smaller places the contribution to the BBE may not be very significant and people may appear to gain more in benefits and subsidies than they provide in taxation. However, this is because the work outside employment is not counted appropriately. There needs to be a valuation of work in other ways than money. With fewer wage labourers, but many workers, such places could provide models of how to bring work to life. The key to the future is the radical reform of the system of taxation which now relates to an outmoded economic formation.

References

Beck, U. and Beck-Gernsheim, E. (1995), *The Normal Chaos of Love*, Cambridge: Polity Press.

Brown, G.W. and Harris, T. (1958), *Social Origins of Depression: A Study of Psychiatric Disorders in Women*, London: Tavistock.

Davidoff, L. and Hall, C. (1987), *Family Fortunes: Men and Women of the English Middle Class*, London: Hutchinson.

Demos Quarterly 2, 1994. Special Employment Issue, Demos, 9 Bridewell Place, London EC4V 6AP.

Gershuny, J. (1995), 'Time Keynesianism', *Demos Quarterly*, 5.

Harman, H. (1993), *The Century Gap*, London: Vermilion.

Hopkins, E. 1974, 'Working Conditions in Victorian Stourbridge', *International Review of Social History*, Vol. 19:401-425.

Hörning, K.H., Gerhard, A. and Michailow, M. (1995), *Time Pioneers: Flexible Working Time and New Lifestyles*, Cambridge: Polity Press.

Humphries, J. (1988), 'Protective Legislation, the Capitalist State and Working Class Men: The Case of the 1842 Mines Regulation Act', in Pahl (ed) (1988).

Kelvin, P. and Jarett, J. (1985), *The Social Psychological Effects of Unemployment*, Cambridge: Cambridge University Press.

Lane, R.E. (1991), *The Market Experience*, Cambridge: Cambridge University Press.

Machin, S. and Waldefogel, J. (1994), *The Decline of the Male Breadwinner. Changing Shares of Husbands' and Wives' Earnings in Family Income*, Discussion paper WSP/103 Suntory-Toyota International Centre for Economics and Related Disciplines: London School of Economics.

Malcolmson, R.W. (1988). 'Ways of Getting a Living in 18th Century England', in Pahl (ed) (1988).

Mendras, H. (1979), *Voyage au Pays de L'Utopie Rustique*, Lyon: Federop.

Offe, C. and Heinze, R.G. (1992), *Beyond Employment*, Cambridge: Polity Press.

Pahl, R.E. (1984), *Divisions of Labour*, Oxford: Basil Blackwell.

Pahl, R.E. (ed) (1988), *On Work: Historical, Comparative and Theoretical Approaches*. Oxford: Basil Blackwell.

Pahl, R.E. (1989), 'From "Informal Economy" to "Forms of Work": Cross National Patterns and Trends', in Scase, R. (ed) *Industrial Societies, Crisis and Divisions in Western Capitalism and State Socialism*. London: Unwin Hyman.

Pahl, R. (1995), *After Success: Fin-de-siècle Anxiety and Identity*. Cambridge: Polity Press.

Social Trends (1996), London: CSO/HMSO.

Winkfield, N. (1995), 'Bad Timing: Attitudes to the New World of Work', *Demos Quarterly*, 5.

Appendix: Defining forms of works by the social relations in which they are embedded

I now put forward my proposal for an analytical framework which would be based partly on an actor's definition of the situation and partly on the understanding of the social relations in which a given task or activity is embedded. Only when both of these objective and subjective conditions are know is it possible to determine what kind of work is being done. However, the charm of my approach is that it provides categories which may be compared cross-nationally. The size of these categories will depend on a whole complex of variables but with some measure of orders of magnitude, a framework for comparative analysis can be established. These social relations can be structured by the patterns of domination generated by the capitalist economic system, the principles of both the market and of reciprocity, and by the social hierarchies of age, gender, kinship, neighbourhood and informal group. An individual may apparently be engaged in a work task but simply observing that individual may provide little understanding of what kind of work it is or, indeed, whether it is work at all. Not all purposeful activity is work; but if it is non-work or play we again cannot be sure until we know more of the social relations in which the play activity is embedded. We see people at an embassy drinks party: one person may be there sharing a convivial activity and engaging in a pure form of sociation or play. Another person may work for the British Council or the embassy staff and is heavily and intensely involved in the employment for which she is paid. There is a distinction between work and play but it is not based on the intrinsic nature of the task or activity. In order to clarify this and to introduce further complexities a particular example may be explored in some detail.

Consider an image of a woman ironing. She is standing by an ironing board on which there is a garment – a blouse or a shirt. Is she at work or is she at play and, if the former, what kind of work is she engaged in? The answer will depend on the social relations in which her task is embedded. Let us explore some possibilities.

First, the woman could be a full-time wage-worker producing garments as a domestic outworker. If she has been hired on a piece-work basis she could have an incentive to iron as many garments as quickly as possible. Alternatively, she may have been hired on a fixed contract with no incentive to increase the number of garments she irons, although there may be some quality control so that the style or quality of her work is more important than her pace. Her approach to her task is likely to be related to the contractual arrangements that exist between her and her employer. She may be working part-time, she may be working shifts which include a period at home, or she may be doing causal work, covering for regular employees at a holiday time or taking on extra work at a particularly busy period. Whatever the precise details, she is, in all these cases, basically a wage-labourer: she is selling her ironing skills to an employer who provides her with the materials and also, possibly, the tools. If she had an accident and lost her sight or injured her ironing arm her labour power would disappear or be reduced.

There is a further twist. We may learn that she is basically a wage-labourer, determined by the social relations in which her task is embedded, but we cannot be sure that her employer is honest. It is possible that this female outworker is not recorded in the firm's official returns to the appropriate government department. This may be a strategy to avoid, on the one hand, the obligation to pay certain taxes or insurance contributions, and also to avoid granting certain rights and benefits to the employee, such as the number of days' holiday with pay, rights to sickness benefit and maternity leave and insurance in the vent of, say, an accident that will not affect the basic social relations of wage-labour; it will however, determine whether it is formally recorded, which, in turn will have fundamental implications for the individual concerned. If the work is done informally this does not, of course, put it in any separate informal economy but it should be described as shadow or hidden wage-labour to distinguish it from the formally recognized and recorded form.

The woman could be preparing the garment for sale but she may own the material and the iron; she may have dyed the cloth, designed the style, or decorated the garment in some distinctive way. She may have her own stall or boutique or she may be selling by contract to specific retail outlets. Whatever the details, she is a self-employed worker engaged in petty-commodity production. She is responsible for her own pace of work and the quality of what she produces. She may employ others who may or may not be members of her family. If the latter she may be engaged in family capitalism with its own distinctive sets of social relations. Again, her activities may be more or less officially recognized and she may prefer to defraud the tax authorities, despite the risks involved. This may involve the simple under-declaring of profits or it may be coupled with paying other people in cash, so that she has no contractual obligations towards them.

So far the woman at the ironing board has been viewed as an income-generating agent. We know nothing about her age, marital status, race, or subjective preconceptions and attitudes. She could be married or single, and in both cases she may or may not have a child. Let us assume that she is ironing the garment for another member of the household in which she lives. What kind of work would that be? Again we need to know more about the nature of the social relations in which the task is embedded. This time we are not concerned with the social relations of capitalist production but with the familiar or patriarchal relations, and these may get very complex. There is a great range of possibilities. The woman may be ironing a shirt for her lover. Her mind is full of loving or erotic thoughts so that the task is highly charged emotionally and provides substantial pleasure as she, perhaps, fantasizes about the person as she irons the various parts of the garment. She may have offered to do the task as an act of love, knowing that her lover was willing and able to do the task himself and, indeed, in the past has done the same for her. The work is thus symbolic: it is work with a purpose, done for love and is similar to the toil of monks or nuns who work, literally, for love as a means of self-expression. The distinction between this kind of work and play is that, in the latter case, the pleasure would be solely in the activity of ironing. It would not matter for whom the shirt was being ironed: the important activity would be the ironing itself and the pleasure would be similar to that experienced by those who play tennis or go fishing as a recreational activity.

However, the woman may have been married for many years to a man she barely tolerates. He insists on a clean, well-ironed shirt every day. He may hit her if she fails in what he claims is her duty. She resignedly goes about her task heavily dominated by patriarchal social relations. The task is a burden and brings no pleasure: she feels constrained, oppressed and resentful. She is but one example of the oppression of women and she may be brooding on the unfairness and injustice of her situation. Even if she is ironing her children's garments the resentment may be much the same if she feels constrained by her domestic role and the social relations established by the power of her spouse.

If the woman is ironing her own blouse then much will depend on the context in which she is to wear it. If, on the following day she has to wear the garment at the office then she is, as it were, working to reproduce herself as a smart worker. She knows that the way she presents herself is part of the way she is able to demonstrate her effectiveness as a worker. She has internalized the expectations of employers and colleagues – whether male or female – and thus feels constrained to dress in a given way. She is thus working for her employer in her own time but, of course, she is also reproducing herself as a worker when she is cleaning her teeth or eating muesli. However, she would do these things even if she were not in employment. Hence, the task of ironing her blouses is more directly related to her employment and she would not do the task if she was on holiday. Some occupations require specific uniforms or work clothes that are provided and maintained by the employer. Other jobs make no demands on their incumbents and the workers may wear what they like. By exploring the task in this way we can see that some women do have extra employment-related work to carry out in their own time. Unmarried men may have the same burden; married men typically pass on the burden to their wives.

It may be that the woman is ironing her elderly mother-in-law's blouse. A combination of social pressures have put her in the position of being responsible for the care of someone who is unable to care for herself. She may be engaged in what is euphemistically termed 'community care'. She is an unpaid community worker and the obligation she is made to feel to care for her husband's mother may prevent her from engaging in paid employment. Such burdens of family and kin are highly gender-specific. Men would not be expected to care for the elderly in the same way and in the case of an unemployed single man with a dependent relative the social services would provide support that would not be available to a woman in the same position. The social relations of family obligation are sharply divided by gender.

Let us now turn away from the labour market and the ageist or sexist domination of the household and consider the situations where the woman is ironing for someone who is not a household member. She might be doing a little causal work as a domestic cleaner and getting extra cash for doing the ironing at home. She would be sharing in the social relations of the casualized lumpenproletariat, however sweetly her employer asked her to do the work. The more likely situation, however, is that she is doing the ironing for a non-household-member without receiving payment. She may be a member of the local dramatic society and the producer has flattered her into pressing the costumes of the leading actors. She may have agreed to do the work calculating that her willingness will put her, as it were, into credit with the producer – she has entered into a relationship based on the norm of reciprocity. Her reasonable assumption is that by giving her time and effort in doing the ironing she will be repaid with a comparable favour in the future. She may be wanting a part in a play; she may hope that the producer will be stimulated by his appreciation of what she has done to notice other more personal qualities; she may want the esteem and support of other members of the dramatic society. Whatever the reward for which she hopes, she will perceive the task as an investment: she is banking reciprocity and she may expect to get her return in due course. If, on the other hand, the producer has looked round the room and simply cajoled or flattered the nearest woman to do a tedious chore, then she has suffered the effects of normative patriarchal oppression (assuming that the producer does not equally victimize men to stay behind to move scenery or to paint the theatre). The woman could, of course, volunteer to iron the garments solely and simply because she enjoys the chance of helping the group. The task is a pleasing relaxation, perhaps, from a mentally exhausting job and she enjoys the chance to share in the collegial style of the amateur dramatic group. She may not care whether or not she is socially rewarded with thanks and gratitude. The activity is genuinely a pleasure and would not, therefore, be classed as work. However, it would cease to be play if, after offering to do the task a number of times, the group started to assume that it was her job and began to apply the pressure of collective domination to trap her into regular labour.

This is not meant to be an exhaustive survey of all the possible patterns of social relations in which the task of ironing could be embedded. It is simply a way of exploring the various structures of constraint that are created by social relations in which wage-labour, domestic labour and communal labour are embedded. It would clearly be quite wrong to say that our busy ironing woman was not working when she was not engaging in wage-labour. However, it is important to recognize that her orientation to the task substantially altered the form of work in which she was engaged. It matters a great deal whether she is a subordinated, physically and economically powerless person living with a domineering husband or someone living with a man in a spirit of partnership. In the former case it could be claimed that she is living in a situation of patriarchal domination, whereas, in the latter case, the lifting of the dominating structure of social relations changes the nature of the task. This point is important. It is not always necessary to change the nature of the task in order to reduce the burden of work but rather, more significantly, it may be more effective to change the nature of the social relations in which the task is embedded. Thus the dramatic society could turn the pleasurable task into work by taking the activity too readily for granted. Similarly, the woman who was producing her own garments for sale on her stall could make some to give to friends or to exchange for their craft products. In such a case principles of altruism and reciprocity would transform a product aimed at the exchange values of the market to something produced solely for its use value to a friend or relative. It is not the nature of the task that determines whether use values or exchange values are being produced: it is a combination of the social relations and the social orientations in which the task is embedded that defines the form of the work. The meanings that individuals bring with themselves as they face a given task are critical. Throughout our example we have been thinking about a woman doing the task. If the example had referred throughout to 'the person' many readers would still assume that it was a woman doing the work. The tyrannies of custom and convention may create work as much as the economic relations of production.

4 Contractualisation, work and the anxious classes

Andrew Sayer

> *Job security is a thing of the past. It's going to be very difficult for young people to assume they will have a certain income cushion, two, five, ten years from now. That makes it more difficult to buy a house, start a family, do all the things which require at least some degree of confidence about the future. Most people will join what I call the anxious class .*
>
> (Robert Reich, US Secretary of Labor)[1]

Introduction

While it is unusual for politicians to be as frank as Robert Reich – at least when they are in government – it is not unusual these days for social scientists to paint a gloomy picture of the future of employment. I am afraid I can't offer much evidence to counter this. It is increasingly difficult for both employers in rich countries and their governments to resist pressures to join a 'race to the bottom', by deregulating employment, and cheapening labour under the guise of the pursuit of 'flexibility'. Alternative policies exist which pursue less damaging forms of competition through upgrading products and skills, increasing worker involvement through improved conditions, raising 'cost recovery' rather than merely cutting costs. However, these tend to favour mainly a fortunate elite of core workers, and many reports seem to suggest that this core is shrinking while peripheries of workers with inferior pay, conditions and security are expanding. Although some workers are experiencing new forms of management which enhance their skills, autonomy and responsibility, others are increasingly subject to quasi-Taylorist management or exposed directly to short-term market pressures of competition and the threat of exit. At the level of concrete examples, the picture is much more complex than this, but I would argue nevertheless that the opposing pulls of the two strategies impinge upon most jobs.

The main focus of the paper is one of the most widely observed changes in capitalist economies: the increased externalisation of work by organisations, or vertical disintegration, in which what were formerly intra-bureaucratic, intra-firm relationships become inter-firm exchange relations subject to competition and exit. This represents a shift from bureaucracies to markets or markets and networks. It

1 See appendix for excerpts from an interview with Reich.

implies an increase in contractualisation and casualisation of work and therefore in insecurity as well as changes in the nature of work tasks themselves. These developments can be found in the public as well as the private sector, though there are differences in the reasons for the changes and in the dominant thrust of the management practices in the two sectors. In this paper I want to look at how these changes are impinging on employment and the quality and experience of work, though inevitably the comments will be patchy as the data is both incomplete and soft. As most of the literature on changes in work and management concentrates on the private sector, I will concentrate on the impact of organisational innovation in the public sector, looking at the new managerialism, quasi-markets, and contractualisation, drawing comparisons with changes claimed to be affecting the private sector. I shall also comment on the competing pulls of anti-Taylorist and (neo-)Taylorist tendencies in the organisation of work in the private and public sectors and the resulting tensions between enhancing workers' skills and discretion and limiting them, between security and casualisation, between strategies of expanding cost-recovery through product innovation and diversification, and strategies of cutting labour costs through de-skilling, etc.

Interpreting emergent tendencies in employment and industry is inevitably a hazardous business, but there are some common pitfalls which can be recognized. The paper therefore begins by noting these and then sets out some major contextual social and economic developments which are conditioning changes in the nature of work. It then discusses some of the changes, firstly in the private sector in relation to vertical disintegration, and secondly, and at greater length in the public sector in relation to quasi-markets and the contractualisation of work. The paper concludes with some remarks concerning work and social settlements.

Hazards: Hype and metanarratives

There are certain recurrent hazards in studies of change in the nature of industry, employment and work. One of these is hype. Usually this involves taking novel, interesting, but often limited phenomena specific to just a few kinds of work, and treating them as innovations which are about to spread and become the norm, perhaps encapsulating the essence of a new era (e.g. 'Toyotism').[2] It secondly involves glossing over the massive material, informational, social-organisational and contextual differences between all the many kinds of employment, which ensure that at any one time there is a considerable variety of kinds of work and organisation.[3] Thirdly it usually involves mistaking synchronic differences for change over time, as if the co-existence of different forms merely indicated a transition between one dominant form and another (Elger and Smith, 1994).

---

2 Often, the innovations are less novel and more restricted than claimed, as shown by Williams et al devastating analysis of Ford before Fordism, with its anticipations of recent Japanese practices (Williams et al, 1993).

3 Recall the absurdity of analyses of 'the capitalist labour process' in the singular!

Another reason for the abundance of hype is the frequent blurring of the boundaries between prescriptive, predictive and descriptive discourse. This is of course inevitable since managers have an interest in putting prescriptions into practice, or at least of adopting the rhetoric of innovation in order to appear progressive. Typically, such is the kudus of technological or organisational innovation and their terminology, that managers are not only keen to adopt the former, but are wont to stretch the terminology to incorporate what they already do, so as to give a progressive image. Moreover, where they do adopt new techniques this invariably involves adaptation and often considerable dilution, so that a diverse range of practices may come to share the same honorific label. The effect of these tendencies is exposed by Williams et al. (1994) whose search for genuine examples of just-in-time organisation turned up far fewer cases than managers and industry commentators claimed.[4] It is not surprising that managers should be guilty of hype, and it is an inevitable hazard in management science, torn as it is between explanation and advocacy, but social scientists' have less excuse for their lack of scepticism.

Worse things happen where commentators – especially in sociology – feel obliged to force the new developments into the metanarrative or binary history of Fordism/post-Fordism, in which – extraordinarily – the future is presented as the opposite of the past, and where, just because certain changes have been noted in a few highly-studied industries, it is assumed the whole of society must be going through similar changes (Sayer and Walker, 1992). At times, proving that a certain innovation is post-Fordist seems to take precedence over actually explaining the phenomena in question.[5] There is already a rich range of theory available for inter-

---

4 It is also illustrated by the example of a British manager who claimed his firm used 'kanban' but who turned out to imagine that this was a way of disciplining workers rather than a means of communication along a production line or chain! (Elger and Smith, 1994)

5 Accounts of 'just-in-time' production exemplify both these problems. Although often assumed to exemplify flexible production, in its root form it is specific to mass production, with smooth – *not* variable or 'flexible' – levels of output. The lack of inventories which could dampen fluctuations means that sudden changes in demand induce enormously inefficient fluctuations between over-extension of the workers and plant and complete idleness. It is therefore less flexible than the old just-in-case system whose reliance on inventories enabled it to respond quickly to changes in demand. Where it scores is in terms of turnover time and quality effects, not flexibility. Often users of the term just-in-time merely mean situations in which *deliveries* are made just-in-time. Yet these can made to and from just-in-case as well as just-in-time production systems. If this distinction is forgotten, then all sorts of fairly limited and ordinary activities which are quite unlike the original model can claim the avant-garde label of just-in-time. Being associated with mass production, just-in-time looks quasi-Fordist, though the opposition to just-in-case production, which was strongly associated with Fordism (at least after the early Ford systems), tempts one to put it on the post-Fordist side of the binary. Such are the problems of binary histories. Definitions of Fordism refer to many different and separable characteristics; just because one identifies large bureaucratic organisations, it does not follow that they are involved in mass production and have Taylorist forms of control over their workers. Equally, just because one finds vertical disintegration, it does not follow that there must be small batch production. However, usages of 'Fordism' which define it on a

preting and explaining economic change, and much of it concerns situations that are common throughout the history of capitalism. While there undoubtedly are innovations in the social organisation of work they are not all subsequently limited to a particular period or stage of development; for example, it is better that terms like 'Taylorism' are read not as denoting particular periods, but merely as referring to certain sets of practices.

The changing context

1. The most longstanding contextual feature, but one which is intensifying and changing its form, is the tension between use-value and exchange-value, or substantive rationality concerning outputs (qualities of product or service) and formal rationality. Sometimes the pursuit of quality in products and services is conducive to balancing the books or making profit in exchange-value terms; sometimes the two are in conflict. This affects both the quantity and the quality of jobs. As we shall see, the public sector in particular is experiencing deepening tensions between use-value priorities – safeguarding the quality of services – and exchange-value in terms of heightened pressure to economise. The key change here has been the extraordinary rise of efforts to impose new forms of economic rationality on institutions and individuals by treating markets – or rather an idealised view of them – as the best form of social regulation.

2. A second feature, similarly not restricted to capitalist economic institutions, is the tension between the benefits of discipline and managerial control on the one hand and discretion or responsible autonomy regarding workers' powers on the other. Again, this often produces double-edged results. Team-working is an excellent example, both enhancing workers' discretion but increasing discipline and intensifying their work (Elger and Smith, 1994). Such tensions are typical of recent developments in work.

3. The third contextual consideration concerns the public sector. In a seminal article published in 1967, William Baumol argued that countries with substantial public sectors faced a serious dilemma: whereas in the private sector, the need to make profit in the face of competition drives firms to favour those economic activities whose productivity can be raised regularly, public services tend to involve activities, such as teaching, whose productivity is difficult to raise without undermining the quality. While there are Taylorist pressures in public services, the nature of the work itself is particularly resistant to them. The result is that over time, public service activities get relatively more expensive, leading to fiscal crises. Yet, precisely because of the difficulty of economizing in much of the public services, they have become targets of government attempts to make them do just that. Furthermore, there is also a macro-economic constraint in that continued high levels of unemployment both keep up the demand for public service work and reduce the tax income available for supporting it.

---

different level in terms of regulation theory have more point, though the connections to usages referring to a Fordist labour process are tenuous (Sayer and Walker, 1992).

4. The future of work depends upon competition not only between firms but between different kinds of capitalism. These in turn depend on how technically and organisationally advanced capital is, on the form of capital-state relations and on different kinds of social settlement or mode of regulation. Following Albert (1993; see also Crouch and Marquand, 1993), it is common to contrast 'Rhenish' or German-Japanese capitalism to Atlantic or neo-liberal capitalism. The former is characterized by: continual up-grading of products, adding value to them instead of merely taking out labour; stable relations between firms involving networks and collaboration as well as competition; close relations with banks acting as committed rather than speculative investors and providing 'patient money'; strong local and central state support for industry, through technical education, strong 'horizontal' institutional organisation of labour and capital, and in the German model if not the Japanese, high standards of state welfare. By contrast the more liberal Atlantic capitalism is characterized by: competitive strategies based on cost-reduction, takeovers and mergers; pressure for wage cuts and strong restrictions on labour organisation; de-regulation of labour, product and financial markets; predominantly uncommitted, speculative investment and short planning horizons; lack of state involvement in development strategies; and minimisation of public welfare systems (as indicated in Britain's refusal of the EU's social chapter).[6]

While this contrast is relatively clear, it must not be allowed to mask the fact that within any one country there are similar contrasts between secure and insecure employment and economic activity. Labour markets in capitalist countries have always and everywhere been dualistic or segmented, but the balance between primary or privileged sectors and secondary sectors varies between sectors, between countries, the simplest difference being between the two capitalisms, and also over time with the shift from a Keynesian welfare states to workfare states (Jessop, 1993). Germany includes not only the exemplars of Rhenish capitalism but a secondary labour market where employment is distinctly insecure, in which ethnic minority labour figures prominently. Likewise Japan's success is not merely due to the usually-cited features – lifetime employment, patient money, state support, high rates of innovation and high quality, high productivity work – but to its cost advantages deriving from its heavy use of small firms with cheap, insecure labour (Williams et al., 1994). It is especially clear in Japan, that the existence of the privileged primary sector is to some extent dependent on its relations with the secondary sector, for absorbing shocks and providing low cost inputs to the big firms. Admirers of Japanese industry and advocates of Japanisation and indeed of German capitalism need to bear in mind these relations. The differences between Rhenish/Japanese and Atlantic capitalism can easily be exaggerated if their secondary sectors (especially the formers') are ignored.

As globalisation develops, the danger is that the race-to-the-bottom will become dominant (Peck and Tickell, 1995) and the quality of employment in leading

---

6 However, in the British case, despite Thatcherism's attempt to roll back the state, such has been the rise of unemployment and demands on the welfare state resulting from the polarisation of income and economic security produced by Conservative policies, that welfare spending has not fallen.

countries will decline. 'Imperatives of global competition, it would seem, are causing nation-states to scrutinize labour regulation and welfare policy less as sources of (national) social integration, more as bargaining counters in the process of (global) economic competition' (Peck, 1996, p.1). The pressures to economize are biting deeper. I would suggest that the future of work depends more on these tendencies and on the relative strength of the two dominant kinds of capitalism, than on technology.

5. The shrinkage of core workforces and the extension of peripheral workforces, the externalisation of economic activities through vertical disintegration, and the pursuit of flexibility are all widely interpreted as responses to increasing competition, uncertainty and insecurity. While this seems plausible, they are also responses which are themselves likely to produce further turbulence and uncertainty (Hutton, 1996). Externalisation and expansion of peripheral workforces increases inequalities and economic insecurity, both for workforces and companies, making them less confident about making long-term investments, and hence depressing demand. Increased short-termism, evident in reductions in investment, training and job tenure, also heightens the insecurity to which it is a response. It further weakens the resistance of workers towards such tendencies, since alternative, more secure kinds of work become rarer. The tendency towards short-termism and heightened insecurity is therefore likely to be self-reinforcing. 'Flexibilisation' is not merely a microeconomic phenomenon – it has macroeconomic causes and consequences.

How far job security can be maintained depends on economic competitiveness, demand and costs, and on macroeconomic circumstances. As Berggren (1995) shows, the post-war social settlement in Japan depended not only on the competitiveness derived from low costs arising from the heavy use of small-firm suppliers with cheap labour, but from the relatively smooth expansion of demand (until recently). This enabled big firms to innovate at a faster rate than was possible in the west. While most literature on innovation in Japan focusses on the organisational and cultural features of Japanese companies which enable them to telescope processes of innovation, it also depends on being able to amortize the investments successfully. By comparison, western firms continually had to delay innovation because of downswings in revenue. The favourable demand conditions experienced by major Japanese companies were not only an effect of their workplace relations, long-term horizons and product strategies, but a necessary condition for their maintenance. Thus, now that Japan is facing downswings in aggregate demand, the familiar features of big company employment policies are in question. (This also tells us something about 'Japanisation' – or the export and adoption of Japanese working practices. While it is common to note the difficulty of exporting or emulating Japanese cultural characteristics, it is less often noticed that there are also *economic* barriers to Japanisation, insofar as Japanese working practices depended on macroeconomic circumstances unlike those in most western industrial countries.)

Vertical disintegration and the private sector

One of the most widely noted changes in the organisation of industry (services as well as manufacturing) has been vertical disintegration, that is forms of industrial organisation in which successive processes are undertaken by separate firms rather than within a single, integrated firm. Where activities within vertically-integrated industries are mostly coordinated through hierarchical, bureaucratic control within firms, activities in separate firms in vertically-disintegrated industries are of course linked by market exchange, albeit often supplemented by networking, involving varying blends of domination, intervention, and collaboration.[7]

There is frequently a certain ambiguity as to whether vertical disintegration refers to an accomplished state or to a process still in train. The primary impact of vertical disintegration *as a process* is an increase in commodity exchange as a mediation of economic activities, allowing disengagement from responsibility by ceding ownership of hived-off activities, and an increase in the possibility of *exit*. Although relational contracting among separately-owned firms is possible and probably becoming more common, the links are usually weaker and more limited than the relations between divisions within single vertically-integrated firms (Sayer and Walker, 1992). On the other hand, growth of networking or relational contracting within an *already*-disintegrated industry – as has happened in the food supply chain and some parts of the clothing industry – obviously does indicate an increase in voice relative to exit. In neither case does vertical disintegration necessarily indicate a greater dispersal of economic power than vertical integration, for it may still be possible for large firms to dominate other parts of their industries without owning them, again as food retailing shows (Doel, 1995).

While the post-Fordist literature emphasizes the growth of networking and the use of voice, the scope for these is of course more limited in vertically-disintegrated industries than within single vertically-integrated firms. In comparison to the latter, the advantage of a vertically-disintegrated structure is that, in addition to the separation of ownership and responsibilities, it allows voice to be backed up by the threat of exit, or at least the hard discipline of dependence on external sales revenue rather than soft budgets from within the firm. Whereas the post-Fordist literature emphasizes the shrinkage of bureaucracies and the development of networks, I would argue that recent changes are marked primarily by the extension of market relations and only secondarily with networks.

On the whole, approaches which characterise the emerging system as 'post-Fordist' or 'flexibly specialized', present a hopeful picture of vertically-disintegrated industries of networked firms, collaborating as well as competing, following strategies which emphasize enhancing skills, flexibility and innovation over cost-

7 Especially within production supply chains, it is common for some products to have only a single supplier, and hence for competition and opportunities for buyers to exit and switch to another supplier to be limited. Hodgson (1988) terms this 'non-market exchange'. Note also, that contrary to the impression given by some of the literature, markets and hierarchies/firms are not simple alternatives for only the latter undertake production. Markets produce nothing; they merely exchange what firms and individuals produce (Sayer, 1995).

cutting (e.g. Amin, 1995; Piore and Sabel, 1984). How this fits with the growth of neoliberal influences in politics is problematic, especially in less successful industrial economies. In contrast, and fitting better with the rise of neoliberalism are accounts which also note increasing vertical disintegration but emphasize marketisation, centre-periphery structures, polarizing incomes, casualisation of labour and declining economic security, reduced innovation due to uncertainty and short-termism, and, in public services like health and education, threats to quality of services and equity principles (e.g. Lovering, 1990; Taylor-Gooby and Lawson, 1993; Hutton, 1996). As Lovering argues, the rhetoric of flexibility is increasingly seen as a way of putting a brave face on economic insecurity and increased pressure to cut costs and liabilities in the face of heightened market uncertainty (Lovering, 1990). Hence the talk of the rise of the anxious classes[8]; the disciplinary role of fear in economic life is regaining importance .

While vertical disintegration is generally attributed to increased uncertainty, and consequent moves on the part of firms to 'go back to basics', hiving off or buying in non-basic activities, it is also common to link this to an alleged shift from mass production to small batch and custom production as the Fordist/post-Fordist metanarrative suggests. Product differentiation may be increasing and minimum economically valuable scales of production falling as a result of more flexible technology and working practices and vastly-improved information systems. However mass production is still alive and well. It can exist in vertically-disintegrated as well as vertically-integrated industries, as the case of Japan shows. Conversely, small batch and custom production are far from new and have often existed within large, hierarchical, vertically-integrated firms (Sayer and Walker, 1992).

Notwithstanding these matters of contention, it does appear that there is also an element of organisational innovation insofar as major capitalist firms have discovered new ways of operating and exercising power. If such firms are sufficiently powerful to dominate suppliers without owning them, then they can be disciplined by the threat of exit. Independent suppliers have to be responsible for their own future and the dominant firms' obligations need not extend beyond those of self-interest, though firms able to operate on longer time horizons, with 'patient money' will take a longer view of the association, exercising voice to deal with short-term problems rather than exiting, as many studies of Japanese capitalism show (e.g. Dore, 1987). Vertically-disintegrated industries may therefore vary in the extent to which exchange relations are stable and embedded in networks, and the type of capitalism within which they operate is likely to influence this, it being more difficult for firms to form stable networks in Atlantic than Rhenish capitalism. In addition to strongly hierarchical industries such as food production there can also be stable relational contracting among firms of more equal power, but again this requires longer term horizons.

While vertical disintegration implies increased use of market regulation it need not imply extensive contractualisation in the strong sense of fixing formal

8 It is possible that such talk exaggerates the problem or its novelty; certainly economic insecurity is nothing new to the working classes.

contracts for the transactions. One of the striking features of recent years is that the growth in relational contracting rarely involves formal contracts, and normally quite complicated 'thick' transactions and forms of collaboration are successfully pursued without them, relying instead on a mixture of trust, shared commitments or lock-in, and domination. As we shall shortly see, this makes an interesting contrast with public services which appear to be moving in the opposite direction.

Vertical disintegration is associated with a core-periphery model of employment and dual or segmented labour markets. These existed with vertically-integrated industries too, but disintegration implies an increase in the size of the periphery, and a consequent rise of fixed contract employment, part-time work and freelancing. Furthermore, there has been a reduction in the middle layers of firm hierarchies ('delayering'). This is a result of several elements: 'downsizing' and increased buying-in of inputs; greatly improved technologies of vertical surveillance; re-organisation of work to devolve certain responsibilities downwards (e.g. through team working) and improved horizontal communication; and bringing higher management closer to front-line or shop/office-floor workers. The devolution of control is often referred to as 'empowerment', but bearing in mind its coupling with reduced security and protection, 'responsibilisation' better captures its double-edged quality. The net result of these changes has been increased economic insecurity and often outright casualisation of labour, together with a widening of differences in incomes and working conditions.

In both private and public sectors these developments have led (albeit by different routes) to the growth of a 'contingent labour pool' estimated to be between a quarter and a third of the labour force in the U.S. (Smith, 1993). There the real wage for manual workers has hardly risen for two decades, while the real wages of the bottom 10% have fallen by a third (Hutton, 1996). In Britain, according to the British census, 28% of the adult working population is unemployed or economically inactive. Another 30% of the employed population is in marginalised, insecure employment or self-employment. The last-mentioned of these nearly doubled to 11.6% in the 1980s, partly as a result of increased contracting out by firms. The fact that half of these work part-time suggests a different picture of entrepreneurship to that pushed by the government. 3.5 million British workers have held full time jobs for less than 2 years, and hence have no access to employment protection. Two-thirds of all new jobs offered to the unemployed are part-time or temporary, so that apart from the long-term unemployed, there is a continual circulation of people between unemployment and temporary, low paid jobs. Most tellingly of all, whereas in 1975, 55% of the adult population held full-time, tenured jobs, only 35% did in 1993 (Hutton, 1996).[9]

The decline of internal labour markets (so-called) means that gatekeepers need feel less constrained by demands for accountability as there are fewer cases of people known to others in the organisations being visibly moved up, down or sideways; workers can simply be hired or their products and services purchased and existing social divisions in the labour market can be exploited rather than

9 Please note that my criticism of casualisation should not be interpreted as an uncritical acceptance of full-time work as the only desirable kind of employment.

challenged (Lovering, 1990). Organising the periphery was never the strong point of trade unions and they have faced enormous difficulties in contesting the deterioration in the quality and quantity of employment; in addition to rising unemployment, deregulation of employment and increased political regulation of their activities, the decline in size of workplaces and in numbers of secure, full-time workers has made organisation more difficult.

Gender and ethnic divisions still map onto the labour market contrasts with depressing regularity. The more secure and better paid jobs in both Rhenish/Japanese and Atlantic capitalism are dominated by male, ethnic majority workers. The less secure and more poorly paid the work, the greater the proportions of female and ethnic minority workers. Where, as is most common, women filled jobs involving routine work, they are most vulnerable to technological unemployment. The uneven rates of change across the different sectors are now less favourable to women than in the 1980s in that growth in service employment has slowed or reversed (e.g. banking). In Britain, the brief flurry of concern in the late 1980s over the 'demographic timebomb' of threatened labour shortages and talk of policies to encourage more women into the labour force was quickly dropped at the end of the Lawson boom.

Where the pursuit of flexibility involves creating new jobs, especially with regard to working hours, it is likely that gender ideologies will influence not only the selection of personnel but the design of the jobs. The polyvalent, or task-flexible workers are overwhelmingly male, while the numerically-flexible workers are more often female (Walby, 1989; Jenson, 1989). While this might be the case for non-professional and non-managerial workers, professional workers are expected to be both polyvalent and flexible in their working hours, which means accepting unrecorded and unpaid overtime as normal. It is typically men who are more flexible in this situation because of their limited involvement in domestic responsibilities (Seron and Ferris, 1995).

Despite the common assumption that temporary and part-time work allow women to fit work around childcare, in Britain most temporary workers do not have children and many part-time workers do not either (Smith, 1993; Hakim, 1995). This so-called flexibility is less a sign of convenience and compatibility with women's domestic burdens – which would in any case accommodate rather than challenge traditional domestic roles – and more a sign of lack of power in the labour market.

As Hakim demonstrates, there has been a tendency to exaggerate the postwar growth of women's involvement in the labour market as a consequence of treating part-time work (which has expanded considerably in Britain and is dominated by women) as equivalent to full-time work (Hakim, 1995). However, even allowing for this, in recent years, women's participation has increased, with the entry of large numbers of highly-educated women (Walby, 1989). In the U.S. the percentage of women in the managerial and administrative workforce rose from 18.5% in 1970 to 39.8% of that workforce in 1989 (Smith, 1993). Graduate women have gained more access to the core workforce, although their distribution has been uneven, being concentrated in more 'feminised' areas such as personnel and involving control of smaller budgets than areas still overwhelmingly dominated by men (Carrier, 1995). However, a further negative qualification to the good news is that the core is now shrinking, and de-layering and externalisation threaten to reverse some of the gains recently made by women. While there is a feminisation of employment in terms of the composition of the workforce, the reduction of job security suggests another sense in which work is being feminised – in that the conditions of insecurity and marginality that have historically been associated with women's employment are coming to be shared by increasing numbers of men too.

The polarisation of income in many industrial countries, including in Britain and the US absolute declines in incomes of the poorest, together with the decline in 'tenured' jobs, have increased the need for two wages per household (Bluestone and Harrison, 1988). The decline of the family wage – invariably a man's wage – is hardly to be mourned, but when coupled with the above trends and reduced welfare support, the consequences are serious: 'With new forms of flexible work that have no long-term employment guarantees and few employee benefits, new forms of redistribution are needed ... Old types of unemployment insurance and retirement benefits linked to continuous and long-term employment do not suffice to guarantee a secure daily life and old age.' (Acker, 1992, p.65).[10] Charles Handy's up-beat vision of the 'portfolio career' will rightly be viewed with suspicion as a new gloss on causalisation and insecurity. For individuals to sustain such a career requires high enough incomes during the periods of employment to allow substantial saving, and/or partners with more secure incomes to fall back on between jobs.

'Culture management', 'Employee empowerment', etc. A more positive story?

I recognise that the previous section makes depressing reading, and is strangely at odds in tone and content with another discourse of employment that has gained prominence in recent years, that of 'culture management', 'learning corporations', 'value-driven companies', 'human resource management', and so on. While these refer to practices in leading firms, they have been surrounded by considerable hype. They are the stuff of airport-lounge management paperbacks, whose sales depend not merely on how well they describe and prescribe efficient and effective management but on making their readers 'feel good about themselves' by endowing managers with charismatic powers. Scepticism is in order.

These practices and discourses stress what labour process theorists call responsible autonomy or delegated responsibility strategies. They are aimed at winning the active consent and involvement of workers – including managers – by encouraging multi-skilling, the exercise of initiative, discretion and responsibility,

10 Furthermore, with the breakdown, reconstitution and diversification of 'the family', the shift towards increased dependence upon wages and salaries (at a time of restricted employment) and reduced reliance welfare support seems irrational to say the least.

and continual learning, as opposed to working by the book or according to habit. They are therefore 'anti-Taylorist' in content and surely desirable for that fact. They concern mainly core workers and managers, for they are unlikely to succeed if workers gain nothing in security, pay and conditions in return for their commitment. Often though, firms attempt to introduce these strategies at the same time as 'downsizing' is going on, and therefore have little chance of winning consent.

Continual training and learning is an essential part of this approach. One of the striking developments in this area is the greatly increased importance attached to communication and other social skills by management, even for technical workers, correctly recognising their importance both for internal efficiency and relations with suppliers and customers (Morgan and Sayer, 1988). Particularly where personal services are involved, there is some truth in the idea that discourse itself is an increasingly important element of the means of production, and that firms are becoming increasingly reflexive about this (Lash and Urry, 1994; Leidner, 1993).

'Culture management' goes further and refers to attempts to drive firms at the level of values, encouraging attitudes that make people work more effectively, identifying with their work and colleagues. Of course, workers are likely to realise that such values and practices are not introduced for their intrinsic worth, but for profit, and regard them with varying degrees of cynicism or approval. The attempt to instrumentalise values for economic ends may actually taint or de-value them. Nevertheless, despite their wholly instrumental character, culture management and human resource management may also allow greater work satisfaction, and may sometimes provide employees with lasting benefits.[11] While such strategies bring benefits to both companies and workers, they are often combined with dualistic set-ups in which non-core workers are subject to more Taylorist control.[12] The division between core and periphery workers means that increases in functional or task flexibility through reduced demarcation applies overwhelmingly to jobs held by men and has not appear to have brought about significant decreases in gender segregation (Jenson, 1989; Walby, 1989).

However appealing the rhetoric of culture management might be its effects are likely to be limited. Firstly, 'the so-called sub cultures found within some organisations are stronger and more enduring than transitory managerial cultural espousals that would overcome them' (Anthony, quoted in Thompson and Ackroyd, 1995). The rhetoric of culture management ignores power in organisations, and existing subcultures are often ones of resistance. Secondly, and more importantly, it remains the fact that the survival of companies still depends above

---

11 Victoria Smith describes the case of some low paid, low status, mainly female and ethnic minority employees who valued a course on communication skills which was intended to make them more efficient by helping them deal with often impatient and irate clients in ways which both placated them and reduced stress levels. Many of these employees found that their enhanced social and communication skills benefitted them outside work as well as inside (Smith, 1996).

12 In light of Whitley's analysis of delegated responsibility systems (see below), an interesting but unsurprising feature of US literature in this vein is its lack of emphasis on long-term employment security and the benefits which long periods of service can bring in terms of highly-developed company-specific skills and know-how.

all on costs and cash, not cultural values. Exchange value, ultimately rules, even if cultural values make some difference. The main point the management literature and its followers overlook is an uncomfortable one for believers in the centrality of management in company performance – that many costs facing firms are beyond managerial control and can make or break firms regardless of their corporate culture (Williams et al., 1994). Thirdly, such management strategies involving exhortations to workers to act as partners and expectations of expanded worker involvement are only likely to work where there is a high degree of employment security, and therefore apply mainly to core workers. Insofar as security depends on market changes beyond the control of management, the viability of the policies themselves depends not merely on management but on wider economic circumstances.

Work systems and their pre-conditions

The above discussion relates to two themes in recent writing on private industry and services, on the one hand concerns with anti-Taylorist work systems which may seem attractive but which affect mainly core workers whose numbers are mostly declining, and on the other, concerns with externalisation which point to an enlarged peripheral workforce, many of whom encounter more Taylorist forms of control, and for whom economic insecurity is the norm. The extent to which work organisation is predominantly Taylorist or involves delegated responsibility (responsible autonomy) control depends on certain enabling conditions. Following Whitley (1996) they include[13]:

Taylorism

- lack of skilled workers and public training
- short-term finance, dominated by capital market, uncommitted investment
- active external labour market for managers so their future is not bound up with a particular firm
- high separation of managers from workers

Delegated responsibility

- availability of skilled workers
- strong public training system
- horizontal organisations encouraging skill development
- dominance of loan capital, long-term loans, committed, knowledgeable investors
- limited external labour market for managers, so committed to firm
- owners committed to firm

13 Whitley points out that the connections involved in these lists only apply at extreme values and may not be reversible.

As Whitley argues, short-term financial imperatives are particularly inimical to the development of skills and trust required by delegated responsibility systems.[14]

Whatever the form of work organisation, what matters ultimately to firm survival is cash and costs, many of which are beyond the control of management, particularly those dictated by the level of wages in the economy. And even with favourable costs, success still depends on strategy; even the best-run, lowest-cost operation may fail if its product strategy is ill-judged.

Again, rather than dating these two work systems and associating them with successive periods, we should recognise the scope for using them across different periods and suspend hasty judgements about whether one will conquer the other. While there are connections between regimes of accumulation and modes of regulation on the one hand and labour processes, they are better captured by analyses such as Whitley's than by the discourse of Fordism and post-Fordism, with its suspect periodisation and forced connections to the mass/small batch production distinction. However, if the dating of work systems has to be left an open question, their location is less indeterminate, precisely because of the uneven geography of their respective enabling conditions. The mutual reinforcements within each set of respective conditions and the incompatibilities between them, means that one or other set of conditions is likely to be predominant in any economy. Nevertheless, some kinds of work may escape the dominant conditioning influences, usually because the nature of the work itself absolutely requires it, or because there are institutions outside the dominant circuits, especially in the case of sources of finance. There may be pockets of highly skilled workers who are relatively unorganised, or firms whose long-term prospects are sufficiently strong to allow delegated responsibility systems within an economy otherwise inimical to them. Conversely, particular kinds of work on volume products where there is little scope for innovation and where task fragmentation affords the most economical form of production, can usually find a low-skilled workforce to employ, even in countries dominated by non-Taylorist work systems. Industrial districts may have delegated responsibility systems dominant in firms at the top of the supply chain hierarchy, and Taylorist and paternalist systems at the bottom.

Ways of managing labour forces also depend on the nature of the work itself – its material, informational and social characteristics. Some work, such as teaching, could not be Taylorized more than marginally because knowledgeable, responsible workers are indispensable for its provision. Other kinds are easily Taylorized and Taylorism may represent an economically superior solution to delegated responsibility or expert personally controlled systems. Nevertheless, while the type of work influences the kind of work system, the above kinds of enabling conditions can to some degree influence the size of sectors dominated by particular types of work. The work systems cannot operate equally well regardless of context. This suggests that types of work which lend themselves most easily to

---

14 Whitley also includes a third category – personally controlled systems – which he divides into two types – expert and paternalist. The latter are common in societies in which paternalist authority relations are strong and horizontal associations (unions and employer associations) weak, and systemic trust low.

Taylorized work will be less common in countries such as Germany than in countries such as the United States. To change the nature of work, in particular to defend or improve the security of work in Atlantic neoliberal systems, one would have to change the enabling conditions, especially the financial context.

Public services

Large numbers of workers in advanced industrial countries are employed in public services. Here too there have been major changes, some of them similar to those in the private sector, others radically, and somewhat ironically, at odds with them. The changes include vertical disintegration, privatisation, the introduction of cost centres and quasi-markets, contractualisation and the rise of managerialism, de-professionalisation, and neo-Taylorism. Public management reform along these lines is common in Europe (Gray and Jenkins, 1993) and is being actively promoted for other countries by the World Bank and the OECD (Mackintosh, 1995). Although these developments have been most commonly evaluated from the point of view of users (e.g. Le Grand and Bartlett, 1993), I shall concentrate on those aspects most relevant to the nature of employment and the experience of work.

The reforms result from three circumstances:

1) the intensification of the Baumol effect, exacerbated in some countries in the case of health by ageing populations;
2) insofar as the public services are within the welfare state, the shift towards a 'workfare state', geared to considerations of international competitiveness rather than internal social welfare and cohesion;
3) the rise of neoliberal influences on policy towards the public sector, actively promoted by the OECD and World Bank.

All the changes involve the intrusion of economic logic into areas formerly relatively insulated from it. Public services have been forced to economise, to raise the importance attached to exchange-value and formal rationality relative to use-value and substantive rationality (quality of service), although there are some efforts to protect and improve the latter too.

In the old welfarist model, public services were under public ownership and bureaucratic control, with extensive influence and autonomy for professionals, and they were financed by tax budgets. Management, or rather administration, was 'custodial', primarily oriented to the conservation of standards of service, and dominated by ex-practitioners who shared the priorities and values of the providers, who in turn exercised 'collegiate self-control' (Ackroyd, 1995). The producer power of professionals ('professional syndicalism' as Walby et al. (1994) call it) was considerable, but supposedly benign, being used to extend and improve provision according to criteria set by the professionals themselves. Finance and income were decoupled from the delivery of the service and the transfer of the former was not seen as a way of controlling the latter (Broadbent et al., 1995).

Hoggett (1990) argues that large state bureaucracies had become unwieldy by the 1970s, with institutions tending to be pulled in different directions by the many power bases of professionals and specialists within them. The new managerialism attempted to police these by increased surveillance, and restrictions on budgets. In Britain the first major challenge to the old model came in the 1980s with the Financial Management Initiative, intended to institute a more independent and less conservative management. For example, in medicine it extended bureaucratic control and managerial authority, including 'an unprecedented battery of measures and techniques for audit, evaluation, monitoring and surveillance' (Flynn quoted in Walby et al., 1994, p.133).

This was followed by the 'Next Steps' initiative, externalising civil service activities in agencies, introducing quasi-markets and a purchaser-provider split (Greer, 1994). Certain professionals and managers would become 'purchasers', controlling their own budget to buy services from others instead of summoning them within a bureaucratic framework without regard to costs. Providers have to perform/deliver certain services measured by various indicators on a contractualised, instead of a bureaucratic basis, and face the threat of exit. Thus social workers have found themselves mainly on the purchasing side, as 'care managers', having now to cost the services they deem necessary for their clients, and buying in the majority of work from external bodies, rather than undertaking therapeutic work themselves.[15] Although such workers have greater 'choice' than hitherto as to the sources of provision, they are more strictly rule-bound and constrained in their decision-making than before, and spending restrictions have forced them to prioritise needs more ruthlessly. Some, such as doctors, inevitably found themselves cast in the roles of both provider and purchaser.

The purchaser-provider split creates only quasi-markets rather than 'normal' markets (i) because the final users or clients are not the purchasers (this being the job of professionals), (ii) because property rights are not usually exchanged, (iii) because there is usually a strong monopsonist, and (iv) because providers are normally not free to move in or out of particular 'markets' but have to stick to delivering a particular set of services. Where quasi-markets have not been created, audits which compare and rank institutions on various indicators and make the results made known to funding agencies and users, can force them to compete. Like workers in private firms, public service workers in particular institutions are being encouraged to see themselves as competing with similar workers elsewhere. In such ways competition and a new economic logic are being forced upon public services.

A common characteristic of the reforms is the development of 'tight/loose' forms of control in place of bureaucratic mechanisms, involving a combination of stricter centralised control of strategy, financial inputs and monitoring and specification of required outputs while freeing up the intervening processes. Budgets are usually set centrally but responsibility for how they are spent is devolved. This gives budget holders or 'purchasers' more freedom but also forces them to exercise

---

15 I am grateful to Roger Graham for discussions on this.

economic self-discipline. Such strategies attempt to increase awareness of market pressures or at least of costs at all levels within organisations, and sometimes encourage greater responsiveness to users too. Purchasing of resources is supposedly brought closer to the points at which the resources are needed, instead of being arranged by intermediaries distant from those specific needs. Given the double-edged character of this form of control we not surprisingly find an opportunistic deployment of the rhetorics of 'responsibilisation' and discipline, on the one hand, and 'empowerment' on the other, echoing the combination of the freedom and the discipline of 'the market'.

These changes were in some ways analogous to earlier shifts in the private sector (Peters and Waterman, 1982), but as we shall see, there are also many differences in the way they have worked out in the public sector. An important attraction of these strategies for the state is that devolution can be invoked to deflect criticism of the state, while offloading decisions on where to make cuts downwards (thereby protecting the centre). Furthermore, in an analogue of de-layering in the private sector, these systems of public sector control have meant that middle level actors and institutions have lost influence. However, in Britain, this was not merely a matter of finding a more efficient way of providing services but one of reducing the power of local democracy, by-passing local governments which were often Labour-controlled. Here, as so often, simple state versus market or firms/hierarchies versus markets formulations which see the two sides as inversely related (the more market control, the less state control) will not do (Auerbach, 1989; Sayer, 1995). In Britain there has been less a shift from state to market regulation than one from permissive state funded professional self-regulation to strongly state-controlled quasi-market regulation (Ackroyd, 1995; Burrage, 1992).

The general reasons for the reforms are diverse, and the priorities among them contested by politicians and observers. For Britain I would suggest the following:

- cutting public expenditure;
- putting into practice neoliberal ideas for improving efficiency, economy and service quality by clarifying objectives (through contractualising services or requiring this for audits), introducing competition, output-related funding, and auditing of performance;
- reducing the power of public service producers, especially professionals;
- reducing local state control of services;
- reducing the responsibilities of the state.

The reforms prioritise economy over efficiency over effectiveness and often pay scant regard for principles of equity that are central to the delivery of public services, indeed in some cases they flagrantly undermine them by encouraging 'cream-skimming'; e.g. avoiding 'difficult' pupils and patients. As in the private sector, there has been a kind of vertical disintegration, although its form and the motives behind it are different. Neoliberal theory has been influential in these developments. The principal-agent distinction informed the introduction of the purchaser-provider split, while public choice theory, with its assumptions that individuals are self-interested and that appeals to professional ethics are merely a cover for producer power, came to influence official views of public services.

Professional ethics and power

As Walby et al. (1994) point out, the traditional commitments and characteristics of public sector professionals – highly motivated, conscientious, flexible, caring about their clients – seem similar to the qualities advocated by new wave management theorists like Peters and Waterman. Public services can claim to have always been value-driven; moreover, in contrast to private business, the values and valuations are normally intrinsic to the 'delivery' of the end-product and not merely a means to the end of making a profit. However, in public services, the direction of change is predominantly *away* from new-wave management's characteristics, indeed some commentators have argued that the reforms amount to neo-Taylorism.

Much public service work involves the exercise of judgement, including moral judgements, about the character of the need and the appropriate response (Ackroyd et al., 1989). Insofar as public services have this normative character, they are likely to differ from private organisations whose priorities concern what goods or services will sell rather than with what services ought to be provided. Commodification of such services brings these two orientations into open conflict, with the instrumental interest gaining ground. However, since all work uses up resources which could be used in other ways, costs and economy can, of course, never be ignored altogether, even in organisations that are not financed by consumer revenue.

The producer power and work autonomy of professionals[16] such as teachers and doctors derives not merely from their self-organisation, closed shops, etc., or from a lack of commodification of their 'product', but from the nature of their work and what it provides. Teaching, medicine, social work and the like are necessarily – and not merely contingently – activities in which the provider has a major influence in deciding what the client/patient/student needs. Different ways of funding and economizing or rationing their resources can influence the way public service workers act but it cannot radically remove the autonomy, power and judgement which derives from their knowledge and normative authority; to do so would effectively stop them working altogether. Delegated responsibility work systems and what Whitley terms 'expert, personally-controlled systems' are therefore to be expected (Whitley, 1996).[17]

---

16 The autonomy of such workers is not necessarily at the level of individuals; self-regulated team working is common in public service work because of the need for corroboration over assessments and for preventing individuals making arbitrary decisions which don't uphold the principles of the profession and organisation. There is nothing new or post-Taylorist about this – it is just a consequence of the nature of the work.

17 Note that producer power and work autonomy need not translate into high pay: pay depends on the scarcity and prestige of the skills and the way such jobs are gendered.

In the light of the impossibility of seriously deskilling public service work it might seem strange that some commentators argue that public services are being Taylorized; e.g. Pollitt (1993). Here it must be remembered that Taylorism is a bundle of measures, some of which are separable. While deskilling is normally out of the question, managerial control can use closer analysis of labour processes, intensifying work through reduction of idle time, setting performance targets and indicators, and paying workers by results.

In principle, managerialism and contractualisation might aim to reduce just those elements of producer power which are not essential for the execution of tasks and which merely give producers a more comfortable life. They may attempt simply to reduce idle time or they may actually police the quality as well as the quantity of work more closely by enforcing certain standards. However, in practice, managerialism and contractualisation can easily reduce the quality of service too. 'Ex ante' bureaucratic and contractual controls are inevitably less flexible and sensitive than expert, individualized control, although there are always risks that the latter will be abused. Thus teachers may be disciplined and controlled more tightly, as has happened in British Colleges of Further Education, but to teach effectively within that intensified work regime they must certainly not be deskilled. Here the imposition of a centralised National Curriculum and regular attainment tests is contested partly because arguably it restricts the quality of the teaching by limiting flexible responses to the varied needs of pupils.

Furthermore, it should be noted that particularly in public services, where inevitably clients have little option but to rely on professionals such as doctors and social workers to pursue their interests on their behalf, managerialism is itself a form of producer power, and one which is hardly challenged seriously by the development of quasi-markets. The public service reforms are less about enhancing user voice and choice and more about asserting the state's interest in controlling expenditure. Insofar as the state still directs public services, the reforms represent more of a change in the form of producer power – from front-line workers to managers interested in economy – than a reduction in that power or a transfer of power to users.

Both neo-liberal and neo-Taylorist reforms ignore the complexities of workplace social relations, norms, beliefs and aspirations, and acknowledge workplace cultures only insofar as they call for a shift to a more market-oriented value system and acceptance of increased managerialism (Pollitt, 1993, p.56).

> The new right's vision of efficient management lacked a coherent model of the highly-motivated, productive public servant. If it had one at all it was a clockwork model that ran on targets and bonus pay [and fear of unemployment], not a flesh-and-blood figure that needed public recognition and self-respect. (Pollitt, 1993, p.115, [my addition])

The idea of people being motivated by the intrinsic value of the work they do and the service they provide is foreign to neo-liberal theory, which sees work as purely instrumental.[18]

Erosion of public service values threatens standards (e.g. increasing exam pass rates), by turning what was hitherto a matter of intrinsic values (how good is this student's work?) into an instrumental matter (how should we mark in order to attract more students?) However, we cannot read off the actual quality of work and the effect of the reforms from these broad features because there are other determinants and constraints – the kind of management, the specificities of the kinds of information, knowledge, materials, technology and social relations involved. Markets and quasi-markets and the economic logic they induce only impinge indirectly on most front-line public service workers, for whom use-value, need and public service considerations are likely to remain uppermost. They do not automatically create the self-interested, financially oriented individuals of neo-classical economics' covert normative theory. Nor can we read off how the changes are interpreted and experienced from abstract principles such as the need to economise or of fairness of treatment and quality of service. While these are liable to influence workers at the level of motivation and self-accounting, there are many other influences upon them and obstacles which make the matter an empirical question.

There is a danger of idealising the situation in public service work prior to financial management initiatives, quasi-markets, etc. Insofar as producer power went beyond the necessary autonomy for providing public services it reflected the protection of self-interest and the lack of pressure to economize. Self-regulation plus 'custodial management' made them remarkably conservative. Although the rhetoric of 'maintaining standards' and 'professional ethics' deployed in defending the status quo is in part a principled response, it also provides a convenient cover for those professionals who care little for them but who merely want a quiet life.

While contractualisation and neo-Taylorist developments which reduce the autonomy of individual workers are common, there are also post-Taylorist, Human Resource Management elements in the reforms which are intended to enhance skills and ability to make decisions, and to increase horizontal communication among workers. But then again, even these developments can be subjected to the Taylorist gaze; audits may count up the number of staff development courses completed by employees, to provide data for influencing subsequent promotion and resource allocation decisions.

Problems of quasi-markets and the purchaser-provider split

The purchaser-provider split can create information and communication problems in that instead of bringing workers and users/consumers closer together, as new wave management recommends, it can actually divide them further by interposing

18 Nevertheless, neo-liberals are not above invoking intrinsic value as a justification for paying less to such workers.

between them externally- or centrally-determined targets defined by institutional purchasers like health authorities (Walby et al., 1994, p.131). Secondly, the purchaser/provider or principal/agent split produces a problematic division of knowledge and responsibility which echoes 'the old policy/administration dichotomy between strategic objective-setting on the one hand and 'management' – the policy neutral business of efficient implementation – on the other.' [It ignores]... 'nearly three-quarters of a century's worth [of analysis] on both sides of the Atlantic – warning that such a hygienic dichotomy is unattainable' (Pollitt, 1993, p.58; see also Broadbent et al., 1995, and Mackintosh, 1995). Under the old model there were few barriers to the exchange of useful information between providers working in related areas. However, auditing and putting people in charge of tight budgets in separate centres is liable to make them reduce such free exchange so as to concentrate on activities that can be audited or which bring in money. It pushes them to put their own self-interest above the public good. In 'hybrid organisations', which are funded partly by revenue from markets as well as from tax budgets, disfunctional changes occur as a result of the differing incentives, for example, workers and managers may be tempted to devote inordinate amounts of time to minor market activities while neglecting the more central tax-financed areas (Mackintosh et al., 1994).

The old bureaucratic forms of control and custodial management were not necessarily much better as regards selfish behaviour. Even in the absence of monetisation, there are always incentives towards selfish behaviour; individuals and groups may still try to take from others more than they give in terms of information and labour. Tensions over such inequalities have always been features of 'horizontal' relations among workers within labour processes involving dense interdependence and inter-personal interaction. Monetisation and cost-centres do not create costs and inequalities where previously there were none, for collegiality was never costless, but they draw attention to them enormously, by quantifying them and making departments account for their members' use and provision of resources. When friends buy each others rounds of drinks they do not normally notice or worry about inequalities in the costs of the rounds. Making the costs public changes the atmosphere and attitudes dramatically. Similarly with quantifying and monetising work.

Any move from bureaucratic and expert personal control to contractualisation is likely to lead to a greater stress on outcomes relative to processes. Whereas in the former, tasks are pushed down the hierarchy to workers who are supposed to follow bureaucratic procedures and professional norms, whose adequacy is seen as the guarantor of the efficiency of the process and quality of the output, contractualisation tends to be more permissive as regards means or process and more regulative as regards ends or output. This may bring some benefits in quality of work but it also ironically adds considerable new bureaucratic burdens involved in assessing alternatives, costing and charging, and monitoring results.[19] While bureau-

[19] This is commonly overlooked because the dominant model of a market for both economists and laypersons is one of a consumer market for a simple, familiar, off-the-

cracies have been broken up in some areas, bureaucratisation has grown in others. The resulting increases in paperwork are widely registered across the public services.

Whether a consequence of contractualisation or of increased monitoring within bureaucracies, setting goals clearly and precisely in advance is not necessarily a virtue for it can prevent flexible, individualised and sensitive response. Thus specifying in advance a 'care package' for an elderly person coming out of hospital makes it difficult for 'providers' in close contact with them who able to assess their changing needs to provide a flexible response. Monitoring and audits also tend to overlook less tangible but often important functions which cannot be measured. Organisations usually have an element of conflict between their goals. The pressure to formulate unambiguous goals may be counterproductive; for example, universities are not only meritocratic (in their examining role) but supportive and redistributive in their educative and pastoral roles and yet despite the contradictions between these it would be imprudent, unfair and possibly immoral wholly to suppress one in favour of the other. This inflexibility of formal contracting stands in ironic contrast to the more flexible and implicit contracting that we noted is common in the private sector. Increased contractualisation in the public sector represents a diminution of trust, though trust is not to be identified automatically with good practice, since people may not be worthy of the trust put in them, indeed this is presumably what neo-liberals suspect. Similarly, formal contractualisation in public service employment relations runs counter to the tendency in the private sector core workforces to make job descriptions as flexible as possible (Morgan and Sayer, 1988).

Audits

Audits are intended to produce data which can be used to evaluate organisations in circumstances where users and funders are not in a position to assess them. Arguably they compensate for the absence of markets and user knowledge.

Auditing produces a bias towards those activities which can be measured, as it uses simple indicators as surrogates for complex, subtle and often individually-tailored, provider-client relationships and processes. This can lead to absurdities and perverse incentives in which professionals devote their energies to meeting the targets rather than meeting needs. Ironically, these problems of the introduction into the state of a quasi-market logic on neo-liberal lines echo the irrationalities of Soviet-style planning in trying to set targets for specific kinds of industry, and which liberal economists love to cite as consequences of the absence of markets.[20]

---

shelf commodity such as potatoes, whose exchange does not require bureaucratic work for the purchaser. Many, if not most, markets are not like this.

20 For example, anecdotes about planners being unsure of whether to give targets to say, nail producers in terms of quantities of nails – which are most easily met by producing lots of small nails – or giving them weight targets – which are most easily met by producing a few very large nails. Such problems are not unique to markets, however; bureaucratic systems have their own internal monitoring mechanisms which

Auditing and inspection can sometimes encourage higher standards of work, but they also induce the expansion of 'front work', that is activities directed solely to producing information and effects required by auditors as opposed to 'the real work' of delivering services, with its complexities, hidden information, and informal understandings (Power, 1995). It may therefore damage productivity. Marketisation and contractualisation have a similar effect in that providers have continually to engage in advertising themselves to win the next contract against competitors. To be sure, complex changing tasks of the sort characteristic of public services need continual negotiation and re-definition among their providers, but this becomes more difficult with the creation of a purchaser-provider split since to varying degrees, it adds a new and possibly unnecessary division of knowledge, labour and responsibility. Stories professional workers tell about their jobs are full of references to these problems.

These changes represent a challenge to professionals and their self-regulation not simply in terms of limiting their autonomy and challenging their monopoly of knowledge, but in challenging professional ethics, in which the quality of the service (which often depends on establishing relationships with clients) and normative issues of equity are prominent.

However, we should not get too alarmed about the effects of the reforms in terms of the quality of public service work, especially its normative side, for the caring role was always limited by budget allocations, albeit not necessarily totally rigid ones. Considerations of formal rationality or exchange-value were always (and always will be) in tension with substantive rationality use-value to some extent. Contractualisation was intended to replace the old, use-value oriented 'custodial managers', who had trained on the job and come to share the same values and assumptions as those whom they controlled, with more independent and innovative purchasers/managers who would act decisively to develop more economical systems. However, the localisation of knowledge in the professionals still makes principals or purchasers who decide what should be provided dependent on the know-how of the providers themselves. The autonomy of public service workers also allows them to influence audits, their criteria and assessments, including the very definitions of quality themselves – thereby making it possible to conceal cost-driven reductions in quality (Pollitt, 1993), and enabling them to claim they have achieved efficiency gains without lowering standards.

It is often said that there is a danger that contractualisation will trigger a reduction of trust and active consent, goodwill and cooperation and encourage cynicism, producing behaviour which has then to be corrected through ever-tighter contractualisation and auditing. Again, the irony is that while public choice theory's views of professionals' behaviour as selfish at base are jaundiced, their embodiment in policies of contractualisation may actually produce the behaviour

can also produce perverse incentives. Thus, in the days before the economic significance of quality was appreciated, quantitative targets were often imposed on workers without regard for quality, thereby encouraging considerable waste. These problems are common in quasi-markets, as well as within bureaucracies or centrally planned economies.

which they predict. On the other hand, there is a danger in romanticising the previous bureaucratic, budget-financed arrangements and overlooking the element of producer-power, and the way that the rhetoric of professional ethics and expertise can be used as a cover for this. The training of professionals is partly a process of socialisation into the ethics of the profession, but this is often an informal and taken for granted process rather than something openly debated. Much of the time professionals are acting in ways which have ethical implications but which do not involve them in consciously weighing these up. Moreover it is often unclear as to whose interests professional values favour, for example, is 'clinical freedom' mainly upheld in the patient's interest or the consultant's? (Walby et al., 1994, 164)

The impact of public sector reforms on employment

The main impact of the public sector reforms on employment has been casualisation, with increasing numbers of workers on fixed term contracts. This is notable in the health services, but also in higher education, which – faced with worsening financial uncertainty – increasingly employs its own graduates on short term contracts, often in contrast to the private sector where longer term loyalty is sought from graduates (Mackintosh et al., 1994). These short-term contracts fall disproportionately on female staff (Newman, 1993).

As with earlier privatisations in Britain, the external provider agencies offer inferior pay, conditions and job security to the in-house/direct labour sector which they largely replace, although in some cases, e.g. social workers, unions have remained strong enough to defend workers quite successfully. National collective pay bargaining has been weakened by decentralized local employment agreements and merit pay has become more common despite being widely seen as unfair. Taylor-Gooby and Lawson (1993, 137) cite estimates that the National Health Service saved £626 million between 1984 and 1991, mainly through driving down wages and conditions of service. The workforce has also been polarised between managers/purchasers and junior and learning grades, with some senior professionals and managers in health and education gaining in income, autonomy and authority over juniors, and managerial consultants and accountants benefitting (Ackroyd, 1995). Meanwhile middle level bureaucrats and professionals have lost out, and again it is these areas in which upwardly mobile female workers have been entering. The change from custodial to independent, economy-driven management, also suggests a more masculine style, although the old management was itself generally patriarchal (Newman, 1993).

The structure and balance of power within the old public service bureaucracies was always shaped by professional groupings, often in rivalry. The new measures have not so much undermined their power as shifted the balance between the groupings. In Britain in the National Health Services there has been particularly strong conflict between managers and professionals with the latter succeeding in incorporating opposition. Of course many workers in the public sector, for example nurses, lack the autonomy and control over others possessed by professional workers. According to Walby et al. (1994) nursing (involving the biggest employment group in the health service) is losing its vocational aspects, and being Taylorized, with some evidence of break-up of teams and removal of nurses from senior positions.[21] Significantly, the new managerialism has been more successful in public services with few professionals; e.g. public housing administration.

In this section I have tried to indicate the general nature of change in public service work, including the quality and experience of work, with particular reference to professionals. While there are similarities – chiefly to do with externalisation, contractualisation and tight-loose forms of organisation – to developments in the private sector, two circumstances make a big difference, namely, the material and informational specificity of public services, especially their normative element, and the continued political mediation and control by the state and reliance on tax revenues.

The tension between the normative principles involved in defending or improving the use-value or quality of public services and the instrumental goals of cutting costs and increasing revenue may seem stark and even dramatic, but the changes to the actual quality and experience of work are likely to be varied and often moderate rather than dramatic. Front-line public service workers cannot simply abandon their normative orientation for it is intrinsic to the work they do and not merely contingently related to it. However they are having to compromise their normative concern from one often presupposing a universal basis to welfare provision to one responsive to income, even though that can produce 'inverse-care effects' whereby those least in need of help receive most.[22] This of course is what the shift from the welfare to the workfare state tends to encourage. Although I have only been concerned with the public service reforms insofar as they affect public sector *workers*, it must be said that the rise of the anxious class derives not only from the contractualisation and casualisation of work with respect to them as workers but on the user side from the attenuation of the public services provided for clients.

Finally, I should point out a major qualification to my argument. While much of what I have discussed amounts to a further commodification of labour, inasmuch as exchange-value considerations have intruded further into public services, absolute cutbacks in welfare services are also *de*-commodifying caring work, by pushing it back into the 'community'. Instead of being provided by paid workers (usually women, usually poorly paid, and with little job security), it falls to unpaid workers – almost invariably women – to look after those formerly cared

---

21 Walby et al. note the 'extraordinary contrast between the individual power of doctors and the collective feebleness of nurses' (1994, p.132).

22 The 'inverse care law', in which the neediest get the least is certainly not new; it was evident during the golden age of the welfare state. For example, in Britain, the structure of housing finance and subsidies has always favoured affluent owner-occupiers over low income groups in rented accommodation. Even within the public-rented sector there was always a bias against those whose rent-paying capacity was low. See Le Grand and Winter (1987).

for by waged workers. In effect some women may not only be losing a wage but gaining a burden.

Conclusions

In Marxist terminology, capitalism is distinguished by the fact that in it, labour-power is a commodity, to be sold freely at whatever price the market will bear. But it is either a highly anomalous commodity or should not properly be called one, for it is not actually produced in order to bring it to sale, and it is of course inalienable from sentient human beings. Polanyi argued that treating workers as if they were commodities by de-coupling any linkage between the level of their wages and the minimum for social reproduction set in force disastrous, destabilizing forces, which divided and de-moralised economy and society, a view echoed more recently in Britain by Hutton (Polanyi, 1944; Hutton, 1996). The main tendencies in the public and private sectors that I have been discussing imply a deepening of the commoditisation of labour. This is evident both in employment contracts and security and in the organisation of work, as exchange-value considerations loom larger in the determination of what work is done and how.

All this points to the need for new national and supra-national social settlements – a new 'mode of regulation' – except that the hollowing out of the state and the forces of globalisation make it harder to create ones which can reverse or compensate for the commodification of labour. These are not simply matters for employers or organised labour. Governments can influence both the quality of employment and the kinds of work system which are dominant. Arguably, through appropriate intervention in financial systems, through certain employment and welfare and educational and training policies, the state can create a climate in which firms and public institutions will mainly take the high road of competition, enhancing skills, and offering more job security and better conditions. But the reversal of the commoditisation of labour and its associated anxiety also requires defence of public services and the welfare state. The growth of what Robert Reich termed the anxious class derives largely from the coincidence of these processes of casualisation of labour power with cutbacks in welfare states. Perhaps the most basic question we can ask about work is whether it is reasonable to make incomes as overwhelmingly dependent on employment as they are now?[23]

References

Acker, J. (1992), 'The Future of Women and Work: Ending the twentieth Century', *Sociological Perspectives*, Vol. 35:53-68.

---

23 Other lines of argument, to do with the break up or diversification of families and the feminisation of poverty, also point to the unsatisfactory nature of the dependence of income on employment.

Ackroyd, S. (1995), 'The new Management and the Professionals: Assessing the Impact of Thatcherism on the British Public Sector Services', Working Paper 24, Work – Organization – Economy Series, Department of Sociology, Stockholm University.

Ackroyd, S. et al. (1989), 'Public Sector Services and their Management', *Journal of Management Studies*, Vol. 26:603-619.

Albert, H. (1993), *Capitalsm Centre Capitalisme*, Paris.

Amin, A. (ed) (1995), *Post-Fordism: A Reader*. Oxford: Blackwell.

Auerbach, P. (1989), *Competition*, Cambridge: Polity.

Baumol, W.J. (1967), 'Macroeconomics of Unbalanced Growth – the Anatomy of Urban Crisis', *American Sociological Review*, June.

Berggren, C. (1995), 'Japan as Number two: Competitive Problems and the Future of Alliance Capitalism after the Burst of the Bubble Boom', *Work, Employment and Society*, Vol. 9:53-95.

Bluestone, B. and Harrison, B. (1988), *The Great U-Turn: Corporate Restructuring and the Polarizing of America*, New York: Basic Books.

Broadbent, J., Dietrich, M. and Laughlin, R. (1995), 'The Development of Principal-agent, Contracting and Accountability Relationships in the Public Sector: Conceptual and Cultural Problems', mimeo, Sheffield University Management School.

Burrage, M. (1992), 'Mrs Thatcher against Deep Structures: The Ideology, Impact and Ironies of her Eleven Year Confrontation with the Professions', Working Paper 92-11, Institute of Government Studies, University of California at Berkeley.

Carrier, S. (1995), 'Family Status and Career Situation for Professional Women', *Work, Employment and Society*, Vol. 9:343-58.

Clarke, J., Cochrane, A. and McLaughlin, E. (eds) (1994), *Managing Social Policy*, London: Sage.

Crouch, C. and Marquand, D. (eds) (1993), *Ethics and Markets*, Blackwell.

Doel, C.M. (1995), *Market Development, Organisational Change and the Food Industry*, Ph.D Thesis, Department of Geography, University of Cambridge, UK.

Dore, R.P. (1987), *Flexible Rigidities: Industrial Policy and Structural Adjustment in the Japanese Economy*, London: Athlone Press.

Elger, T. and Smith, C. (1994), *Global Japanization*, London: Routledge.

Florida, R. (1995), 'Toward the Learning Region', *Futures*, Vol. 27:527-536.

Gray, A. and Jenkins, B. (1993), 'Markets, Managers and the Public Service: The Changing of a Culture', in Taylor-Gooby, P. and Lawson, R. (eds) (1993), *Markets and Managers: New Issues in the Delivery of Welfare*, Buckingham: Open University Press.

Greer, P. (1994), *Transforming Central Government: The Next Steps Initiative*, Buckingham: Open University Press.

Hakim, C. (1993), 'The Myth of Rising Female Employment', *Work, Employment and Society*, Vol. 7:97-120.

Hakim, C. (1995), 'Five Feminist Myths about Women's Employment', *British Journal of Sociology*, Vol. 46:429-456.
Hodgson, G.M. (1988), *Economics and Institutions*, Cambridge: Polity.
Hoggett, P. (1990), *Modernisation, Political Strategy and the Welfare State: An Organizational Perspective*, Studies in Decentralisation and Quasi-Markets No. 2, School for Advanced Urban Studies, University of Bristol, UK.
Hutton, W. (2nd edn, 1996), *The State We're In*, London: Vintage Books.
Jenson, J. (1989), 'The Talents of Women, the Skills of Men: Flexible Specialisation and Women', in Wood, S. (ed) *The Transformation of Work*, London: Unwin Hyman.
Jessop, B. (1993), 'Towards a Schumpeterian Workfare State? Preliminary Remarks on Post-Fordist Political Economy', *Studies in Political Economy*, Vol. 40:7-39.
Lash, S. and Urry, J. (1994), *Economies of Signs and Space*, London: Sage.
Le Grand, J. and Winter, D. (1987), 'The Middle Classes and the Welfare State under Conservative and Labour Governments', *Journal of Public Policy*, Vol. 6:399-430.
Le Grand, J. and Bartlett, W. (1993), *Quasi-Markets and Social Policy*, London: Macmillan.
Leidner, R. (1993), *Fast Food, Fast Talk*, Berkeley, CA.: University of California Press.
Lloyd, C. and Seifert, R. (1995), 'Restructuring in the NHS: Labour Utilisation and Intensification in Four Hospitals', *Work, Employment and Society*, Vol. 9:359-378.
Lovering, J. (1990), 'A Perfunctory Sort of Post-Fordism: Economic Restructuring and Labour Market Segmentation in Britain in the 1980's', *Work, Employment and Society*, Special Issue, 9-28.
Mackintosh, M. (1995a), 'Competition and Contracting in Selective Social Provisioning', *European Journal of Development Research*, 7 (1), 26-52.
Mackintosh, M. (1995b), 'Putting Words into People's Mouths? Economic Culture and its Implications for Local Governance', Paper prepared for the ESRC Conference on Local Governance, Exeter, September 19-20th.
Mackintosh, M., Jarvis, R. and Heery, E. (1994), 'On Managing Hybrids: Some Dilemmas in higher Education Management', *Financial Accountability and Management*, Vol. 10:339-353.
Mayston, D. (1993), 'Principles, Agents and the Economics of Accountability in the New Public Sector', *Accounting, Auditing and Accountability Journal*, Vol 6:68-96.
Morgan, K. and Sayer, A. (1988), *Microcircuits of Capital: 'Sunrise' Industry and Uneven Development*, Cambridge: Polity.
Newman, J. (1993), 'The Limits of Management: Gender and the Politics of Change', in Clarke, J., Cochrane, A. and McLaughlin, E. (eds), *Managing Social Policy*, London: Sage.
Peck, J. (1996), 'Permeable Welfare?: Workfare Politics and the Deconstruction of Canada's Work-welfare Regime', Paper presented to the conference 'Crises

of global regulation and governance', Athens, Georgia, USA, April 6-8, 1996.

Peck, J. and Tickell, A. (1995), 'Searching for a New Institutional Fix: The *after* Fordist Crisis and Global-local Disorder' in Amin, A. (ed), *Post-Fordism: A Reader*, Oxford: Blackwell.

Penn, R. (1992), 'Flexibility in Britain during the 1980's: Recent Evidence', in Gilbert, N. et al. (eds), *Fordism and Flexibility: Divisions and Change*, Basingtoke: Macmillan.

Peters, T. and Waterman, R.H. (1982), *In Search of Excellence*, London: Harper Collins.

Piore, M. and Sabel, C. (1984), *The Second Industrial Divide*, New York: Basic Books.

Polanyi, K. (1944), *The Great Transformation*, New York: Rhinehart.

Pollitt, C. (1993, 2nd edn), *Managerialism and the Public Services: Cuts or Cultural Change in the 1990's*, Oxford: Blackwell.

Power, M. (1995), *The Audit Explosion*, London: Demos.

Sayer, A. (1995), *Radical Political Economy: A Critique*, Oxford: Blackwell.

Sayer, A. and Walker, R.A.(1992), *The New Social Economy: Reworking the Division of Labor*, Cambridge, MA: Blackwell.

Seron, C. and Ferris, K. (1995), 'Negotiating Professionalism: The Gendered Social Capital of Flexible Time', *Work and Occupations*, Vol. 22:22-47.

Smith, V. (1993), 'Flexibility in Work and Employment: The Impact on Women', *Research in the Sociology of Organizations*, Vol. 11:195-216.

Smith, V. (1996), 'Employee Involvement, Involved Employees: Participative Work Arrangements in a White-collar Service Occupation', *Social Problems*, Vol. 43:166-179.

Stover, D.L. (1994), 'The Horizontal Distribution of Female Managers within Organizations', *Work and Occupations*, Vol. 21:385-402.

Taylor-Gooby, P. and Lawson, R. (eds) (1993), *Markets and Managers: New Issues in the Delivery of Welfare*, Buckingham: Open University Press.

Thompson, P. and Ackroyd, S. (1995), 'All Quiet on the Workplace Front? A Critique of Recent Trends in British Industrial Sociology', *Sociology*, Vol. 29:615-633.

Walby, S. (1989), 'Flexibility and the Changing Sexual Division of Labour', in Wood, S. (ed), *The Transformation of Work*, London: Unwin Hyman.

Walby, S. et al. (1994), *Medicine and Nursing*, London: Sage.

Whitley, R.D. (1996), 'The Institutional Structuring of Collective Actors and Work Systems in Market Economies', Paper presented to workshop on 'Dominant Institutions, Governance Structures and Work Systems', ESF Programme on European Management and Organisations in Transition, Barcelona, January 25-27th 1996.

Williams, K. ct al. (1993), 'Ford versus Fordism: The Beginning of Mass Production?', *Work, Employment and Society*, Vol. 6:517-555.

Williams, K. et al. (1994), *Cars: Analysis, History, Cases*, Providence: Berghahn.

Appendix

Robert Reich, US Secretary of Labor, interviewed by Details magazine, cited by The Guardian, 2.1.96

Q. So what's the future of work going to look like?

A. A combination of job hunting and a lot of uncertainty, and the absolute necessity of learning on the job.

That sounds more like Blade Runner .... will we be more likely to have, say, ten jobs in a lifetime instead of two or three?

A. Yes. Expect to spend much of your twenties and early thirties moving from job to job, and also from skill to skill. People are moving across the boundaries of occupations at a much faster rate.

Q. When is technology your enemy?

A. If you're working in an organisation where management use it simply to control employees. Take the back offices ... where large numbers of people sit all day long simply typing at keyboards, putting data into computers. Often they are monitored electronically. They cannot take more than a three-minute bathroom break. In these environments technology is trapping people, it's ... oppressive.

Q. Do you think we'll all be freelancing in 20 years?

A. Well, we're heading in that direction. Large companies are outsourcing – that is, subcontracting more of what they're doing to small businesses and freelancers. And let's not romanticise freelancing. Most freelancers would rather have more job security. And their time is not their own. You're at the beck and call, any hour of the day, of organisations that need your services. A freelancer, an entrepreneur, an independent contractor may be spending a significant part of their day making choices about healthcare, pensions, doing paperwork, or just drumming up the next job.

Q. So job security will basically be obsolete?

A. Job security is a thing of the past. It's going to be very difficult for young people to assume they will have a certain income cushion, two, five, ten years from now. That makes it more difficult to buy a house, start a family, do all the things which require at least some degree of confidence about the future. Most people will join what I call the anxious class ...

Q. Corporations seem to have all the power these days ... How can a worker protect him or herself from being exploited?

A. The best protection is having skills that are in demand. There's no substitute for being someone whom the market needs. I spend a lot of time on the road, moving around the country talking to people ... What you have to do is look at the faces of people at their workplaces. That's what I do.

Q. And what do you see there? The truth?

A. Anxiety.

5 Blaming the benefit: The costs of the distinction between active and passive programmes

Adrian Sinfield

The subject of income maintenance for those out of work is generally regarded a technical issue to be left to the appropriate official and other experts. In consequence there is little awareness of how the discussion of this issue has become focussed on relatively narrow issues relating to work disincentives and hardship. It has not been recognised that this narrowing has important implications for the ways we perceive and respond, not only to the experience of unemployment, but also to broader issues relating to society, state and the citizen, and to questions of justice, need and desert. This chapter uses the analysis of one particularly influential report on benefits for the unemployed to start to draw out these wider issues in a consideration of the functions that a benefits system might fulfil.

The dominating concern with work disincentives

When some thirty years ago I first became involved in research into the social impact of unemployment and the ways in which policies affected the experience, I quickly became aware of the Swedish perspective on what were then called 'active manpower policies'. In the late 1960s OECD took up this theme and many reports emerged from the Manpower and Social Affairs Division under its Swedish director, Gösta Rehn, strongly supported by the Deputy Director, Sol Barkin, a trade unionist from the United States. The essence of this approach was a total labour force strategy which aimed at keeping unemployment low and equipping people, whether currently in work or not, with the appropriate skills to enable them to contribute. Benefits were relatively neglected because the very great majority of those becoming unemployed were not expected to remain out of work very long with this strategy. But income support was still seen as an integral constituent of the overall active policy, and not set apart from it. This is borne out in, for example, OECD's series of 'reviews of manpower and social policies'. In fact, in the Swedish review in 1963 the term 'active' only seems to be used by the OECD examiners and not by the Swedish authorities, and the term 'passive' does not appear at all (OECD, 1963).

Today the levels of unemployment across Europe are very much higher than they were in the 1960s, and there is very much less optimism that governments can play an important part in controlling and reducing them. In these circumstances discussions and policy making in many countries about measures to combat unemployment have taken on an increasingly different tone from the past. Benefits have come to be presented as 'passive' in contrast to the other, 'active' measures such as training, retraining and placement.

There has been increasing concern expressed by many, both inside and outside government, about the ways in which the benefit system influences unemployment. One particular theme seems to have become dominant. 'Typically economists', and many others, 'have seen unemployment compensation as having a negative effect on the labor market, with high benefits causing the unemployed to be less willing to accept jobs and inducing those in employment to quit to become unemployed' (Atkinson and Micklewright in a critical review of the evidence, 1991, p.1679). At least part of the explanation of higher unemployment is its longer duration, and it is argued that this could be tackled by some reduction or curtailment of benefits and/or the insistence on tighter conditions for their continued receipt. These proposals tend to be accompanied by calls for a shift of government resources from the 'passive' support of benefit systems to 'active' labour market policies.

An important example of this is provided by *The OECD Jobs Study* of 1994. In the much-quoted introductory volume, part III provides the 'Main Planks of a Strategy' 'designed to improve the ability of economies and of societies both to cope with, and benefit from, change, by: enhancing the ability to adjust; and increasing the capacity to innovate and be creative' (OECD, 1994a, p.43):

> Unemployment insurance and related benefit systems were originally designed to provide temporary income support to the unemployed during the process of finding a new job. With the growth of long-term and repeat unemployment, these systems have drifted towards quasi-permanent income support in many countries, lowering work incentives. To limit disincentive effects – while facilitating labour market adjustments and providing a necessary minimum level of protection – countries should legislate for only moderate levels of benefit, maintain effective checks on eligibility, and guarantee places on *active* programmes as a substitute for paying *passive* income support indefinitely. (ibid., p.48, emphasis added)

The more detailed discussion is provided in the second of the two substantial volumes of background material, *Evidence and Explanations: The Adjustment Potential of the Labour Market* (OECD, 1994b). It is to be found mainly in chapter 8, 'Unemployment and Related Welfare Benefits', with some further analysis elsewhere, especially in the final section on the interaction between taxation and benefits of chapter 9, 'Taxation'.

I have chosen to focus on the OECD analysis both because of the general importance and significance given to this study and because of the very considerable influence given to this organisation nationally and internationally. Drafts of its reports are carefully considered and commented on by officials from the relevant government departments in the individual countries. It is difficult to say how close its views come to representing what is most agreed-upon within its member countries, or at least the dominant view in their debates, but it is clearly very mindful of governments' representations in preparing its final, published reports. After publication these also receive close consideration from governments and others in the twenty-seven member countries, and indeed more widely – for example, in the new democracies. They are often invoked to support changes in government policy. In addition, I would want to point out that this particular study provides a careful, documented account of evidence on the work disincentive effect of unemployment benefits.

The main OECD chapter on benefits 'examines the case that unemployment benefits have affected the level of unemployment, as well as its duration and incidence across population groups', but this is then carefully qualified. 'The hypothesis here is not that unemployment benefits (or other structural factors) may cause movements in unemployment independently of movements in GDP, but rather that they may contribute, for example, to the unexpected depth or prolonged nature of a recession which, as seen from the point of view of macroeconomic variables, shows higher inflation or a weaker consumption or export performance than anticipated' (OECD, 1994b, p.171). 'Comparison suggests that, although there is not an immediate statistical link between unemployment rates and unemployment benefit entitlements, the hypothesis of a longer-term link is plausible' (ibid.), and this statistical work is supplemented by further analyses. The whole provides the evidence for the strategy statement quoted above.

The analysis of unemployment benefits is introduced by three sentences outlining the objectives in providing such benefits:

> The rationale for unemployment insurance benefits is to relieve people who have lost a job through no fault of their own from immediate financial concerns, and thus allow efficient job search. Insurance benefits, therefore, have an economic efficiency as well as a social equity objective. For assistance benefits the social role, in reducing poverty among unemployed people and cushioning the adverse effects of high and rising unemployment, comes to the fore although the efficiency objective, in facilitating job-search which might otherwise become increasingly difficult, should not be neglected.
>
> (OECD, 1994b, p.171)

After this initial comment, the writer appears to pay no attention to the functions of unemployment benefits other than their efficiency in the very limited sense of whether or not they act as work disincentives: if they do not, the assumption seems to be that they are efficient. I do not think that the 'social equity objective' is mentioned again and the 'social role', 'reducing poverty' and 'cushioning the adverse effects of high and rising unemployment', receives no further discussion. From the chapter as a whole the 'social role' would appear to mean the prevention of hardship, but what in turn is meant by hardship is left unclear. There is no reference to the nature, type or extent of hardship (let alone poverty) experienced by people out of work. Indeed the presumption seems to be that benefits are quite sufficient to avoid any such problem.

Hardship is mentioned in the conclusion to one part of the examination:

> Thus, it is important to understand relationships between benefit entitlements, benefit administration and unemployment rates in more detail, *to get the best compromise between the concerns of hardship and the equally important concern with disincentive problems.* (OECD 1994b, p.181, emphasis added)

This is a particularly important, and revealing, passage in the analysis. Anyone coming to this sentence in isolation would, I believe, be very likely to assume that it is the issue of disincentive problems, not hardship in unemployment, which has been receiving less attention, either in this paper or more widely. In fact, the whole analysis is concentrated on disincentives to work, and there are only a few references to hardship in the forty-three pages of the text of the chapter and virtually none in the following twenty pages of annexes and notes. This is not to say that the issue of work disincentives is not one important factor which should be taken into account, but to emphasise that it is only one of these factors: others deserve as careful consideration before that one is given so much weight.

Except when hardship refers explicitly to children, there is no further discussion of what this term means. The mention of children and hardship at one point is itself remarkable for the way it is presented. In a section discussing benefit administration, it is stated:

> in the case of assistance benefits for heads of household, rigorous administration is hard to implement. If benefit is refused or reduced on the grounds that the head is not available for work, dependants (mainly children) suffer hardship, *unless they are taken into care at great expense.*
>
> (OECD, 1994b, p.201, emphasis added)

Clearly the hardship envisaged here is essentially in financial terms. Social workers and child psychologists are well aware that separating children from parents can itself create other forms of hardship and should only be undertaken in the most exceptional circumstances in the best interests of the child. The public cost of caring for children away from their family is acknowledged, although the implication does seem to be that this is the basic reason for not doing so, rather than any effect on the children or family. Maybe this passage should not be taken too seriously, but it is one of the few occasions where any reference to hardship, poverty or deprivation is made. (It seems reminiscent of the proposal from the radical Republicans in the United States to terminate welfare benefits to encourage more self-support by introducing 'adoption or foster care for some [children]; for the rest orphanages', quoted in *The Economist*, 19 November 1994, p.62).

At best hardship is defined residually. But, in reading and rereading the chapter, I found it difficult not to conclude that hardship is not really considered at all: the result is a very one-sided account of the role and effect of benefits on work disincentives. Instead of an equally balanced discussion of hardship and incentives, there are a remarkable couple of paragraphs in the section on benefit administration which is headed 'Anecdotal evidence'. The first begins:

> There is a tradition in the social sciences of dismissing anecdotal evidence as misleading. However, with unemployment rates close to 10 per cent, most people have many among their family, friends and close acquaintances who are or have been at some time unemployed. With common sense interpretation, these personal experiences as well as reports based on journalistic inquiries are among the best sources of information on how people become unemployed, their income situation and work motivation.
>
> (OECD, 1994b, p.202)

This is then followed by examples from three countries of 'concealed unemployment among beneficiaries' with fraudulent claiming of benefits.

The sensitive and scientific use of qualitative evidence is well established in many of the social sciences. There are some notable examples in research on people out of work, much of which touches on the very points with which the OECD analyst is concerned (for example, Liebow, 1967; Marsden, 1982; Wadel, 1973; Pahl, 1984; Ritchie, 1990; Wight, 1993; Jordan et al., 1992). Unfortunately, the anecdotal material here was not carefully related to, and used to throw light on, the existing literature on 'how people become unemployed, their income situation and work motivation' (OECD, 1994b, p.202). In fact, with one valuable exception, there is no reference to the body of research. The research cited is drawn from a very interesting discussion of the attitudes of the unemployed in the 1990 Netherlands Social and Cultural Report (SCP, 1990, pp.92-98). The OECD writer concludes his discussion:

> this report notes that 'All three studies produce a modal group which indeed corresponds with how one generally imagines the unemployed to be and which is oriented towards the labour market and gainful employment. The estimates of the size of this category vary from 45% to 60%'. *Only this group would appear to be eligible for benefits.*
>
> (OECD, 1994b, p.202, emphasis added)

This last sentence is a quite remarkable one which reveals a very specific and limited view of the role of unemployment benefits. From my own reading of the Netherlands report it is not at all clear to me that there is any justification for such a conclusion. Certainly no evidence is given in that report to support it.

The OECD writer continues:

> However, not much such research seems to exist from other countries, so it is not clear how far the categories above, or the proportions of unemployed in each of them, might apply elsewhere. (ibid.)

This statement is also surprising because there is now a very significant corpus of research in some countries, although it has been sadly neglected in others. Indeed some of that work was explicitly designed to examine just the questions with which the writer is concerned, and it did so with very great care. In general the research evidence does not support the views expressed in the OECD chapter. In Britain, for example, the Department of Health and Social Security spent what was then regarded as an exceptional amount of its research budget on a cohort study which has received much recognition here and abroad for the path-breaking and thorough construction of its work (Moylan, Millar and Davies, 1984). This detailed analysis over time of the incomes in and out of work of people experiencing unemployment demonstrated the disadvantages experienced by those suffering from unemployment and did not support the policy concern with work disincentives.

One of the largest labour market studies ever to be carried out in Britain was the Social Change and Economic Life Initiative financed by the publicly-funded Economic and Social Research Council and carried out by a multi-disciplinary team based in six different universities across Britain. Its examination of the experience of unemployment in the six contrasting labour markets specifically considered the extent to which the attitudes and motivation of the unemployed affected their re-employment. The final sentences of the analysis deserve to be quoted in full as they catch very well the general tenor of primary and longitudinal research which has actually taken account of the attitudes of those who return to work as well as those who remain unemployed:

> Finally, for the greater part of the unemployed, there was no evidence that differences in either employment motivation or in the flexibility of attitudes to job search affected the time that it took people to find work again. Rather our evidence points to the importance for job chances of the availability of particular types of work, of the resources that can be provided by the household to facilitate job search, and of the structural misfit between the low qualifications possessed by the unemployed and the sharp rise in qualifications required by the changing nature of work in industry.
>
> (Gallie and Vogler,1994, pp.152-153)

The inadequacy of attitudes to employment as a clear indicator of who returns to work is repeatedly stressed elsewhere.

The questions of why people work, and when it is worth working, have been systematically analysed in recent years. At what point is disposable income out of work high enough to constitute a disincentive to look for or take a job, or to stay in one? And at what point does it become a 'significant disincentive'? A multi-disciplinary review of the evidence in 1994 stressed the dangers of governments giving too much attention to policies designed to create financial incentives and not enough to the many non-financial considerations which affect people's labour market decisions (Bryson and McKay, 1994; see Goodwin, 1972, for a valuable earlier study in the United States).

This point is particularly relevant to analyses such as OECD's because of the weight which is given to the issue of work disincentives. It is not that the issue is unimportant, but that it has to be related to others. In addition, disincentives are spoken of in this and other reports as if they either existed or they did not. There is insufficient attention given to the significant qualification emphasised by Atkinson and Micklewright in their examination of the issue: 'Our review of the evidence leads us to conclude that there may be adverse effects [from benefits] on the incentive for the unemployed to leave unemployment but that these are typically found to be small': they then go on to stress that 'a richer view of the relationship between unemployment and the labour market' enables recognition of 'some of the ways in which [benefits] may have a positive, rather than a negative, impact' (Atkinson and Micklewright, 1991, p.1722).

The need for a broader view of efficiency

Study of the evidence on the experience of unemployment shows that consideration of the efficiency of a benefits system simply in terms of work disincentives and the speed with which people out of work stop claiming benefits is a very limited measure, and a broader one is needed. A good benefits system may save people out of work from having to accept the first job which becomes available, whatever it is, because of the extreme financial pressures. While this is clearly one of the most worrying aspects of benefits for some, there are advantages if unemployed people are able to exercise some choice, where it is available, and so select employment more suitable to them. This has benefits for them and for the company which they join. There is less likely to be a mismatch so that the new worker is likely to stay longer, and there is less risk that any training or retraining invested in him or her is wasted. These are all gains for the economy and the society as a whole, and it should be remembered that this is one of the basic reasons why unemployment insurance was introduced.

This argument indicates that research should ask more searching questions, and not just how quickly unemployed people cease to claim benefits. What happened to them? And what part did benefits play in affecting what happened to them? If they returned to work, what sort of work did they find? How quickly were they able to recover from the impact of being out of work? How long did that new job last? If it was brief, did it nevertheless provide a springboard to a better job, because those in work generally have an advantage over the unemployed in competing for jobs? Or did they become unemployed again, and did this repeated unemployment become a stage on the way to prolonged unemployment? If they did not return to work, were they effectively forced out of the labour force into early retirement, with the risk of poorer health and greater dependence upon other public benefits and services in the future? For those who remain unemployed, what jobs did they seek, with what effect? Were they offered any, and why did they reject them? These are all questions on which longitudinal surveys in particular can throw some light.

The effect of the benefits system then becomes one among many factors to be taken into account. Review of research on the experiences of unemployment indicates that the concern with work disincentives has played a major role in setting the agenda for many studies. As Atkinson and Micklewright have argued, the consequential 'polarization of policy choices ... is a dangerous oversimplification'.

'This takes a too limited view of the labour market. ... It is necessary to distinguish several different labor market states, and not to consider only employment and unemployment' (Atkinson and Micklewright, 1991, pp.1679-1680). One author underlined the need to locate study of the experiences of unemployed people in the context of a changing labour market by subtitling his paper on the social psychology of the labour market, 'Or why we need to understand the labour market before we can understand unemployment' (Burchell, 1992). Throughout this and many other analyses in recent years there has been increasing, or renewed, emphasis on the need to accompany research into the problems associated with long-term unemployment with more research into repeated short-term unemployment and the impact on mental health of 'cumulatively disadvantaged careers of unemployment, substandard scheme attendance and psychologically poor jobs, all characterized by relative poverty' (Fryer, 1992, p.266; see also Burchell, 1994).

In fact I have not been able to locate any evidence from any country that many of the unemployed do turn down many jobs when unemployment is running at the current high levels. The actual pattern appears to be much closer to the UK experience which has been analysed by Michael White, drawing on the substantial number of studies which he and others have undertaken at the Policy Studies Institute over many years:

> Finding a new job, even for those who succeed within a fairly short time, for most people involves taking a cut in pay. There are long-term costs even for those who do not experience long-term unemployment. Unemployment disrupts and downgrades working lives and in very many cases leaves behind permanent and cumulative disadvantages. (White, 1991, pp.19-20)

This is confirmed by other studies which take a longer-term view of the impact of labour market change and unemployment.

This was well documented by the studies of unemployment in the recessions of the 1930s. As one particularly fine study commented, those out of work:

> are not simply units of employability who can, through the medium of the dole, be put in cold storage and taken out again immediately they are needed. While they are in cold storage, things are likely to happen to them.
> (Pilgrim Trust, 1938, p.67)

There is disturbing evidence accumulating from a number of countries which calls attention to the hardships experienced by people out of work and their families and raises searching questions about the adequacy of present systems of benefits to alleviate these hardships, let alone prevent them. Poor benefits may lead to prolonged unemployment and eventually withdrawal from the labour force due to poor health. They may reduce people's ability to cope with the pressures of being out of work. They may fail to prevent poverty and may cause people to take unsatisfactory jobs which endanger them. This is all the more likely when forms of employment protection and measures relating to health and safety at work have been cut back. Longitudinal studies have now confirmed in very detailed fashion that unemployment increases the risks of ill-health and earlier death (Townsend, Davidson and Whitehead, 1992).

The fact that there can be effects on the families of the unemployed is acknowledged by the writer of the OECD chapter who is concerned that:

> assistance benefit administrations often feel unable to be rigorous in the ways suggested here because they see a need to protect children. However, short-term accommodation in this area can have undesirable long-term consequences, through its effect on unemployment rates and because children are disadvantaged by growing up in a benefit-dependent household.
>
> (OECD, 1994b, pp.212-213)

As with so many other statements, there is no evidence to support this claim. However, if there is a disadvantage, does it result from the fact that those living in the household are receiving state benefits or from the impact of unemployment, perhaps combined with the fact that the benefits which are received may not provide enough for an adequate standard of living and for sufficient participation in society?

There is no discussion in the OECD chapter of what constitutes adequate benefit levels and no attention given to the importance of this question. And the limited nature of this criterion for public benefits should be noted. If you tell friends on your return home that your holiday was 'adequate', you are not saying that it was 'good'. So even by the criterion we apply to state benefits for the unemployed, we are not envisaging a particularly generous provision. However, in the OECD chapter there is no discussion of whether or not benefits are adequate for carrying out their 'social role': they are only considered in terms of 'generosity'. This concept first appears in quotes (OECD, 1994b, p.172), but there is subsequently no explicit definition. The presumption from the text must be that the measure is the percentage of earnings replaced by the benefit. What is meant by OECD's recommendation of 'only moderate levels of benefits ... providing a necessary minimum level of protection' (1994a, quoted on p.42) remains undiscussed throughout the four volumes of *The OECD Jobs Study*.

There is also no research evidence cited here which supports the claim that 'transfer-dependency ... has become an important phenomenon' (OECD, 1994b, p.172). Equally, there is no recognition that the belief that people remain and 'rest on benefit', as one UK Minister for Employment put it recently, is itself a well-known and recurrent phenomenon in at least some market economies (Katz, 1989). If nothing else, this makes it all the more important to obtain systematic evidence that 'transfer-dependency' is actually happening to a significant extent before proposing policy changes based on this view. In my attempts to review the research in a number of countries, I have not been able to locate any evidence.

By contrast there is a growing wealth of evidence that the impact of financial hardship on children can be considerable. This is well explored, for example, in *Children in Poverty* where research from many disciplines is brought together to show the effects, both immediate and longterm, of being brought up in poverty in the United States (Huston (ed), 1991). The risks of both illness and death are greater (see also Townsend, Whitehead and Davidson, 1992). 'The health problems of poor children have long-range effects on their cognitive, social and emotional development' (Huston (ed), 1991, p.15). Longitudinal studies show that children growing up in persistent poverty are themselves likely to be less well-educated, to have higher rates of unemployment and to be more likely to be caught themselves in the more serious poverty trap of poorly paid, insecure and dead-end work (ibid., p.291). Even those experiencing poverty more briefly with a parent's temporary unemployment are also at greater risk. The concluding chapter sums up the evidence:

> Economic circumstances affect children by influencing the physical environment in which they live, the health conditions into which they are born, their parents' stresses and coping mechanisms, the schools they attend, and the explicit and implicit messages surrounding them about what the future has to offer. (ibid. 1991, p.310)

Huston also makes the point that discussion of child poverty and the solutions to it have often been overtaken by short-term economic concerns with reducing benefit-dependency that may make conditions worse for children (ibid., p.311). Quite apart from the impact of the hidden injuries of growing up in poverty on individual lives, there are obvious costs for governments and the wider society which should encourage greater priority to ensuring that risks such as unemployment do not expose families to poverty (see also on the United Kingdom, Bradshaw, 1990).

In 1992 the *Journal of Occupational and Organizational Psychology* devoted a Special Issue to research on unemployment and mental health from a number of countries which was edited by David Fryer, a social psychologist with a considerable record of research in this area (1992). In his editorial he emphasises the continuities in research since the innovative study in Marienthal (summarised in Jahoda, Lazarsfeld and Zeisel, 1933 and 1972). The issue contained the report of a study based on a representative sample of over 3,000 households in urban and rural Ireland which ended:

> The original Marienthal conclusion, that the deterioration in mental health among members of households affected by unemployment is intimately related to the erosion of economic resources, appears to be no less true today. (Whelan, 1992, p.342)

And the author began his report:

> A compelling case can be made that, with hindsight, the most striking feature of the current literature on the consequences of unemployment will be seen to be its remarkable lack of emphasis on poverty. (ibid., p.331)

It may well be argued that benefits are so much higher in most European countries than they are in Britain, Ireland and the United States that the issues of hardship emphasised in this paper are of little general relevance. However, from my enquiries, there does not appear to be much research evidence to support such a view. Constantly poverty has been discovered after it has been the experience of a significant number for a significant period, and this is more likely to be true if the group are liable to be seen as less deserving – and this would particularly apply to people out of work (Brown, 1990; Macarov, 1970).

It is interesting that nowhere in *The OECD Jobs Study*, not even in chapter 9 which specifically considers the interaction between benefits and income tax, and the problems of the 'poverty trap' and 'unemployment trap', is there any mention of the 'non-take-up' of benefits. This is an issue much exercising those who are concerned about the persistence of poverty, not least among those out of work. How far this is revealing of a particular perspective on unemployment and the unemployed it is difficult to say, but acknowledgement that many of the people who are out of work are in fact failing to claim means-tested benefits to which they are entitled does not fit easily with the general tenor of the chapter. The limited amount of evidence actually collected on non-take-up is stressed in recent studies (van Oorschot, 1995; and Eardley et al., 1996, pp.106-108, a study partly sponsored by OECD). In the United Kingdom, where data are probably the fullest, there may be as many as one household not receiving a means-tested benefit to which they are entitled out of work for every three receiving the benefit. In countries where assistance benefits are based on local schemes with different levels of benefit and different criteria for receipt, the proportion of those eligible who do not receive the benefit for whatever reason is likely to be higher.

The functions of a benefits system

Because of the concentration on the need to avoid disincentives, the positive functions of the public provision of benefits during unemployment receive virtually no attention at all in the OECD analysis. And I should repeat here that I deliberately chose this study not simply because of the influence which OECD can exercise but because it was a carefully developed and analytical account of the subject. It would not have been at all difficult to identify other discussions of the same themes, but most of them would have been of much poorer quality and largely confined to one nation's data. Many might however have been much more entertaining because of their swashbuckling disdain of evidence and their partisan and ideological view of the need for control in the labour market. Some fit into what could be called 'poor law' thinking associated with the pre-democratic policies of the nineteenth century and earlier in most countries. Indeed, one specifically calls for the restoration of the 'less eligibility' policy of the notorious English Poor Law Amendment Act of 1834 to ensure that the incomes of the unemployed should be below that of the lowest-paid worker (Miller and Wood, 1983, pp.72-73).

Even in the OECD report there is no consideration of the state benefits system as some form of compensation which constitutes societal recognition that there are at least some social costs borne by individuals and their families during unemployment. This is rejected by the bald and undiscussed conclusion on the last page of chapter 8: 'In a role of pure compensation for job loss, employer-financed severance payments are preferable' (OECD, 1994b, p.213). But there is no consideration of the experience of these schemes and the extent to which they provide adequate compensation for all losing their jobs. In most countries these schemes are related to the length of service for a company and to the current level of pay. Those who have experienced earlier redundancies are more vulnerable to subsequent unemployment and are often particularly disadvantaged in pay-offs. They may have established no or very little right to compensation, and evidence shows that those with shorter service are often more vulnerable to being made redundant, especially where both employers and trade unions accept 'last-in first-out' as part of seniority-based procedures. There is also no discussion of the fact that many workers becoming redundant receive little or nothing from their employers.

How efficient these schemes are judged to be should also take account of the concealed cost to the government and taxpayer of the generous tax reliefs for severance payments. In most countries the cost of these tax expenditures are not published: contact with colleagues in a number of countries has elicited many stories of generous tax-assisted payments but no evidence on the public cost of these subsidies through the tax system. In the United Kingdom in recent years these tax expenditures have exceeded the total cost of the National Insurance unemployment benefit scheme (Kvist and Sinfield, 1996, p.25). Yet they operate as 'upside-down benefits' which confer more advantage on the better-off among those leaving jobs and provide very little for those who are most vulnerable to poverty – a form of 'reverse targeting' which is totally counter to the government's reform of the unemployment insurance benefit to concentrate its help on those most in need. The effect is that the cost to the UK Treasury through tax reliefs for the 'private' severance schemes has become twice the cost of the insurance element in the public benefit after recent policy changes.

The neglect in the OECD report of any form of explicitly-financed public compensation for unemployment reflects a limited view of the causes of unemployment. It fails to recognise that unemployment is a characteristic of the sort of societies in which we live, and not simply of those people who happen to be out of work at any particular time. Despite the very limited references to the 'social role' of benefits, the ways in which the unemployed are described and discussed reveals at best a sceptical view of the hardships of unemployment. There is no acknowledgement of issues of social justice, rights and citizenship (Wikeley,

1989). The importance of public benefit systems as an expression of social solidarity with those experiencing a risk is not considered (ILO, 1984, paras 39 and 219; Micklewright, 1990, pp.3-4).

In many ways this limited view of benefits represents a step backwards, ignoring the reasons for introducing national programmes of unemployment insurance. Yet the history of social security systems reveals that benefits for the unemployed have always occupied a very precarious position. This risk was often recognised later than the other insured risks such as invalidity or retirement, and almost always needs have been met in a more limited way (Kaim-Caudle, 1973, chapter 7; Clasen, 1994; Sinfield, 1983).

The value of benefits in easing the impact of greater job insecurity both for individuals and for the economy is also not discussed. Recent UK surveys of perceptions of those in work show that they expect greater job insecurity and so are more reluctant to consider changing jobs, moving house and making major investments. The 1995 British Lifestyles report, for example, concluded that 'the recession of the early 1990s has affected people's spending' (*The Guardian* 24 January 1996). The response to greater insecurity is likely to be even sharper when benefits are not seen as adequate. It acts as a brake on economic growth because workers are not moving to more productive work and because reduced consumption itself is deflationary.

There is also no attention to the actual deflationary effect of reducing benefits. Again the United Kingdom can provide an instructive example where the sharp reduction in the spending power with an increasing number of poor people may well have acted to weaken any consumer-led boost to the economy. Cutbacks in the British social security system totalled more than 1 percent of GDP in the 1980s, and these alone would have acted to slow growth (Hutton, 1995, p.179).

A good benefit system may attract people into the labour force, or keep them in longer, with the result that they finish up in employment (Micklewright, 1990, pp.3-4). One part of the gain to the wider society is the contribution they then make in taxation and insurance contributions, and in higher indirect tax yields as their standard of living, and so purchasing-power, goes up with their employment.

The significance of a benefits system for those in work may be considerable. At all times workers may be more ready to accept the risks of change if they believe that the rest of society is prepared to provide what they see as a reasonable level of support (NEDC, 1963). This can be seen as part of an implicit social contract. This collective recognition that social costs should not be allowed to lie where they fall is one of the central functions of social security systems –

> partial compensations for disservices, for social costs and social insecurities which are the product of a rapidly changing industrial-urban society ... part of the price we pay to some people for bearing part of the costs of other people's progress. (Titmuss, 1968, chapter 11, p.133)

By contrast the alienation which may result when a significant part of the society sees, or believes, that it is being excluded can be very costly to the efficient and effective working of an economy:

> The collapse of social cohesion that comes when the market is allowed to rip through society has produced a fall in the growth rate: marginalisation, deprivation and exclusion have proved economically irrational.
>
> (Hutton, 1995, p.175).

The weight of this argument was recognised very clearly over twenty years ago in the terms of reference to the Swedish Royal Commission on Long-term Employment in March 1974 when unemployment was then 2%:

> In a society where unemployment is accepted, great material and social gaps develop, resulting in the mutual isolation and alienation of different groups. Any social order not based on full employment must imply a restriction of living conditions and a squandering of human resources.

There will be serious costs to governments which give too much weight to the work incentive issue and cut benefit entitlements in line with the reductionist arguments. If incentives are not as important as it is argued, then unemployment will not fall and public spending will not be reduced or freed for other purposes. In addition, the experience of the United Kingdom indicates that there could be significant long-term costs for government and for society as a whole which result from increased poverty and deprivation (for one review of the costs of the wider impact of unemployment, see Sinfield, 1984).

The longer-term social effects may also impinge on working relationships. It has been argued that the restrictive practices of the trade unions in the high employment years after 1945 were a reaction to the ways in which workers had been treated during the interwar recessions (Burkitt and Bowers, 1979, p.13; Hyman, 1979, pp.290-293). The advantages of social cohesion and relative consensus of an integrated, corporate welfare state such as Sweden could be weakened, if not destroyed, by the narrow calculations of 'rational economic man' (Sen, 1992; see also Kalecki, 1943; and Ganssmann's discussion of the 'pull-down effects' of the welfare state, 1991).

While benefit systems are coming in for close scrutiny, there appears to be a more relaxed, even complacent, view of the labour market measures, often routinely abbreviated to ALMPs (Active Labour Market Policies). A recent exception to this in Sweden is illuminating. A study reported in the 1995 *Swedish Economic Policy Review* found that 'participants in the four ALMPs examined seem to exit to regular employment at a lower rate than nonparticipants'. This is described as 'the most disappointing finding', seeming to support 'the hypothesis that the overall volume of programmes may introduce inefficiencies' (Ackum Agell 1995, pp.92-93). This point was picked up with concern many times in this issue of the journal, one of two devoted to unemployment, although I am told that the author has subsequently rejected this interpretation of the data. In the 1995 publication there did not appear to be any discussion of the many other criteria which need to be employed in evaluating the efficiency and effectiveness of any labour market measure, as with the benefits programme. How good, or even adequate, were the jobs to which participants and non-participants went; how long did the jobs last; who became unemployed again; and, if so, for how long and how many times?

More analysisis is needed before too much reliance is placed on the speed of return to employment alone. Focus on that to the exclusion of all else recalls Peter Blau's study of the US state employment service office in *The Dynamics of Bureaucracy* where the use of the number of job placings to evaluate, reward and promote staff encouraged them to devote greater effort to quickly pushing poorly-skilled unemployed into routine, short-term jobs again and again rather than spending time finding people more appropriate, longer-term work. This especially worked to the cost of those jobseekers with disabilities or handicaps (Blau, 1963; see also Cohen, 1965). A subsequent article in the *Swedish Economic Policy Review* revealed the very high risk of repeated unemployment in Sweden which has remained unrecognised, as in most countries, because of the lack of regular data on the recurrence of being out of work (Ackum Agell et al., 1995). And its discussant, Tor Eriksson, reflected that 'the high frequency of recurrent unemployment ... reinforces the picture of a low Swedish unemployment rate [in the past] being concentrated on few persons' (Eriksson, 1995, p.131). Once again the causes of repeated unemployment require investigation, including the stimulus of labour market or social security programmes in pushing people into short-term and dead-end work.

The assumption that training programmes are in themselves a good thing because they are 'active' still seems to be accompanied by too little attention to their context and the long-term impact. Schemes are better than nothing, one is often told, even if they do not lead to some form of regular employment. Not surprisingly, the nature and quality of the training, how it is rewarded and how it is implemented can all have their impact (Finn, 1987). People who lack marketable job skills can still have the skill to recognise when they are being put through an inferior course and may be swift to conclude that they are regarded as inferior too. Social policy is full of examples of where services designed for poor people are poor, and so reinforce the problems people are already enduring from their poverty (Miller, 1993).

This was well-documented in one of the outstanding studies of the American War on Poverty which pointed out:

> Disillusionment is not apathy, and to confuse them only complacently displaces the responsibility for failure. ... Indeed, it was not amongst the poor, but amongst the staff of the institutions which served them, that apathy and indifference more often frustrated progress. (Marris and Rein, 1967, p.90)

The disillusionment of those who come to see themselves as pushed through a course, or a succession of them, when no-one expects them to find work, can lead to cynicism and alienation, especially when the experience is frequently repeated.

This risk may be particularly great for marginal groups in the labour force who are more vulnerable to repeated and prolonged unemployment.

Points such as these, which seem to have been neglected in *The OECD Jobs Study*, have been picked up in the editorial to OECD's 1995 *Employment Outlook* which provided a well-judged and analytical discussion of 'Making active labour market policies more effective' (1995, pp. vii-xii). There is some particularly useful discussion of the need 'to be clear about the criteria to use in evaluating ALMPs', and 'the urgent need for more and better evaluation of ALMPs' is well emphasised (ibid., p. xi). However, the whole editorial concludes: 'The case remains compelling for a switch of resources from passive income support to ALMPs which have proven to be effective' (ibid., p. xii). Once again the option is presented in terms of shifting from one to the other, without any recognition of the important role which good income support policies can play in tackling the problems of unemployment, complementing good ALMPs. In consequence there is no discussion of how the best elements of both can be combined to improve labour market strategies.

The need for a fuller debate on benefits for people out of work

My discussion has led me to argue that the distinction between 'active' and 'passive' programmes as operated at present is both mistaken and misleading. It is mistaken because there are many features of the benefits system which can assist and promote activity and tackle other problems associated with unemployment and labour market change in a more positive way which brings benefits and reduces costs in the long-term. Equally, there are aspects of so-called ALMPs which can work against renewed employment activity and the best interests of the individual and the wider society, as I have indicated. But I would emphasise that my intention is not to question the value and importance of good schemes of this type as part of a response to unemployment, but rather to demonstrate the shortcomings in the limited way in which benefits systems are considered.

The current usage of the terms 'active' and 'passive' is misleading because of the way that they resonate politically. It is hard, if not impossible, to conceive a ministerial statement in favour of passive measures at the expense of active ones. In consequence, what is classified as passive seems eternally condemned to lower priority with second-class status and funding at best, and to stigmatising dismissal, ever-tightening and humiliating conditions and continual cuts, if not abolition, at worst. There is the danger that the current application of the two terms will provide one more case-study for Murray Edelman's *Political Language* which he neatly subtitled, 'Words that Succeed and Policies that Fail' (1977).

I would argue that it is much better to distinguish between 'positive' and 'negative' aspects of programmes, whether they be labour market measures or benefit systems, than to attempt to distinguish 'active' from 'passive'. Good policymaking needs to identify priorities and then to strengthen those elements of policy which support these objectives most effectively – and not rest upon assumptions about active and passive which may have little substance in reality. Before we accept strategies such as the OECD one set out at the start of this chapter, we need a much fuller discussion than we have had for many years of the criteria which are appropriate for the assessment of benefits for people out of work. What *mix* of what type of benefit, employment, training and other policies are most helpful in reducing and preventing unemployment and its harmful effects on those who directly experience it, their families and the rest of society? And how can their combination most effectively support the broader strategies that are needed to make a substantial impact upon the level of unemployment?

Any measure which helps those vulnerable to unemployment to cope with the pressures out of work would seem to be very useful to the individual and to society as a whole. It would at the very least help governments to keep down the long-term costs of unemployment in terms of higher public spending on a whole range of services. Those who tend to dismiss this as a moral plea which cannot be afforded in present economic realities' have overlooked or discounted the economic and other costs which not providing a good benefit system may incur. But the way that the discussion of benefits for unemployed people has shifted touches on much broader issues related to views about the causes of unemployment, the role of the state, and the rights and duties of the citizen in a modern democracy. It is hard to escape the view that 'the unemployed' are not considered as citizens in much of this policy debate: 'the workless tend to be viewed as worthless' (Marsden 1982, p.2).

•••

The concentration on two words, active and passive, and on one chapter of a study for a contribution to a volume with such a wide and all-embracing remit as this one may need special justification. My purpose has been to bring out the very specific ways in which the agenda is being limited in discussions of not only benefits but also people out of work. By focussing on work disincentives and discounting other aspects of the experience of unemployment, and by treating those out of work in an individualistic way that takes little note of the level of demand at local or national level or of the wider social costs of unemployment, the discussions serve to reduce the political and policy significance of unemployment and the unemployed.

The salience of the discussion of benefits to strategies to tackle the overall scale of unemployment was recognised by William Beveridge:

> The dangers [of a generous scheme of benefits for the unemployed] lie not so much in the risk of demoralising recipients of relief, so that they do not look for work, as in the risk of demoralising Governments, employers, and trade unions so that they take less thought for the prevention of unemployment.
>
> (Beveridge, 1930, p.294)

And this, it might be added, was written at a time when, according to his biographer, he was in an individualist rather than collectivist mood. Experience of the recent debates would lead me to qualify this in one important respect: it is the perception that benefits are high which is crucial. How that perception is created deserves further analysis.

The total effect of OECD's blinkered account, given its influential standing, is to contribute in a significant way to 'agenda-setting' on both an international and national scale. It is an outstanding example of the 'mobilisation of bias' which may reinforce current policy directions in many countries.

There are two secondary themes which this analysis raises. The first is the questions it poses about the role played by such international bodies as OECD and other external groups in helping to set the agenda of national debates, whether policy-related or other. This is not necessarily a new development, but it is becoming an increasingly important and influential one with the growing power of international agencies (Townsend, 1993). It is also important to take account of private bodies such as the Manhattan Institute and the Heritage Foundation in the United States who have exercised considerable influence with well-financed sponsorship of free-market thinking (Marmor and Plowden, 1991; Katz, 1989). They have been particularly influential in disseminating and exporting notions of 'underclass' and 'benefit-dependency', the latter of which appeared to be taken up uncritically in the OECD report.

There is a certain irony that OECD should be developing this position more firmly, just when the World Bank, which has been long criticised for its limited, economistic and asocial analyses of problems and for recommendations of market-only counterpolicies, is showing signs of recognising the importance of policies which sustain solidarity and social cohesion (Deacon, 1995).

The other minor theme is the ways in which economists continue to exercise a dominant influence among social scientists in policy debates. This too is by no means new, particularly in the general area of labour markets and employment. However, despite some outstanding exceptions, the range of economic debate has narrowed in recent years, and the range of policy and other social science debates has become correspondingly further restricted. I would suggest that we need to give more attention to examining the political construction of knowledge on these issues, and the relative lack of success of other approaches to economics and of other social sciences in informing and generally contributing to both public and policy debates. This chapter would indicate that these other approaches provide a different view of unemployment and the unemployed which leads to a different balance of policy emphases from that set out by many governments and by OECD in its *Jobs Study*. This could be revealed particularly clearly in a broader-based cost-effectiveness analysis (see, for example, the rights-based approach in Neuburger and Fraser, 1993).

It is relevant that analyses of work disincentives are seen as technical and apolitical presentations (Macarov, 1970). By contrast, a challenge such as this one tends to be viewed as highly political. This in itself reveals the perspective from which the rights and needs of people out of work are usually considered: it is one which reinforces the social and political construction of the undeserving poor from the able-bodied out of work.

If this view of work and unemployment is left unchallenged, it is possible that the dominance of this particular discourse on what manner of income maintenance is appropriate will help to shape the ways in which working relationships are developed as we go into the twenty-first century. Those who are most vulnerable to unemployment are likely to be those whose experience will be most affected. However, as I have tried to indicate, the discourse also touches upon much broader issues about society, state, power and the citizen which have important implications for the sort of society we live in. The basic distinction was nicely caught by William Beveridge in *Full Employment in a Free Society* (1944), the book which he saw as the essential complement to his wartime Plan on social insurance. His language may reflect another era, but the contrast between the two views of not only unemployed people but also the working relationship is clear: 'It may be that cattle must be driven by fear. Men can and should be led by hope' (Beveridge, 1944, p.250).

Acknowledgements

I would particularly like to thank Dorothy Sinfield for her valuable assistance and Michael Adler, Jochen Clasen, Zsuzsa Ferge, Dan Finn, Jon Kvist, Ruth Lister and John Veit-Wilson for their very helpful comments on an earlier version.

References

Ackum Agell, S. (1995), 'Swedish Labor Market Programs: Efficiency and Timing', *Swedish Economic Policy Review*, Vol. 2:65-98.

Ackum Agell, S., Björklund, A. and Harkman, A. (1995), 'Unemployment Insurance, Labour Market Programmes and Repeated Unemployment in Sweden', *Swedish Economic Policy Review*, Vol. 2:101-128.

Atkinson, A.B. and Micklewright, J. (1991), 'Unemployment Compensation and Labour Market Transitions: A Critical Review', *Journal of Economic Literature*, Vol. 14:1679-1727.

Beveridge, W. (1930), *Unemployment: A Problem of Industry*, London: Longmans, second ed.

Beveridge, W.H. (1944), *Full Employment In a Free Society*, London: Allen and Unwin.

Blau, P.M. (1963), *The Dynamics of Bureaucracy*, Chicago: Chicago University Press.

Bradshaw, J. (1990), *Child Poverty and Deprivation in the UK*, London: National Children's Bureau.

Bryson, A. and McKay, S. (1994), *Is it Worth Working*? London: PSI.

Burchell, B. (1992), 'Towards a Social Psychology of the Labour Market: Or why we Need to Understand the Labour Market before we can Understand Unemployment', *Journal of Occupational and Organizational Psychology*, Vol. 65:345-354.

Burchell, B. (1994), 'The Effects of Labour Market Position, Job Insecurity, and Unemployment on Psychological Health', in Gallie, D., Marsh, C. and Vogler, C. (eds), *Social Change and the Experience of Unemployment*, Oxford: Oxford University Press.

Burkett, B. and Bowers, D. (1979), *Trade Unions and the Economy*, London: Macmillan.

Brown, J.C. (1990), *Victims or Villains? Social Security Benefits in Unemployment*, York: Joseph Rowntree Memorial Trust.

Clasen, J. (1994), *Paying the Jobless: a Comparison of Unemployment Benefit Policies in Great Britain and Germany*, Aldershot: Avebury.

Cohen, H. (1965), *The Demonics of Bureaucracy*, Ames, Iowa State: University Press.

Deacon, B. (1995), 'The Globalisation of Social Policy and the Socialisation of Global Politics', *Social Policy Review*, Vol. 7:55-76.

Eardley, T. et al. (1996), *Social Assistance in OECD Countries: Synthesis Report*, London: HMSO.

Edelman, M. (1977), *Political Language: Words that Succeed and Policies that Fail*, New York: Academic Press.

Eriksson, T. (1995), 'Comment on Ackum Agell et al', *Swedish Economic Policy Review*, Vol. 2:129-133.

Finn, D. (1987), T*raining Without Jobs: New Deals and Broken Promises*, London: Macmillan.

Fryer, D. (1992), 'Introduction to Marienthal and Beyond', *Journal of Occupational and Organizational Psychology*, Vol. 65:257-268.

Gallie, D. and Vogler, C. (1994), 'Unemployment and Attitudes to Work', in Gallie, D., Marsh, C. and Vogler, C. (eds), *Social Change and the Experience of Unemployment*, Oxford: Oxford University Press.

Ganssmann, H. (1991), 'Pull-down Effects, Unemployment and Interests in the Welfare State', in Adler, M. et al. (eds), *The Sociology of Social Security*, Edinburgh: Edinburgh University Press.

Goodwin, L. (1972), *Do the Poor want to Work?* Washington DC: Brookings Institution.

Huston, A.C. (ed) (1991), *Children in Poverty: Child Development and Public Policy*, Cambridge: Cambridge University Press.

Hutton, W. (1995), *The State We're In*, London: Jonathan Cape.

Hyman, H.H. (1979), 'The Effects of Unemployment: A Neglected Problem in Modern Social Research', in Merton, R.K. et al., *Qualitative and Quantitative Social Research: Papers in honor of Paul F. Lazarsfeld*, New York: Free Press.

ILO – International Labour Office (1984), *Into the Twenty-First Century: The Development of Social Security*, Geneva: ILO.

Jahoda, M., Lazarsfeld, P.F. and Zeisel, H. (1972), *Marienthal: The Sociography of an Unemployed Community*, (first published in German, 1933), London: Tavistock.

Jordan, B. et al. (1992), *Trapped in Poverty? Labour-market Decisions in Low-income Households*, London: Routledge.

Kaim-Caudle, P.R. (1973), *Comparative Social Policy and Social Security: A ten-country study*, London: Martin Robertson.

Kalecki, M. (1943), 'The Political Consequences of Full Employment', *Political Quarterly*, pp.322-331.

Kamerman, S. (1995), 'Social Security: Has Proved its Worth – now it must Adapt', in ISSA, *Social Security Tomorrow: Permanence and Change*, Geneva: International Social Security Association.

Katz, M. (1989), *The Undeserving Poor: From the War on Poverty to the War on Welfare*, New York: Pantheon.

King, D. (1995), *Actively Seeking Work? The Politics of Unemployment and Welfare Policy in the United States and Great Britain*, Chicago: University of Chicago Press.

Kvist, J. and Sinfield, A. (1996), *Comparing Tax Routes to Welfare in Denmark and the United Kingdom*, Copenhagen: Danish National Institute of Social Research.

Lane, R.E. (1991), *The Market Experience*, Cambridge: Cambridge University Press.

Levy, D. (1988), 'Moore's American Cure for Britain's "Dependency" habit', *The Listener*, 18 February, pp.4-5.

Liebow, E. (1967), *Tally's Corner: a study of Negro streetcorner men*, Boston: Little Brow.

Liebow, E. (1970), 'No Man can Live with the Terrible Knowledge that he is not Needed', *New York Times Magazine*, 5 April.

Macarov, D. (1970), *Incentives to Work*, San Francisco: Jossey Bass.

Marmor, T.R. and Plowden, W. (1991), 'Spreading the Sickness', *The Times Higher*, 25 October, p. 17.

Marris, P. and Rein, M. (1967), *Dilemmas of Social Reform*, Harmondsworth: Penguin.

Marsden, D. (1982), *Workless*, London: Croom Helm.

Micklewright, J. (1990), *The Reform of Unemployment Compensation: Choices for East and West*, London: LSE, TIDI 149.

Miller, R. and Wood, J.B. (1983), *What Price Unemployment? An Alternative Approach*, London: Institute of Economic Affairs.

Miller, S.M. (1993), 'The Politics of Respect', *Social Policy*, Spring, pp. 44-51.

Moylan, S., Millar, J. and Davies, R. (1984), *For Richer, for Poorer? DHSS Cohort Study of Unemployed Men*, London: HMSO.

NEDC – National Economic Development Council (1963), *Conditions Favourable to Faster Growth*, London: HMSO.

Neuburger, H. and Fraser, N. (1993), *Economic Policy Analysis: A Rights-Based Approach*, Aldershot: Avebury.

OECD (1963), *Labour Market Policy in Sweden*, Paris: OECD.
OECD (1994a), *The OECD Jobs Study: Facts Analysis Strategies*, Paris: OECD.
OECD (1994b), *The OECD Jobs Study: Evidence and Explanations*, Parts I and II, Paris: OECD.
OECD (1995), 'Editorial', *Employment Outlook*, July.
Pahl, R. E. (1984), *Divisions of Labour*, Oxford: Blackwell.
Pilgrim Trust (1938), *Men Without Work*, Cambridge: Cambridge University Press.
Ritchie, J. (1990), *Thirty Families: Their living standards in unemployment*, London: HMSO.
SCP – Sociaal en Cultureel Planbureau (1990), *Social and Cultural Report 1994: The Netherlands*, Rijswijk: SCP.
Sen, A. (1990), 'Individual Freedom as a Social Commitment', *The New York Review of Books*, 14 June, pp.49- 54.
Sennet, R. and Cobb, J. (1973), *The Hidden Injuries of Class*, New York: Vintage Books.
Sinfield, A. (1983), 'Unemployment', in P.A. Kohler and H.F. Zacher, (eds), *Beitrage zu Geschichte und Aktueller Situation der Sozialversicherung*, Berlin: Duncker and Humbolt.
Sinfield, A. (1984), 'The Wider Impact of Unemployment', *High Unemployment: A Challenge for Income Support Policies*, Paris: OECD.
Stewart, G. & Stewart, J. (1988), 'Targetting Youth or How the State Obstructs Young People's Independence', *Youth and Policy*, Vol. 25:19-24.
Titmuss, R.M. (1968), *The Commitment to Welfare*, London: Allen and Unwin.
Townsend, P. (1993), *The International Analysis of Poverty*, New York: Harvester Wheatsheaf.
Townsend, P., Davidson, N. and Whitehead, M. (1992), *Inequalities in Health*, Harmondsworth: Penguin.
van Oorschot, W. (1995), *Take It or Leave It: a study on non-take-up of social security benefits*, Aldershot: Avebury.
Wadel, C. (1973), *Now whose Fault is that?* Newfoundland: Memorial University.
Whelan, C.T. (1992), 'The Role of Income, Life-style Deprivation and Financial Strain in Mediating the Impact of Unemployment on Psychological Distress: Evidence from the Republic of Ireland', *Journal of Occupational and Organizational Psychology*, Vol. 65:331-344.
White, M. (1991), *Against Unemployment*, London: PSI.
Whiteside, N. (1991), *Bad Times: Unemployment in British and Social Political History*, London: Faber and Faber.
Wight, D. (1993), *Workers not Wasters: Masculine Respectability, Consumption and Employment in Central Scotland*, Edinburgh: Edinburgh University Press.
Wikeley, N. (1989), 'Unemployment Benefit, The State and the Labour Market', *Journal of Law and Society*, Vol. 16:291-309.

6 How to get rid of unemployment and transform work into play

Gunnar Adler-Karlsson

Suffering is Man's lot
and Man must bear it
(Buddah & Kazantzakis)

But now we need no more threnodies,
but visions of how to improve Man's lot,
even if only by a tiny little bit!
(GA-K.)

Unemployment – the necessary social progress

Philosophical points of departure

As life gets its value from death, human progress is created by human suffering. Suffering has always been a part of the human condition. For instance, in the forms of both work and that lack of work which is called unemployment.

We don't want to work. We want to play. But we have to work. In order to get to work, we must either suffer unemployment or change work into play.

Essence Number One of our problem is to avoid a bigger suffering by accepting a smaller one, of buying less of long-term suffering at the price of more short-term suffering. Essence Number Two is to transform work into play, following Schiller's famous statement that 'man plays only where he is human in the full meaning of the word, and he is wholly human only where he plays'.

Those are my philosophical points.

If they are correct, one important conclusion follows: *our big problem is not to create more jobs, but to find a new income distribution system that gets us to work without the threat of misery and permits us to play also on the labour market.*

Just as we try to avoid the subject of death, however, most participants in the normal debate about work and unemployment strenuously try to avoid the subjects of both suffering and play. That is why they stutter.

Let me explain.

Human progress is created by human suffering

If you cut through the details of the statistics provided by S. Kuznets and A. Maddison and others on economic growth, you find a long-term development of the Western world which looks approximately like this:

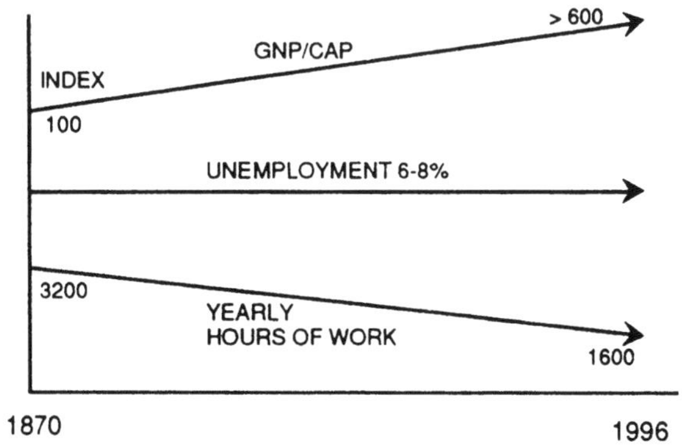

Figure 6.1 Essential development 1870-1996

The GNP per person has increased more than sixfold since 1870. The yearly load of working hours per employed person has been roughly cut in half.

Human progress is often seen as a higher standard of material living and more leisure in which to enjoy the wealth. If that definition of progress is accepted, the top and bottom lines show the enormous progress that the Western capitalist democracies have made.

The middle line represents unemployment. We started to measure it in the 1850's. Since then it has been structurally stable around 6 to 8%.

All the three lines vary, of course, with the business cycles. Unemployment varies the most. The world record, to my knowledge, came in the early 1930s, when 36% of the Dutch and 44% of the German labour force were reported unemployed.

Why did unemployment not rise over time, as Marxist analysis predicted, or fall and disappear, as liberals and democratic socialists hoped?

My answer is that *unemployment is an absolutely necessary form of social progress in our mixed capitalist system.*

Why progress?

'Social progress' – are you kidding? Are you telling us that the perhaps fifty million Europeans who, at one time or another, have been hit by unemployment since the early 1970s have been enjoying some perverse form of 'progress'? How cynical can you be?

Well, 'the right to unemployment is one of the joys of a free economy', said one of president Eisenhower's advisers once, when he saw it in Detroit. Why?

We have good written sources on our cultural progress for the last 4000 years. During 3850 of them, slavery has been a fully normal and conventional social institution.

Slavery, in my understanding, was not an institution for the punishment of the slaves, but of the sloppy. Everybody who was *not* a slave was meant to be scared of becoming one and therefore work as hard as hell.

This has been true from the 'trans-Tiberim' legislation in Rome, 452 BC, to the debt bondage of, for instance, Charles Dickens' father in the early 19th century AD, the same suffering that inspired his contemporary, Karl Marx, to his hate.

When slavery was abolished, by Quaker criticism in the 1600s, the Philosophers in the 1700s, in Russia in 1861 and the USA in 1865, unemployment took over its function as a disciplining rod.

The social function of unemployment is to scare all those who have a job to work very hard, lest they lose their jobs.

In order to be truly efficient as a slave whip, unemployment should also be combined with misery, at least with psychological, but preferably with material misery.

The early communists reacted against this truth of the capitalist system. After 1917 they did away with unemployment in the Soviet empire. On paper. And got tremendous economic inefficiency. Which they tried to mend by the even worse misery of Siberia. The communist labour system surely deserves the name of 'national slavery', that is, feudal slavery writ large.

Italians, with their superrealistic Machiavellian cynicism, claim that in order to get lazy men to work you have to have 'o miseria, o Siberia', either misery or Siberia!

However that may be, it is hard to find any societies since Rome that have not had either classical slavery, national slavery, or unemployment.

If this is so, it follows that those who want to reintroduce classical slavery, as well as those who may want to take another try at communist national slavery, evidently have a right to protest.

But shouldn't the rest of you join me in seeing unemployment as a form of social progress?

Why necessary?

Because we don't want to work. But we have to work. In Paradise we were spoiled. No work was necessary. But then Man fell. God chased him away. God condemned us to earn our bread in the sweat of our brows. Fallen man has followed up on that by giving life-sentences of hard labour to those criminals who were not beheaded. Work was the second degree of punishment, after the gallows.

Read Aksyonov's *Generations of Winter* about work in Kolyma, and you'll understand. Or consider the threat of a new form of *'debt prison'* to get the homeless to work in Austin in Texas in the year of 1996![1]

We don't want to work. Especially not when we are forced to work in a disciplined manner for others.

But we have to work!

Why do we have to work? We work to satisfy our basic needs.

What are they? Food, sex and power.

How do these affect work?

The need for food forces us to work for ourselves.

The sex urge forces us to work for our children and the global population explosion.

And the need for power forces us to work for others.

Out of paradise in Africa?

The myth of the expulsion from Paradise might have something to do with one of the most important events in human history. There are calculations which indicate that when we were hunters and gatherers, living of the fruits of natural nature, there was space for only some ten million individuals.

What we know of primitive men indicates that they worked for their material needs for no more than two or three hours per day, some 700 or 800 hours per year. That may be what we are willing to do, without external constraints, when food and fruits are in abundance.

When we reached ten millions, the fruits of nature became scarce. That may be when the myth was born that God kicked us out of his abundant Eden, a garden free of labour, into agriculture that requires the sweat of our brows, lest we starve to death.

Those who do not own a garden that is big enough to provide for their needs are forced to work for their own living. As somebody put it recently: 'Unless people are independently wealthy, they're going to work, they're going on welfare or they're going to steal. There are no other alternatives'.[2] I fear it is typical for the Western debate to forget the most normal alternative in history, most common even today: they may be left to starve and suffer in silence!

Only one reminder of this fact: On December 21st, 1995, the U.S. House of Representatives by 248 votes against 178 approved a bill to overhaul the U.S. welfare system. The day after, the Senate followed with 52 votes for and 47 against.

President Clinton said he would veto the bill, but he accepted much of it.[3]

One of the provisions of this bill was that it prohibited the states from giving welfare to a family 'for more than two years at a time', for 'a maximum of five years', or for families 'who have additional children' when they are on welfare. It

---

1 *Washington Post* 951226, p. A14.
2 Richard Reeves in *IHT* 951129, op-ed.
3 *Washington Post* 951222 & 23.

also mandates an obligation for states 'to get half of all families on welfare into jobs by 2002'.

Professor Laurence M. Mead, a labour market expert, even 'much respected by Republican conservatives', warned that the states would not be able to create the jobs.

Assume this bill becomes law.[4] Assume also, which seems likely, that the states are unable to create the jobs required.

What, then, would a small family do, when they have been on welfare for five years in all, or after two years without a job, when they get a new child but neither welfare nor jobs?

How do we tackle the potential material suffering that is likely to arise, not least among innocent children?

Cain

The story of Cain and Abel contains the seed of the next reason why we work. In the famous story, God told Abel that he was Number One and Cain that he was Number Two. But Cain wanted power. To get it, he killed his brother. Later, Cains permitted Abels to live, on the condition that they accepted becoming slaves.

Slaves work hard. As we already said, such has been the human condition for 3850 out of the last 4000 years. Which has scared all others to work hard for their employers, lest they lose their job and fall into misery.

Slavery has now been abolished. Raw power is less naked than before. People are 'free' to work. They get paid for it. But, seriously, isn't the Marxian concept of 'wage slavery' a bit justified? If it isn't, why have 'free' labour and their unions accepted the heavy redistribution of income that has taken place after 1973?[5]

The need for food forces some to work, and to work hard in a disciplined manner for others. Which some don't like. Such work is often, at least subjectively, felt as suffering. Sometimes it is, even in objective terms.

The third reason for work is rarely considered at all. Even if it might be the most important of all.

We were expelled from Paradise, I assume, when we reached ten million people in 'natural nature' some ten millennia ago. Today we increase the global population by nine times as much, by 90 million individuals every single year for the foreseeable future. Even the most optimistic prognoses, that by the IIASA[6], implies a yearly growth of some 80 million per year.

---

4 Since this was written, it has become law!

5 For both figures and explanations, see for instance: Simon Head, 'The New, Truthless Economy'. *The New York Review of Books*, Feb. 29, 1996, pp. 47-52, one of hundreds of similar articles.

6 Wolfgang Lutz suggested in February to the AAAS-congress in Baltimore that the population would stop growing around 2050 at a level of 10 billion. Sv.D. 960217, p.9.

What was true 10,000 years ago is equally true today. If 'reproductive success' guides us, like all other animals; if we cannot restrain our global sex urges; and if we do not accept nature's harsh redundancy principles and simply let most children die, then it follows that we have to work to find food for another 80 or 90 million humans beings every year for the next fifty years.

That may be the most important driving force behind global economic and political integration – or division of labour – but with players who are unconsciously driven to this deterministic behaviour which is creating one world, or none.[7]

The necessity of unemployment

Politicians don't want to take responsibility for what voters don't like. Thus they try to explain away unemployment as a temporary 'failure' of the system. They never want to admit that the economic growth, for which they claim credit is based upon suffering.

To me it seems a fact that the human progress we discussed above (in Figure 6.1), the increase in material standard and decrease in yearly labour time, has been strongly stimulated by the constant threat of slavery or unemployment, depicted by the middle line in the figure. Because unemployment is the bottom step of the incentive ladder that gets us all to work.

Or, seen from a contrary perspective, had we had full employment all the time since 1870, without any threat of unemployment, productivity might have been much lower, our material levels of living much below what we now have, working hours much above, and a considerable number of people who now live might not have been born or survived childhood.

The suffering of the unemployed fulfils a most important function in society. It gets the others to perform efficiency.

The unemployed are thus so important to society that they should get double as high a wage as the others!

However, if they did not suffer, they wouldn't fulfil this function. Thus they must instead be threatened with misery, slavery, homelessness, contempt and debt prison. Even in the 1990s!

Human progress always builds upon human suffering. So it was when we were expelled from Eden. So it still is, even in the richest nations of the world, at the close of the second millennium after Christ.

Until we openly recognise this ugly fact, no Theseus will be able to slaughter the suffering-demanding Minotaur of unemployment.

That is the firm conviction behind this 'cynical', or, if you so prefer, realistic paper.

---

7 My theory behind this comment is to be found in 'A Monotheistic Theory of Power, or 10,000 years in 10 pages'. Stockholm, 1994.

The present dilemma

Some history

In 1923 German super-inflation culminated, with price increases of thousands of per cent per week. The German economy was thrown into total chaos. In 1933 Hitler was democratically elected to power in Germany. Many believed, and still believe, there was a causal connection. Six years later war broke out. This is the important background for understanding the policy of the German Bundesbank in the 1990s!

At the end of World War II, the Western powers in Bretton Woods tried to forestall monetary chaos of the 1923 German type by creating a system for international monetary cooperation. To start with, it functioned fairly well. It stabilised currencies enough to permit a growing liberalisation and growth of world trade.

This is the period of the intensive Cold War.. This had two consequences.

Partly in order to avoid any growth in the communist parties in the West, democratic politicians created the welfare state and promised more than they could finance without inflation. And in order to fight back the potential 'domino effects' of the Vietnam war, the United States resorted to the old policy of 'debasement of the coinage'. It printed paper money to finance the war, money that undermined the Bretton Woods' ultimate guarantee, the right for central banks to exchange dollars for gold at the U.S. Treasury at the stable price of 35 dollars an ounce.

On August 15th 1971 the Bretton Woods system died. President Nixon unilaterally declared that the U.S. would not any more exchange its gold for dollars bills.

The basis for renewed super-inflation had been laid. Commodity prices went up right away and in 1973 came the first oil crisis, creating serious chaos in the world monetary system.

What very few people are aware of is that at the time of the second oil crisis in 1979-80, we had a world record in global inflation. Never before, as Robert Triffin shows, had we had such high inflation all around the globe.

The central bankers in the United States and Western Germany, however, not only knew, but also reacted to it.

The decision to create unemployment

The present unemployment is not only a consequence of a 'failure' of the market system to maintain reasonably full employment.

It is also, to a large extent, the consequence of a conscious decision by the leading central bankers of the world to create short-term human suffering in order to avoid infinitely more of it in the long run. It was even possibly done with the connivance of leading economic politicians who might have realised the necessity of the policy, but who refused to take any responsibility for its ugly results.

We know extremely little about the details. We know, however, that the central bankers of the Group of 10, plus the one from Switzerland, have been meeting ten times a year in or near the Bank for International Settlements in Basle. In utmost secluded forms,[8] these gentlemen have made a non-legally binding, but firm 'gentlemen's agreement' to stop the acceleration of heavy inflation. Basically, it seems, in the early 1980s they promised each other not to permit ministers of finance to finance their budget deficits by 'printing money' in the central banks.

This now forced politicians, who for a generation had justified the sloppy handling of their budgets with reference to the Keynesian theory for avoiding unemployment, to turn to the normal capital markets to finance their deficits. Demand for capital rose, supply did not. It followed that the price of capital, the rate of interest, went up. The real rate of interest rose to levels hardly seen after 1945 and rarely seen in history.

The natural results were a decrease in investment, extreme difficulties for the poor nations to pay their huge debts, a few Western bank crashes, bankruptcies of a considerable number of speculators, the Wall Street crashes of 1987 and 1989 with repercussions on all the financial markets of the world, and, most important for the masses, a big increase in unemployment.

Since then we have had some 8 to 12% unemployment in much of Europe.[9]

The case of Sweden in Europe

For a number of years Sweden seemed lucky, but it wasn't.

Sweden remained outside all monetary cooperation in Europe. To gain domestic election advantages, its politicians profited recklessly from a serious classical debasement of the coinage combined with a series of devaluations between 1976 and 1982. In this way Sweden did not have its unemployment crisis until ten years after Denmark.

Far from being a model for the others, Sweden cynically utilised those 'competitive devaluations' which destroyed the inter-war economy in Europe and which again, if the EMU is a flop, is scaring us.[10]

Sweden avoided some suffering from unemployment by throwing it on others.

This also has some importance for the present situation.

---

8 I have been told that when Bengt Dennis, the Swedish central banker, was sick, no deputy was sent to Basle. Only one single individual should know what was happening. In 1995 the U.S. Congress asked the Federal Reserve, who had participated in Basle for more than 15 years, if the U.S. was also participating in this monetary cooperation! It has been kept secret!

9 For detailed figures, see e.g. EU, *The European Economy*, No. 12, December 1995, table 18, ISSN 0379-2056.

10 See e.g. Guido Brunner, 'Germany pays a high price as anchor of currency system'. *IHT* 960219, p.6.

Since Sweden became a member of the European Union, it has been trying to sell the EU some variation of neo-Keynesianism in order to get full employment. Its spokesmen, including the prime minister, have suggested that this should be a goal which is as important as monetary union. Some degree of inflation could be accepted too, they hinted, in the good tradition of the last decades of Swedish monetary counterfeiting.

Opposition from the United Kingdom and Germany, and also within BIS cooperation, has been strong. Lately, however, in January 1996, Kohl has stolen the electoral popularity of the Swedish issue, but turned its content upside down. The key words of the German proposals are now 'deregulation, deconcentration and flexibilisation', something that Swedish labour unions abhor.

Neither of these proposals will solve the underlying problems. If realised they would distribute human suffering differently, the Swedish less, the German more on the unions.

Recognise reality!

Both proposals are, however, only temporary ways of handling the 15-year-old unemployment crisis in Europe. Neither of them tackles the basic issue.

The basic issue will never be tackled unless and until we become honest about the fundamental fact: human suffering in the form of unemployment fulfills a most important disciplining function in our economies. It gets the potentially lazy, the free riders, to work. It prevents super-inflation that might lead to disastrous political results. And it creates the preconditions for rising material standards and increasing leisure.

The suffering of unemployment is good for our economy. As slavery has been for some 4000 years.

Given (the lack) of human intelligence, we have not been able to find any alternatives.

Which shouldn't prevent us from trying again!

Two unemployment problems

If we want to tackle the unemployment problems in a realistic manner, we should start from a simple fact: we have two, not one, problems of unemployment.

For fifteen years we have been suffering from some 8 to 12% unemployment in Western Europe. Roughly half of that, I would suggest, is connected to the long-term suffering, necessary to get our system to function in a stable, non-inflationary, disciplined manner. It is the same level as that in the United States.

On top of that we have another half, connected to the short-term problems. They may, indeed, be troublesome in their own right. It is the accelerating Schumpeterian 'creative destruction' which is a natural result of domestic restructuring and reengineering in all nations, connected with a tremendously rapid rate of technical change. It is the opening up of the world markets for both goods and capital, making it possible for good entrepreneurs to exploit cheap labour in any part of the world. In Western Europe this is particularly serious after the fall of communism, which has opened up a close, well-trained and very cheap labour force to the dynamic West European companies. The growth of world population with close to 100 million individuals in 1995 is another factor pressing down the value of human work.

All this has exerted a strong downward pressure on the inflexible wage levels, on the high welfare costs and on the many despiriting public regulations in Western Europe. Reluctance to decrease welfare and increase wage gaps have resulted in high unemployment in spite of good profits in the companies.

The public debate has concentrated almost exclusively on this, the second group of problems. I have nothing to contribute to this stuttering.

The existence of the first problem, the suffering from unemployment necessary to get our system to function at all, is hardly ever recognised. It is, of course, extremely sensitive for the politicians responsible. It comes up only in the secluded and refined discussions about NAIRU in technical circles in IMF and OECD. Most people, even most labour market politicians, haven't the foggiest idea about the Non-Accelerating Inflationary Rate of Unemployment.

Considering this situation, I would like to make three suggestions:

1. We must be honest about the necessity, and even the positive contribution from the human suffering of unemployment and misery.
2. We should attack this suffering in a manner that might decrease it.
3. If we were able to find a new solution to the underlying long-term unemployment, some of the short-term problems might be easier to handle.

Based on these hunches, I would like to propose a number of concrete ideas.

Towards a 'provisional utopia'

The idea has been advanced many times. I got it from the first winner of the economic Nobel Prize, Jan Tinbergen, who in the 1960s told me that it was his youthful dream which he had got from his teacher at the beginning of the century.

Everybody should have his basic material needs covered by a basic income, or a citizen income, guaranteed by his State. From this follows:

Proposal No. 1:

The European Union should introduce a basic income for all European citizens. It would be the politically most 'sexy' thing they could do!

Why? For three strong reasons.

First, because no rich society, wanting to call itself civilised, should permit its citizens to fall into outright misery and starvation.

If that happens it is bound to lead to problems of a dangerous sort. It sometimes seems to me that this is the situation towards which we now are drifting. Some unemployed, even if only a few, become completely marginalised, fall into the underclass,[11] start to hate, are enlisted in some fanatical sect, get drugs, get hold of miniature terror instruments, and cause much evil.

Secondly, because it would simplify things. It would relieve us of a very big and troublesome bureaucracy now administering an enormous panoply of subsidies to help the unfortunate. It would also decrease the present risks of abuse and arbitrariness on a huge scale.

Thirdly, because it would create a degree of freedom from material fears, potentially liberating for play the spirits of those who wanted so to be liberated.

A number of subsidiary reasons could be listed. They are well summarised in the papers from BIEN, the Basic Income European Network, under the leadership of Professor Philippe van Parijs[12] in Belgium.

A guaranteed basic income would solve the first of our basic human needs, that for food.

Proposal No. 2:

The basic income should be low. It should cover the basic necessities of life, giving a normal human being a healthy life, but not much more.

The present Swedish level of material living is, at least, ten times higher in real terms than that at which some of my grandparents grew up in the 1870s. A level at which some of them lived to be 90.

If, as Figure 6.1 suggests, we are six times richer than our forefathers in 1870 as a European average, this might be another clue to how high the basic income should be.

I would suggest that the level of the basic income might be something like one fourth of the present OECD average, not higher.

Why this niggardly attitude?

First, because we are lazy. The problem of free riders is eternal. If we don't fix the level at a rather low point, the laziness of the free riders will become a serious problem. Lots of people will be satisfied with the basic level and become completely pacified in front of the infotainment of the monitors. And we do need much hard human work to solve the problems of the population explosion.

Secondly, because we don't trust our States any more. The tasks of the States should be kept to a minimum. We want to forget that most of the genocides of this century have been managed by big States, often with a socialist leaning. '*Arbeit macht frei!*' We want to forget the horrible abuse of power that big States have engaged in. And we don't want to believe that the corruption which also exists in a considerable number of Western States, even in the last decade, is normal. But we feel it!

The Augustinian opinion that 'a government without justice is nothing but a robber band', strengthened by the Machiavellian idea that all governments are

11 The concept is ugly, but a reality, see e.g. Ken Auletta, *The Underclass*. Random House 1982, and Andrew Hacker, 'The Lower Depths', *NYRB* 820812, pp.15-20.

12 Those who are interested can write to van Parijs, 3 Place Montesquieu, B-1348 Louvain-la-Neuve.

without justice, has squeezed out the Hegelian belief that the State is something good, a protector of its citizens. We don't believe in the strong State any more.

Thus, if the State is to guarantee the basic income, it should be at a low level.

Thirdly, all income levels are relative. Poverty is a relative concept. That is widely realised. But so is wealth, even if less widely realised. If we don't fix an absolute level for the guaranteed basic income, related to a healthy survival level, possibly even in real terms in kind, we will fall into an eternal political debate on how high it should be.

This is a problem of 'responsibility'. In Sweden the State has for decades also tried to guarantee high income levels, already reached by the citizens, against too deep a fall in case of unemployment or other misfortunes. That is politically attractive. But, in fact, it is a compulsory insurance scheme, blowing up both the size, the power and the responsibility of the State.

Indeed, such insurance schemes will certainly be necessary also in the future.

Why, however, should they not be private? Why shouldn't the individual who has a good income put aside some of it in a private insurance, or in other saving funds for a rainy day? And why shouldn't the voluptuous ones, those who consume all their current income, be permitted to fall to the basic income level, when misfortune strikes?

Why shouldn't the individual bear such a responsibility for himself and his family?

Proposal No. 3:

To earn the right to a basic income, every citizen should have the legal duty to work for the State for a short period of his or her life.

The idea of a citizens' income has been advanced many times. But rarely has it been combined with this demand, for a compulsory civil service. I am convinced, however, that this is an absolutely necessary complement.

Why?

First, because in principle there are no rights without corresponding duties, 'free lunches' do not exist. Someone always pays for them. And that someone always demands some work.

This lies deep in human nature.

'I cannot accept that one who eats my food doesn't work' says Telemachus in the 19th song of the Odyssey, when he wants to hide the identity of his returning father among the spongers around Penelope.

'The man who will not work shall not eat', said St. Paul in his second letter to the Thessalonians, 3:10.

The requirement from Homer and St. Paul that those who don't work shan't eat, is equally strong today as it was two or three thousand years ago.

Secondly, it is demanded by work ethics. If the lazy free riders, even if they were few, received a basic income without doing anything for it, why shouldn't everybody?

To keep the basic work ethic high, this requirement of a few years' compulsory work is a must! Which doesn't mean it should be organised like a slave market; it could even be more humanely arranged than the present wage-slave market.

Third, because then everybody would get at least a short period of work in his or her life. Everybody would get the feeling that 'I have myself justified my basic material existence'. Nobody would be forced to suffer unemployment and feelings of valuelessness all through life.

Fourth, because this compulsory civil service could replace much of the extremely irritating, annoying and work-ethic-destroying taxation system, which is now the spear-head of the so-called public sector, taking away all Hegelian trust in the State.

Fifth, because it might contribute to a solution of the migration problems. Immigrants would know that they had do to the years of compulsory civil service before they could enter any other system of benefits.

Sixth, because freedom is a very precious thing.

An old Swedish labour leader, Gunnar Nilsson, used to define material freedom as 'having so much money in the bank, that you can tell anybody to go to hell!'

My system creates the potential for such a freedom. This is true at least for those who can master their feelings of jealousy and envy. If you have your material base secured, you are *objectively* free!

How long should we be forced to work?

One per cent of the American labour force produces food in abundance for the U.S. population and roughly half of the world's exportable grain surplus. In Western Europe the big problem is to get the few remaining farmers *not* to produce. Nourishing food for everybody is no problem.

Warm but simple jeans, T-shirts, sweaters, and the like, can be equally simply produced in long series.

Simple standardised housing, much of it out in the now abandoned countryside, might cost somewhat more, but not prohibitively so.

It is the luxury and all the new and unnecessary gadgets that today demand work; it is the high volatility in the demand for these goods that creates unemployment. But it cannot be considered either a human right or the obligation of the State to provide luxury and unnecessary gadgets for people. That is a problem for the individuals on a free market.

The production of the simple necessities of life is, on the contrary, easy and stable, and surely does not require more than ten per cent of the present OECD-labour-time averages.

If we now work for forty years, between 20 and 60, four or five years of compulsory work would thus be enough to pay for the life-long basic income.

Proposal No. 4:

Concentrate education on 'the three R's' and on a deep understanding of the Human Condition. Leave vocational education to the market.

Why?

All politicians talk of education and training as solutions to the unemployment problems. They are not.

The present policies in education have three grave faults.

The first is that for the best students education is seen as a preparation for the labour market. Thus it is channelled into a utilitarian content in which 'Computer literacy' is more important than Homer and Shakespeare.[13] 'Where is the wisdom we lost to knowledge, and where is the knowledge we lost to information'? T.S. Eliot once asked. These students are transformed into economic-growth-zombies.

Secondly, because for the bottom fifth of the students, both schools and universities are transformed into 'parking lots for the unnecessary', as I once called a book of mine.[14] They are just kept there, like puppies in a kennel, without much hope of ever being able to utilise their academic knowledge in any future work.

To give them some both emotional and rational self-understanding, it would be much better to let them study the Human Condition in the classical literature!

Thirdly, because many educational programmes today are little more than programmes of hidden income redistribution.

As long as youngsters can be fooled into believing that they are engaged in some useful preparation for a good future, they keep calm and don't rebel.

And as long as the tax-payers can be fooled into believing that they are paying for some useful preparation for a better future for us all, they grudgingly accept to pay for it.

But this myth of education as a way of creating useful employment is already crumbling.[15] Sooner or later it will be abandoned, the tax-payers will refuse to go along and the youngsters will rebel.

Before we reach that point, it would be good to have my system in place!

Fourth, because my system is, certainly, far from an ideal system. The only thing I claim for it is that it is the least ugly economic system that is intellectually available at present. If we are not content with the present one.

Because of that, all young people will need a good grounding in the Human Condition, in understanding why we have to work; how we are created unequal; why we will always have gaps in wealth and power; how we can counteract the eternal tendencies to abuse the wealth and power of those who get it; why we must learn to restrain both our food and our sex urges; and why we must submit to, possibly suffer, a few years of compulsory work.

Which can be defended by the freedom in which it will result! Because everybody will have the material freedom to tell anybody to go to hell!

Proposal No. 5:

Let men and women live 35 active years in – almost – full liberty.

---

13 See *IHT* 960215, 'Classics Optional, Teachers Say'.

14 *Skolan – parkeringsplats för onödiga eller vägen till det inre reviret?*, Stockholm 1983.

15 See e.g. *Oxford Review of Economic Policy*, Vol. 11, No. 1 and Barry Bluestone in *The American Prospect*, Winter 1995.

When the stomach is satisfied, when some insight in the Human Condition has been gained, when the maximum five years of compulsory work has been done, the stage is set for free activity in play-like forms during the remaining 35 years of an active life.

The Cain-mentality, the urge to be Number One, the wish to be Best as well as the desire for women and gold will guarantee that lots of strong people will spontaneously continue with competitive production, useful inventions, and hard labour.

As they have paid most of their taxes through their years of compulsory work, they will now be able to do what they want to do without being disturbed by the present highly irritating bureaucracy and informer system, in which Western tax authorities often are seen as close cousins of the East German Stasi.

The only serious rule they will have to obey is the good old liberal restriction that you may not physically harm your fellowmen.

Thus, there is much in these proposals for the strong. But also for the weak.

There will be lots of less strong individuals who will not be subjectively content with the level of living permitted by the objectively satisfactory basic income. They will want to earn more income in the private affluence sector created by the strong. Now they will be in a much better bargaining situation with the strong entrepreneurs than any union can give them.

'I'll do this job for you', they can always say, 'on such and such conditions. If you don't fulfil them, I'll live on my basic income instead'.

This would be a great improvement on the present labour market.

Don't forget that today it is the fear of *unemployment in misery* that is the ultimate stick for disciplining materially un-free individuals to accept conditions that they don't like. Now, at least the fear of misery is gone!

Conclusion

Couldn't these five proposals together create a liberating economic system in which the internal desire to transform work into play could be realised?

As only the highly motivated will work in it, wouldn't it be possible in this way to get an extremely productive economy, so efficient that we will easily be able to feed the new five or six billion human fellow beings, who will come during the next two generations?

Shouldn't we hope in this way to give them all a fully human life, such as Schiller was dreaming of: '*man plays only where he is human in the full meaning of the word, and he is wholly human only where he plays*'?

All for the price of five years, at most, of a legal duty to work!

If you don't like this system, don't just criticise it. Suggest a better remedy to the present evils yourself! Because remember: the intensive stuttering about the present unemployment problems will not help us.

If you are vaguely tempted by my proposals, help me to improve upon them!

And if you like them, try to contribute to the building of a bridge between the present one and this hopefully better and more human system!

Are we determined for unemployment?

Let me end this paper on an even more philosophical note.

Determinism is a problem that few dare to tackle. Politicians are useless if they have no power, media uninteresting, and the normal man insulted. 'Don't I have my free will?!'

Well, at the individual level a certain amount of free will may exist. Even if a leading expert believes more in the concept of 'near-determinism'.[16]

At the collective level, however, especially in the long run, the middle line of Figure 6.1 does indicate that a certain amount of determinism has ruled the development. As do the enormous failures to change the human condition in this century. We seem to have been fighting a vain war against our, whatever we do, ever recurring animal nature.

Lenin wanted to get rid of unemployment and inequality in Russia. Both Stalin and Khrushchev hoped to 'catch up with and overtake' the most developed capitalist nations.

Today, capitalist Russia is one of the most unequal and backward nations of Europe, with lots of unemployment.

Hitler wanted to create a system that would last 'a thousand years'.

It lasted twelve.

The Swedish social democrats have for twenty years shrugged off all warnings that their full employment policy was doomed.

Now, Sweden has at least fifteen per cent real unemployment.

Margaret Thatcher's pet idea was to cut down the size of the public sector.

When she left, it was about as big as when she came.

Ronald Reagan's major election promise, when he won, was to cut the U.S. budget deficit.

When he left, it had ballooned into the double.

Man, even a Woman, even the most powerful among us, seem unable to realise their professed pet ideas.

Why?

Do forces exist which are both stronger and more complex than Man's restricted intelligence can grasp?

Is this also true for the control of the business cycle and unemployment?

In the 1980's, Christina Romer of Princeton published a series of important papers. She showed that the business cycles in the 40 years *after* 1945 had been of about the same magnitude and latitude as during the 40 years *before* the first world war in 1914. This proved to be true, measured in several different ways.

---

16 Ted Honderich, *A Theory of Determinism*, Oxford 1988.

With particular respect to unemployment, Romer demonstrated that the ups and downs in this series between 1948 and 1982 – a period of intensive Keynesian attempts to control them – were about the same as during 1866 and 1914[17], when politicians did nothing.

This problem of determinism, I believe, should be taken much more seriously than it, so far, has been.[18]

Every single drop of water in the falls may imagine itself to be different from all the others and to have a free will. But Niagara falls lies where it lies, and flows like it flows, without much concern for the speeches of politicians.[19]

Assume that social forces exist which we neither understand nor can control. Assume also that the level of employment is one result of their workings.

If politicians then *pretend* that they can create full employment – when they cannot – thereby taking responsibility for the level of unemployment, they will be blamed for it in a much harsher manner than if they did not pretend to have such power.

In this way not only the politicians, but also the democratic system will lose its credibility.

Wouldn't it be better for the credibility of our precarious democracy if the politicians restricted themselves to taking responsibility for a basic income level – which they surely are able to do – and, for the rest, leave it to the workings of the free market system to take responsibility of the level of (un)employment?

I believe it would. And, in a way I believe this might be *the* most important benefit of the system proposed in this paper.

Because if it is part of the Human Condition to have a certain amount of suffering, politicians should certainly try to diminish it as much as is realistically possible. That is what I hope my system would do. But when that is done, and all attempts to break the determinism seem vain, why not let determinism rule for a while?

Don't forget, it took more than 4000 years to get rid of slavery!

Why pretend to be an omnipotent God? As all forms of hubris always have been, such attempts will sooner or later be punished.

---

17 Christina D. Romer, 'Spurious Volatility in Historical Unemployment Data'. *Journal of Political Economy*, Feb. 1986, pp.1-37.

18 Romer's articles were extensively quoted in my *Lärobok för 90-talet*, Stockholm 1990, see p.91, but as far as I know, nobody listened, not even when I warned about unemployment like in the 1930's. Now we are approaching it.

19 In a thick book which attempts to replace the paradigm of Keynes, *Structural Slumps. The Modern Equilibrium Theory of Unemployment, Interest, and Assets*, Harvard 1994, Edmund S. Phelps et al. have given good arguments for suspecting that most conventional attempts by governments, at least so far, to lower unemployment simply result in a decrease in the work ethic and the will to work!

7 The work ethic under challenge?

Knut Halvorsen

Introduction

The key question to be addressed in this paper is whether specific work and unemployment experiences or non-work (social) contexts have a greater effect on employment commitment (Bielby and Bielby, 1989; Row and Snizek, 1995). In particular, I shall test the (so called) feminist orthodoxy which according to Hakim (1995) is critical of a dualistic understanding of men's and women's employment patterns and employment commitment. The dominant opinion is that sex differentials in work commitment have faded away (Gallie and White, 1993; Ellingsæter, 1995), while others (Reskin and Padavic, 1994) have dismissed sex differences in work commitment as implausible and out of date ideas.

In many Western countries there is a fear that the welfare system discourages work ethic values (Barbash, 1983) and that this weakened work involvement will negatively affect the country's international competitiveness and economic progress (Andrisani and Parnes, 1983; Sipilä, 1995). It has also been alleged that most unemployment is voluntary and due to lack of work motivation. The unemployed do not put enough effort into the search for a job (Noelle-Neuman and Gillies, 1987). Generous welfare benefits make people unwilling to perform tiring or dirty tasks. Besides, it is maintained that there is no longer a stigma involved in accepting the 'dole'. Therefore, the unemployed lack a commitment to the ideology of employment (Howe, 1990). Others maintain, on the contrary, that low work involvement is the result of unfavourable labour market experiences and unemployment (Habermehl, 1988).

So far, there has not been any study in Norway focusing especially on the relationship between employment status and employment commitment, with the exception of Ellingsæter (1995). This paper employs various data sets and indicators of employment commitment and their association with employment status to demonstrate that indicators used to operationalise employment commitment impact on the conclusions that can be drawn.

In the next section, work involvement is discussed in the broader context of the work ethic and employment regimes and theories of how attitudes are developed. The following section presents the data, the operationalisation of employment commitment and hypotheses. Then we consider the above questions by a) looking at employment commitment from 1986 to 1995, b) comparing the unemployed and working populations and people on the edge of the labour market (social assistance recipients, sole parents and young disabled persons), and c) doing a multivariate analysis of variations in employment commitment in the working age population.

Several data sets are used to throw light on the themes addressed in this paper. The most important ones are the level of living surveys of 1991 and a Gallup type survey conducted on behalf of INAS (Institute of Applied Social Research) in the fall of 1995.

Background: Scandinavian employment regimes and the dominant work ethic

Having a paid job is regarded as a dominant value in Western societies. This is true, of course, because paid work (employment) is the most important source of income, but paid work also has other intrinsic rewards, such as providing a moral income (Wadel, 1973). Historically, the main premise of the work ethic was the core of moral life (Barbash, 1983). For the unemployed to be regarded as deserving they have to conform, or at least claim to conform, to the dominant value of work (Howe, 1990) and the ideology of self-reliance (Schram, 1995). Alternative values pertaining to work are found, for example, among unemployed young people (Grotenhuis and Meijers, 1994). Nevertheless, most young people seem to be very committed to paid employment – and not just for financial reasons (Rose, 1985). On the other hand, a decline in the work ethic over time has been reported in some studies (see for example Zetterberg, 1977; Otto-Brox, 1991; Hakim, 1991; Offe, 1994), but this is strongly contested in others (Barbash, 1983; Applebaum, 1992).

Several primary causal factors have been suggested to explain a decline in the commitment to work. First, the mass unemployment caused by the advent of new technology displacing human labour, raises questions about the future of paid work in society. Early retirement schemes and generous unemployment benefits have also contributed to welfare dependency. Providing support for the needy has simultaneously undermined the incentive to work (Andrisani and Parnes, 1983). Massive unemployment may have contributed to a normalisation of the unemployment situation. Less time is spent in paid work, and more time in leisure. When one works fewer hours, work identity decreases (Bratt, 1988). Society offers alternatives to work such as life-long education, sports and consumption. Increased consumption leads towards an orientation to enjoyment: 'I shop therefore I am' (Bocock, 1993:106). Youth sub-cultures and lifestyles have developed. Postmodernists tend to regard 'consumerism' as opposed to the work ethic (Bauman, 1992). Identity is associated with property and consumption rather than production, but this does not have to be the case. The two can reinforce one another (Applebaum, 1992), work more to earn more money to consume more, i.e. work and consumption are two sides of the same coin: 'The work and spend culture' (Cross, 1993). If the cash/work nexus is broken as a result of proposals put forward by 'post-industrialists' such as basic income, this may effect the work ethic in the long run; but as long as work means more goods and services to consume (economic growth), and people prefer these things as a source of happiness (goods fixation) rather than more leisure and a clean environment, the value of work will remain high.

Countries like Norway are called 'labourers' societies' (Arendt, 1958) or employment regimes of the Scandinavian type (Esping-Andersen, 1993) because paid work (wage labour) and a policy of full employment are regarded as cornerstones of society in general and of the welfare state in particular (Korpi, 1983). The Scandinavian welfare state contributes to a maximisation of jobs (and commodification) through high public employment, an active labour market policy and by making it possible to be temporarily absent from work through paid sick and parental leave (decommodification). All able-bodied persons have not only a right to work (at least an opportunity to work), but also an obligation (duty) to work. The work ethic holds that labour (and especially paid work) is good in itself. It also seems to be a precondition for being part of mainstream society and not being socially excluded (Pixley, 1993; see, however, Andersen and Hoff, 1995). Through public employment and the provision of child care facilities the Scandinavian welfare state has contributed to an increased labour force participation for women (Ellingsæter, 1995).

The labour movement and the social democratic parties (and governments) have been strong supporters of the work ethic and of the ideology of full employment (Frogner, 1995; Terum, 1996). The obligation of the political authorities to create opportunities for employment was added to Norway's constitution in 1954. Norway has one of the world's highest labour participation rates, both for men and women (OECD-Economic Outlook, December 1993). The long-term trend is a big increase in the participation rate for women, from about 55% in 1980 to 63% in 1994, and a decline for men during the same period from 79 to 74%. In 1993 about 30% were public-sector employees. In that year nearly half of the working females were working less than full-time (=36 hours per week) (Ellingsæter, 1995). Over same period the labour force participation for young people aged 16-24 fell dramatically. The same is true of disabled persons (St.meld.no. 35 for 1994-95). The composition of the population outside the labour force changed; there was a decline in the proportion of people supported privately, such as housewives, and an increase in the proportion supported by the welfare state, such as students, single mothers, the disabled, early retirees and old age pensioners. Finally, the unemployment rate increased each year from 1988 to 1993, when it reached a peak of 5.5%. In addition, about 2.8% of the labour force were enrolled in labour market programs in 1993 (Kommunal- og arbeidsdepartementet, 1995). The main purposes of these programs are to enhance the work motivation of the unemployed and to maintain the (ruling class) ideology of paid work (Øian, 1994). There is, thus, a marked relationship between the provision of welfare, attitudes to work and labour market policy. Social policy aims to reinforce the work ethic and the norms of self-sufficiency and to enforce low-wage work. (Piven and Cloward, 1972)

Given this background, it is not surprising that in 1986, 86% of women and close to 90% of men (ages 16-74) agreed (wholly or partly) with the following statement: 'All able-bodied adults should support themselves with income from their own work' (NAVF koordineringsundersøkelse, 1986). This statement measures a general employment value (work ethic) rather than the respondents' commitment to employment. It not only touches on the intrinsic aspects of a job as a source of reward and personal fulfilment, but can also be linked to the rewards that paid work brings to society (Giorgi and Marsh, 1990).

The positive appraisal of employment is not solely derived from the Scandinavian Welfare Model, but also seems to be related to Norway's culture and history (Stjernø, 1995). Even though the country has a high gross national product and is thus affluent, which according to Furnham et al. (1993) could imply a low work ethic, there is still strong support for the view that everybody should take care of themselves and be self-reliant (Halvorsen, 1996c). It is a general social norm that one should not live off other people (Elster, 1989).

Yet, the attitudes to women and paid work are somewhat ambiguous. Responsibility for the provision of care (for small children and sick siblings) is a legitimate reason for not having paid work. Changes are under way, however; in 1980 almost half the population of Great Britain accepted the notion that 'Women cannot combine a career and children.' By 1987 only one-third of the adult population agreed with a similar statement: 'Women should not try to combine a career and children' (Jowell et al., 1988, according to Hakim, 1991). Studies from 1989 (ISSP, The International Social Survey Program) indicate that in Germany, Great Britain and the United States, the attitudes of both men and women reflect a substantial preference for a primary family role for women, especially when young children are in the picture (Alwin et al., 1992). Similar attitudes are found in Norway: 45% of the respondents believed that the best thing for a family with small children was for the mother to stay at home while the father worked full time, 31% believed that the mother should have a part-time job and the father a full time job, 21%that both parents should have a part-time job, and only 3% that both parents should have a full-time job. In a recent survey, 47% of the males and 57%of the females agreed with the statement: 'In the end, family life suffers when women have full time work.' (Gallup, 1995). By contrast, 29% of all mothers with small children are currently employed in a full-time job (NSD, 1995). The most important factor for explaining women's attitudes to working mothers is their own educational background. Well-educated women are more likely to favour paid work for mothers. Apart from the level of education of their spouse, what matters most to men seems to be whether their own mother worked during their upbringing (Knudsen and Wærness, 1996).

The work ethic is reinforced by the three public discourses on unemployment (Vennesland, 1992; Ågotsnes, 1993). It seems that public attitudes are shaped by the attitudes of the governing elite (Martinussen, 1988), as expressed through the media:

1) The government is committed to the policy of full employment. The right to work and the obligation of able-bodied persons to work is emphasised: 'Work for all is our main objective.' Work is praised and idealised, while unemployment is regarded as a waste of resources (NOU 1993:11, St.meld.no 35 for 1994-95.) . The work ethic is reinforced by the industrial-achievement welfare state model (Halvorsen, 1993). The welfare institutions differentiate between the deserving and the undeserving for eligibility for cash benefits and thereby reinforce the disci-

plining forces favouring paid employment. Until 1991 at least, the welfare state model in Norway was characterised by a substantial expansion of the right not to work without any substantial income loss, but since 1991 this trend has been reversed by the introduction of 'workfare' (work for the dole) arrangements which are intended to draw people out of welfare and into paid work. The unemployed have a duty not to challenge the prevailing work ethic. Unemployment benefits are regarded as 'passive support', and the social democratic government wants to cut down expenditures on these benefits and spend the money instead on 'active support' for the unemployed (NOU 1992:26, St.meld.no. 35 for 1994-95).

2) With few exceptions, the media present unemployment as a clear evil, as 'social death'. Researchers studying the consequences of unemployment have willingly contributed to this discourse, which has been shaped by the initial assumption of their research that 'evil begets evil' (Jamrozik, 1985). This point of view has a long tradition in research on unemployment: 'even a bad job is better than unemployment' (Jahoda, 1982). Unemployment is regarded as a non-role. Research issues, methods and theories are such that they tend to concentrate on the negative side-effects of joblessness, especially in periods of high unemployment (Colbjørnsen, 1992; Furnham, 1994).

3) Employers contribute to the public discourse on unemployment. From their point of view, unemployment is due to laziness or a lack of motivation to work. A recent study conducted in Norway shows that employers have a negative attitude to the unemployed: a significant proportion of employers think that the unemployed have low work involvement (selectivity effect), which could reduce their chances of being hired by employers with negative attitudes toward the long-term unemployed (Larsen, 1995).

These particular discourses on employment and unemployment are based on the more fundamental ideologies of individualism, self-reliance, dependency and deservedness (Howe, 1990; Schram, 1995).

Theoretical perspectives on how attitudes to work are shaped

To what extent do attitudes shape our behaviour and to what extent are they a reflection of our experiences? Two contrasting hypotheses have been put forward to explain the direction of causality: the 'work shy' hypothesis (social selection) versus the 'habituation-effect' (a learned value which is gained through habituation to work). It could also be a dual process. We shall pay particular attention to the argument that women have traditionally had to balance their commitment to paid work with family obligations, which may result in an ambivalence towards paid work.

Are work attitudes useful for explaining people's behaviour? People may voice opinions that do not bear any relation to their actual choices about working or not working (Hakim, 1996b). Do attitudes change in accordance with people's changing experiences of work and unemployment, or are they stable over time? Attitudes do not seem to change easily. They are regarded by some as a stable personality characteristic and should therefore remain unresponsive to variations in employment status, at least in the short term (Jackson, Stafford, Banks and Warr, 1983). This study found small changes in employment commitment, namely a slight drop in commitment for those who became unemployed and a slight increase for those who resumed employment (ibid. 532; see also Jackson, 1994). Banks and Henry (1993) found that employment commitment fell among a cohort of young people from 1987 to 1988/89, although there was a positive correlation at times 1 and 2. On the other hand, it seems that people adjust their attitudes to reflect their experience and actual behaviour (Bem, 1967; Kelvin and Jarret, 1985), and also that involvement in particular work and family roles leads to identification with these roles (Bielby and Bielby, 1989).

School-leavers have been socialised into a work-oriented society (Hovde, 1983, 1986). The need for a positive identity, and, in the case of young people, parental pressure normally result in a strong commitment to work (Furnham, 1994). A solid finding is that alternative values to work originate from a growing sense of discouragement or expulsion from the labour market (Grotenhuis and Meijers, 1984; Hannan, O'Riain and Whelan, 1994; Furnham, 1994). Young people's jobs are likely to be characterised by low wages, insecurity, and unpleasant working conditions (Hendry, Raymond and Stewart, 1984). Low work commitment has also been found among older people anticipating retirement. Lower levels of education also seem to reduce people's commitment to employment (Gallie and Vogler, 1994; Ellingsæter, 1995). Furthermore, it has been demonstrated that conservative political attitudes are positively correlated with high work motivation in Protestant countries, while strong religious faith is negatively correlated with high work motivation, but this factor was only significant (at the 0.05% level) for Sweden (Lindseth, 1993).

Women generally have lower work commitment than men (Lindseth, 1993), and part-time workers have markedly lower work commitment than full-time workers (Bielby and Bielby, 1989; Hakim, 1991, 1995, 1996b. See, however, Ellingsæter, 1995). The gender differentials in work commitment are explained by the fact that women more often work part time in less skilled and lower paid jobs (Hakim, 1991; Bielby and Bielby, 1989). As opposed to this 'social structural model', differences between the sexes can also be explained by 'the gender socialisation model'. According to this theoretical model, women tend to place greater importance on intrinsic job features than men. An implication of this model is that women's work involvement is determined before they enter the labour force. In line with this model, it can be hypothesised that women's work involvement will be more strongly influenced by non-work factors than will men's work involvement (in accordance with the hypothesis posed about gender differences in work values by Rowe and Snizek, 1995).

In light of the public discourses on unemployment, it is not surprising that most people score high on measurements of employment commitment. Responses in surveys may simply be an echo of the public discourses on unemployment, not an internalised part of the personality. We do not know much about the reference groups through which these public discourses are filtered. In most cases attitudes are shaped by personal work experiences, past and present, and expectations for the future (Ellingsæter, 1995), but it may be difficult to interpret the findings of surveys: is high work motivation an internalised attitude, an echo of public discourses or perhaps both? When people are found to have high work involvement, it may have been influenced by what they read in the newspapers, heard on the radio or saw on television. If we presume that everyone is influenced to the same extent by these public discourses, the reported variations in employment commitment must still be trusted, though the absolute level may be too high. It is also plausible that the unemployed who want to be regarded as deserving, will conform to these public discourses to a greater extent. That enables them to distance themselves from the voluntary, and hence 'undeserving', unemployed (Howe, 1990). There are probably discourses among the unemployed themselves (Wadel, 1973; Howe, 1990; Smith, 1994), but in Norway we have no knowledge of conversations among the unemployed, nor do we know whether they help shape attitudes to any significant extent.

Data, measurements and hypotheses

Employment commitment can be viewed as a component of the Protestant work ethic (Furnham, 1990; Giorgi and Marsh, 1990). The positive assessment of work is influenced by a *secularised* version of the Protestant work ethic, according to Max Weber (Ezzy, 1993).

Although commitment to work is at the heart of the Protestant work ethic (PWE), it is possible for someone to be highly committed to work without sharing other PWE beliefs (Furnham, 1990:130), such as morality, reward or leisure. This analysis attempts to find a valid measure for the 'meaning' of work (Haller and Rosenmayr, 1971), or 'work as a central life interest' (Ellingsæter, 1995:284). 'Commitment' is defined 'as the binding of an individual to behavioural acts' (Bielby and Bielby, 1989:777). The employment commitment scale must be distinguished from the scale of commitment to or involvement in a specific work role (work values) (Andrisani and Parnes, 1983; Randall and Cote, 1991; Jackson, 1994; Harding and Hikspoors, 1995; Rowe and Snizek, 1995), occupation, career, organisation or workplace (Cohen 1995). We want to test the intrinsic value of work as an institution (formal employment), not the value of any particular job. Employment commitment is thus more abstract and general than, for example, job or organisational commitment (Cohen, 1995). Work is a worthwhile activity in its own right, not just the means to material comfort or wealth (Barbash, 1983; Mueller et al., 1992). We are looking for a valid measure of attitudes or preferences as regards conventional market work, not informal work (Ferman, 1983). So far we have treated work and employment as synonyms, but there is a clear distinction between these two concepts: 'Employment is a contractual relationship in which money is exchanged for the exertion of effort, while work is a non-contractual activity' (Jackson, 1994). In the following pages (paid) work is treated as synonymous with employment.

Over the years work involvement (employment commitment) has been measured by asking respondents to indicate their level of agreement with three to eight items on 5-point or 6-point scales (Lodahl and Kejner, 1965; Warr and Jackson, 1983; Rowley and Feather, 1987; Hannan and O'Riain, 1993), or with only one statement (Gallie et al., 1994; Ellingsæter, 1995; Hakim, 1996a).

In the Norwegian level of living surveys conducted in 1991 an adjusted work involvement scale was used. Six different statements about work were used to construct the scale:

- Having a job is very important to me.
- Even if I won a large sum of money, I would work.
- I should hate being on the dole. (I detest/would detest/being unemployed.)
- I would soon become bored if I had no work to do.
- Work is/has been among the most important things in life.
- Even if unemployment benefits were high, I would prefer to work.

The scale is based on a slightly different version of the employment commitment test constructed by Warr et al. (1979; see also Jackson, Stafford, Banks and Warr, 1985). It has been used in Sweden (Isaksson and Svedberg, 1989; Marklund, 1993) and in a slightly different version in Norway (Underlid and Thuen, 1991; Claussen, 1994).

The respondents could agree or disagree with each item. We have used five response categories ranging from one to five, with those who 'agreed completely' scoring five and those who 'disagreed completely' scoring one. Those who neither agreed nor disagreed with the statement or who gave no answer were assigned the value three, which is the value in the middle of the scale. Work was defined as paid work, and the interviewers were instructed to define work as paid work rather than work in general. In this article we present mean scores of work involvement so that the maximum possible score is 5, and the minimum is 1. This index had an acceptable internal consistency with a Cronbach's alpha of 0.76 (Spector, 1992) in the sample of the long-term unemployed, and 0.76 in the sample of the ordinary population.

Factor-analysis of the employment commitment scale in the survey of the long-term unemployed revealed that it is a reliable composite measure. Only one factor was extracted, with an eigenvalue of 3.04. The factor explained 50.7 % of the variation. The only factor that was extracted loaded strongly on all six of the variables entered.[1]

---

[1] Factor pattern and factor structure after Varimax rotation; work; involvement scale; variables reflecting opinions on:

Structure matrix variables	*Factor loadings*
– Having a job is very important to me	0.72898
– Even if I won a large sum of money, I would work	0.70647
– I should hate being on the dole	0.79041
– I would soon become bored if I had no work to do	0.70048
– Work is among the most important things in life	0.65809
– Even if unemployment benefits were high, I would prefer work	0.67809

We are unable to report a test-retest correlation, because the questions were only asked in the first interview of the panel-survey of the long-term unemployed in 1991/92. However, in a study of social assistance clients in the Nordic capitals, respondents were interviewed after a one-year interval. The correlation between the work involvement at time 1 and time 2 was 0.65, which shows that there is consistency over time in attitudes to work (Marklund, 1993). Similar stabilities over a period of time have been reported by Jackson et al. (1983), and by Isaksson and Svedberg (1989).

The criterion-related validity of the scale can be determined by testing hypotheses about how the scale relates to other variables, i.e. to what extent do those who answer differently behave differently? (Furnham, 1990). Certain groups of respondents will score higher on the scale than others. We hypothesise that working people generally have higher work involvement than non-working people, but we cannot ascertain whether high work involvement, e.g. among the unemployed, is the result of a retrospective idealisation of work, an echo of public discourses on unemployment (i.e. they claim to conform to appropriate attitudes in order to be regarded as deserving), or a resigned adaptation to a marginalised situation in relation to the labour market. Di Fazio's study of the Brooklyn longshoremen found that after some years of joblessness, these men had lost their desire to do labour (Di Fazio, 1985). The predictive validity can be tested, for example, by measuring the extent to which employment commitment predicts voluntary unemployment, which, to a certain extent, it does (Halvorsen, 1995a).

In order to make comparisons between 1991 and 1995 and to conduct a multivariate analysis of the whole working age population, we have also used a single-item measurement (the so called 'lottery-win' question), namely 'I would prefer to work even if I won a great sum of money.' People are thus asked what they would do if the purely financial incentive to work were removed (Hakim, 1996b). In the last section of this paper this is contrasted with another indicator of employment commitment, namely 'work is/has been among the most important things in life.' Both of these single-item measurements are also items in the index described above. The first question is hypothetical and future-oriented, while the latter is more related to the present (and past) commitment to work.

Hypotheses

The evidence from previous research gives some support to the importance of attitudes for labour market behaviour, but also indicates that there is a reciprocal relationship between attitudes and economic outcomes. The influence may work in the opposite direction as well – i.e. favourable labour market experiences may encourage commitment to the work ethic, while unfavourable labour market experiences may have the opposite effect (Andrisani and Parnes, 1983; Bielby and Bielby, 1989; Ellingsæter, 1995). Fraccaroli (1993) found, for example, that

---

All factor loadings are positive and their values are above 0.4, which is regarded as necessary as a rule of thumb.

unemployed young people who found employment were more like to perceive intrinsic value in work. Commitment to and identification with the work role develops when individuals become engaged in this role (Bielby and Bielby, 1989).

The hypotheses for this study are inspired by those posed by Bielby and Bielby (1989), Furnham (1990), and Gallie et al. (1994) and concern correlations between labour market participation, family roles, political attitudes and employment commitment:

a) Working people have greater employment commitment than the unemployed and those outside the labour force.

b) Among working people, those in highly skilled jobs have greater employment commitment than those in low-skilled jobs.

c) Among working people, those who work full-time have greater employment commitment than those who work part-time.

Data on work commitment offer evidence that women as a group give less priority to paid employment than do men (Hakim, 1991, Alwin et al. 1992. See, however, Ellingsæter, 1995). Since the latter must often temper their interest in their work with family responsibilities (Bielby and Bielby, 1989), we also assume that

d) Men have a greater employment commitment than women.

e) Women's employment commitment is more strongly influenced by non-work factors than men's.

Further, we assume that political attitudes are correlated with employment commitment. Conservatives have the greatest employment commitment (Furnham, 1990) since they seem to be the strongest supporters of the ideology of self-reliance (Halvorsen, 1996c), so

f) Conservatives have greater employment commitment than others.

Descriptive statistics

Among people of working age we generally find a high personal employment commitment. Table 7.1 demonstrates that there have not been any major changes in employment commitment in the population from 1986 to 1995.

Regardless of when and how employment commitment was measured, the differences between the sexes are small and non-significant. Over the last ten years employment commitment seems to have been high and stable. The lower employment commitment in the 1989-survey may be due to the slightly different wording of the statement as compared with the surveys of 1986, 1991 and 1995. The differences in employment commitment in 1991 and 1995 (18-40 years) are significant for men ($p<0.01$) and for everyone ($p<0.01$), but not for women. A decline in employment commitment for men and a small increase for women has also been found in Great Britain (Hakim, 1996b).

Table 7.1
Employment commitment for people of working age 1986-1995.
Percentages (M = male, F = female, T = total)

	1986 1)			1989 2)			1991 3)			1995 4)		
Age group	M	F	T	M	F	T	M	F	T	M	F	T
18-40	89	86	87				92	90	91	87	89	88
20-66	86	85	86							88	87	87
16-64	87	88	88	68	71	69				88	87	87
(number)	(519)	(416)	(935)				(876)	(877)	(1753)	(664)	(747)	(1411)
	(724)	(616)	(1346)							(1185)	(1202)	(2387)
	(801)	(694)	(1495)	(822)	(778)	(1600)				(1222)	(1250)	(2472)

1) Source: NAVF's koordineringsundersøkelse 1986: % who said they would have paid work (full-time or part-time) even if they did not need the money
2) Source: SSB: Arbeidslivsundersøkelsen (Work Conditions and Working Experiences) 1989, quoted after Ellingsæter, 1995: % who agreed to the statement: 'I would have liked to have paid work even if I did not need the money'
3) Source: SSB: Level of Living survey 1991: % who agreed to the statement: 'Even if I won a large sum of money I would work'
4) Source: Gallup 1995 for INAS, same statement as 3)

Expressive (non-financial) attitudes to work in Norway can be compared with those in Germany and Great Britain where only 52 and 59% respectively said that they would prefer to work even if they did not need the money, as opposed to 73% in Norway (The International Social Survey Program, 1989; Stjernø, 1995). In Norway 63% held the opinion that work is a person's most important activity compared with only 38 and 39% respectively in Germany and Great Britain (Stjernø, 1995). A comparative study of social assistance clients in the Nordic capitals also found that the level of work involvement on the average was greater in Norway than in Denmark, Finland and Sweden (Marklund, 1993). These results indicate the strength of the work ethic in Norway. Work is perceived not only as an instrument for earning money, but also as a meaningful activity in itself. There is a long-term trend towards more varied and interesting jobs, but also towards more stressful work. Wage earners also tend to be more concerned about the work environment and whether the job is interesting, rather than if it is highly paid (Iversen and Midtlyng, 1994). However, we cannot rule out that even in Norway a minority are marginalised with respect to meaningful work (Applebaum, 1992), which could induce a weak work involvement.

Table 7.2 gives an overview of the distribution and mean scores on the work involvement scale for samples of long-term unemployed (ages 20-59), social assistance recipients (ages 18-49), single parents (ages 18-60), young disabled persons (ages 18-40), and the general population (ages 18-40).

Table 7.2
Work involvement scale mean values and distribution of scores for various categories. 1991.
(Percentages and mean values)

Score ↓	Ordinary population	Long-term Unemployed	Social assistance recipients	Sole parents	Young disabled
1 - 2.5(low)	2.5	3.2	5.1	2.7	15.3
2.6-3.5	7.3	11.5	78.3	8.2	10.3
3.6-6 (high)	90.2	85.3	16.6	89.1	74.3
	100.0	100.0	100.0	100.0	100.0
Sum mean score	4.43	4.37	3.17	4.37	4.07
Std.deviation	0.63	0.71	0.46	0.68	1.16
(number)	(1742)	(687)	(1184)	(792)	(536)

(Sources: Level of living surveys 1991)

All categories except social assistance recipients report a high average work involvement. With the exception of that one category, there are great similarities in the distribution of scores (a 2-tailed test only gave significant differences in overall mean scores between social assistance recipients and the other categories, and between young disabled persons and the other categories). So far we can conclude that the work involvement for most of the population is very high. Only about 10% seem to have a very low work involvement (i.e. scores less than 3.6 on the employment involvement scale). The low employment commitment among social assistance recipients could be explained by their low labour force participation rate, but even recipients with paid work had a far lower average employment commitment than the ordinary population (results not shown). It may be that working individuals with a social assistance allowance are marginalised with respect to meaningful work. Very few of these recipients had full time tenured work (Halvorsen, 1996a). For all samples reported in Table 7.2, the age differences are small and non-significant, whereas gender differences are significant when the employment commitment index is used (results not shown). In general, men had a higher employment commitment than women, with the exception of young disabled persons and social assistance recipients, where the differences were not significant at the 0.05% level. This is contrary to what we found when we used the single item measurement of employment commitment (see Table 7.1). We shall return to these anomalies in the last section of the paper.

There also seem to be differences in employment commitment between working, unemployed and non-working individuals (Table 7.3). The differences between those working and not working are in the expected direction, especially for females. In general, however, the differences between employed and unemployed are small, as was also found in the U.K. (Jackson, 1994).

Table 7.3
Work involvement scale for persons (age 18-40) working, unemployed and outside the labour force differentiated by sex. 1991.
(Mean values)

Employment status→ Sex ↓	Working now	Unemploy-ed in 1990 /working now	Unemploy-ed in 1990/ not working now	Outside labour force	All
Males	4.60	4.57	4.50	4.40	4.55 (863)
Females	4.36	4.35	4.22	4.13	4.30 (867)
Total	4.50	4.47	4.35	4.25	4.43
(number)	(1090)	(173)	(118)	(345)	(1730)

Labour force participation, F-value for males = 6.788, $p < 0.001$, F-value for females = 7.910, $p < 0.001$

Source: Level of living survey 1991, ordinary

Based on a Gallup survey conducted in the fall of 1995, Table 7.4 reveals a similar pattern to that reported in Table 7.3 for persons aged 20-66. Employment commitment is measured here by only one of the statements used in the employment commitment index, because not all the other statements were included in this survey.

The differences found in Table 7.3 between those who are working and those who are not working are confirmed in Table 7.4. The gender-based differences are generally smaller however, and non-significant, with the exception of homemakers, where males had a lower employment commitment than females.

Our findings differ with the results of two British studies made in 1986 and 1992, in which the unemployed had a higher employment commitment than the employed, even after age and sex differentials were taken into consideration (Gallie et al., 1994), nor do they agree with the findings of Ellingsæter (1995), in which employed women in particular had a higher employment commitment than employed men.

If present and previous work experiences matters, it can be assumed that employment commitment varies with occupation. Table 7.5 reports variations of this sort.

Among respondents who gave their occupation, the gender-based difference in employment commitment is small and not significant, but employment commitment varies with occupation and there is also an interaction effect between occupation and gender. For both males and females the lowest employment commitment was found among unskilled blue collar workers. On average, the lowest work involvement was found among persons from low-rank positions, with the exception of persons (especially females) in liberal professions (doctors, dentists etc.). The highest employment commitment was found among self-employed men and female technicians and engineers. Within particular occupational categories the genderbased differences were significant at the 0.05 level for skilled workers and self-employed persons only. Females working part-time in unskilled blue collar work had the lowest employment commitment (a mean score of 4.02 as compared to 4.63 for men in the same category), whereas self-employed men working full-time had the highest employment commitment (a mean score of 4.95) (results not presented). Ellingsæter (1995) also found a clear correlation between occupational status and work commitment, with blue collar workers recording the lowest commitment and high-salaried employees the highest, with similar patterns for men and women.

Table 7.4
Proportion of the population of working age (age 20-66) who agreed with the statement 'Even if I won a large sum of money, I would work'. 1995.
(Percentages and mean values[1], in brackets)

Employment status ↓	Females	Males
Working full- time	90 (4.57)	90 (4.58)
Working part- time	87 (4.43)	88 (4.41)
Unemployed	85 (4.43)	86 (4.53)
Homemaking	82 (4.33)	73 (4.22)
Student	93 (4.64)	92 (4.59)
Sick/disabled/early retired	76 (4.21)	74 (4.24)
Total	87 (4.48)	88 (4.54)
(number)	(1172)	(1143)

χ^2 Employment status p<0.001, gender ns
Gender: F-value=0.0047, df 1, ns, Employment status: F=5.723,df 5, p<0.001, no 2-way interaction significant

1) Mean values are calculated in a manner similar to that used for each item in the employment commitment index (Table 7.3) using five response categories ranging from one to five, where those who agreed completely scored five, and those who disagreed completely scored one. Those who neither agreed nor disagreed with the statement or who did not answer were assigned the value three.

(Source: Gallup, 1995)

Table 7.6 indicates that there is a gender difference in employment commitment using the single-item statement: 'work is/has been the most important activity'.

It seems that the single-item measurement used in Tables 7.4 and 7.5 is not as valid a measure of gender-based differences as the employment commitment index (see Table 7.3) or, for that matter, as the single-item measurement used in Table 7.6. An index is better at revealing nuances and ambiguities in attitudes. Furthermore, it turns out that the gender-based differences were generally greater in response to the other statements. This was particularly true for the statement: 'work is almost the most important thing in life' (see Table 7.6), which, as a single-item measurement, is probably a better indicator of employment commitment reflecting 'work as a central life interest' than the statement, 'I would prefer to work even if a won a great sum of money'. It becomes clearer that women working part-time (and homemaking men and women) are less committed to employment than persons in the other categories.

Table 7.5
Employment commitment: Proportion who agreed with the statement 'I would work even if I won a great sum of money' differentiated by occupation and gender. Population aged 20-66.
(Percentages and mean values[1])

Occupation ↓	Females		Males	
Apprentice	(100	4.60)	(73	4.30)
Unskilled worker	85	4.30	83	4.33
Skilled worker	96	4.79	83	4.31
Salaried worker	92	4.56	93	4.66
Technician	(100	4.93)	94	4.76
High salaried worker	89	4.51	94	4.71
Manager	90	4.66	93	4.77
Self-employed	(79	4.42)	100	4.96
Liberal occupations	(90	4.24)	90	4.56
Other	90	4.58	90	4.56
All	90	4.53	90	4.57
(number)	(745)		(873)	

(number < 20 in brackets)

1) See note table 7.4.

$\chi 2$, Occupations: females n.s., males df 9, p<0.001

Gender: F-value 2.99, df 1 ns, occupation: F-value 3.19, df 9, p<0.01, 2-way interaction: F-value: 2.15, p<0.05

(Source: Gallup, 1995)

To sum up so far: Although there are gender-based differences, they are generally small and more often than not insignificant. The differences in employment status and occupation are greater than the differences between men and women. The data presented so far support the hypothesis that working people have greater work involvement than non-working people. We found that both males and females outside the labour force had lower work involvement than those who were working but the unemployed did not seem to have significantly lower employment commitment than the employed, with the possible exception of the long-term unemployed. We have also demonstrated that whether or not there is a gender-based difference in employment commitment depends on the way in which employment commitment is measured. We shall return to this question in the next section. We now turn to multivariate analysis in order to examine the relative importance of the explanatory variables in explaining variations in employment commitment among people of working age.

Table 7.6
Proportion of the population (age 20-66) who agreed with the statement 'Work is/has been about the most important thing in life' distributed according to employment status and gender. 1995.
(Percentages and mean values[1], in brackets)

Employment Status ↓	Females	Males
Employed full-time	65 (3.84)	77 (4.09)
Employed part-time	58 (3.50)	78 (4.19)
Unemployed	72 (3.91)	77 (4.14)
Homemaking	55 (3.53)	59 (3.73)
Students	63 (3.64)	62 (3.65)
Sick/disabled/early retirees	65 (3.87)	76 (4.18)
All	65 (3.71)	76 (4.07)
(number)	(1140)	(1117)

1) See note Table 7.4

$\chi 2$ (gender all) $p<0.001$, Gender: F-value: 11.593, df 1, $p<0.001$, employment status: F-value 3.667, df 5, $p<0.01$

(Source: Gallup, 1995)

Multivariate analysis: What factors explain variations in employment commitment among people of working age?

The analytical model used as a point of departure for the multivariate analysis is based on theories about how the attitudes presented in sections one and two are formed, on the hypotheses put forward in this paper, and on previous empirical findings. The dependent variable is the single-item statement, 'Even if I won a large sum of money, I would work'. Those who agreed completely or partly with this statement were assigned the value of 1, while other responses were given the value of 0. Since this is a dichotomous variable, we have used a logistic regression. The explanatory factors are divided into five groups.

The first is associated with background factors, such as gender, age and educational level. We expect individuals with higher education to have a stronger employment commitment. As for age, we expect to find the lowest employment commitment among the youngest and oldest respondents. Females are expected to have a lower employment commitment than men.

The second group of factors is related to previous work and unemployment experiences. Employment commitment comes from involvement in work roles (Bielby and Bielby, 1989). We therefore hypothesise that homemakers and the sick, the disabled and early retirees, in particular, are less committed to work than people in the other categories. We do not have relevant information about the previous number of years spent working though this factor seems to be associated with employment commitment (Ellingsæter, 1995), so we have had to use previous unemployment as a proxy (i.e. a substitute variable). One line of argument is that those in work take the benefits of employment for granted while those without work tend to idealize paid work (Gallie et al., 1994). An alternative explanation could be that those who have been without work for a while tend to reject work values in order to cope with the unemployment situation. The variables used are: present unemployment (a category of the variable 'present employment status') and whether or not the respondent had been unemployed during the past two years, which was entered as a dummy variable. Present employment status has five categories: working part-time, unemployed, homemaker, student, and sick/disabled/early retiree with working full-time used as a reference category.

The third group of factors are household circumstances, such as marital status, breadwinner status and whether one lives with children under 7 years of age. We hypothesise that especially females who are married and/or have small children and/or who have a male breadwinner are less committed to work than others, whereas these factors do not influence men's employment commitment to the same extent. This hypothesis reflects the findings of Bielby and Bielby (1989) that women give the family priority when determining the relative importance of their work and family roles, whereas no definite conclusion can be drawn for men.

The fourth factor is related to political attitudes. Political attitude is measured with a question about which political party the respondent would vote for if there were an election. Voting for the Labour Party is used as a reference category, since it represents a social democratic work ethic, as explained in the introduction.

Finally, we have analysed the influence of a fifth group of factors, namely contextual factors. Bearing in mind theories about the influence of reference groups on norms, we assume that employment commitment is influenced by social networks. We assume that employment commitment is weaker in local communities where unemployment is quite common than it is in communities where it is perceived by the respondent as uncommon.

The results of the logistic regressions are reported in tables A and B in the appendix. We first ran the logistic regression for the whole sample. When we checked for other relevant independent variables, the gender-based differences were non-significant, and the coefficient had a negative sign, which meant that men had a lower employment commitment than women. The only explanatory variables of significance were marital status (being married increases the likelihood of high employment commitment), age (the 40-49 age group had a significantly higher employment commitment than the reference category aged 60-66), employment status (homemakers and the sick, the disabled and early retirees had a lower employment commitment than the full-time employed) and political attitude (those who vote for Christian Democratic Party had a significantly lower employment commitment than the reference category which consisted of those who vote for the Labour Party). Those who vote for the Conservatives (Høyre) are more committed to employment than those in the reference category, but the coefficient was only significant at the 10% level.

We then analysed males and females separately in order to determine whether factors associated with employment commitment are similar or differ for men and women. As demonstrated in Table 7.B (appendix), the main finding is that previously married females who are homemakers and/or vote for the Christian Democratic Party are less likely to be committed to work, whereas the opposite is the case for women with a higher education and/or women who are married or have never been married.

As for men, the age group of 40-49 was significantly more likely to have a high employment commitment than the reference category (age group of 60-66). In addition, male homemakers and sick, disabled and early retired males were more likely to have a low employment commitment than males in the reference category (full-time employed). Furthermore, married men were more likely to have a high employment commitment than previously married men, but the coefficient is only significant at the 10% level. The differences in employment commitment between (full-time) employed and unemployed seem to disappear in multivariate analyses, since neither the coefficients for females nor those for males are significant at the 10% level. Unemployed men had a equally high employment commitment as employed men nor does previous unemployment seem to be significantly associated with a low employment commitment.

The question of whether or not unemployment in the community was common did not seem to be significant. It was positive, as expected, for women, but not for men. Thus, there is no strong evidence for the development of a 'culture of dependency'.

Discussion and conclusion

Overall, both employed and unemployed persons in an 'employment society' such as Norway have a high employment commitment. Differences in employment commitment tend to be minor, and big variations in employment commitment with respect to sex, age, education level, employment status and household circumstances only occur to a limited extent. It may be possible to explain these small variations with the public discourses on employment. It appears that those who are working full-time and who have had no unemployment experience generally have a somewhat greater work involvement than the unemployed, or at any rate the long-term unemployed. The lowest work involvement was found among persons more permanently outside the labour force, such as young disabled persons and social assistance recipients, homemakers, the sick, the disabled and early retirees, and previously married elderly women. With the exception of males aged 40-49, who had significantly higher employment commitment than the reference group (aged 60-66), we did not find any age-based differences in employment commitment. It thus seems that young people are just as committed to employment as older ones. However, this statement will be qualified below.

The gender-based differences in the multivariate analysis (although not significant) point in the same direction as those found by Ellingsæter (1995) in a multivariate analysis of the whole working age population (age 16-64). Men had a slightly lower employment commitment than women. Another similarity with the findings in her study is that persons with higher education are more likely to be committed to employment than persons with only primary or upper secondary education. As a measure of employment commitment, Ellingsæter used a slightly different statement from ours, namely, 'I would have liked to have paid work even if I did not need the money'. The age groups employed were also somewhat different, there were no controls for children under the age of seven in the household, and marital status was only differentiated into two possible values: married or unmarried. She only differentiated between those who were currently employed and those who were not employed (for the whole sample), whereas in our study we used several categories for employment status, as she did when the analyses were conducted separately on men and women. More important, however, her analysis included the number of previous years worked, whereas ours included periods of unemployment during the previous two years.

As for marital status, we found that previously married women were more likely to have a low employment commitment than both unmarried and married women. This could be due to unobserved heterogeneities among the previously married, especially those who were separated and/or divorced. Unlike Ellingsæter (1995), however, we did not find did that married men had a higher employment commitment than unmarried or previously married men, but she was unable to confirm her finding in a linear regression. Homemakers of both sexes were more likely to have a low employment commitment than the full-time employed, but the coefficient for women was not significant at the 0.05 level. With the possible exception of female, unskilled, blue-collar workers (results not shown), part-time workers (men and women) were no more likely to have low employment commitment than full-time workers. It could be argued that the commitment of a part-time worker to a part-time job is not as great as the commitment of a full-time worker to a full-time job (Hakim, 1995). Unfortunately, we do not know whether the responses to the statements about employment commitment referred to full-time or part-time work. The survey in 1986 (see Table 7.1) found that the majority of women would actually prefer part-time work (even if they did not have to worry about money). This, combined with the results presented in Table 7.6 demonstrating that women are less inclined than men to rate employment as the most important activity in life, indicates that our measurement of employment commitment with the statement 'I would prefer to work even if I won a great sum of money', may attribute a higher priority to employment than female part-time workers and homemakers actually do in reality.

Both unemployed men and women had a surprisingly high employment commitment (see Tables 7.4 and 7.6), which contrasts somewhat with what we found earlier for the 18-40 age group (see Table 7.3). It must be kept in mind that the survey in Table 7.2 (column two) is of the long-term unemployed. It may be that the (short term) unemployed are idealizing that which has been taken away from them, while the long-term unemployed have had to readjust their employment commitment in order to maintain their self-respect. In the study of the long-term unemployed in 1991 (who had been unemployed an average of 1.7 times during the last five years and an average of 14 months per unemployment spell, see Halvorsen, 1995b), there was a much lower proportion of both males and females who agreed with the statement in Table 7.6 (64 and 47% respectively) (Halvorsen, 1996b, forthcoming). Thus, it seems that the long-term unemployed (and especially females) have a lower employment commitment than all the unemployed. This could indicate a selection effect or a causation effect. Those with low employment commitment are more likely to become unemployed, for instance, because they quit their job voluntarily. They are also more likely to stay unemployed because they are better able to cope with unemployment and search for a job less intensively. Long-term unemployment, however, could also result in a resigned adjustment to a life that does not include paid work. On the basis of retrospective information given by the respondents in the survey of the long-term unemployed, it seems plausible that low work involvement could at least partly be the reason why a small minority of them were unemployed. Those (few) with low work involvement tend to quit their jobs voluntarily and also seem to be less eager to get a new job (Halvorsen, 1995a). The fact that those with low work involvement are less likely to be re-employed also supports this conclusion (Halvorsen, 1994).

It seems that people who are highly skilled, have senior positions or run there own business have especially high work involvement. Other studies have demonstrated that those who enjoyed autonomy in their job had the greatest job satisfaction (deVaus and McAllister, 1991; see, however, Bielby and Bielby, 1989). This is an indication that high work involvement is at least partly influenced by (favourable) work experiences (Ellingsæter, 1995). This is supported by variations in employment commitment in the different occupational categories shown in Table 7.5. Having a higher education also increases the likelihood that women will be committed to work, but this is not the case for men.

From the correlations presented here, we can only speculate about the causal directions. Cross-sectional data cannot show that low work involvement is an effect of previous work or unemployment experiences. We need longitudinal data of marginalised categories, such as the long-term unemployed, for example, if we are to ascertain the direction of causality between employment commitment and employment status, but the low employment commitment among unskilled workers indicates that such causal effects may exist. However, it could also be argued that persons with low employment commitment choose undemanding jobs 'with no worries or responsibilities' and are therefore concentrated to lower grade and lower paid jobs (Hakim, 1995:434). The gender-based differences are small, but our findings indicate that females have a somewhat more ambiguous attitude to employment than has been acknowledged by those who are opposed to a dualistic paradigm for explaining women's and men's employment patterns (see, for example, Ellingsæter, 1995; Ginn et al., 1996). Some women still prefer part-time work to a greater extent than men and some do not see work as the most important activity in life, probably because of their dual role as providers of care and workers. Hakim (1996a) maintains that a substantial proportion of women still regard homemaking as women's principal activity. Our data indicate that this is only the case for a minority, regardless of how employment commitment is measured, and with the proportion of traditional housewives declining (and more obtaining higher education), the level of work commitment among all women of working age will increase (Ellingsæter, 1995).

That a gender-based difference is not an artefact is supported by the finding in the 1986 survey that more women than men would prefer to work part-time. Furthermore, when the statement 'Work is the most important activity in life', was entered as the dependent variable in a multivariate analysis with the same independent variables as in Table 7.A of the Appendix, females were more likely (odds ratio 1:2) than men to have a low employment commitment (but the coefficient is not significant at the 5% level): i.e. a gender-based difference in the opposite direction to that presented in Table 7.A. In particular women working part-time are less likely than full-time working women to be committed to employment for non-economic reasons, whereas this was not the case for men working-part-time (results not shown). This contrasts with what Ellingsæter (1995) found. Hakim (1996a) maintains that there are qualitative differences between the orientation to work of women working full-time and those working part-time in the sense that the majority of the latter regard breadwinning as primarily the responsibility of men, whereas women working full-time reject this proposition. Still, these gender-based differences in employment commitment are small. The similarities between men and women are more striking than the observed differences.

Moreover, using 'work is the most important activity in life' as a dependent variable also indicates that young people were significantly less committed to work than older ones (results not shown). This could be due to both an age effect and a cohort effect. Young people are, in fact, just as committed to employment as older ones, but they are less inclined to regard it as the most important activity in life. It also matters whether or not the respondent is the main or sole breadwinner.

One may question the validity of some of the indicators used in previous studies, especially the single-item ones, which seem unable to reveal people's ambiguous attitudes to employment. Based on our combined findings, a tentative conclusion can be drawn that women are just as likely to regard employment as an important activity in life as men, but they are less likely than men to regard employment as the most important activity in life. They are more likely than men to want to balance their commitment to paid work with their commitment to children and family. In the future, it is more likely than not that more men will do the same, though this prediction depends to a certain extent on whether employers are providing 'family friendly' policies.

We have found support for hypothesis a) (Working people have a higher employment commitment than the unemployed and those outside labour force), with the exception of students, and where the unemployed refers to the long-term unemployed. Our findings also support hypothesis b) (Among working people, those in highly skilled jobs have a greater employment commitment than those in low-skilled jobs), but, with the possible exception of females, not hypothesis c)

(Among working people, those who are working full-time have a greater employment commitment than those who are working part-time).

Support or rejection of hypothesis d) (men have a greater employment commitment than women) is dependent on the way in which employment commitment is measured. This was not the case for hypothesis e) (women's employment commitment is more strongly influenced by non-work factors than men's) because motherhood (here measured with the parameter of whether one is living with children of pre-school age) or marriage does not correlate with low employment commitment regardless of how it is measured. These findings are consistent with those of Ellingsæter (1995). On the other hand, the fact that females who vote for the Christian Democratic Party have a low employment commitment supports hypothesis e). This party is a strong advocate of traditional family values and the traditional division of labour between the sexes, with mothers looking after their own children at home. The majority of women who vote for this party, accordingly, have traditional attitudes to sex roles; 89% agreed with the statement: 'It is, after all, the family who have to suffer if women have full-time work' as compared, for example, with 52% of the women who voted for the Labour Party (i.e. the Social Democrats) (Gallup, 1995).

We only find limited support for hypothesis f) that conservatives have a higher employment commitment. On the one hand, those who vote for the Conservative Party are more likely to be committed to employment than those who vote for the Labour Party, but, on the other hand, those (females) who support The Christian Democratic Party (which, politically, is relatively close to the Conservatives) are less likely to have a high employment commitment.

There is little support for the 'gender socialisation model', which implies that women's work involvement will be more strongly influenced by non-work factors, but there is some support for the 'social structural model', which hypothesises that employment commitment is influenced by actual work experiences. We cannot regard work orientations as immutable (Ellingsæter, 1995; Bruegel, 1996). Since there are more females with higher education working full-time in skilled occupations, and thereby having a longer working career, they would most likely regard employment as their most important interest in life to the same extent that men do, whereas traditional attitudes to employment would tend to be concentrated to a gradually decreasing number of (older) homemakers.

One conclusion to be drawn from this study is that it is unlikely that low work involvement among those outside the labour force will undermine the work ethic and thus the foundation for the Norwegian welfare state. This feedback effect of labour market experience on work involvement means that the work involvement of individuals is not beyond the reach of public policy measures. A meaningful job or higher education would most likely be the most important factors for maintaining a high employment commitment in our society.

If people remain outside the labour force for years, however, or are in marginal jobs (low paid, insecure jobs), there is a risk of a decline in their work involvement as a result of a resigned adjustment to an unsatisfactory life situation. Yet it is unlikely that a 'culture of dependency' consisting of people who reject dominant work values is about to develop. In order to give more reliable evidence of a culture of dependency we need longitudinal data for marginalised groups, such as social assistance recipients. We also need longitudinal data if we want a more precise answer to the question of whether attitudes to work are the cause or the effect of marginality to the labour market.

Acknowledgements

The data from the surveys of 1986 and 1991 used in this paper were obtained through Statistics Norway and put at our disposal by Norwegian Social Science Data Services (NSD). The Gallup 1995 survey was put at our disposal by Lars Gulbrandsen, INAS, Oslo. Neither of these agencies is responsible for the analyses presented. The study was financed by a Research Council of Norway grant under its 'Velferd og samfunn' programme, and by the Ministry of Government Administration and the Ministry of Local Government and Labour. This paper was written while the author was on study leave from Oslo College as a visiting scholar at the Social Policy Research Centre at the University of New South Wales in Sydney, Australia. We would like to thank Rolf Rønning of Lillehammer Regional College, Anne Lise Ellingsæter at the Institute for Social Research in Oslo and Arne Mastekaasa of the University of Oslo for useful comments on earlier drafts of this paper.

References

Ågotsnes, K. (1993), 'Å stanse i spranget. Refleksjoner omkring arbeid og arbeidsløshet', *Plan and Arbeid* 5/6.93.

Alwin, D.F., Braun M. and Scott J. (1992), 'The Separation of Work and the Family Attitudes towards Women's Labour Force Participation in Germany, Great Britain, and the United States', *European Sociological Review*, Vol. 8:13-37.

Andrisani, P.J. and Parnes, H.S. (1983), 'Commitment to The Work Ethic and Success in The Labour Market. A Review of Research Findings', in Barbash J. et al. (eds), *The Work Ethic – A Critical Analysis*, Madison, Wisconsin: Industrial Relations Research Associations.

Andersen, J.G. and Hoff, J. (1995), *Likhed i den politiske deltakelsen*, Aarhus: Aarhus Universitet.

Applebaum, H. (1992), *The Concept of Work*, New York: State University of New York Press.

Arendt, H. (1958), *The Human Condition*, Chicago: The University of Chicago Press.

Banks, M.H. and Ullah P. (1988), *Youth Unemployment in the 1980s: Its Psychological Effects*, London: Croom Helm.

Banks, M.H. and Henry, P. (1993), 'Change and Stability in Employment Commitment', *Journal of Occupational and Organizational Psychology*, Vol. 53: 187-196.
Barbash, J. (1983), 'Which Work Ethic', in Barbash J. et al. (eds), *The Work Ethic – Critical Analysis*, Madison, Wisconsin: Industrial Relations Research Associations.
Bauman, Z. (1992), *Intimations of Postmodernity*, London: Routledge.
Bem, D. (1967), 'Self-perception on Alternative Interpretation of Cognitive Dissonance Phenomena', *Psychological Reviw*, vol. 74.
Bielby, D.D. and Bielby, W.T. (1989), 'Family Ties: Balancing Commitment to Work and Family in Dual Earner Households', *American Sociological Review*, 54: 776-789.
Bocock, R. (1993), *Consumption*, London: Routledge.
Bratt, C. (1988), 'Arbeidsglede og arbeidsfientlighet – lønnsarbeid som sosial inegrasjon', in *Sosiologisk Årbok 1988*, Oslo: Universitetet i Oslo, Institutt for Sosiologi.
Bruegel, I. (1996), 'Whose myths are they anyway?: a comment', *British Journal of Sociology*, 47:175-177.
Claussen, B. (1994), *Deprived of work and health? A two-year follow up of long term unemployed from Grenland, Norway 1988-90*, Research Report No F 1-1994, Oslo: National Institute of Public Health.
Cohen, A. (1995), 'An Examination of the Relationships Between Work Commitment and Nonwork Domains', *Human Relations*, Vol. 48:239-263.
Colbjørnsen, T. (1992), 'Hvor står forskningen om mestring av arbeidsledighet?', in NAVF: *Hva kan arbeidsledighetsforskningen fortelle oss?*, Oslo: NAVF, Rådet for samfunnsvitenskapelig forskning.
Cross, G. (1993), *Time and Money. The Making of Consumer Culture*, London: Routledge.
Di Fazio, W. (1985), *Longshoremen. Community and Resistance on the Brooklyn Waterfront*, Massachusetts: Bergin and Carvey Publ.
Ellingsæter, A.L. (1995), *Gender, Work and Social Change. Beyond Dualistic Thinking*, Report 95:14, Oslo: Institute for Social Research.
Elster, J. (1989), *The Cement of Society*, Cambridge: Cambridge University Press.
Esping-Andersen, G. (1993), 'Three Post-industrial Employment Regimes', in Kolberg, J.E. (ed), *The Welfare State as Employer*, New York: Sharp.
Ezzy, D. (1993), 'Unemployment and Mental Health: A Critical Review', *Social Science and Medicine*, Vol. 37:41-52.
Ferman, L.A. (1983), 'The Work Ethic in the World of Informal Work', in Barbash, J. et al. (eds), *The Work Ethic – A Critical Analysis*, Madison, Wisconsin: Industrial Relations Research Associations.
Fraccaroli, F. (1993), 'The Experience of Unemployment and Meanings of Work', *Stodi di Sociologia*, Vol. 3:159-176.
Frogner, T. (1995), *Ideenes kraft og politikkens grenser*, Oslo: Forum.
Furnham, A. (1990), *The Protestant Work Ethic*, London: Routledge.

Furnham, A. (1994), 'The Psychological Consequences of Youth Unemployment', in Petersen, A.C., and Mortimer, J.T. (eds), *Youth Unemployment and Society*, Cambridge: Cambridge University Press.
Furnham, A. et al. (1992), 'A Comparison of Protestant Work Ethic Beliefs in Thirteen Nations', *The Journal of Social Psychology*, Vol. 133:185-197.
Gallie, D. and White, M. (1993), *Employee Commitment and the Skills Revolution*, London: Policy Studies Institute.
Gallie, D. and Vogler, C. (1994), 'Unemployment and Attitudes to Work', in Gallie, D., March, C. and Vogler, C. (eds), *Social Change and the Experience of Unemployment*, Oxford: Oxford University Press.
Gallie, D., Cheng, Y. and Tomlinson, M. (1994) in White, M. (ed) *Unemployment and Public Policy in Changing Labour Market*, London: Policy Studies Institute.
Ginn, J. et al. (1996), 'Feminist Fallacies: A Reply to Hakim on Women's Employment', *British Journal of Sociology*, Vol. 47:167-174.
Giorgi, L. and Marsh, C. (1990), 'The Protestant Work Ethic as A Cultural Phenomenon', *European Journal of Social Pscychology*, Vol. 20:499-517.
Grotenhuis, H.T., and Meijers, F. (1994), 'Societal Consequences of Youth Unemployment', in Petersen, A.C. and Mortimer, J.T. (eds), *Youth Unemployment and Society*, Cambridge: Cambridge University Press.
Habermehl, W. (1988), 'Die Arbeitsmoral der 'Arbeidslosen' Kommentar zu Karl-Heinz Reuband: Die Arbeitsmoral der Arbeitslosen', *Kölner Zeitschrift für Soziologie und Sozialpsychologie*, Vol. 40:370-375.
Hakim, C. (1991), 'Grateful Slaves and Self-made Women: Fact and Fantasy in Women's Work Orientations', *European Sociological Review*, Vol. 7:101-121.
Hakim, C. (1995), 'Five Feminist Myths about Women's Employment', *British Journal of Sociology*, Vol. 46:429-452.
Hakim, C. (1996a), 'The Sexual Division of Labour and Women's Heterogeneity', *British Journal of Sociology*, Vol. 46:178-188.
Hakim, C. (1996b), *Key Issues in Women's Work*, London: Athlone.
Haller, M. and Rosenmayr, L. (1971), 'The Pluridimensionality of Work Commitment', *Human Relations*, Vol. 24:501-518.
Halvorsen, K (1993), *Innføring i sosialpolitikk*, Oslo: TANO.
Halvorsen, K. (1994), 'Kommer langtidsarbeidsløse tilbake i lønnet arbeid?', in *Søkelys på arbeidsmarkedet* 2/94.
Halvorsen, K. (1995a), 'Impact of Employment Commitment on Experiences of Unemployment and Job Search Behaviour', Paper, unpublished draft.
Halvorsen, K. (1995b), 'Ledighetsmønstre blant langtidsarbeidsløse', *Samfunns-speilet*, 3/95:13-15.
Halvorsen, K. (1996a), 'Utsatt posisjon i arbeidsmarkedet: en hovedvei til bidragsavhengighet', in Halvorsen, K. (ed), *Mestring av marginalitet: Å leve og overleve som sosialklient*, Oslo: Cappelen Akademisk Forlag.
Halvorsen, K. (1996b), 'Variations in Employment Commitment among Long-term Unemployed', unpublished draft.

Halvorsen, K. (1996c), 'The Concepts of Self-reliance and Dependency in Contemporary Discourses on Welfare – Sympolic Purposes and substantial Consequences', Paper presented at The Scandinavian Journal of Social Welfare symposium, Stockholm, September 4-5.

Hannan, D.F. and O. Riain, S. (1993), *Pathways to Adulthood In Ireland: Causes and Consequences of Success and Failure in Transitions Among Irish Youth*, General Research Series, No. 161, Dublin: The Economic and Social Research Institute.

Hannan, D.F., O Riain, S. and Whelan, C.T. (1994), 'Youth Unemployment and Psychological Distress in The Republic of Ireland', Paper presented at 23rd International Congress of Applied Psychology, Madrid July 17-22.

Harding, S.D. and Hikspoors, F.J. (1995), 'New work values in theory and in practice', *International Social Science Journal*, Vol. 14:441-455.

Hendry, L.B, Raymond, M. and Stewart, C. (1984), 'Unemployment, school and leisure: An adolescent study', *Leisure Studies*, Vol. 3:175-187.

Hovde, S. (1986), 'Arbeidsvillig ungdom søkes', unpublished manuscript, Oslo: University of Oslo, Department of Sociology.

Howe, L. (1990), *Being Unemployed in Northern Ireland*, Cambridge: Cambridge University Press.

Inglehardt, R. (1990), *Culture Shift in Advanced Industrial Societies*, Princeton: Princeton University Press.

Isaksson, K. and Svedberg, L. (1989), *Permanent tillfällighet – om arbete och socialbidragstagande i en klientgrupp*, Forsknings- och utvecklingsbyrån vid Stockholms socialförvaltning – Socialt arbete, FoU-rapport nr. 112, Stockholm.

Iversen, G. and Midtlyng , E. (1994), 'Urolig arbeidsmarked, stabilt arbeidsliv?', *Samfunnsspeilet*, 4/94:22-27.

Jackson, P R. (1994), 'Influences on Commitment to Employment and Commitment to Work', in Bryson, A. and McKay, S. (eds), *Is it Worth Working?*, London: Policy Studies Institute.

Jackson, P.R. et al. (1983), 'Unemployment and Psychological Distress in Young People: The Moderating Role of Employment Commitment', *Journal of Applied Psychology*, Vol. 68:525-535.

Jahoda, M. (1982), *Employment and Unemployment*, Cambridge: Cambridge University Press.

Jamrozik, A. (1985), 'Unemployment: Social Implications of Its Structure and Dimensions', in Western, J. and Nayman, J.M. (eds), *A Sociology of Australian Society*, Sydney: Macmillan.

Jowell, R., Witherspoon, S. and Brooke, L. (1988), *British Social Attitudes – the 1986 Report*, London: Gower.

Kelvin, P. and Jarrett, J.E. (1985), *Unemployment: Its Social Psychological Effects*, Cambridge: Cambridge University Press.

Knudsen, K. and Wærness, K. (1996), 'Barnet lider av at mor er yrksaktiv ...', *Sosiologisk Tidsskrift* 1/96:3-23.

Kommunal- og arbeidsdepartementet (1995), *St.pr.p.nr. 1 (1995-96) for Budsjett-terminen 1996.*
Korpi, W. (1983), *The Democratic Class Struggle*, London: Routledge and Kegan Paul.
Larsen, K.A. (1995), 'Arbeidsgivernes holdninger til å ansette arbeidsledige', *Søkelys på arbeidsmarkedet*, årgang 12:37-45.
Leana, C.R. and Feldman, D.C. (1990), 'Individual Responses to Job Loss: Empirical Findings from Two Field Studies', *Human Relations*, Vol. 45:1155-1181.
Lindseth, O.H. (1993), *Samme himmel, samme samfunn?* Master Thesis in Sociology, Trondheim: Institutt for sosiologi og statsvitenskap, Den Allmenvitenskapelige Høgskolen, Universitetet i Trondheim.
Lindseth, O.H. and Listhaug, O. (1994), 'Religion og arbeidsverdier i 1990-årene: En komparativ studie av Vest-Europa og Nord-Amerika' *Søkelys på arbeidsmarkedet* No. 1:13-21, Oslo: Institutt for Samfunnsforskning.
Lodahl, T.M. and Keiner, M. (1965), 'The definition and measurement of job involvement', *Journal of Applied Psychology*, 49:24-33.
Marklund, S. (1993), 'Work, Work Involvement and Persistent Poverty', in Fridberg, T. (ed), *On Social Assistance in the Nordic Capitals*, Copenhagen: Socialforskningsinstituttet.
Martinussen, W. (1988), *Solidaritetens grenser*, Oslo: Universitetsforlaget.
Mueller, C.W., Wallace, J.E. and Price, J.L. (1992), 'Employee Commitment', *Work and Occupations*, Vol. 19:211-236.
Noelle-Neuman, E. and Gillies, P. (1987), *Arbeitslos. Report aus der Tabuzone*, Frankfurt Am Main: Verlag Ullstein.
NOU 1992:26 *En nasjonal strategi for økt sysselsetting i 90-årene.*
NOU 1993:11 *Mindre til overføringer - mer sysselsetting.*
Norsk Samfunnsvitenskapelig Datatjeneste (1995), *Survey of family and sex roles, spring 1994*, NSD Brukermelding 2/95.
Offe, C. (1984), *'Arbeitsgesellschaft', Strukturproblemen und Zukunftperspektiven*, Frankfurt am Main: Campus Verlag.
Øian, H. (1994), 'Lønnsarbeidets illusjoner', *Samtiden*, 3:73-80.
Otto-Brox, H. (1991), 'Jugend und Arbeit: Ein Forschungsüberblick', *Zeitschrift fur Berufs- und Wirtshaftspedagogik*, Vol. 87:208-224.
Piven, F.F. and Cloward, R.A. (1972), *Regulating the Poor: The Functions of Public Welfare*, New York: Panteon Books (updated 1993: Vintage Books).
Pixley, J. (1993), *Citizenship and Employment. Investigating Post-Industrial Options*, Cambridge: Cambridge University Press.
Randall, D.M. and Cote, J.A. (1981), 'Interrelationships of Work Commitment Constructs', *Work and Occupations*, Vol. 18:194-211.
Reskin, B.F. and Padavic, I. (1994), *Women and Men at Work*, Thousand Oaks, Ca: Pine Forge.
Rose, M. (1985), *Re-working the Work Ethic: Economic Values and Socio-cultural Politics*, London: Batsford.

Rowe, R. and Snizek, W. (1995), 'Gender Differences in Work Values', *Work and Occupations*, Vol. 22:215-229.

Rowley, K.M. and Feather, N.T. (1987), 'The Impact of Unemployment in Relation to Age and Length of Unemployment', *Journal of Occupational Psychology*, Vol. 60:323-332.

Schram, S.E. (1995), *Words of Welfare. The Poverty of Social Science and the Social Science of Poverty*, Minneapolis/London: University of Minnesota Press.

Sippilä, J. (1995), *Välfärdsstatens återkomst?* Nordisk Socialhögskolekomités konferanse, Aarhus.

Smith, R. (1994), *The political sub-culture of young unemployed Australians*, Doctoral Thesis, Dep. of Government and Public Administration, University of Sydney.

Spector, P.E. (1992), *Summated rating scale construction*, London: Sage.

Stjernø, S. (1995), *Mellom kirke og kapital*, Oslo: Universitetsforlaget.

St.meld. nr. 35 (1994-95), *Velferdsmeldingen*.

Terum, L.I. (1996), *Grenser for sosialpolitisk modernisering*, Oslo: Universitetsforlaget.

Underlid, K. and Thuen, F. (1991), 'Arbeidsinvolvering ved arbeidsløyse', *Nordisk Psykologi*, Vol. 43:161-173.

Vaus, de D. and McAllister, I. (1991), 'Gender and Work Orientation', *Work and Occupations*, Vol. 18:72-93.

Vennesland, K. (1992), 'Forskning om mestring av arbeidsløshet innen AHS-gruppen ved Universitetet i Bergen', in NAVF: *Hva kan arbeidsledighetsforskningen fortelle oss?*, Oslo: NAVF, Rådet for samfunnsvitenskapelig forskning.

Wadel, C. (1973), *Now,Whose Fault is That?*, Social and Economic Studies No. 11, Toronto: Memorial University of New Foundland.

Warr, P. (1982), 'A national study of non-financial employment commitment', *Journal of Occupational Psychology*, Vol. 55:297-312.

Warr, P., Cook, J. and Wall, T.D. (1979), 'Scales for the Measurement of some Work Attitudes and Aspects of Psychological Well-being', *Journal of Occupational Psychology*, Vol. 52:129-48.

Warr, P. and Jackson, P. (1985), 'Factors Influencing the Psychological Impact of Prolonged Unemployment and of Re-employment', *Pscychological Medicine*, Vol. 15:795-807.

Zetterberg, H. (1977), *Arbete som livsstil i konkurrens med andra livsstilar*, paper presented at Siviløkonomforeningens høstkonferanse, Bergen.

Appendix

Table 7.A

Likelihood of agreeing with the statement 'I would work even if I won a great sum of money', Population of working age (20-66 years). 1995.

Logistic regression, parameter estimates (n=2175)

	B	S.E.	Exp(B)
Constant	1.20	.40	
Sex (1=man, 0=woman)	- .27	.16	.76 ns
Age			
20-29	.39	.29	1.47 ns
30-39	.40	.27	1.49 ns
40-49	.48	.25	1.80 *
50-59	.31	.25	1.36 ns
60-69 (ref.category)			
Education			
Basic	-.30	.23	.74 ns
Further	-.31	.18	.73 ns
Higher (ref.category)			
Marital status			
married/cohabitating	.70	.22	2.01 **
unmarried	.45	.26	1.57 ns
previously married (ref.category)			
Children under 7 years in household (1=yes, 0=no)	.09	.20	1.09 ns
Main breadwinner (1=yes, 0=no)	.26	.18	1.30 ns
Present activity (employment status)			
working part-time	-.33	.23	.72 ns
unemployed	-.18	.32	.83 ns
homemaking	-.67	.23	.51 **
student	.32	.32	1.38 ns
sick/disabled/early retired	-.63	.23	.53 **
working full-time (ref. category)			
Respondent unemployed during last two years (1=yes, 0=no)	-.17	.16	.85 ns
Whether being unemployed is common or not in the community (1=common, 0=uncommon)	-.01	.22	.99 ns

Table 7.A, cont:

Political affiliation			
dont know/will not vote	-.05	.19	.95 ns
Venstre (Liberals)	.24	.39	1.18 ns
SV (Socialists)	.13	.31	1.13 ns
SP (Agrarian)	.11	.30	1.12 ns
RV(marxists)	-.89	.55	.41 ns
KrF (Christian Democrats)	-.55	.28	.58 *
Høyre (Conservatives)	.45	.25	1.58 ns
FrP (Radical Righet)	-.31	.23	.73 ns
AP (Social democrats)(ref.category)			

- 2 Log likelihood: χ^2=1522.955, df 2149, p=0.001

*= p<0.05, **=p<0.01, ns=not significant

Table 7.B

Likelihood of agreeing with the statement 'I would work even if I won a great sum of money', Population of working age (20-66 years). 1995.

Logistic regression, parameter estimates

	Men (n=1089)			Women (n=1086)		
	B	S.E.	Exp(B)	B	S.E.	Exp(B)
Constant		1.46	.55		1.67	.57
Age						
20-29	.24	.42	1.27 ns	.42	.43	1.5 x
30-39	.23	.39	1.26 ns	.55	.40	1.73 ns
40-49	.74	.38	2.10 *	.39	.36	1.48 ns
50-59	.54	.38	1.72 ns	.01	.35	1.01 ns
60-69 (ref.category)						
Education level						
Basic	-.08	.32	.93 ns	-.61	.34	.54 ns
Further	-.16	.24	.85 ns	-.57	.28	.57 *
Higher (ref.category)						
Marital status						
married/cohabitating	.60	.33	1.81 ns	.71	.36	2.03 *
unmarried	.08	.39	1.09 ns	.90	.39	2.45 *
previously married (ref.category)						
Children under 7 years in household (1=yes, 0=no)	.04	.30	1.05 ns	-.02	.28	.98 ns

Table 7.B, cont:

Main breadwinner (1=yes,0=no)	.06	.26	1.06	ns	.21	.31	1.23	ns
Present activity								
working part-time	-.06	.51	.93	ns	-.32	.28	.73	ns
unemployed	02	.44	1.03	ns	-.55	.48	.58	ns
homemaking	-1.12	. 53	.32	*	-.49	.28	.61	ns
student	.57	.47	1.78	ns	-.03	.47	.97	ns
sick/disabled/ early retired	-.97	.33	.38	**	-.40	.35	.67	ns
working full-time (ref. category)								
Respondent unemployed during last two years (1=yes, 0=no)	-.17	.30	.84	ns	.13	.36	1.14	ns
Unemploment in the community (1=common, 0=uncommon)	-.36	.23	.70	ns	.06	.24	1.06	ns
Political affiliation								
dont know/will not vote	-.12	.27	.89	ns	.01	.27	1.01	
Venstre (Liberals)	.52	.63	1.68	ns	.03	.52	1.03	ns
SV (Socialists)	-.39	.44	.67	ns	.47	.47	1.61	ns
SP (Agrarian)	.87	.55	2.39	ns	-.41	.38	.66	ns
RV(Marxists)	-.57	.89	.56	ns	-1.07	.72	.34	ns
KrF (Christian Democrats)	- .11	.49	.90	ns	-.79	.35	.45	*
Høyre (Conservatives)	.49	.33	1.63	ns	.47	.38	1.60	ns
FrP (Radical Right)	- .19	.32	.83	ns	-.40	.34	.67	ns
AP (Social democrats)(ref.category)								
- 2 Log likelihood:		735.778				759.539		

DF 1024, p>0.001 DF 1061, p>0.001

*= p<0.05, **=p<0.01, ns=not significant

PART II.
FAMILY AND GENDER

8 Gender relations and research on work

Sheila Allen

Introduction

The study of paid and unpaid labour under conditions of late twentieth-century capitalism raises in acute form the limitation of social theories regarding gender and work. There has been a general assumption that in industrialised societies men work and women care for families. It is not surprising therefore that industrial sociology ignored, or treated as an exception, women's labour market work and completely neglected other forms of work. Its conceptual frameworks ensured that women's paid and unpaid work fell outside the normal perceptions of how structures and processes operated. Nowhere has the effect of male dominated social science been more obvious than in the lack of understanding and explanation, or even adequate description, of women's work. More than this, however, there has been an almost total neglect of gender relations.

In this paper I examine some of the mainstream theoretical and methodological conventions which have resulted in the invisibility of the gendered structuring of work and the consequent ignoring of the different experiences and meanings of work. I discuss some of the ways in which feminist scholarship attempts to develop more encompassing analytical concepts and categories free from these flaws. Some of the data are from research projects in which I have been engaged. One concerned women in business enterprise, the second women in mining communities and the third was into homeworking labour.[1] All were conducted from within conceptual frameworks which owed much to my experience of the women's movement and the literature produced by feminists, both contemporary and those of earlier generations. Each project demonstrated the lack of attention previously given to gender in the sociology of work and the need to incorporate it in a constructive way into a new sub-discipline.

It is one of the strengths of feminist scholarship that it argues for and undertakes a re-examination of all areas which had become locked into virtually self-contained disciplines and sub-disciplines. By asking and exploring questions which cross over conventional boundaries erected by so much academic social science, it creates less rigid and constraining vocabularies, more adequate theorising and improved methods of data collection. It is however necessary to

1 The *Women In Mining Communities* research (1985-88) was funded by the Economic and Social Research Council and carried out with G.M. Littlejohn and D. Warwick. The *Women In Business Enterprise* project was funded by The Leverhulme Trust (from 1988-91) The first stage of the *Homeworking in West Yorkshire* research was funded by the Social Science Research Council (now the ESRC) from 1979-81 and by the University of Bradford Research Committee 1983-85. My thanks are due to these bodies for their financial help.

acknowledge that the deficiencies of social science reflect the marginalisation and lack of recognition given to women's work in society. Their activities are ignored or marginalized, continuously and consistently, by language, by ideologies and by material conditions. The cultural struggle to improve social science and the political struggles to reduce gender inequalities are interrelated. And as in all fields of enquiry, knowledge and power are intertwined.

Narrow concepts, broader concerns

The development of discrete categories of work and workers, consequent on ideological changes accompanying industrialism made the association of women and work normatively unaccepted and unacceptable. The very definitions of work narrowed, so that most commonly it was equated with full-time, regular, paid employment. These provided social scientists with an escape from any serious consideration of much of the work women do and the conditions under which it is done. This conceptualisation lasted well into the third quarter of the twentieth century so that unpaid work was non-work and the links between women and paid work, where recognised, were conceptualised as exceptions and conditional in form. The concrete links varied with the social and economic structures of households, familial ideologies and with the structures and processes involved in the demands for labour. The conditions which both separate women from and integrate them into different forms of work in contemporary Western societies include kinship networks particularly relations with husbands, partners, fathers, children, elderly parents and parents-in-law and sick or handicapped relatives; authority structures, especially those of the state and religious bodies in determining the obligations of wives and mothers and husbands and fathers; and the availability, organisation and systems of sanctions and rewards of men's paid work. Gender relations therefore lie at the heart of the divisions of labour and sociological theorising, investigation and explanation need to incorporate them.

The social construction of twentieth century man as breadwinner and woman as housewife and mother has been so pervasive that questions about gender differences went unasked. The differences were recorded as normal, indeed natural. One of the most fruitful developments in sociology over the past two decades has been the gendering of approaches to the world of work. While the term still creates problems for those who look for precise, abstract definitions it is the case that work is no longer simply equated with paid full-time, permanent, regular employment, carried on outside the home and recorded in official statistics.

Much of the initial impetus for this development came from the re-emergence of women's movements. Questions about the work carried out largely by women in and for the domestic unit were broached. The domestic labour debate raised the issue of how family-society relationships were to be adequately theorised. Centring specifically on the relations of productive and reproductive labour shifted the debate away from the plight of the 'housewife', characterised as isolated, increasingly functionless, prone to depression, (a problem to herself, her children and her spouse), to that of the political economy of the household, the industrial sociology of housework and the relation of unpaid to paid work (Coulson et al., 1975; Gardiner, 1976; Seccombe, 1974). This challenged the structural-functionalist approach which had dominated sociology for decades and the conjugal family was portrayed, as the dominant form, as functional for industrialism, as characterised by strict role segregation and specialisation between the spouses and generations: the husband, as economic provider, working outside the home, and the dependant wife engaged in bearing and rearing children and attending to the needs of her spouse (Parsons, 1943). This was not a description, but a theory of the dominant trends in the relations between kinship and the economy in industrial societies.

The strait-jacketed intellectual tradition which developed from this theoretical exposition had immense influence. A dominant orthodoxy of role segregation and mechanistic gender socialisation was erected. This still informs large areas of work on sex roles by feminists as well as others, because it fits so well into the voluntaristic, individualistic portrayal of the development of Western industrialism. Some feminist critics objected not to the theoretical approach itself but, as they saw it, to the fact that women had not shared equally with men in the escape from family control and dependency offered by industrialism. The root and branch challenge from the domestic labour debate and from those who drew on a materialist perspective opened up a range of theoretical questions. They rejected the separation between home-family and work-economy and engaged in relating reproductive and productive labour in the structuring of households and markets. They directed attention towards the interrelation of patterns of exploitation and subjugation and contributed in some measure to a new approach to all forms of work. However, they offered little to the theorising of gender or the different meanings work carried for men and women.

It was from another body of research, that of attempts to theorise the informal sector, that these were developed.[2] Debates on the informal sector in industrialised societies emerged in the 1970s with the decline of many basic industries, shipbuilding, steel and coal, largely male preserves, as well as textiles and engineering. The growth in the service sector, which provided part-time employment for women, also slowed down. The recession in the 1970s, accelerated by economic policies to reduce inflation, brought large scale unemployment and interest in the informal sector was prompted in part by the belief that unemployment could be reduced by a shift to informal sector working (Gershuny and Pahl, 1979/80). Theorising the relation of the formal and informal sectors proved as problematical in Western capitalism as it is in the Third World (Allen and Wolkowitz, 1987a; Bromley and Gerry, 1979; Moser, 1978; Young, 1978). Many forms of work outside mainstream employment were classified as informal. These included subsistence work (for individual or household provisioning), reciprocal work between kin, friends and neighbours ranging from caring work to repair and maintenance tasks; self-employment, and second jobs (Allen, 1982; Pahl, 1984).

[2] Initially much of this research related to the Third (developing) World. Models were adopted of formal and informal sectors in attempts to explain the relations of the industrialising sector to the much more widespread informal economy.

While raising many as yet unresolved theoretical issues, research in the informal sector shifted the sociological perspectives on work and employment opening up for investigation a range of economic activities formerly ignored or marginalized by industrial sociology and economics (Mingione, 1985; Redclift and Mingione, 1985). In particular gendered divisions of labour became more central and those theoretical approaches which were predicated on the separation of home and work and of market relations from kinship relations came under critical scrutiny. Essentially it was argued that household divisions of labour, market relations and processes of capital accumulation are integral parts of one gendered system to be analysed as a totality (Mies, 1986; Redclift and Sinclair, 1991; Young et al. 1981)

Who works? Who counts?

Over the past two decades women social scientists have raised questions about women's economic contribution, as employees, paid workers, family supporters and voluntary workers (Allen, 1982, 1983; Amsden, 1980; Waring, 1988). By so doing, previous writing on the subject, much of which had been some long out of print and never, incorporated in industrial sociology was made visible (see, for instance, Gilman Perkins, 1898; Schreiner, 1911; Tilly and Scott, 1987; Vincius, 1985; Visram, 1986; Zetkin, 1984).

Almost everywhere women are to be seen carrying out work of many different kinds, at all hours of the day and night, sometimes with their children, sometimes not. They work in cities, towns, villages and remote rural areas. They can be almost any age, they may be married, single, divorced, separated for long periods from male partners in areas of migrant labour, or migrants themselves. They may live alone, with or without children, or in small or large family groups; at their place of paid work or separated from it. One element they share in common, is work.[3]

What distinguishes the genders is first their structural location in the labour market where both vertical and horizontal segregation is the norm (Walby, 1988); secondly economic activity is much more likely to be officially recorded for men than for women (Allen, 1993; Nuss and Majka, 1983; Waring, 1988); thirdly whereas men are defined by their occupations, women are primarily defined in terms of kinship and life-stage relationships; and fourthly the share of women's unpaid economic contribution differs not only in volume from men's, but is obligatory and yet unrecognised as work. The first difference carries a whole range of inequalities in remuneration and prestige and affects, not just work expectations and experiences, but has wide ranging consequences for all aspects of the relative positions of men and women.

Much was made during the 1980s of the increasing participation of women in self employment and small business enterprise in Western Europe and North

[3] The invisibility of child labour in the dominant approaches to the sociology of work is even greater than that of women's, for much the same reasons. This can not be discussed in this paper although it should be noted that child labour is also gendered.

America, but as with women's economic activity more generally, the statistics on which such claims are based present many problems. The unreliability of official statistics as an indicator of volume is illustrated by a survey conducted in the European Economic Community which found the numbers of women who worked independently, or ran their own business, or worked in their partner's business was higher by some *10 million women* than those recorded in official Eurostat figures (EEC, 1987). In Eurostat definitions they are not employed, therefore economically inactive and so excluded. Such deficiencies in official statistics are widespread. In Britain, the Labour Force Survey and the Inland Revenue adopt different criteria in defining economic activity and so regularly produce widely varying numbers of self-employed and business owners (Allen and Truman, 1992). In both the homeworking and the mining communities research women who worked in their partner's business, as book-keepers, tax accountants or secretaries, described their work as 'helping'. These data did not emerge as responses to questions on their working lives, but either as explanations of why they did *not* work or as details of their domestic obligations.

These examples reveal a common ideological construction which leads to the systematic under-recording of women's economic activity, and a lack of recognition of the interrelated structuring of gender and work. Consequently, not only is women's contribution invisibilised but the economic realities of male business activity continue to be misunderstood.

Material from some of the interviews in mining communities illustrates how both men and women's views are embedded in the dominant ideology and the care which has to be taken in collecting and interpreting data. Women would say, for instance, that they had not worked since marrying or having children. They refer instead 'to helping on the market' or going to the club 'to give a hand'. Although working several shifts a week as bar staff or regularly on market stalls each weekend, these were not regarded as having a job and certainly not a *real* job by the women, their partners or families. Spouses of women who did a wide variety of paid work on a part-time or seasonal basis systematically responded that their wives did not work. The marginalisation of some forms of paid work in popular discourse is frequently reinforced by the methods used to collect data. Where only the male is interviewed or both partners are interviewed together, where the wording of questions does not take account of the meanings of colloquialisms or the latter are not understood by the interviewer, distortions of women's economic activity occur.

Women's paid work whether it is part of the formal labour market, business ownership, self-employment, sub-contracted labour, or casualised income generating activities, is for the majority of women additional to that *expected* of them, as daughters, wives, mothers and sisters; in short as unpaid domestic labourers.

Analyses of homeworking in thc 1970s showed the difficulties of maintaining boundaries between these familial expectations and paid labour carried out at home. For most of the 20th century it was either ignored or portrayed as a pre-industrial relic, as 'spare-time' work, as not a real job, as predominantly an ethnic minority activity, or as a convenient option willingly undertaken by women 'trapped' in their homes. Subsequent investigations and analyses demonstrated how persistent and widespread this form of paid labour is on a global scale; and how the terms and conditions under which it operates are explicable only within a context of the sexual division of labour in the household and the segregated and segmented labour markets of patriarchal capitalism (Allen and Wolkowitz, 1987a; Boris and Daniels, 1989; Brown, 1974; Hope et al., 1976)

The location of work

In the past decade the economic changes, referred to as re-structuring, have been accompanied by an ideological shift in the depiction of work locations. Related in part to technology, but also to the cost effectiveness for enterprises of externalising production, outsourcing the goods they sell and contracting out the services they use, new ways of thinking about work and a new rhetoric on the future of work were introduced. One of these related to where work is or will be done. The 'tele-cottage', in which 'distance working', 'networking' and 'telecommuting' would be carried out were put forward as beneficial for firms and for workers (see for, instance, Atkinson, 1984; Handy, 1984). The consequences of such changes, it was argued, would bring greater flexibility and autonomy for people no longer constrained to travel to the office or to work set hours, and for those with domestic obligations greater possibilities of combining these with earning a living.[4] Thus home as a work place was acknowledged, not only as acceptable, but as preferable in many respects. No longer could sociologists maintain that 'The typical and statistically normal state of affairs in an industrial society is that people do not work where they live' (Berger, 1964). This clear illustration of the narrow definition of work, challenged on other grounds by both the domestic labour debate and the informal sector discussions, came under further attack as the home was projected as the new site of work. The public-private dichotomy, at least in relation to work, appeared to be disappearing as professional men, executives, computer software designers and marketers joined the ranks of those whose work had long been based in domestic premises.

To assess the meaning and social consequences of this change we need to consider the relevance of gender. This dimension has been largely ignored in the re-structuring discussions. The 'future of work' based in the home is predicated on unrealistic assumptions about power relations within households between men and women and between those who produce goods and services and the structuring of markets in which they are sold. It is in the context of these relations that the growth of small businesses, homeworking and distance working which have been central to political strategies for economic recovery in market economies need locating. The obligations in relation to unpaid domestic labour, the claim to and

---

4 I am concerned here only with one aspect, that of the ideological shift, and not with examining the extent to which work has been relocated or the conditions under which this has taken place. For a discussion of the conditions see Allen and Wolkowitz, 1987a.

use of space and the conception of time are material to understanding the way that gender impacts on this change.

Flexibility

Flexibility of time and of the conditions which structure the labour contract are two of the main ways that men and women are likely to experience home based work differently. To take an example from women's experience of homeworking we can see that productive and reproductive work intermesh on a daily basis and according to the life-stage. The popular image is that they combine child care and household chores with paid work in an easy going manner, attending to each as they determine. Preparing meals, shopping, taking the children to school, feeding the baby are fitted around their 'work' or they can do their 'work' as the meals cook, the baby sleeps, the children play. This image manages to demean both productive and reproductive labour. It ignores the deadlines set for delivering whatever goods or services are being produced for income and the attention these require and the schedules involved in reproductive labour over which individual women have only very limited control. High levels of stress reported in many studies along with long working days and weekend work, contrast sharply with the freedom and choice depicted by those advocating home based work. Flexible working in this sense results in an intensification of labour where the boundaries to paid work disappear and it becomes as reproductive labour has always been, timeless.

Seen from a women's perspective, time flexibility whether zero hour contracts or those stretching over longer periods, specifying annual or monthly hours are equally problematic (Allen and Wolkowitz, 1987b; Forman et al. 1989). For those with responsibilities for care work and servicing the freedom to benefit is limited by continuing and continuous obligations determined by the needs, expectations and schedules of others. The flexible arrangements assume a voluntaristic, individuated world in which working time is confined to remunerated labour and no other forms of work exist. Obligations to others disappear. It is on this basis that the ideologies of choice, autonomy and the relative freedom from alienated labour rest.

Men, whose obligations for reproductive work are bounded by custom and convention may choose to engage in it, but not at the expense of or along with their productive work. This is facilitated by a spatial separation in domestic premises, where men have workshops, studies or offices as designated spaces for working, off limits to household and family members while women's paid work takes place in the family's living space, on the kitchen table, in the corner of the sitting room or under the staircase. Such differential and unequal arrangements are so taken for granted that their sociological significance is frequently overlooked.

Throughout the industrial period women have been a flexible labour force, in formal employment and other forms of work. The gendered ideology that they did not work reinforced the ways in which flexibility operated in the labour market and the household with far reaching consequences for women workers, creating highly disadvantageous pay levels and working conditions and a lack of recognition of women's unemployment. They experience a wide range of working patterns: early morning, evening, night and split shifts spread over a seven day week; seasonal, part-time or full-time work, periods without work and periods of extremely long hours. Such patterns of 'flexibility' are due more to the demands of employers and the market than to the needs or wishes of the women themselves (Allen, 1989a). In dual labour market models these conditions attach to jobs in the secondary market, but such models do not explain the gender allocation between primary and secondary jobs. Insecurity, uncertainty and irregularity in the labour market are not confined to women, nor do they apply to all women, but for men such conditions are construed as exceptions, as short-term, or as political and economic problems to be confronted and resolved at least in the eyes of 'good' employers, trade unions, and politicians. For women, they are seen as appropriate, as normal even as freely chosen to fit with their primary obligations, which lie not in labour market work but in the home and the family.

Family: Beyond stereotypes

The lack of research which centres on gender impoverishes the understanding of economic activity and reduces the possibilities of explaining its links to family and kinship. Examples from two research projects which treat women as well as men as social actors illustrate these points. The first relates to mining communities and the second to business enterprise.

Much social science research on mining areas begins with an assumption of 'occupational communities', producing ideal typical constructions of families, households and of men and women. Stereotypical representations of 'the miner' and 'the miner's wife and family' have endured in social science and in popular mythology over decades and few have looked beyond these. As Harwood (1985) points out such blanket terms, blinds us to much of the life in these communities. 'Women in coalfield communities become miners' wives, daughters and sisters. ...'. The reality of women's own lives, varied, colourful, and exciting, becomes blurred to the point of invisibility and so half the population disappears off the historical map (1985:25). There can be little doubt that as a major employer of male labour, coal-mining had a substantial influence on the local culture and the social organisation of family life. However, the conventional wisdom that strict role segregation obtains in all spheres of life, producing *particular* forms of gender segregation and consciousness and that women, once married, neither work nor expect to work relies almost wholly on male centred accounts. For instance, 'The family is normally a group of father, mother and children, all dependent on the wages of the father. This is especially true of a mining community like Ashton, where facilities for the employment of women have always been slight' (Dennis et al. 1956:174).

In the first part of our research into mining communities we took women as our main respondents, unlike the majority of other studies which rely on men alone for information.[5] In terms of women's working lives very different pictures emerge. We recorded work histories, current employment patterns and all forms of paid work and evaluated official labour statistics for the areas in the light of our respondents' presentation of their own lives.

These show not only a wide variety of paid work being undertaken by women, but a minority of them with uninterrupted labour market activity throughout their adult lives. When women married and bore children then a narrowing of the geographical location and a drop in the status and pay of their jobs occurred. Where jobs were scarce, greater degrees of flexibility in working patterns emerged. Most of the women were highly disadvantaged in working conditions, with little or no protection against sickness, and without rights to redundancy, unemployment pay, maternity leave or pensions. In those respects they do not differ from other women of their class.

Other data indicate that the range of kin obligations and the reciprocity between neighbours were such that they did not fit the conjugal family model with its depiction of economic dependency on the husband/father and its distortion of the relations between kin and economic activity (see Allen, 1989/96; Measham and Allen, 1994). Patterns of financial and social indebtedness and survival skills, with kinship networks, cross generations and genders can not be neatly pigeon – holed as *either* economic activity ***or*** family they are both. Our findings signal the need for a change in research methods and in the assumptions which underlie research design. With regard to flexibility of labour time, location and conditions, the unitary, conventional conceptions of the sociology of work are too restrictive to take into account networks of social reciprocity. The household and the domestic domain is fundamental to the analysis of the economic system' (Redclift, 1985: 95).

Sociological research has been dominated by the view that working class households exhibit high levels of gender role segregation and male dominance and that these were most marked in areas of heavy industry, including mining, where it was argued there was a strict division of labour creating separate worlds for men and women.

Campbell (1993) writes of miners as the 'archetypical proletarian, the archetypical patriarch', of 'the absolute power of men' and that 'No group of men has been so sustained by women's self denial. No group of men has been so cold and confident in its exclusion of women, yet so dependent on their support'. These views are widely accepted and obscure much of women's working lives, the relations between kin and the variety of experiences and attitudes in coalmining communities.

---

5 We interviewed 123 women and 31 men from 124 households separately. Discussions were held with 16 key informants, including women who had been activists in the 1984/85 strike and many conversations took place during the course of the research at meetings, conferences and informal social gatherings.

Two questions about such views are relevant to the present discussion. The first is how far this was confused in our research and secondly what is the relation between household divisions of labour and the economic activities of men and women. The restructuring of economies involving large reductions in the labour requirements of heavy industry, the promotion of self employment and business enterprise, new forms of labour contracts and the home as a workplace, make these investigations.

In the mining research there was a small, but systematic discrepancy in the responses of men and women to questions about responsibilities for household tasks, including childcare, with women claiming more responsibility than men. However, while both agreed that women did the bulk of the housework, half the men claimed to share childcare equally. What is most surprising when this general picture is analysed in terms of class differences is that the gender segregation of domestic tasks was clearest in the middle class non-mining households and least in the most working class locality.[6] Attitudes to labour market work among women also showed class differences. Working class women without jobs regarded themselves as unemployed, were looking more actively for jobs and attributed their unemployment to labour market conditions not domestic duties. Middle class women accepted more readily that childcare duties and/or partners' preferences were reasons for 'not working'. It was only middle class women who said they had 'no wish to work' and who saw their lack of labour market involvement as a choice.

In the research on women in self employment and small business the results also raise questions about several aspects of gender relations, household divisions of labour and women's experiences which show many similarities with those in mining communities. In terms of flexibility of time, working patterns, location of work, labour market constraints and domestic divisions of labour there were few, if any, differences between the majority of women in both contexts. Almost all were subject to life stage factors, so that those with dependent children or caring for elderly parents were subject to more constraints than the single woman business owner and lacked the networks on which women in mining communities could call. This distinguishes them from male business owners as O'Connor and Ruddle found. 'For male entrepreneurs, [business and family] priorities are clearly defined ..., and business roles do not conflict as the wife takes responsibility for the organisation and running of the home. Women entrepreneurs ... find themselves trying to balance the combined roles ...' (1988:24). Our findings confirmed this picture, with none of the business men having responsibility for household management. The majority rely on partners/spouses (and in one case a mother) taking complete responsibility and none employed paid domestic help. Only 20% of business women had any kind of unpaid help and 25% of the total paid for assistance with domestic tasks or caring obligations. Women of any age who did not have a partner to look after, though all had some domestic responsibility, had

6 One out of the four localities researched had been selected because it had fewer mining households and a greater concentration of middle class households, measured by the male partner's occupation and other socio-economic indices.

more options and divorce or widowhood were among the main factors which allowed businesses to be started or successfully developed. These women were more like their male counterparts in the hours they devoted to business activity, their ability to raise capital and their inclination to take risks in extending their enterprises. Carter et al. (1988) pointed to some of the issues that women face at different life stages if they become business owners and the range of coping strategies they employ. The complexities of these are for the most part left unexplored in research on business enterprise which concentrates on business*men*, produces stereotypes of individual, abstract, genderless entrepreneurs or hides the unpaid contribution of women to the firm and the household in the blanket term family. Women business owners or potential business owners of all kinds share several common experiences which separate them to greater or lesser degree from men. Their access to capital, to collateral and credit, to training and technical know-how and to many sectors of industrial or other economic activity are more restricted than they are for men (Allen and Truman, 1993). These restrictions are in large part related to gender segmented and segregated social and economic structures and the ideologies which surround them. An example from the Netherlands demonstrates that those judging credit worthiness hold traditional views on the sexual division of labour and entrepreneurship. Women seeking loans are asked to show their husband's pay slip or, [if unmarried] evidence of a financial guarantee from their father, whether they have children or plan to have them and are expected to prove how they can resolve combining business activity and child rearing. As a *real* entrepreneur works full-time, marriage, pregnancy and children make women unsuitable subjects for loans (Koper, 1993:64). 'Starting up a business in Dutch society is still associated with characteristics like 'resolution', 'ambition', 'self-confidence' and 'perseverance' which are seen as largely male attributes' (ibid. p.67). Such views and practices are not uncommon in industrial societies nor among those who control credit in development programmes.

To re-shape our analyses of business activity much can be learned from the fragmentary, but growing body of work on women's engagement in it. To be researched not as a new phenomenon or one restricted to advanced economies, but within a global perspective as one of many forms of economic activity undertaken by both men and women. The relevance and weight to be assigned to gender in explaining it can not be determined *a priori*, but it can not be explained at all unless both men and women are subjects of the research and the blanket term family abandoned.

Concluding comments

Economic restructuring, recession, the international division of labour and the globalisation of capital have been recurring themes in economic sociology in the 1980s. The implication of these for sociological theory and for social organisation have been widely discussed (Sayer and Walker, 1992). There is, however, confusion, ambiguity and above all uncertainty about the nature and meaning of the changes and how they are to be theorised. Two approaches to the transition will be looked at briefly: those of post-structuralism/post modernism and the more orthodox/modernist variety. Although there are many different shades of emphasis within both, here I am concerned only with those particularly relevant to analysing economic activity.

In its criticism of general theory postmodernism stresses the need for contextualised and situated knowledge, an end to grand theory and the rejection of statements claiming the authority of science. Cultural politics, discourse and localised, fragmented experience and meaning are placed in opposition to structure, the objective bases of power and the means by which it is exercised (Seidman and Wagner, 1992). It is relatively easy to criticise post- modernist writings from a sociological perspective and from a feminist standpoint (see Brodribb, 1992 for one form of feminist critique). Many of the ideas put forward as new have been part of sociological dialogues from the classical theorists onwards. The notion of culturally and historically specific theory/knowledge is a case in point. The argument that modernist theories left out whole social categories (women, racial minorities, gays and lesbians, and so on) may be correct, and has been pointed out many times, but simple listings of such categories do not amount to analysis. To analyse requires conceptual tools to build theories by which to understand social and economic life. These are not provided in postmodernism. The insistence that social, political and economic relations are fragmented may not be wrong as a worm's eye view of the world, but is certainly inadequate, even descriptively, in the face of the centralisation and concentration effects of globalised economic power *and their localised impacts* (Sadler, 1992). Theorising gender in relation to the restructuring of work, in its narrow or broader conceptualisations, involves frameworks which include global, regional and national as well as local dimensions.

Postmodernist discussions raise again many enduring and unresolved questions in the social sciences. As noted above these have been part of sociological debate throughout its existence (Gouldner, 1971). Furthermore the ideas and insights in many feminist writings, on substantive areas, on methodology, theory and knowledge production are central to these questions (Rose, 1994; Smith, 1987; Spender, 1983; Stanley, 1990; Sydie, 1987). All these insist that to understand and explain social processes gender has to be incorporated from the beginning and not regarded as an add on.

Another response has been to remain within the contours of dominant sociological paradigms. Those established during the twentieth century drew variously and selectively on earlier theories, particularly those of Durkheim, Marx and Weber. The most common, especially those developed in the period from the 1940s to 1960s when a series of sub-disciplines emerged and more or less firm boundaries were erected between sociology and other social sciences, lacked the breadth of the concerns of the earlier theorists, the depth of their empirical referents and their engagement with moral and epistemological questions. Even those who took a broader and more critical perspective, debating dual labour market models, deskilling, the labour process and the degradation of work in the 1970s, remain wedded to models which do not require them to go beyond Fordism and

Post-Fordism. Several issues discussed in this paper indicate that I find this mode far from satisfactory.

These include the narrowness of conceptualising work in dominant approaches, the voluntaristic underpinnings of discussions about women's lack of integration into primary sector employment or entrepreneurial activity, the stubborn resistance to incorporating research findings on the inadequate methods of statistical recording of economic activity, and the failure to challenge the distortions these create. The class blind or biased nature of some analyses of women's work and gendered divisions of household labour are a mark of the lack of success in integrating gender and class into theorising work in all its forms.

The reasons the two approaches are found lacking in theoretical purchase can be touched on only briefly. These are to do with the aims of theorising, its political as well as philosophical underpinnings (see Turner, 1992 for further discussion) and the issue of moral concerns. One aim of theorising gender relations is to understand and explain how these have been constructed and reconstructed to produce inequalities, what the consequences of these inequalities are and how they can be changed. There is a political agenda here which requires explicit acknowledgement for it influences the ordering of research priorities and the conceptualisation of areas of study. For example, for those looking for ways to change the position of women, explaining their unequal location in the labour market led to bringing domestic activities out of social science oblivion, breaking the boundaries separating the subdisciplines of family and work and the reshaping of research agendas.

There is then a moral agenda related to oppression and exploitation which has been historically associated with much of feminism. A gendered sociology of work cannot overlook this constructed reality common to women, whatever differences exist within this category.[7] Sexual divisions and equalities are a typical, normal, familiar way of organising social relations. The acceptance of these divisions as natural in much orthodox social theory belittles their importance. Such historically constructed realities are open to social change as much in gender relations as in any other sets of relations. Through its questioning and critique of the sociology of work, a key location of exploitation/oppression, feminism has addressed possible alternative ways of social organisation.

A social science agenda has emerged which starts from a recognition that theorising without gender can not produce anything other than a very inadequate sociology of a men's world. Analysis demands that theorising does not neglect the complex interrelations of major social divisions, of class or race, for instance, as well as gender. To privilege gender ontologically is to disregard how these other divisions impact differentially within and between genders, how all are constructed together historically and experienced together in concrete situations. The theoretical task is to specify how they articulate in contrasting contexts. In other

---

7 The recognition of differences between women is important, but as Maynard (1994: 22) argues '... to focus on this alone is to marginalize other issues ... It is not the case that women are constructed differently in any absolute way and clearly evident that they share experiences across cultures. Nor is it necessary to abandon categories such as woman ..., in order to recognise that they are internally differentiated'.

words diversity among women (and men) is not to be ignored, nor allowed to obliterate shared patriarchal subordination (or in the case of men shared patriarchal power).

Many of these ideas have been extensively discussed in sociology, especially but not only by feminist sociologists. However, they have not been systematically incorporated into theory building and do not inform much empirical investigation. They are not in the mainstream of the sociology of work. Taken as a whole they provide possibilities for understanding the changing economic and social dimensions of work not apparent in either post-modernism or the established or more critical 'modernisms'.

References

Allen, S. (1982), 'Women in Local Labour Markets', in Laite, J. (ed), *Bibliographies on Local Labour Markets and The Informal Economy*, London: Social Science Research Council.

Allen, S. (1983), 'Production and Reproduction: The Lives of Women Homeworkers', *The Sociological Review*, Vol 31:649-65.

Allen, S. (1989a), 'Flexibility of Work and Working Time: A Gendered Approach', in Buber Agassi, J. and Heycock, S. (eds), *The Redesign of Working Time: Promise or Threat?*, Berlin: Sigma.

Allen, S. (1989b), 'Gender and Work in Mining Communities', paper presented to the *British Sociological Association Annual Conference*, Plymouth.

Allen, S. (1993), 'Counting Women's Labour', paper presented to *The Fifth International Conference on Interdisciplinary Women's Studies*, Costa Rica.

Allen, S. and Truman, C. (1992), 'Women, Business and Self-employment: A Conceptual Minefield', Arber, S. and Gilbert, N. (eds), *Women and Working Lives – Divisions and Change*, Basingstoke: Macmillan.

Allen, S. and Wolkowitz, C. (1987a), *Homeworking: Myths and Realities*, Basingstoke: Macmillan.

Allen, S. and Wolkowitz, C. (1987b), 'Women's Working Time', paper presented to *The Third International Conference on Interdisciplinary Women's Studies*, Dublin.

Amsden, A.H. (ed) (1980), *The Economics of Women and Work*, Harmondsworth: Penguin.

Atkinson, J. (1984), *Flexibilty, Uncertainty and Manpower Management*, Sussex: Institute of Manpower Studies, Report No. 89.

Berger, P.L. (1964), *The Human Shape of Work*, New York: Collier-Macmillan.

Boris, E. and Daniels, C.R. (eds) (1989), *Homework: Historical and Contemporary Perspectives on Paid Labour at Home*, Urbana: University of Illinois Press.

Brodribb, S. (1992), *Nothing Mat(t)ers: A Feminist Critique of Postmodernism*, Melbourne: Spinifex Press.

Bromley, R. and Gerry, C. (1979), *Casual Work and Poverty in Third World Cities*, Chichester: Wiley and Sons.

Brown, M. (1974), *Sweated Labour: A Study of Homework*, London: Low Pay Unit, Pamphlet No. 1

Campbell, B. (1993), 'Dependable Props of the Ashington Pit', *The Independent*, 8 December.

Coulson, M., Branka, M. and Wainwright, H. (1975), 'The Housewife and her Labour under Capitalism – a Critique', *New Left Review*, Jan-Feb.

Dennis, N., Slaughter, C. and Henriques, F. (1956), *Coal is Our Life*, London: Eyre and Sprottiswoode.

EEC (1987), *Non-Salaried Working Women in Europe: Women Running Their Own Businesses or Working Independently – Women Involved in Their Husband's Professional Activity*, Brussels: Commission of the European Communities.

Forman, F.J. with Sowton, C. (eds) (1989), *Taking Our Time: Feminist Perspectives on Temporality*, Oxford: Pergammon Press.

Gardiner, J. (1976), 'Political Economy of Domestic Labour in Capitalist Society', in Barker D.L. and Allen, S. (eds), *Dependence and Exploitation in Work and Marriage*, London: Longman .

Gershuny, J. and Pahl, R.E. (1979/1980), 'Work Outside Employment: Some Preliminary Speculations', *New Universities Quarterly*, XXX1V, Winter.

Gilman, C.P. (1898), *Women and Economics*, Boston: Small, Maynard and Company.

Gouldner, A.W. (1971), *The Coming Crisis Of Western Sociology*, London: Heinemann.

Handy, C. (1984), *The Future of Work: A Guide to a Changing Society*, Oxford: Blackwell.

Harwood, C., (1985), 'A Woman's Place ...', in *Striking Back*, South Wales Area: WCCPL and NUM .

Hope, E., Kennedy, M. and de Winter, A. (1976), 'Homeworkers in North London', in Barker, D.L. and Allen, S. (eds), *op cit*.

Koper, G. (1993), 'Women Entrepreneurs and the Granting of Business Credit' in Allen, S. and Truman, C. (eds), *Women in Business*, op cit.

Maynard, M. (1994), ' "Race", Gender and the Concept of "Difference" ' in Feminist Thought', in Afshar, H. and Maynard, M. (eds), *The Dynamics of 'Race' and Gender*, London: Taylor and Francis.

Measham, F. And Allen, S. (1994), 'In Defence of Home and Hearth? Families, Friendship and Feminism in Mining Communities'' *Journal of Gender Studies*, Vol.3:31-46.

Mies, M. (1986), *Patriarchy and Accumulation on a World Scale*, London: Zed Books.

Mingione, E. (1985), 'Social Reproduction of the Surplus Labour Forces: The Case of Italy' in Redclift, N. and Mingione, E., (eds), *op cit*.

Moser, C. (1978), 'Commodity Production: Dualism or Dependence in Urban Development', *World Development*, V1, 9.

Nuss, S.A. and Majka, L. (1983), 'The Economic Integration of Women: A Cross National Investigation', *Work and Occupations* Vol 10, No. 1, pp. 28-48.
Pahl, R.E. (1984), *Divisions of Labour*, Oxford: Basil Blackwell.
Parsons, T. (1943), 'The Kinship System of the Contemporary United States', *American Anthropologist*, Vol.45:22-38.
Redclift, N. (1985) 'The Contested Domain: Gender, Accumulation and the Labour Process', in Redclift, N. and Mingione, E. (eds), *op. cit.*
Redclift, N. and Mingione, E. (eds) (1985), *Beyond Employment: Household, Gender and Subsistence*, Oxford: Blackwell.
Redclift, N. and Sinclair, M.T. (eds) (1991), *Working Women: International Perspectives on Labour and Gender Ideology*, London: Routledge.
Rose, H. (1994), *Love, Power and Knowledge*, Bloomington: Indiana University Press.
Sadler, D. (1992), *The Global Region*, Oxford: Pergamon.
Sayer, A. and Walker, R. (1992) *The New Social Economy*, Oxford: Blackwell.
Schreiner, O. (1911), *Woman and Labour*, London: T. Fisher Unwin.
Seccombe, W.(1974), 'The Housewife and her Labour under Capitalism', *New Left Review*, Jan-Feb.
Seidman, S. and Wagner, D.G. (eds) (1992), *Postmodernism and Social Theory*, Oxford: Blackwell.
Smith, D.E. (1987), *The Everyday World As Problematic*, Milton Keynes: Open University Press.
Spender, D. (ed) (1983), *Feminist Theories*, London: Women's Press.
Stanley, L. (ed) (1990), *Feminist Praxis*, London: Routledge.
Sydie, R.A. (1987), *Natural Women, Cultured Men*, Milton Keynes: Open University Press.
Tilly, L.A. and Scott, J.W. (1987), *Women, Work and Family*, London: Methuen and Co.
Turner, J. (1992), 'The Strange Life and Hard Times of the Concept of General Theory in Sociology: A Short History of Hope', in Seidman, S. and Wagner, D.G. (eds) *op cit.*
Walby, S. (ed) (1988), *Gender Segregation at Work*, Milton Keynes: Open University Press.
Vincius, M. (1985), *Independent Women*, London: Virago.
Visram, R. (1986), *Ayahs, Lascars and Princes*, London: Pluto Press.
Waring, M. (1988), *If Women Counted: A New Feminist Economics*, London: Macmillan.
Young, K. (1978), 'Modes of Appropriation and the Sexual Division of Labour: A Case Study from Oaxaca, Mexico', in Kuhn, A. and Wolpe, A. (eds), *Materialism and Feminism*, London: Routledge and Kegan Paul.
Young, K., Wolkowitz, C. and McCullagh, R. (eds) (1981), *Of Marriage and the Market*, London: CSE Books.
Zetkin, C. (1984), *Selected Writings*, New York: International Publishers.

9 Negotiations about family responsibilities within dual-earner families

Ulla Björnberg and Anna-Karin Kollind

Introduction

This paper will address theoretical aspects of informal work within dual-earner families. The basic idea behind the problems in focus is that conditions for negotiations within families are in a process of change due to many structural and cultural circumstances. We are approaching the problem area with a gender perspective in a context of family sociology, and the types of questions that we are asking are fundamental to an understanding of the changing conditions for the ways in which families function in contemporary society. How do men and women deal with issues of family obligations or family commitments concerning the provision of practical support? How do men and women differ in their capacities to handle power, autonomy and dependence within a family circle?

In the paper we present a theoretical approach for a study of how men and women negotiate responsibilities and the division of time, money and love: in particular, how the outcomes of the negotiations are justified and argued for as being reasonable and fair or unreasonable and unjust.

The project is anchored in an ongoing discourse on how family relations are changing in contemporary society. Many discussions of modernisation and individuation tend to focus on the fact that individuals seem increasingly to be giving up traditions and long lasting social relationships, for instance local ties and family ties. With the growth of the welfare state and modernised family laws, the institutionalisation of the family has changed (Théry, 1993). It has changed from being conceptualised as a societal contract with more or less moral obligations into a private project with personal commitments.

Feminist theories have suggested that, basically, women and men have different rationalities behind their actions (Gilligan, 1982; Chodorow, 1978). The rationality behind men's activities in relation to women is to preserve their autonomy and to gain love and care as far as this does not interfere with their autonomy. The rationality behind the activities of women is to give love and care and to sustain social cohesion within families and other social networks. Women tend to pursue a rationality of care and responsibility. We ask ourselves to what extent such ideal types correspond to concrete actions in everyday life settings. The dichotomy has a theoretical value but the empirical reality can be expected to present a more complex pattern. For instance, are women always oriented towards upholding social relationships? To what extent do women as well strive for autonomy? There are reasons to believe that both women and men are exposed to contradictory demands and constraints in solving problems in everyday life, and these contradictions and constraints are related to changing conceptions of the family. They are also related to new conceptions of professional cultures or, rather, to the fact that professional cultures in a wide sense have become integrated into family life.

Our theoretical approach is divided into different dimensions. First we discuss families as social groupings with regard to conceptions of morality and to the classical theory of reciprocity in social relationships. What kind of social group is a family? To what extent are family relations guided by morality of a more general kind? To what extent do general norms of reciprocity act on family members? The next section deals with different rationalities of action and various forms of reciprocity in social relationships, discussed in terms of economic systems or rationalities. The third section concerns principles of justice and family relations. The principles of justice are related to the rationalities of action and thus develop these a little deeper.

In the fourth section we discuss power within families from a gender perspective. We examine different approaches concerning the ways in which women are subordinated to men. The fifth section deals with the relationships of autonomy and care from a gender perspective. The question here is whether autonomy is incompatible with a caring and mutual relationship. In the final section we consider the integration of family and employment and ask to what extent different professional cultures have an impact on the ways in which legitimacy is perceived in contemporary families. All the sections are summarised in a concluding section.

Morality and reciprocity in family relationships

Are relationships in contemporary families justified by general moral codes or ideologies for what family members should do to one another? How are such codes connected with everyday practices in families?

A reasonable supposition is that there are certain moral guidelines for family relationships which tend to transcend more immediate feelings of justice in everyday life in families. The actions of family members are in a sense performed in the context of a family pact or a family culture, where certain values function as moral guidelines in the relationships of everyday life. Research undertaken by Finch and Mason (1993) has led to the conclusion that there is a certain set of norms in society which make family members take on certain expectations about what they should do to one another. These norms are given as general guidelines, but are transformed into commitments in the concrete relationships between the individual family members through their negotiations over the distribution of tasks and responsibilities. This means that general norms or obligations are not experienced as binding by the individual family members. Rather, what they find to be important are the dynamic interplay between the persons involved in everyday relationships and the sense of commitment and personal responsibility which emanates from these (Finch, 1989).

Sense of commitment is explained with reference to Alvin Gouldner's 'norm of reciprocity' (1973a), as follows. When a person (A) gives an advantage to another person (B) there is a sense of indebtedness, or an obligation to reciprocate is evoked by the person receiving (B). Person A will have a certain power over person B during the time between the gift-giving and the reciprocation. The implication is that B has acquired a feeling of commitment, which is also experienced as an indebtedness. In personal interactions over time, certain patterns of commitment and indebtedness are developed. According to Gouldner, those to whom a person feels indebted are not abandoned, since it would be morally incorrect to abandon people to whom one has a debt. It would mean a loss of social/moral capital invested in the social networks around the persons involved. However, if the person finds that the accumulated debts are too many, he/she will regard people to whom he/she is indebted as having acquired too much power over him/her and this might force B to conclude that he/she will have to withdraw completely from the relationships, including the social network surrounding person A.

We suggest that some kind of norm of reciprocity is valid in all social relationships. If so, this implies that family members, like all other group members, make evaluations concerning balance and reciprocity in their actions towards one another, in either the short term or the long term. Relationships between family members are sustained through chains of gifts and debts. Being in debt is linked with a feeling of obligation and giving is associated with an expectation of return, sooner or later. Returning a debt is again the starting point for a new indebtedness (Bloch, Buisson and Mermet, 1992).

When we apply these theoretical statements to the exchange of services, care or provision among adults at the community and family level, the central components in the negotiations will appear as a tension between autonomy and dependence, symmetry and asymmetry. A person who is offered care might not accept if he/she is not able to return it in some way. As long as a person feels able to restore a balance, he/she will feel independent and not in debt. This feeling of independence is important in intergenerational relationships between adults. The old parents are anxious not to be too dependent upon their kin (Finch, 1989).

Moral obligations are sustained and reinforced by society to the extent that asymmetrical relationships are deemed necessary or profitable by the powerful groups in society. They are sustained in order to legitimise asymmetrical relationships. Thus, family obligations were codified in law and sustained by a patriarchal ideology in order to maintain a system for the provision of support and care of dependants as kin, and not primarily as citizens.

Patriarchy is no longer codified in law and no longer sustained by institutionalised practices. Still, however, family relationships are sustained through gender identities and values and expectations which blur the process of assessing the proper value of actions in terms of reciprocity. For instance, men (and to a certain extent women) tend to regard housework as obligatory or even natural for women, something which 'rests with her' (Haavind, 1994). Thus, the fact that the wife does the bulk of household chores does not necessarily evoke a sense of indebtedness from the husband or male partner in the household. This means that in family relationships, the evaluation of the net balance is a matter of a subjective feeling which is not shared. Gifts and debts are also mixed up with feelings allied to love and pure altruism – that giving is unconditional under certain circumstances (Gouldner, 1973 b).

In general, however, and despite the fact that it is possible to find empirical examples of unconditional, self sacrificing, non-calculating family relationships, there are reasons to reject the thesis that reciprocity is only to a minor extent a component in family relationships. Several empirical studies lend support to the hypothesis that kin relationships are contained within a reciprocal system (Hochshild, 1989; Finch and Mason, 1989, 1993; Moxnes, 1990; Haavind and Andenæs, 1994; Bloch, Buisson and Mermet, 1992). The more family relationships are subject to de-institutionalisation and the more they are embedded within an image of the family as a project where responsibilities, tasks and even money are matters to be negotiated, the more family relationships are subject to the 'norm of reciprocity'. This is the overarching hypothesis for our study and our objective is to study how men and women are differentiated in terms of the rationalities used to justify the division of labour and money between them.

Rationalities of action and family relations

In families, there is a considerable exchange of work, services, money, help and support, affection, love, critical remarks, punishments etc. Such exchanges often continue for many years, sometimes, as in the case of parents and children, throughout a lifetime. According to the norm of reciprocity, it is important that the persons concerned experience the exchanges they are involved in as balanced. However, the principles according to which such a balance is reached and evaluated cannot be taken for granted. There are different principles or, as we prefer to call them, rationalities guiding exchanges of acts.

In our opinion, it is essential to distinguish between different kinds of rationalities by which the exchanges are evaluated as balanced or unbalanced. Our belief is that families differ in the ways exchanges are organised. Also, we presume that what is regarded as an ideal form of exchange varies between families. In order to clarify our point, we will give some examples of how money might be distributed and exchanged between husband and wife.

The first example concerns a couple where each partner's income is regarded as his own or her own means, except what is reserved for common expenses. In this relationship it is quite possible and reasonable to borrow money from each other and to be in debt to each other. If there is no equalisation, this type of exchange order might mean that one of the partners, often the man as we know, has more money for his personal expenditure than the other partner, because of differences in income. If equal sharing is an important goal for the partners, the distribution might be of another kind, where each gets an equal amount for personal expenses, regardless of differences in income. But also in the latter type of distribution, our second example, some of the money is regarded as hers or his, and the principle of borrowing and getting into debt is possible between the partners. However, in a third example, this kind of relationship is not possible or even reasonable. Here, no differentiation is made by the couple between his and her money. Since incomes are regarded as common property, neither can tell how much belongs to one or the other, and no borrowing can occur.

These examples are intended to illustrate some basically very different principles and ideals of exchange in money matters between spouses. Issues concerning the kinds of principle that are most common in different groups, ages, cultures etc., or the possibility of mixed forms, are of no relevance here since our examples are more idealised than empirical descriptions. In each of these examples there is a norm guiding the distribution and exchange of money but the norms and ideals differ. What for one couple seems to be a natural way of sharing might, to another couple, appear as a repugnant, or at least an uninviting, form of exchange.

To oversimplify, we can differentiate between an 'I-oriented' principle in the first two cases, and a more 'we- or group-oriented' one in the last case. Where an 'I-orientation' is predominant, the needs and preferences of the husband and wife are separated from what they have in common. The limits between what is mine and what is yours are rather strictly defined, and there are limits between individuality and commonality. In principle at least, the spouses provide each other with space to decide on expenditures without asking for the point of view of the other. When matters of money are governed by a 'we-orientation' the limits between what are my preferences and what are ours are blurred. Since the guiding principle comes close to the idea that what is mine is yours, the space for each spouse to decide on his or her own is much more limited.

This rough differentiation between an 'I-' or 'we-orientation' is connected with an age-old sociological discourse on the processes of individualisation. In the basic concepts of Durkheim, Tönnies, Weber, Mead, Parsons and Etzioni we find features of both orientations. In an attempt to synthesise various strands of these theoretical ideas, Fiske (1991, 1992) suggests that in the social world there are four elementary forms of social relations. These forms of relation, or types of interaction and reciprocity, can be observed in every known culture, in all civilisations. Although this typology is all-encompassing in its claims, our ambition here is to restrict the presentation to the give-and-take processes between family members, especially between husband and wife.

In one of the types, termed by Fiske 'communal sharing', belonging to a group is heavily emphasised. The exchange is grounded in belonging to a certain group, being one of 'us', and what one gives and what one gets are not grounded in any explicit balancing. The old communist utopian ideal is relevant here; to each according to his or her needs, from each according to his or her capacity. In this kind of exchange one does not keep an account of how much each gets or gives, and is not even prepared to perceive actions between members of the specific group in terms of exchange. An example from the emotional sphere is the ideal of romantic love. The concept of selfless love and mutual caring, of sharing values, interests, space and bodies, of an intimacy which means the merging of selves in a deep belonging that transcends each separate individual, is a variant of 'communal sharing'.

Another example is provided by Cheal (1988) in his description of gift relations in modern societies. In several empirical studies of gift exchange between relatives and friends, he has found that gifts are regarded as an important means of shaping endurable social relations, and ensuring belongingness. Cheal does not deny that gifts can also be used as means to achieve power and status, in the way Mauss (1925/1972) showed, or that gifts are given because it is part of a ritual, or out of a feeling that one owes another a present in return. But he emphasises that gift-giving is not necessarily connected with such interests and that the dominant interest among the individuals he has studied was to shape and demonstrate group relations and solidarity. Cheal's view of exchanges of gifts in families and among friends, then, is very close to what Fiske discerns as 'communal sharing'.

Characteristic of the second form of elementary social relations are exchanges based on considerations of costs and benefits: 'market-pricing' in Fiske's vocabulary. In this kind of relationship services, work, things, or other valuables such as sex and care are exchanged for something else that is regarded as equivalent – money, work, services, other valuables and so on. The parties in the relationship look for proportion between what is received and what is given, each having a wish to get the most out of the deal. Bargaining, bartering, negotiations, treaties and contracts are typical elements in this type of exchange, as well as calculations of advantages and drawbacks. In the personal sphere, plenty of examples of 'market-pricing' can be found in marital arrangements between partners from wealthy families. Negotiations between the partners and their families regarding money, estates, services etc., with the aim of gaining as many benefits as possible, fit this pattern.

Gary Becker's study of the family (1981/1993) is an excellent example of this sort of rationality. In Becker's analysis of the family as a macrosocial system, the relative benefit of alternative actions for the household or the individual is always at the centre. It is irrelevant whether the analysis concerns the choice of marital partner, the division of household labour, divorce, the relation between parents and children, polygamy or altruism, the thinking in terms of cost and benefit is always present. At bottom, there is an assumption that human beings have a calculating attitude to most of their relations, including their family relations. An interesting aspect of Becker's analysis is his assumption that, for households to be efficient, at least one person in the family has to be altruistic in his orientation. A calculating self-interest that dominates all activities of the family members will be destructive for the whole group. In order to counteract this, at least one family member must find it valuable to give more than he gains. Thus, Becker here introduces an element of reciprocity as a one-way flow of generosity. In other words, according to his analysis, the 'market-pricing' exchange is not able to create the type of solidarity and group cohesion needed for a family to function.

Obviously, these two forms of social relations are close to what in classical sociology is associated with the relations of Gemeinschaft and Gesellschaft. The third form is different, however, and has affinities with the norm of reciprocity as defined by Gouldner. The model for this form, called by Fiske 'equality-matching', is one of balance and mutualities. In these relations there is an egalitarian motive, with the goal of even matching. Fairness, equality and balanced reciprocity are a guiding theme. For instance, if I invite you to dinner, I expect to be invited back in due course. The dinner could be 'repaid' in some other 'currency', but it has to be perceived as roughly equivalent. If the dinner were paid back in money, the relationship would be transformed, changed in the direction of 'market-pricing'. In the family sphere, the ideology of contemporary marriages is a good example of 'equality-matching'. It says that spouses should have the same rights, do equal amounts of child care and housework, and have an equal say in decisions. Relations between friends might be regarded as the prototype of this kind of relationship.

A large part of the discourse on family matters in our time revolves around issues concerning supposed changes towards a symmetrical family (Young and Willmott, 1973), or concerning a lack of fundamental change towards equality between spouses (Haavind, 1987). Another important theme is that of socio-psychological tension between man and woman at a time of transition when demands for democracy are reaching deep into intimate relations (Hochschild, 1989; Giddens, 1992). In spite of this huge interest in the issue of an equal relationship between spouses, we more seldom find analyses of what such a relation might mean. Several researchers assert that this kind of relation is vulnerable (Fiske, 1991; Gouldner, 1973a; Sahlins, 1965/1988). According to them, it is a delicate matter to balance the give-and-take between two people, when no measures of evaluation can be taken as a standard and outspoken bargaining is not looked upon as acceptable. There is an inherent instability in these relations because of the constant risk of an equal relation being transformed into an unequal one. The relation very easily tips over into an unbalanced (dis)advantage, which happens when one party has got the better of the other and the other has become 'indebted'. However, in his discussion of reciprocity in marital alliances in primitive societies, Sahlins asserts that 'the lack of precise balance is socially of the essence', because it provides a very important basis for social bonding. 'If neither side is 'owing' then the bond between them is fragile. But if accounts are not squared, then the relationship is maintained by virtue of 'the shadow of indebtedness'' (1965/1988, p.222). Whether such reasoning is applicable to attempts to achieve equality in family life in our time is still an open question for us.

The final form of elementary social relation distinguished by Fiske is a hierarchical one ('authority-ranking'), which can be based on a diversity of variables, like age, gender, birth and blood, wealth, charisma, wisdom, etc. As we all know, family relations are, to a considerable extent, ranked according to age, order of birth and gender. Parents control their children, and elder sisters and brothers often have a higher status than younger ones. Generally, the husband has more control over the property, with the final say on major decisions, broader powers etc. Moreover, he is regarded as the one with special responsibilities for the welfare of wife and children. It is this genderised ranking pattern that is challenged by the above-mentioned ideology of equality.

A common model of exchange between related parties with different status is that superiors receive more from inferiors than the latter get back. This kind of exchange, with the opportunity for the 'higher-ranked' to get what they wish from the 'lower-ranked', is reciprocated, at least implicitly, by a norm of responsibility to provide for the needs of inferiors. This, however, is not the only known pattern of reciprocity between parties of different rank. In primitive societies, excesses of generosity have been shown to be an important means of asserting authority, a pattern which at the same time is often part of a coercive social structure. This certainly exists in modern societies, too. In politics, for example, giving advantages and favours is often used as a means of mobilising followers, building authority, and even immobilising opponents. A somewhat trivial example from the emotional sphere is the traditional courtship between man and woman. In this phase of the relationship, the man is the giver; he is the one who pays for dinners at restaurants, purchases presents, gives compliments, opens the doors and provides favours of different kinds. By playing the role of the chivalrous, polite and generous party, the man arguably creates a relation of ranking. By accepting his benign offerings, the woman contributes to the status of the male and in return gives her own female deference. Courting games like these are made possible by an already existing ranking order. A courting woman, who in a similar way generously uses money and flattery, would not in return bring about an equivalent male deference (Heen, 1995).

Fiske's distinctions between fundamental forms of social relations, with varying rationalities for exchanges, must of course be regarded as ideal types. In the real world, forms may be mixed and one or the other might be more or less dominant. In our culture, as compared to other known cultures, a calculating form of exchange is rather prevalent. Our assumption is that these rationalities and forms of reciprocity can also be found in all family relations, but with varying dominance for one or the other.

At the beginning of this section, we presented three ways of organising the distribution of money between spouses. These were supposed to exemplify the kinds of divergent rationalities in reciprocal interaction discussed above. According to an on-going Swedish study, married women seem to have less money for their own use, and more money problems, than do married men. Could this indicate a consistent pattern of uneven distribution of money between husbands and wives in Swedish marriages (Nyman, 1996)? Does this reflect uneven earning capacities in women and men, and patterns of expenditure for household issues where women are responsible for everyday consumption whereas men can use money for long-term savings or personal use? Another study has shown that a system of separation between his and her money is more common in couples without children. When children arrive, there is generally a change towards some kind of pooling of resources. In reconstituted families, however, a continued separation between his and her money is more frequent (Bernhardt, 1996). How does this happen and how do men and women reason in these diverse situations?

In family contexts, money is not just plain money; it is also interwoven with work, time and especially love. Under certain conditions, a husband's washing-up might be seen, by him or his wife, as a sign of love. A wife, working full-time and taking care of housework and children in order to give her husband time to study, might see all this as her way of contributing to their community, as her way of expressing love. A woman's decision to spend evenings together with her female friends might be regarded by her husband as a token of vanishing love. In the family sphere ordinary activities involving time and money have several levels of meaning and cannot be separated from a moral order of love, duties and rights.

We believe there are great differences between families concerning what is regarded as the real, good, natural way to organise the mobilisation, distribution and sharing of such valuables as time, money, work and love. Of course, differences between spouses in these respects can be assumed to be commonplace and important sources of marital clashes, conflicts and tensions. We also assume that families – and family members – differ in preferences and ideals as regards the principles of sharing, exchange, distribution and justice.

Principles of justice in family relations

Principles of exchange in families or other groups are related to principles of justice, in the sense that what is exchanged has to be seen as fair and legitimate. Remuneration, punishments, objects, money, gifts, attention, responsibility, time and love are examples of important values which are distributed and exchanged within families and all these values are subject to evaluations of justice. Conceptions of fairness, righteousness and justice are regarded as very important by all members in families, as in many other social contexts, but the implementation of principles of justice or fairness has its own rationality in social relationships.

Some illustrations can be given. Distribution according to need in a family could mean that the smallest child is given more ice cream than the others, because the child needs energy to grow stronger. Another child is given more because he has performed well in school (distribution according to merit). If all the children are given an equal share, the principle is equality, regardless of performance or need. If the oldest child is given more than the others, the principle applied is status or ranking order (Kellerhals, 1989; Fiske, 1991; Eckhoff, 1971). These examples illustrate the links between rationalities applied in exchange and reciprocal relationships which were discussed above.

On the basis of a review of research on distributive justice, the Swiss sociologist Jean Kellerhals (1989) has elaborated a model for studying justice arguments in families. In his view, evaluations of justice are basically relational and they are primarily aimed at reproducing a certain group structure and promoting group cohesion. As a corollary of this purpose, the judgements which family members make about justice do not follow fixed preconceptions about fairness, but are formed according to specific circumstances and situations.

In his further discussion, Kellerhals suggests that the cohesion of families can take on different styles, or as we prefer to call it, family cultures. In order to classify family cultures, he refers to three dimensions: 'Cohesion', 'Integration' and 'Principles of Regulation'.

'Cohesion' indicates the extent to which the family is individualised towards the 'us' in the family. At the individualised extreme, the group consists of autonomous individuals, each pursuing his/her own interests with their own time schedules and activities, expressing personal opinions and life styles. The cohesion in individualised families is characterised by complementarity or confrontations. Cohesion is weak. At the other extreme, the members are group-oriented and experience themselves as having joint interests. The group has superiority over individual needs and interests. The consensus of the group in terms of values and interests against the social surroundings is of the highest priority.

'Integration' refers to the extent of closure or openness to the environment. A very closed family is characterised by self-reliance and expresses suspicion of those who do not belong to it. In a family which is characterised by a high degree of openness, the members are other-directed and take great pleasure in having many visitors.

'Principles of regulation' refer to the style of control within the family. At one extreme, the regulation of the behaviour of family members is governed by strict rules and normative patterns set by authorities within the family; at the other, rules are always negotiated and debated according to highly communicative behavioural patterns.

These three dimensions are combined into styles of family cohesion, or family cultures. In some families, the members are autonomous and open to the environment. These family cultures tend to regulate internal behaviour through communication, but probably internal communication is quite low. Some combinations are hard to imagine, such as families with autonomous individuals and with a high degree of closure against the environment. It is also unlikely to find families with autonomous individuals where behaviour is regulated by strict rules. The important point is not primarily to stress all possible combinations of family styles, but the fact that certain family cultures are based on certain action strategies whereby the family culture is reproduced. Principles of justice or fairness applied in families are examples of such strategies. This means that families create their own rationality concerning justice and righteousness.

This suggestion can be illustrated by Kellerhals' own empirical studies of families (1989). He found that working-class families tended to have a cohesion where group orientation was emphasised. Negotiations within the families were normative and rule-oriented, and reasoning on justice emphasised status, property and rank rather than performance and needs. Among higher officials cohesion had a more individualised and autonomous style. Negotiations were centred on thinking in terms of cost benefit, and external criteria were used in evaluations of justice.

Ways of justification are, then, related to dominating patterns of reciprocity, types of cohesion and principles of regulation in families. But they are also influenced by what kind of reasoning is culturally legitimate. During this century, democratic ideologies have contributed to a shift in thinking about distributive justice within political institutions. There has been a change from applications of principles based on rank and status towards principles of equality and performance. This is reflected in family law: principles of justice under patriarchy were based on status, but principles of equality have become more prevalent in modern law and the wife is granted the same rights as the husband. These formal changes do not imply that ranking order and status have vanished as principles, but they have lost legitimacy. Still, power relations within families are highly intricate and rest on informal conceptions of principles of justice, and on the way in which they are implemented in negotiations in families in everyday life.

While asymmetries in economic resources between spouses in former times could be justified by referring to the ranking order, namely the husband's rights as a husband and a man, the legitimate character of this kind of justification has become much less certain. Instead, other more legitimate principles of justice have to be used to defend similar types of difference between husband and wife. Justice according to performance or merit might be such a principle, where a fitting argument might be that the one who earns or owns the most should also have the bigger share.

In developing the 'norm of reciprocity', Gouldner refers to morality and rumour which function as a glue in the chains of gifts and debts in social relationships. Justice is one way of dealing with morality in social relationships. Thinking or acting in terms of justice is, however, a principle which can be distinguished from principles of care. According to Carol Gilligan, individuals who argue on the basis of the principles of the 'equality ethic' are concerned about assessing balanced relationships. In the application of the equality ethic, inequality is a moral problem. Morality which is centred on principles of the 'care ethic' is concerned with social relationships as such: caring about somebody, listening to others and being engaged in other people's problems. Disconnection and abandonment pose a moral problem for a person who acts according to the 'care ethic'. To be moral is to be attentive and responsive in social relationships. Gilligan has made several empirical studies and concludes that all social relationships include both types of moral judgements, but one principle tends to dominate over the other (Gilligan, 1988). Men tend to argue in accordance with the equality ethic, and women with the care ethic but the gender differences are not very strict (Lyons, 1988).

The equality ethic and care ethic refer to two different conceptions of 'responsibility'. The equality ethic refers to responsibility conceived as 'commitment to obligations'. The person acts out of a sense of duty and obligation arising from norms which are shared with persons with whom he/she is in daily interaction. In contrast, the care ethic refers to responsibility based on an urge to be 'responsive in relationships'. To act responsibly is to listen actively to the needs and feelings of the persons with whom one is in interaction, and to be prepared to do something about them. The individual takes the initiative in being attentive to the needs, thoughts and feelings of others and is willing to influence these according to his/her capacity.

To conclude, justice and reciprocity are connected with conceptions of responsibility as moral commitments and social contracts while responsiveness is connected with love and a sense of empathy. Gilligan does not discuss whether there are expectations about returns in social relationships where responsiveness is the moral rationality, but she stresses the fact that mutuality is a prerequisite in social relationships based on responsiveness.

In their models, Gilligan and Kellerhals have different approaches and modes of understanding the ways in which individuals deal with social relationships in contemporary families. Kellerhals regards ethics as a result of family culture as such. The family culture is an expression of a rationality to reproduce a certain pattern of social relationships. Gilligan's relational perspective is more person-oriented. In her model the individual is a moral actor regardless of the social setting in which the person acts. The interesting point in her theoretical analysis is that she connects ethics with other concepts, such as those of responsibility and of the self in social interaction, i.e. the relationship between autonomy, dependence and equality. Before developing these themes, we would like to discuss our views of power in families.

Theoretical perspectives on power in families

Patriarchy as a major structure for imparting legitimacy to power relations and authority over women has in several respects been eroded as a formal system – at least in Sweden. For instance, in the family, paternal authority and the formal power of men over the incomes and property of their wives have disappeared from the laws along with several other patriarchal rules concerning the civil status of children. Yet, despite changes in the law which have made women equal in civil status to men, their social citizenship rights have remained largely subordinate to those of men. Empirically there are numerous examples of women with subordinate positions economically and socially within families. Power relations within families are the result of tacit agreements or even negotiations between men and women where certain basic conditions have been very resistant to change. Such is the case with the basic idea that the wife or female partner has the primary responsibility for the care of home and household, children and other relatives. This responsibility almost always rests with her whilst the husband can choose his terms for sharing the care of home and children. As a bread-winner, the man is expected to have the main responsibility for supporting the family. He is also expected to represent the family outwards, and to make the big decisions.

There is, today, a vast body of literature attempting to explain the asymmetries in the division of work between men and women, as well as in power relations and in love. Money and property are regarded by many feminists as a basic component in the unequal balance of power between men and women in households. According to some opinions, the male in families gains authority from his physical strength (Pateman, 1988). Others have argued that, in a culture where the ideology of rationality takes precedence over one of emotionality, men achieve authority through the way they reason in terms of principles and rationality (Seidler, 1995). Broadly speaking, two perspectives for explaining the asymmetries between the sexes can be discerned in feminist literature. One emphasises processes of socialisation as the main force in creating asymmetrical relations between men and women whilst the other stresses social structures which systematically block access for women to education, work and family on equivalent conditions to those of men. Here, women's shortage of resources with regard to economy, power, status, and privilege is explained by patriarchal structural relations (Komarovsky, 1991).

Chodorow's (1978) very influential work is an attempt to integrate these two perspectives, although her theory is firmly based on psychoanalytical views of object-relations and focuses on processes of socialisation. Starting-points for her theory are two universal facts: the subordinate position of women in all known societies, and the fact that all over the world women, often mothers, take care of small children. According to Chodorow, this institutionalised way of organising child-care contributes to a fundamental difference in male and female identities, which explains the devaluation of femininity and females that can be seen everywhere. Female-led mothering creates very different conditions for identity construction in little boys and girls. Whilst the girl, in creating her gender identity, can keep to an already existing self-image related to what her mother represents, the boy has to deny the feminine elements in his construction of a male gender identity. When turning from mother to father as a primary object of identification, the boy must dissociate himself from what mother and femininity represent. The fact that masculinity, then, is essentially formed as a negation of femininity is the psychological and emotional basis of male devaluation of femininity.

Hence, Chodorow's theoretical story tells us that mothering, as an institutionalised social relation, creates a kind of fundamental difference in gender identities that brings about polarisation between men and women and a ranking order with men in authority, an order which tends to reproduce – eternally as it seems – female mothering and male devaluation of femininity. In this theory, the general asymmetry between the sexes has its origin in family life, primarily in the relations between mother and children. Thus, mothering is looked upon, on the one hand, as an important source of most virtuous qualities, like self-definition in relation to the needs of others, capacity for closeness and mutual dependency, all qualities considered essentially feminine, and on the other, as a source of female powerlessness.

This stress on motherhood as a key factor in creating power asymmetries is criticised by Miriam Johnson (1988). The two important roles of women, being a mother and being a wife, are here confused. It is in wifely relations to men that women are 'weak', not in motherly relations to children and men. According to Johnson, Chodorow and others underestimate the role of the 'male peer group' in the activity of devaluing women. Male identity is constructed in processes of competition, achievement, and dissociation from everything that is female. Small boys and grown-up men prove their masculinity not primarily in relation to girls and women, but to other males. The 'male peer group' is the most important social group for such contests, where a major goal is not to be like a girl, not to be a sissy, showing weakness, dependency, and so on. In this context, heterosexuality becomes a means to demonstrate dominance and masculinity to other men. To objectify woman, to turn her into an object of sexuality with no human dignity, is part of the means of strengthening male identity in the peer group. Johnson, then, accepts Chodorow's thesis that the construction of male identity is based on the negation of femininity. However, she does not accept the idea of motherhood as a socially structuring factor in this process, but suggests 'the male peer group' is the most significant agency. To her, 'wifehood', not motherhood, is the Achilles' heel of women.

A similar view is to be found in a more structural, feminist analysis by Delphy and Leonard (1992). To them, a family household is an economic unity, organised as a hierarchical system of work-relations. In this system, it is primarily the men who benefit from the work of other dependent family members, especially from that of the women. Husbands have the legitimate right to appropriate the work of their wives. In this context 'work' refers to everything men and women do at home, i.e. housework, care, nursing, emotional work, and taking responsibility. Emotional work entails being considerate, caring, supporting, confirming others, creating solidarity and emotional bonds, and being sexual. Although, in practical matters, the husband delegates this kind of work to his wife, he governs her work and appropriates it. Of course, women might work at home out of love and respect, but their main reason for doing this work is that they are wives. The unpaid work done by wives for their husbands is regarded by Delphy and Leonard as the most important cause of the subordinate position of women in families. Through the work of women a surplus value is created that contributes to asymmetric ownership in families, husbands usually owning much more than their wives.

Delphy and Leonard see marriage as the most important social institution that conditions the biased distribution of power in families. In their view, it does not really matter if women are employed, have incomes of their own, have a good education and high-status jobs. Of course, these kinds of conditions give women more autonomy and a better bargaining position. Still, their subordinate position remains. The proof of this, the authors assert, is that married women's employed work has, in reality, led to a double workload, regardless of their incomes and social status in work, and even if housework has been delegated to other women. The rather gloomy conclusion is that, for a woman to avoid subordination, she has to evade heterosexual marriage.

These three types of feminist theoretical discussion on power and gender relations have at least one thing in common. All of them heavily emphasise family relations as the reason why women have less power than men in society. Social relations within the family, within married couples, have far-reaching consequences for women's subordinate position, not just in the family but also in the wider society, i.e. in the labour market, in politics, in business and so on. The authors provide provisional answers to such questions as why the kind of interaction between wife and husband emerges that Bell and Newby (1976) refer to as the 'dialectic of deference', in which the wife tends to relate to her husband as a servant to his master, a farmworker to his farmer.

In their discussions of power, these feminists focus on structural relations between men and women rather than on the diversity of ways in which these relations can manifest themselves in various concrete marriages. In our study, however, we have to delve into the problem of the meanings of concepts like power, influence, dominance, authority, and subordination, and also into issues of how to know when different kinds of subordination and superordination are manifested in concrete situations of interaction within families and couples. We cannot take as our point of departure the fact that women never possess any power in marriage. Neither can we rule out marriages where husband and wife continuously, perhaps in very different ways, struggle over influence. And some couples certainly reach some kind of balance of power.

In marriages and relationships today, men and women in their private lives try, in one way or another, to handle a strange mixture: a new ethos of equality in intimate relations, an ideal of romantic love, elements of a still vivid patriarchalism, which is partly unrecognised, and all this in a context of social regulations that pretend to be gender-neutral. What kinds of strategy are chosen? How do women strengthen their position in the family? Do they wish to be as independent and autonomous as men are, and does this restrict their willingness to care and nurture?

Autonomy and dependence in families

Power and autonomy are held in esteem within social relationships, whereas being an object of power and being dependent are not highly esteemed. Thus, it could be expected that individuals in interaction tend to act with the purpose of avoiding dependence and obtaining as much power as possible, reproducing a rationality of action in order to sustain a certain amount of power and independence. We tend to regard autonomy and dependence as polarised entities along a one-dimensional scale. Gilligan challenges this conception by introducing two different concepts: 'separateness' and 'connectedness'.

Following an action strategy which is geared towards separateness implies that the individual tends to draw borderlines for his/her dependence on others in order to remain as independent as possible in social relationships, i.e. to avoid being led into debt. Such a strategy means that reciprocity and balancing are important rationales for social interaction. Hence, the self is defined in terms of duties and obligations in relation to roles and positions. The purpose in social interaction is to maintain distance, autonomy and independence. In contrast, following an action strategy which is geared towards connectedness implies that the individual is interactive. Responsiveness is the rationale for action, as opposed to reciprocity. The self is defined in terms of listening to the voice of the other. Dependence is not regarded as a matter of subordination, but as a matter of strength. In terms of responsiveness, autonomy and independence are regarded as negative, as social isolation without support from individuals in the social surroundings. In that sense, dependence is regarded as positive.

This approach to an understanding of the relational concepts means that autonomy can be linked with positive and negative 'risks'. The positive ones are liberty and independence, and the negative helplessness and social isolation. Social interactionism is associated with social support and social resources, but also with subordination and manipulation. The negative aspects can, however, be avoided, which would mean that an autonomous position can be reconciled with an orientation characterised as 'connected'.

For a discussion of this possibility we would like to refer to another dichotomy within a related conceptualisation, namely rationality versus emotionality, or instrumentalism versus expressionism. Expressionism has many connotations, such as emotionality, dependence, passivity and incompetence (which is a logical corollary when expressionism is contrasted with instrumentalism). Instrumentalism connotes qualities such as efficiency, reason, analytical thinking, foresightedness.

Expressionism means being relational. In our culture this is often linked with passion and short-sightedness, even chaos and incomprehensible behaviour – i.e. the opposite of being rational. However, empirical research suggests that, while 'autonomy/dependence' is a relational dimension, instrumentalism/expressionism are not opposed poles on a one-dimensional scale. Thus a person can be expressive or emotional as well as instrumental. A person can relate to others in an autonomous way and still be expressive. Further, it is possible to be both instrumental and expressive (Johnson, 1988).

In our interpretation, this reasoning is supported by the arguments of Gilligan. Being responsive in relationships and being connected does not imply that a person is monitored by emotions. On the contrary, it is being able to understand what the other person thinks and feels, and finding adequate ways of responding to these. Understood in this manner, responsiveness in relationships is an intellectual process where emotions are dealt on a level similar to that of logical reasoning.

The capacity to be responsive in relationships is, however, not easily acquired. In her research on girls, adolescents and women Gilligan has suggested that in the patriarchal cultural order girls are taught subordination and during this process they are subjected to the voice of 'others' rather than their own voice. They develop from being authentic to being other-directed as a result of norms about being nice, kind, silent, not opposing others. The cultural prescriptions for girls promote behaviour which is not authentic and the paradoxical consequence is that young women distance themselves from true relationships 'for the sake of relationships'. Being honest and speaking with their own voice means, for the girls, that they will risk being regarded as cruel and selfish, and such behaviour will be punished by exclusion. Thus young women tend to develop a high sensitivity to what can be regarded as proper behaviour and skills in interpreting what others wish them to do. Through this process they distance themselves from their own experience, which they tend to regard as irrelevant.

In mature age women have developed strategies to more or less successfully deal with the conflicts between 'authenticity' and 'normative direction'. Four major strategies can be differentiated (Attanuci, 1988): a strategy of autonomy, which implies that the women has a feeling of being separated from the surrounding social networks, whereby these will be regarded in terms of contracts and commitments; a self-sacrificing strategy, which implies that the woman subordinates herself to the conditions of others and is directed by their needs and wishes; egoism, which means that the woman only identifies her own needs and acts on her own terms, whilst regarding others as having obligations towards her; and mutuality, which is the strategy of being responsive in relationships. Here both the self and the surrounding networks are handled in a communicative way. By being true to the self and listening to one's own voice, one is guided by past experiences. This does not mean closing one's ears to the voices of the others, but it is a necessary condition that the others are similarly responsive in relationships. Hence we call this relationship strategy 'mutual integrity'.

Gilligan and her colleagues have provided empirical and theoretical insights which, in turn, open up a departure from the dichotomous views on the relationships of autonomy and dependence, or of social interactionism and subordination and being steered by others. For the individual to be socially interactive, she/he must listen to her/his own voice and rely on her/his own knowledge and experiences. Further, it is necessary that the individual can listen to the voices of others and find out how to respond to these. It does not imply that the individual is emphatic in reading the feelings of the other and transforming these feelings into their own feelings. It is rather a matter of developing a capacity to acknowledge the feelings and needs of the other and to respond to them. Nor does it mean that the individual accepts being steered by norms and prescriptions which have been filtered through patriarchal culture. A strategy of responsiveness in relationships is, in our view, a way to become a self-reliant woman without having to accept the premises of patriarchy including the prevailing ideals of autonomy and independence.

Work, gender and rationality

Like Young and Willmott (1973) and other sociologists, we consider economic conditions and the position of individuals in the socioeconomic stratification as being of primary importance for changing gender relations in society. Paid employment is a social practice which contributes to displacements in symbolic borderlines between masculinity and femininity in dual-earner families.

A question of interest for our study is whether it is possibility to discern a connection between a professional culture within different professional strata and the ways in which argumentation is pursued within families. In Kellerhals' studies, referred to above, justifications in middle-class families tended to be characterised by autonomy and performance, whilst rationality in working-class families tended to emphasise privileges and the group as a whole. Similarly, Bernstein's research (1977) on social class and forms of control in child-raising can be mentioned. He suggests that working-class families use a positional argumentation in regard to their children, whereas middle-class families use a personalised style of arguing. In working-class families, reference is made to how things are: 'You must do what mum tells you, just because she tells you to'. In middle-class families, reference is made to the children themselves, their feelings, personality or social relationships to the mother or others as persons: 'I understand your feelings, but I know that you could be harmed if you do as you wish'.

In discussing the relationship between professional culture and family orientation, two perspectives can be discerned. It could be asked whether the profession as such socialises individuals (through the educational process) not only professionally but also politically and in private life. For instance, do lawyers, psychologists and technicians have different social and political orientations? It could also be that individuals deal with their professional identities in certain ways which, in turn, will have an impact on their orientations in social, political and private matters. Do, for instance, lawyers in the business field, develop different orientations to lawyers working as judges in court? If this is so, the individual's location in the professional structure will influence their attitudes in moral and social issues.

The influences of professional cultures on the social, political and private orientations of individuals have been dealt with only sparsely in the literature. An approach in this direction is provided by Brint (1994), who has developed a typology of professions and the cultural orientations which tend to accompany them. He distinguishes five professional spheres: (1) A sphere where activities are aimed at doing business and reproducing capital, that is, concentrated on money and profit-making. (2) A sphere where activities are aimed at applying science – the branch within business where new products are developed. (3) A sphere devoted to creating and mediating information, culture and communication as pictures or texts. (4) A sphere oriented towards regulating civil life, administering and organising activities – where law and accounting are important kinds of professional knowledge. (5) Finally, a sphere where services, caring, and curing other persons are the major concerns. Brint suggests that individuals within each sphere will develop a specific societal and cultural orientation in harmony with the dominant rationality in that sphere. For instance, a lawyer in a private organisation will be mainly oriented towards making money. His perspectives on political and cultural matters will tend to be more influenced by money-making than by his legal profession as such. In empirical studies Brint has found that professions in a sphere where activities are geared to doing business and reproducing capital display a distinct professional ethos compared to professions in spheres where activities are oriented towards applying science, or where services, caring and curing other people are major concerns. He does not discuss the implications of these findings for family orientations.

Another approach to the link between family orientation and profession has been used in interpretations of the sharp gender division on the labour market between traditional male and female spheres. The choices that women make when they choose to take up care and education as professions have been explained by assuming that they choose to do work similar to what they do at home, but that they wish to get paid for it. Also men who have chosen to work within the public sphere are supposed to develop a more family-oriented style than other men. As far as women are concerned, it is almost taken for granted that there is a positive association between their professional orientation and their family orientation. Women, it is suggested, choose employment which harmonise with their feminine identity, seen both individually and culturally.

Such types of work in Sweden are mainly organised within the public sphere, where the dominant ethos is to satisfy needs and not to make profit. It has been shown empirically that men who are employed within the public sphere take parental leave to a greater extent than men working within the private sphere. This has been interpreted to mean that, within the public sphere where many activities are oriented towards administration and the satisfaction of needs without reference to making profit, people have acquired a greater tolerance and understanding of men's wish to develop as fathers. Further, the public sphere is dominated by women and this, it is suggested, has a positive impact on attitudes towards reproductive work within families. Within the public sphere, employers have for much longer adapted their work organisation to the fact that staff take parental leave and have family responsibilities. Besides, men working in professions which have been labelled as typically female occupations also take parental leave to a greater extent than other men. Empirical studies on the relationship between work-place cultures and family identities suggest that people in male work-place cultures also have more traditionally male ideals for family life than those working in female or gender-mixed work-place cultures (Holt, 1994). A further observation is that men who choose to be active and caring fathers give as their motive the desire for personal development and for the acquisition of more social competence. It has been suggested that this is a consequence of the fact that, in contemporary working life, greater demands are made on people's ability to handle social relationships due to more communication and more services. Many men have found that they can develop social skills by developing as persons – an advantage which women used to have through their social orientations in families and social networking (Björnberg, 1994; Holter, 1994).

Similar arguments have been put forward by Hochshild (1983) in a book on the expansion of service occupations and its implication for the social orientations of people with such jobs. Modern companies are increasingly employing client- and service-oriented staff in all occupational strata. One of the greatest assets for the company is the ability of the staff to be friendly towards clients and to act as if clients have a personal value, the ability to work with disciplined emotions and always to be pleasant and service-minded. Also in educational programmes for many of the new professions, people are taught to discipline their emotions and to control their personal feelings. In some programmes, students are taught to express emotions which are labelled as 'proper' emotions, i.e. a direct steering of emotions in certain directions. In a professional context the disciplining of emotions has an exchange value, but in private life it carries a use value. Hochshild suggests that this development tends to commercialise human emotional life, thus making it calculating and profit-oriented with consequences for behaviour in private life as well. There is a risk that this transference of emotional control on a commercial level to a private level will mean that we lose the capacity to listen to our own voice.

What might the implications of this aspect of work orientation be for family relations, for parent-child relationships and for the relationships within couples? Hochshild suggests that parents' occupations will have implications for how they raise their children, because the occupations provide some sort of model for the parents in their image of how the children should behave. She argues that individuals involved in emotional work teach their children to accept personal authority, whereas individuals in occupations without the emotional component are geared to positional argumentation and pay less attention to the personal and emotional aspects.

At many work-places today, organisational changes are leading to fewer hierarchies and status orders and the implication is that male dominance over women is diminishing. Further, these changes imply that technical rationality, which has been central to modern culture and of the greatest importance for the construction of gender structures and gender identities, is being challenged in new organisations. This development is linked to the fact that many new professions and expert roles lack the sort of social authority associated with wealth or status and corporate power. This argument has been put forward by Connell, who refers to the fact that both men and women have expert positions in many modern enterprises. In knowledge-intensive work organisations such as advertising, consultancy and journalism, or work-places concerned with service or welfare, the organisations are less hierarchical and co-operation between members of the staff is promoted. In these types of work-place a culture is developing where traditional masculinity with great emphasis on technical rationality has been eroded. For many men, this development involves contradictions which they have to handle. Some men choose to reconstruct their male identity and adapt it to a new reality, whilst other men forcefully resist the changes.

In his analysis, Connell's point of departure is that, in contemporary Western culture, great changes are taking place in gender relations, with the result that many traditional fields for the construction of male identities are being challenged. During the development of bourgeois industrial society, reason – technical rationality and logic – was a central component for lending legitimacy to patriarchy. Nowadays reason or rationality is being used by women to challenge male dominance over women, and to argue for equality, equal treatment in law and equal opportunities on the labour market. Thus what was always the cornerstone in the construction of male identity is being used to erode or deconstruct masculinity. Much of this is going on in working life, particularly in modern occupations. By means of different male biographies, Connell shows how men, through their past experiences, adapt their construction of the male identity and choose those social contexts which lend support to their strategies (Connell, 1995).

In this review of research we find many inputs for understanding how work experiences could have an impact on private life and the construction of masculinity and femininity. The review provides numerous examples of how the 'social dimension' at many work-places, and in several occupational strata has a socialising function which implies that people are trained to handle social relationships and control their emotions.

Since the relationships between work culture and family culture are complex, it is hardly likely that occupational experiences would have a unidirected influence on how family relations are perceived. Individuals form their biographies and choose occupations which confirm their ideals or ambitions for private life but, due to changes in working life, they are also forced into situations where they have to choose. These changes concern not only organisations but also expectations related to their professions, which demand great involvement in professional activities and a large amount of psychological energy, which in turn may have an impact on the ways in which the individual perceives other aspects of his/her social reality.

Summary and conclusions

This paper began with a number of questions concerning commitments and negotiations in contemporary families regarding the distribution of time, money and caring. These matters belong to work within the informal sphere, where families constitute the most important social setting. The problem of informal work has received increasing attention against a background of shifting gender relations and demographic changes such as ageing, sinking birth rates, and rising divorce rates. Welfare states all over the Western world are being forced to reduce the provision of public services, and many expectations are being directed towards communities and families for the provision of care and services of different kinds.

This development has inspired our questions about informal work in families and social networks in contemporary society. We plan a project where the basic issues are: What meaning do family relations have for young people today? What are family members prepared to do for one another in dual-earner families? What are the basic rationalities in informal work? Our aim is to understand the division of informal care, distribution of money and time as men and women negotiate against a background of the changes that are taking place in working life, particularly regarding gender relations.

We assume that families differ considerably as regards conceptions of what is just or unjust, moral or immoral in negotiations on time, money, and care. We believe that there are reasons to assume the existence of varieties of 'family cultures' in these respects. In some families, for instance, there is a pronounced orientation towards equality justice, whereas in other families there is more of a distinct orientation towards reasoning and judgement in terms of cost and benefit, input and output. Further, we ask whether diverse occupations and work-places in the labour-market influence rationalities in families. Does occupation have an impact on the ways people perceive and deal with their family life? Do people working in the sphere of health and care have different views on care and justice in families from people working in business? Thus, our concern is not only the impact on the division of informal work of shortage of time, levels of salaries, and types of exhaustion emanating from jobs, but also how the cultural aspects of professions and occupations influence family life.

Families are informal units built up by women and men, boys and girls, within different gender structures. When developing our theoretical approach, we have found it necessary to link conceptualisations regarding reciprocity in social relationships, economic activities and rationality in different systems, distributive justice, gender and power in families and the tension between autonomy and dependence.

Informal work in families is basically identified with a gift economic rationality, where work and distribution are linked with motives of sustaining sociality. According to the norm of reciprocity, gift-giving, like other economic activities, has its specific forms of rationality with tension between autonomy/independence and dependence/powerlessness. In families women tend to be givers but dependent, which is a contradiction if we follow the logic of the theory. This contradiction can be partly explained as being a result of a mixture of two economic rationalities, those of gift economic and of market-economic thinking. The gift economy in families is associated with distribution according to rank and status. In marriages, men are given more status because they earn more money and have the merit of just being men, who have been assigned a higher value than women in society and in families. Thus women have to give more than they receive in order to bring about balance. What women give is time and care, which means being available on terms set by those in the family who receive care. This promotes dependence for the giver unless there is a break with the terms set by others. These terms are set through norms which are internalised by women as women, perceptions about how women should be and what they should do. These norms are integrated in a patriarchal value system and sustained by women themselves in their social networks and by men in theirs .

In marriage, men act with a patriarchal rationality which, in turn, is linked to a market-economic way of reasoning. Exchange is linked to merit and formal rules, which is a different scale of judgement compared with the scale of the gift economy. Exchange is also linked with a rationality of justice, with logical reasoning about principles. The rationality of justice is regarded as more valuable than rationality linked to the care ethic. Thus, it can be concluded that, when the two rationalities are mixed, the justice and exchange order will be given a higher value than the care and gift-giving order.

It is our point of departure for the study that gender relations are in a process of change. Women are gaining more independence while having more access to jobs, money and political influence. Thus, women are becoming increasingly integrated into market-economic ways of reasoning. What implications does this development have for women's way of arguing about the distribution of time, money and informal work? What alternative arguments are there? Does it mean that women are trying to gain autonomy on terms similar to those of men, that men persist in fighting the phantom of being less autonomous? We think that Carol

Gilligan has provided a solution to this problem with her conceptualisations about care ethics and justice ethics, autonomy and connectedness. Being responsive in relationships does not mean giving up the self but developing self-reliance and mutuality, which is quite a different thing. We think, with Gilligan, that the ways in which concepts are dichotomised lead into blind alleys, especially in theorising about gender relations. A more fruitful strategy is to study how both men and women in diverse contexts combine their approaches to ethics and rationalities.

References

Attanuci, J. (1988), 'In Whose Terms: A new Perspective on Self, Role, and Relationship', in Gillian, C., Ward, J.V. and McLean Taylor, J. (eds), *Mapping the Moral Domain. A Contribution to Women's Thinking to Psychological Theory and Education*, Cambridge, Mass.: Harvard University Press.

Becker, G. (1993), *A Treatise on the Family*, Cambridge: Harvard University Press.

Bell, C. and Newby, H. (1976), 'Husbands and Wives: The Dynamics of the Deferential Dialectic', in Barker L.D. and Allen, S. (eds), *Dependence and Exploitation in Work and Marriage*, London: Longman.

Bernhardt, E.M. (1996), 'Non-standard Parenting among Swedish Men', in Björnberg, U. and Kollind, A-K. (eds), *Men's Family Relations*, Stockholm: Almqvist & Wiksell.

Bernstein, B. (1977), 'En sociolingvistisk aspekt på socialisation med viss hänsyn tagen till den individuella inlärningsförmågan', in Loman. B. (ed), *Barnspråk i klasssamhälle*, Lund: Liber Läromedel.

Björnberg, U. (1994), 'Family Orientation among Men. Fatherhood and Partnership in a Process of Change', in Brannen, J. and O'Brien, M., *Childhood and Parenthood*, Institute of Education and University of East London.

Bloch, F., Buisson, M. and Mermet, J-C. (1992), 'From Disjointed to Joint Parenthood', in Björnberg, U. (ed.), *One Parent Families*, Amsterdam: SISWO.

Brint, S. (1994), *In an Age of Experts. The changing Role of Professionals in Politics and Public Life*, Princeton, N.J.: Princeton University Press.

Brown, L.M. and Gilligan, C. (1992), *Meetings at the Crossroads. Women's Psychology and Girls' Development*, Cambridge, Mass.: Harvard University Press.

Cheal, D. (1988), *The Gift Economy*, London: Routledge.

Chodorow, N. (1978), *The Reproduction of Mothering. Psychoanalysis and the Sociology of Gender*, Berkeley: University of California Press.

Connell, R.W. (1995), *Masculinities*, Berkeley: University of California Press.

Daatland, S-O. (1983), 'Eldreomsorg og eldres omsorg', in Wadel, C. et al. (eds), *Dagliglivets Organisering*, Oslo: Universitetsforlaget.

Delphy, C. and Leonard, D. (1992), *Familiar Exploitation. New Analysis of Marriage in Contemporary Western Societies*, Cambridge: Polity Press.

Eckhoff, T. (1971), *Rettferdighet ved utveckslinq og fordeling av verdier*, Oslo: Universitetsforlaget.
Finch, J. (1989), *Family Obligations and Social Change*, London: Polity Press.
Finch, J. and Mason, J. (1993), *Negotiating Family Responsibilities*, London: Routledge.
Fiske, A.P. (1991), *Structures of Social Life. The Four Elementary Forms of Human Relations*, New York: The Free Press.
Fiske, A.P. (1992), 'The Four Elementary Forms of Sociality: Framework for a Unified Theory of Social Relations', *Psychological Review*, Vol. 99:689-723.
Giddens, A. (1992), *The Transformation of Intimacy. Sexuality, Love & Eroticism in Modern Societies*, Cambridge: Polity Press.
Gilligan, C. (1982), *In a Different Voice*, Cambridge, Mass.: Harvard University Press.
Gilligan, C. (1988a), 'Two Moral Orientations', in Gilligan, C., Ward, J.V. and McLean Taylor, J., *Mapping the Moral Domain*, Cambridge, Mass.: Harvard University Press.
Gilligan, C. (1988b), 'Remapping the Moral Domain: New Images of Self in Relationships', in Gilligan, C., Ward J.V. and McLean Taylor, J. (eds), *Mapping the Moral Domain*, Cambridge, Mass.: Harvard University Press.
Gouldner, A. (1973a), 'The Norm of Reciprocity', in *For Sociology. Renewal and Critique in Sociology Today*, London: Allen Lane.
Gouldner, A. (1973b), 'The Importance of Something for Nothing', in *For Sociology. Renewal and Critique in Sociology Today*, London: Allen Lane.
Haavind, H. (1982), 'Makt og kjærlighet i ekteskapet', in Haukaa, R., Hoel, M. and Haavind, H. (eds), *Kvinneforskning. Bidrag til en samfunnsteori*, Oslo: Universitetsforlaget.
Haavind, H. (1987), *Liten og stor. Mødres omsorg og barns utviklingsmuligheter*, Oslo: Universitetsforlaget.
Haavind, H. and Andenæs, A. (1994), 'Care and the Responsibility for Children: Creating the Life of Women Creating Themselves'. Unpublished.
Heen, H. (1995), 'Money, Gifts and Gender', in Borchgrevink, T., Holter, Ø.G. (eds), *Labour of Love. Beyond the self-evidence of everyday life*, Aldershot: Avebury.
Hochshild, A.R. (1983), *The Managed Heart. Commercialization of Human Feeling*, Berkeley: University of California Press.
Hochschild, A. (with Machung, A.) (1989), *The Second Shift. Working Parents and the Revolution at Home*, London: Piatkus.
Holt, H. (1987), 'The Influence of the Work-Place Culture on Family Life', in Carlsen, S. and Elm Larsen, J. (eds), *The Equality Dilemma. Reconciling Working Life and Family Life, Viewed in an Equality Perspective*. Copenhagen: The Danish Equal Status Council.
Holter, Ø. and Aarseth, H. (1993), *Menns Livssammenheng*. Oslo: Ad Notam.
Johnson, M.M. (1988), *Strong Mothers, Weak Wives. The Search for Gender Equality*, Berkeley: University of California Press.

Kellerhals, J., Coenen-Huther, J. and Modak, M. (1988), *Figures de l'équité. La construction des normes de justice dans les groupes*, Paris: PUF.
Komarovsky, M. (1991), 'Some Reflections on the Feminist Scholarship in Sociology', *Annual Review of Sociology*, Vol. 17:1-25.
Lyons, N. Plessner (1988), 'On Self, Relationships, and Morality', in Gilligan, C., Ward, J.V. and McLean Taylor, J. (eds), *Mapping the Moral Domain*, Cambridge, Mass.: Harvard University Press.
Mauss, M. (1925/1972): *Gåvan*, Uppsala: Argos.
Moxnes, K. (1990), *Kjærnesprengning i familien? Familieforandring ved samlivsbrudd og dannelse av nye samliv*, Oslo: Universitetsforlaget.
Nyman, C. (1996), 'Inside the Black Box. Intra-household Distribution of Consumption in Sweden', in Bihagen, E., Nyman, C. and Strand, M., (eds), *Three Aspects of Consensual Poverty in Sweden*, Umeå: Studies in Sociology, No 109.
Pateman, C. (1988), *The Sexual Contract*, Cambridge: Polity Press.
Sahlins, M. (1988), *Stone Age Economics*, London: Routledge.
Seidler, V. (1995), *Unreasonable Men. Masculinity and Social Theory*. London: Routledge.
Théry, I. (1993), *Le démarriage*, Paris: Editions Odile Jacob.
Young, M. and Willmott, P. (1973), *The Symmetrical Family: A Study of Work and Leisure in the London Region*, Harmondsworth: Penguin.

10 Gender, segmented labour markets, continental welfare states and equal employment policies, the case of Spain[1]

Celia Valiente

A first glance at the position of women in the Spanish labour market would lead us to conclude that a significant advancement has taken place at least in the last three or four decades. The Spanish female activity rate[2] has constantly increased, and it is now 35% (Eurostat, 1996b; 1995 data). The former pattern of most women leaving the labour market (if ever present there) when they got married or had the first child seems to have been reversed, since currently many young women remain in the labour force after marriage or the first delivery (CES, 1994b, p.11), as can be seen in Table 10.1. In comparative terms, part-time work is still less widespread in Spain, where it accounts for 17% of female employment, 3% of male employment, and 7% of total employment – the equivalent European Union (EU) average percentages are 31%, 3%, and 16% respectively (Eurostat, 1996b; 1995 data). This means that even if the percentage of women who belong to the active population is lower in Spain than in most EU member states, most Spanish women who work for wages have full-time jobs which provide them with a higher degree of economic independence than jobs in other EU member states, where part-time employment is much more prevalent. In all countries, women are overrepresented among workers who earn the lowest salaries. In Spain, low-earners are protected by a statutory national minimum wage, which is the same for all sectors and all jobs, and which might be improved by collective agreements (there is a reduced minimum wage for workers under 18 years) (OECD, 1994, p.148).

Nevertheless, the aforementioned advancement of women in the Spanish labour market is more modest than what a superficial observation would lead us to think. As explained in the first section of this paper, the first reason is that the labour market is not homogeneous but a segmented space made up of different sectors. Each sector is composed of a different type of worker and functions according to its own logic. Women are underrepresented in the sector in which workers enjoy better working conditions, and are overrepresented in the remaining sectors,

1 I would like to thank Javier Astudillo, Juan C. Rodríguez and Salvador Seguí for their valuable comments on an earlier draft. It was presented at the meeting of the European Science Foundation Network on Gender Inequality and the European Regions, Mekrijärvi (Finland), September 19-22, 1996.

2 The female activity rate is the proportion of active women (employed and registered unemployed) in the female population of working age (women aged 15 or over, for Eurostat statistics).

where working conditions are worse. As described in the second section, another reason is that in Spain the welfare state is heavily transfer-oriented (the main benefits are monetary transfers for some people who fail to earn an income in the market), and provides very few social services. Thus, people who have caring responsibilities (usually women) get hardly any assistance from the state to help them combine their professional and family responsibilities. The third section of this paper argues that the equal employment policies elaborated in Spain in the last two decades have had little impact in changing the subordinated position of women in the labour market because these policies have not challenged either the segmentation of the labour market or the aforementioned characteristics of the welfare state. The fourth section argues that for several reasons the labour market and the welfare state have provided a different set of opportunities and constraints for women of different cohorts. Secondary sources constitute the main data for this paper.

Table 10.1
Female Activity, employment and unemployment rates by sex and age, Spain, 1994

Age	Activity	Employment	Unemployment
16-19	20.9	8.7	58.1
20-24	55.6	30.3	45.5
25-29	73.6	47.8	35.0
30-34	64.6	45.1	30.2
35-39	61.7	46.1	25.3
40-44	55.1	42.5	22.8
45-49	45.5	37.2	18.3
50-54	35.2	29.1	17.4
55-59	26.0	22.1	14.9
60-64	15.2	13.9	8.7
65-69	3.0	3.0	3.3
70-	0.5	0.5	0
Total	36.9	26.0	29.5

Source: Calculated by the author from INE [Instituto Nacional de Estadística] 1996. *Encuesta de Población Activa: Resultados detallados, segundo trimestre 1996*. Madrid: INE, pp. 44, 152, 334.

Female activity rate: proportion of active women in each age group.
Female employment rate: proportion of employed women in each age group.
Female unemployment rate: proportion of unemployed women among the active women of each age group.

I. Segmented labour markets

As in the majority of countries, most individuals in Spain achieve economic independence by working and earning wages, due to the absence of a universal system of income support (O'Connor, 1993).

Labour market segmentation (LMS) theories developed in opposition to the neo-classical model of the labour market (a unitary market governed by salary fluctuations, in which salaries are fixed at the intersection of the demand and supply of labour). LMS analysts empirically observed the existence of different labour compartments (or segments), which are characterised by different rules of entry, working conditions, salary levels, degree of stability in employment, and promotion and training opportunities. Within each segment workers compete for jobs, salaries and working conditions. There are barriers against the mobility of workers across compartments. LMS theories explain the existence of different compartments in the labour market beyond the existence of imperfections in the functioning of the market (caused, for instance, by the intervention of the state), which is the explanation provided by neo-classical analysts. LMS theorists argue that the existence of different labour markets is the result of a number of different factors, among them, the strategies of employers (or firms); the role played by the state as employer; state regulation of the labour market; workers' collective actions; or the functioning of other institutions (e.g. the family, in which different people develop different attitudes and roles, which will be later reflected in their market behaviour) (Dex, 1991 [1985], pp.151-163; Doeringer and Piore, 1971; Piore, 1971; Wilkinson, 1981).

From a gender point of view, the labour market is divided up differently in different countries. First, analysts have identified a fundamental division between part-time and full-time workers in some countries, for instance, Great Britain. In comparison with full-time jobs, the majority of part-time jobs are characterised by lower pay, lower training and lower career prospects, and have fewer welfare state benefits attached. Part time jobs also tend to exist in a smaller range of occupations, and are overwhelmingly performed by women (Lewis, 1992; O'Connor, 1993; Ruggie, 1984).

There is another type of differentiation in the labour market (from the gender point of view) in some countries, for instance in Scandinavia. Proportionately more jobs in the public sector are today performed by women, while many more jobs in the private sector are performed by men. Many state jobs are in the area of public social services. In these times of welfare state retrenchment it is reasonable to suspect that losses in 'female' jobs are going to occur (Langan and Ostner, 1991, p.135).

In Spain, the crucial divisions in the labour market are neither between part-time and full-time jobs, nor between the public or the private sectors. Pérez-Díaz and Rodríguez (1994) convincingly argued that the Spanish labour market consists of four different spaces: space 1 (permanent workers); space 2 (temporary workers); space 3 (workers in the informal economy); and space 4 (people who do not perform paid work). These four spaces are populated differently by men and women. It is to the description of these four spaces that we now turn.

Space 1, which is also called the 'core', consisted in the mid-1990s of almost 6 million workers with indefinite-duration jobs, that is, somewhat less than two thirds of the workers of the formal economy (but a minimal proportion of new hiring). Some (slight) gender differences existed with regard to permanent employment. Permanent employment accounted for 67% of male employment and 62% of female employment (Eurostat, 1996b; 1995 data). Core workers are protected by high severance payments, and generally speaking receive higher salaries than other workers. Permanent contracts were strongly promoted under the former right-wing authoritarian political regime (1936-1975), when most family needs were thought to be satisfied by the salary attached to the indefinite-duration job of the male breadwinner rather than by social policy, and when free mobility of labour was conceptualised as an inherent source of social disturbance, which policy-makers attempted to make disappear. In fact, until the mid-1980s, and with the exception of some seasonal activities such as tourism or agriculture, permanent employment was mandatory (Dolado and Jimeno, 1996, p.6; Pérez-Díaz and Rodríguez, 1994).[3]

Space 2 is composed of about 3 million workers with fixed-duration contracts, that is, more than one third of the workers in the formal economy. In Spain, the percentage of temporary wage-earners out of the total of wage-earners (35%) is not only by far the highest in the EU, but it is more than double the second highest (16% for Finland) and the EU average (14%). There are also some slight gender differences in this regard, since temporary employment accounts for 33% of male employment and for 38% of female employment (Eurostat, 1996b; 1995 data).

It is politically very difficult to reduce the high severance payments and the higher salaries associated with indefinite duration contracts, because permanent workers are the majority of workers, the majority of trade union members, and a significant number of voters in political and union elections. Therefore, the different governments in post-authoritarian Spain have only attempted very timid reforms of the regulation of indefinite duration jobs, but in 1984 permitted fixed-term contracts for all types of activities, whether temporary or not (with much lower employer contributions to the social security system than for indefinite-duration contracts).[4] The number of fixed-term contracts have sharply raised since 1984, and the vast majority of the people employed since then, many of whom are the young, have signed temporary contracts. In the second quarter of 1996, fixed-

---

3 Permanent contracts were also widespread after World War II in the decades of economic growth and (male) full employment in many Western countries governed by democratic regimes.

4 The relaxation of the rules protecting jobs for the new workers, 'while leaving intact the job protection of existing job holders' was a labour policy that was established in many European countries in the 1980s, although the relaxation took different forms (e.g. the absence of labour law in relation to many of the new contracts such as in the UK, or allowing temporary contracts such as in Spain) (Cousins, 1994, pp.55-56).

term employment accounted for 86% of the total employment of people aged 16-19 years, for 73% of people aged 20-24, and for 51% of people aged 25-29.[5]

In general, temporary workers earn lower salaries than permanent workers due, among other things, to the lack of seniority and discrimination, and receive less training. Fixed-term contracts are more common in some sectors of the economy (agriculture and construction) than in others (manufacturing). Nevertheless, it should be stressed that very often permanent and temporary workers work for the same firms or state departments and even perform the same tasks (Bentolila and Dolado, 1993; 1994; Bentolila, Segura and Toharia, 1991; Dolado and Bentolila, 1992; Jimeno, 1993).

There is a high turn-over of workers with temporary contracts for three reasons. First, temporary contracts have low or no firing costs. Second, a person can be hired on a temporary basis up to a certain number of years. Afterwards, the firm either has to hire the person on a permanent basis or dismiss him/her (and hire another temporary worker after a mandatory waiting period). This latter option is the most usual, since the conversion rate of temporary into permanent contracts is very low (about 10-15%). Third, the fact that temporary workers are, in some cases, protected by unemployment benefits after their dismissal makes it easier for employers to dismiss them, and for temporary workers to accept the dismissal. Therefore, being temporarily employed in the formal economy and unemployed for some intermittent periods has become a 'permanent' condition for many young workers, who might also participate in the underground economy (Bentolila and Dolado, 1993, pp.117-119; Dolado and Bentolila, 1992, p.15).[6]

Space 3 is the informal economy. In the mid-1980s between 1.5 and 2.5 million people worked in this sector (Pérez-Díaz and Rodríguez, 1994, p.31). It is worth mentioning that informal workers are not only those officially unemployed but also some of those permanently or temporarily employed in the formal economy, who moonlight (Bentolila and Blanchard, 1990, p.239). Women are a significant proportion of informal workers. It has been calculated that, in the mid-1980s, roughly the same number of men and women were employed in the informal economy, while about 75% of the formal jobs were performed by men. Informal jobs are more prevalent among very young women, among married women, and among the least educated women (Ruesga, 1991).

Space 4 comprises, among others, the registered unemployed, whose number has oscillated between 2 and 3.5 million people since the 1980s (Pérez-Díaz and

5 The proportion of temporary employment is considerably smaller for the remaining age groups. Fixed-term employment accounts for 28% of total employment of people aged 30-39, for 19% of people aged 40-49, for 15% of people aged 50-59, and for 11 of people aged 60 or over – calculated by the author from data contained in INE (1996:237-238).

6 As this is being written (March 1997), employers and trade unionists are negotiating a reform of the labour market in order to modify the regulation of permanent and temporary contracts. The negotiations have not been concluded, so I will leave the discussion of this for another paper.

Rodríguez, 1994, p.32). The Spanish unemployment rate[7] (23%) is the highest in the EU, and is more than double the EU average (11%) (Eurostat, 1996b; 1995 data). Two experts on the labour market have this to say about the Spanish unemployment rate:

> An initial reaction to these figures is to take them with disbelief on the grounds of the existence of a large black economy which acts as a 'shock absorber'. Nonetheless, the official unemployment rate is approximately correct: taking account of the underground economy and correcting for some technical problems in the elaboration of the Spanish Labour Force Survey will reduce this rate by 3 points at most.
>
> (Dolado and Jimeno, 1996, p.2)

Gender differences are considerable here, since the female unemployment rate (registered unemployed women as a percentage of the female active population) is 30%, while the male unemployment rate (registered unemployed men as a percentage of the male active population) is 18%. The Spanish female unemployment rate (30%) is not only the highest in the EU, but it is almost twice as high as the second highest (16% for Italy and Finland), and is more than double the EU average (12%). Moreover, Spanish women are overrepresented among those suffering what has been termed 'the worst types of unemployment': those unemployed for long periods, and those who are first-time job seekers (Cousins, 1994, p.55). 60% of unemployed women (and 49% of unemployed men) have been unemployed for twelve months or more. 27%of unemployed women (and 17% of unemployed men) are first-time job seekers (Eurostat, 1996b; 1995 data). In fact, many women enter the labour market not by starting a job but by registering as unemployed in the employment office.

In Spain, some of the registered unemployed receive unemployment benefits because they have previously worked and made the required contributions to the social security system. In 1995 approximately over 60% of non-agricultural unemployed workers received unemployment benefits (Dolado and Jimeno, 1996, p.5). Women are economically less protected than men by the state in case of unemployment. For instance, in 1995 unemployed women received contributory unemployment benefits over a shorter period than unemployed men (15.3 and 17.2 months respectively – MTAS, 1996, p.794). Unemployed women receive, on average, lower contributory benefits than men (2,569 and 3,155 pesetas respectively, gross average amount per day – MTAS, 1996, p.795; 1995 data).

Generally speaking, in collective bargaining, the main unions have defended the interests of core workers, that is, the preservation of their stability in employment and higher wages. Although the trade union membership as a percentage of wage earners is in Spain among the lowest in the EU (11% in 1990) (OECD, 1994, p.184), the laws which regulate work council elections and collective bargaining

7 The unemployment rate is the proportion of registered unemployment in the active population (the employed and the registered unemployed).

place a lot of importance on main unions, and the coverage of collective bargaining is high, about 70% in the mid-1990s (Dolado and Jimeno, 1996, p.6). Collective bargaining is often studied in Western Europe as a process that is dominated by 'insiders', who are last period employees, protected by high dismissal costs and with the specific skills necessary for the functioning of firms. Insiders defend their interests and disregard the interests of 'outsiders' (the unemployed who want to be hired). In Spain not all last period employees are insiders but only those with indefinite-duration jobs. Due to the average short duration of fixed termed contracts[8] and to the fact that temporary workers are less unionised than core workers, it is very unlikely that temporary workers participate in the committees which take part in collective bargaining. If the firm or the sector is in trouble, temporary workers could always be paid less, forced to work longer hours, and/or easily dismissed (Bentolila and Dolado, 1993, 1994; Dolado and Bentolila, 1992; Dolado and Jimeno, 1996, pp.6-7).[9]

II. Continental welfare state in Spain

According to Esping-Andersen's typology of welfare states in industrial capitalist countries,[10] that of Spain (and Italy, France and West Germany, among others) is of a continental type. In continental welfare states, social rights are linked to occupational categories and status (for instance, there are different insurance schemes for different types of workers). They (and their dependants) are the beneficiaries of the main social programmes. The redistributive effects of social policy are minimal. One result of this social policy is a certain degree of decommodification, that is, 'the degree to which individuals, or families, can uphold a socially acceptable standard of living independently of market participation' (Esping-Andersen, 1990, p.37. Provision of welfare benefits is mainly public. The welfare state aims at reinforcing the traditionally crucial role of the family as welfare provider. Thus, the

---

8 The average length of new temporary contract is very short: 3 months and 9 days (Missé, 1997, p.64).

9 There are signs of a limited change in the actions of trade unionists in collective bargaining. For instance, newspapers report that, due to the high rates of unemployment and temporary employment, trade unionists at the level of the firm are becoming more willing to accept salary moderation or other employer demands in exchange for the employers' commitment to job creation and the transformation of temporary into permanent contracts (see, for instance, *El País* 24 February 1977, p.65, for an example of this kind of agreement in the automobile industry).

On the other hand, it has been argued that, in general, Spanish trade unionists have defended the interests of the unemployed and the temporarily employed when they participate not in collective bargaining, but in policy-making, for instance, pressurising the government to increase the level and coverage of unemployment benefits.

10 Esping-Andersen (1990, pp.3-4) analysed the variation across welfare states along three dimensions: the type of social rights; the type of stratification that the welfare state produces; and the interrelation of the state, the market and the family in the provision of welfare.

state tends to intervene only when the capacity of the family to act as social provider is exhausted (Esping-Andersen, 1990, pp.27-28, 48).[11]

In Spain, as in any other continental welfare state, participation in the labour market is the main route of access to welfare state benefits, since, generally speaking, most of these have been historically given to workers (and their dependants) who have made the required contributions to the system (Guillén, 1992, p.12; 1996). The two main exceptions to this general rule are health care and compulsory education (for people who are 6-16 years old), which are programmes of universal coverage.

Historically, adult women have had access to all types of welfare state, not only via labour market participation but also via marriage, or more broadly speaking via family ties (Lewis, 1992, p.161; Orloff, 1993, p.308). Nevertheless, it is important to note that in former times marriage provided access to very few benefits in Spain (mainly to health care and survivors' benefits). Similarly, nowadays widow(er)'s pensions are the only important benefit to which women (and men) are entitled via marriage. Moreover, in all types of welfare states benefits acquired via marriage are less generous than benefits acquired via labour market participation (Orloff, 1993, p.315).[12]

In all societies, women are those who overwhelmingly provide care for people who, for any reason, need the care of others, such as the frail elderly, the disabled, the ill or small children (Orloff, 1993, p.313). This provision of care is, in some cases, conflictual or even incompatible with the requirements of the performance of paid work. Of course, it cannot be argued that women have a subordinate position in the Spanish labour market just because a significant number of them perform (unpaid) care work for others. In fact, some women do not provide care for other people at all, while others do so for limited periods of their lives. The reasons which account for the different positions of men and women in the labour market are multiple. Nevertheless, other things being equal, a welfare state which

---

11 Two other types of welfare states exist in the classification made by Esping-Andersen (1990:, pp.7-28): the social democratic and the liberal welfare states. In the social democratic welfare state, which exists in Scandinavia, universal benefits are numerous. De-commodification is high. Social programs are directed to all social classes. The purpose of social policy is to attain equality. The state provides generous care services for children, the elderly and other people in need of care.

In the liberal welfare state, which exists in the United States, Canada and Australia among others, 'means-tested assistance, modest universal transfers, or modest social-insurance plans predominate. Benefits cater mainly to a clientele of low-income, usually working-class, state dependants'. De-commodification is very low. The state encourages market provision of welfare.

12 For example, in Spain on November 1, 1996, the average widow(er)'s pension (acquired via marriage) was 47,900 pesetas (2,521 Swedish crowns), while the average contributory old age pension (acquired via labour market participation) was 78,400 pesetas (4,126 Swedish crowns) (MTAS, 1997:490). All numerical data in this paper are given in monetary terms, in Spanish pesetas and in Swedish crowns (converted at the March 1997 rate of 1 Swedish crown=19 pesetas).

For a description of the requirements to receive the aforementioned pensions, see also notes 19 and 20.

provides numerous social services facilitates female labour force participation more than a welfare state which does not provide these services, because the former saves women from providing care for others (on an unpaid basis).

The Spanish welfare state, as any other of continental type, only facilitates the participation of women in the labour force to a limited extent, because the welfare state is heavily transfer-oriented and offers very few social services.[13] In the early 1990s, approximately one tenth of the welfare in continental welfare states was dedicated to social services (health care excluded), while the figure was one third in the social democratic welfare states (Esping-Andersen, 1995, p.2).[14] Let me illustrate this point with the example of the policies for two groups of the population in need of care: children under six, when mandatory school starts; and the elderly. This makes my analysis different from most feminist researchers (O'Connor, 1993; Orloff, 1993; Ruggie, 1984) who only focus attention on the policies related to the care of children. This narrower focus is inappropriate for studying Southern Europe (and probably every other country as well), where families (that is, mainly women) are generally in charge of the care not only of small children, but also of any adult who, for whatever reason (e.g. illness or disability), needs the care of other people.

II.a Public policies for children under six

My next point is that parents receive modest aid from the state for children under six:[15] paid maternity leave and non-paid parental leave as a substitute rather than as a complement to child care; hardly any child care services for children aged two or under; means-tested child allowances; and low tax exceptions for dependent children and for child care. The main exception to this general rule is the relatively generous supply of pre-school services for four- and five-year-old children, services which are conceptualised by policy-makers not as gender equality programmes (with the aim of promoting the participation of mothers in the labour market) but as educational programmes for the benefit of minors (especially of those who come from less privileged families) (Valiente, 1995).

As for paid-maternity leave, working mothers who have been previously employed and have contributed to the social security system for at least 180 days within the five years previous to child birth are entitled to 16 uninterrupted weeks of paid leave. The number of years contributed and the level of contribution (which is proportional to the salary) are used to calculate the so-called regulatory

---

13 For an analysis of the Spanish welfare state with the analytical focus on gender, see Cousins (1995) and Guillén (forthcoming).

14 If health care is excluded, social services include, among other things, 'day care and youth services, care of the aged and disabled, home help services, and the like, but also employment-related services such as rehabilitation schemes and employment exchanges' (Esping-Andersen, 1995, p.2).

15 This has also been the conclusion of comparative research on support for children. See, for instance, Bradshaw et al. (1993).

base (base reguladora). The amount received during parental leave is 100% of the regulatory base. The right to return to one's job is guaranteed. Since 1989, if both parents perform paid work, the father may take up to four of the final weeks leave (in this case the mother must return to work).[16] There is also provision for up to three years of non-paid parental leave for working mothers or fathers. The right to return to one's job is only guaranteed during the first year. The right to a job in the same professional category is guaranteed during the second and third years. The period of leave is counted as effectively worked in terms of seniority (Guillén, forthcoming). The fact that, after this leave working women receive hardly any help from the state to combine family and work responsibilities has led some observers to conclude that in continental welfare states maternity and parental leaves are a substitute and not a complement to child care (O'Connor, 1993).

The main policies for children under six are educational preschool programmes for children aged four or over. In the academic year 1992-1993 the percentage of children who attended public preschool programmes was: 67.7 for five-year-old children; and 66.1 for four-year-old children. The extent of such programmes is quite high in comparative terms. In contrast, the percentage of children aged three or under cared for in public centres was very low: 0.3 for those under one year old; 1.3 for one-year-old children; and 3.0 for two-year-old children; and 24.3 for three-year-old children, as can be seen in Table 10.2. The table also shows that children younger than three are not taken care of in private centres either.

Foreign observers are often impressed by the extent of pre-school programmes for four- and five-year-old children, and emphasise that, in this regard, Spain is ahead of other countries, like the United Kingdom (see, for instance, Cousins, 1994, p.51). Nevertheless, it should be stressed that pre-school programmes are educational programmes that have been established with the purpose of attaining equality among children from different social classes. These are not at all gender equality programmes established to provide child care for working mothers (or parents). Pre-school programmes cannot then be used by parents as perfect substitutes for child care, since pre-school hours are shorter than working hours (and sometimes much shorter and interrupted by a break). It should be remembered that in Spain most women who work for wages do so on a full-time basis.

It is important to note that private child care or preschool centres are *de facto* hardly regulated by the state. Moreover, paid care provided in private premises (in the child's or the childminder's home) is not regulated by the state at all. The Spanish non-regulation of private centres and private care in homes contrasts with the efforts made by most Western governments to control such sectors, although it is known that the implementation of these regulations is always uneven and in part unsuccessful, especially as regards care provided in homes (Valiente, 1995).

---

16 The number of fathers who take the last weeks of maternity leave is insignificant. The Spanish Labour Force Survey (*Encuesta de Población Activa*) provides data desegregated by sex of wage-earners who are not working during the week when the survey questionnaire is administered. In the second quarter of 1996, 99% of wage-earners who were not working due to maternity leave were women, and the remaining 1% were men (INE, 1996: 205).

Table 10.2
Percentage of children under 6 who attend centres, by age of child, and type of centre, Spain, academic year 1992-1993

Age	Total	Public centres	Private centres
less than 1	0.6	0.3	0.3
1 year	2.8	1.3	1.5
2 years	8.7	3.0	5.7
3 years	46.0	24.3	21.7
4 years	97.1	66.1	31.0
5 years	100	67.7	33.1

Source: Calculated by the author from data contained in INE (1994, p.27; 1995, p.5) and MEC (1995, p.91).

In Spain child allowances (except for handicapped children) are means-tested, the income threshold established in the means test is low (slightly above the national minimum wage) and their level is relatively modest in comparative terms (Guillén, forthcoming).[17] This means that child allowances are not at all an important monetary transfer, which might be used to pay for child care. The same could be said with regard to tax exemptions for dependent children and for child care expenses, whose amount is also relatively low.[18]

To summarise, after the 16 weeks of paid maternity leave (for those who work for wages and have made the required contributions to the social security system), working women receive very little help from the state to combine work and family responsibilities: unpaid parental leave; pre-school services for children

17 Child allowances (*prestaciones familiares por hijo a cargo*) amounted to 36,000 pesetas (1,895 Swedish crowns) per year in 1995 per dependent child younger than 18 years. These allowances were given to family units whose yearly income was lower than 1,080,540 pesetas (56,870 Swedish crowns). This income threshold increased 15 per cent for each dependent child since the second.

Child allowances for handicapped children are not means-tested and their yearly level is higher.

18 Those who pay the personal income tax (*Impuesto sobre la Renta de las Personas Físicas*, IRPF) can benefit from tax exemptions for each dependent child. A child is defined as a person up to the age of 30 who lives with his/her parents and whose income does not reach a certain level. In 1997, this tax relief amounts to 21,100 (1,110 Swedish crowns) for each of the first two children, 26,700 (1,405 Swedish crowns) for the third child, and 31,000 (1,674 Swedish crowns) for the fourth child and the following.

In 1997, IRPF tax payers may be the beneficiaries of tax exemptions for 15 per cent of the amount of child care expenses (of the under-threes) up to a maximum of 25,000 pesetas (1,316 Swedish crowns). The yearly income of the tax payer should be lower than 2,000,000 pesetas (105,263 Swedish crowns) or 3,000,000 pesetas (157,895 Swedish crowns) if both parents pay IRPF taxes jointly. Both parents have to work for wages. In the fiscal year 1993, 106,299 IRPF tax payers were the beneficiaries of this tax exemption. The average tax exemption was 11,835 pesetas (623 Swedish crowns) (MEH, 1995:108).

aged three or over (pre-school hours are usually shorter than working hours); means-tested child allowances; and modest tax relief (for dependent children and child care expenses).

II.b Public policies for the aged

Because the Spanish welfare state is so heavily transfer-oriented, it is important to study the income that the aged receive from state transfers. Since the retirement age in Spain is 65, in this paper the elderly are defined as those who are 65 years old or older. In Spain, most of the aged derive their main income from state pensions. Most analysts agree that, generally speaking, the economic situation of the elderly is very varied, but has improved significantly for many of them in the last two decades. If old people have been previously employed and have made the required contributions, they are entitled to contributory retirement pensions.[19] Contributory retirement benefits are very generous, if benefit levels are not measured in absolute terms but as a percentage of net earnings. Nevertheless, what is usually less emphasised is that, in many cases (but with important exceptions), if the elderly person is in need of care, these contributory retirement pensions are not high enough to purchase all the caring services needed at the market-rate, and that their beneficiaries are partly (or totally) dependent on the care of (usually female) relatives (Esping-Andersen, 1995). The same is, of course, true for the other main source of income of the aged in Spain, contributory widow(er)'s pensions,[20] and also for the two types of means-tested retirement benefits which exist for some of the people outside the contributory system: non-contributory and assistential benefits. Moreover, in some of these means-tested programmes the means test (imposed not on the applicant but on the family unit) is much less strict when the old person lives with their children or parents than when s/he lives alone.[21] In other words,

19 In order to receive a contributory retirement pension, a person has to have contributed at least 15 years (at least two of these have to have been included within the eight years previous to the retirement). See note 12 for the average contributory retirement pension.

20 In order to receive a widow(er)'s pension, a person has to have been married to an employed person who had contributed for at least 500 days within the five years previous to death. The amount of the pension is 45 per cent of the regulatory base, that is, almost half of the contributory retirement pension. See note 12 for the average widow(er)'s pension.

21 In order to receive a non-contributory old age pension the yearly income of the claimant must be below a certain level. This is the total amount of the pension for claimants living alone. If the claimant lives with other people (whether relatives or not), the incomes of all of them are counted. All these incomes must again be below a certain level: the sum of the amount of the pension plus 70% of the pension multiplied by the number of people who live with the claimant minus one. Nevertheless, there is an exception to the general rule: when the old person lives with their children or parents. In this case all aforementioned limits are raised 2.5 times. In 1996, the monthly amount of a non-contributory old age pension was 35,580 pesetas (1,873 Swedish crowns.

the state sometimes provides clear incentives for old people to live with their relatives.

The system of contributory retirement and means-tested old age benefits is not universal in Spain. People who have made the required contributions receive contributory benefits, and people who have not made the required contribution but live in family units whose level of income is low according to the means test receive means-tested benefits. Thus, people without the required contributions but whose family unit has a level of income higher than the income threshold established in the means test do not receive any benefit. Gender differences are conspicuous in this regard since this last group of people consists mainly of old women who have been housewives during most of their adult lives and whose family unit has an income level higher than that established in the means test, probably because such family unit is composed by one or more wage earners or recipients of welfare benefits (Durán, 1995, pp.467-468). In 1994, 97% of men and 66% of women (both older than 65 years and who did not perform paid work) received a state pension. Less than half of these women received a pension based on their own contributions while the rest received widow's pensions. 1.2 million of women aged 65 or over did not receive any state pension (CES, 1995, pp.414).

Although theoretically the elderly might live in centres, where they receive the care needed, in practice most of the elderly live in their homes or in the homes of their relatives but not in centres. In 1994, approximately 2.8% of the elderly were cared for in public or private old people's homes (CES, 1995, pp.445-446).

The most common type of family in Spain is the nuclear family. It is formed by a couple who live with one or more children. The extended family, where other relatives live with one or two parents and dependent children, is clearly less common.[22] In fact, the elderly living with their adult children is not the option preferred by either party. The former prefer to live in their own homes as long as possible (CES, 1995, pp.447-448); De Miguel, 1994, pp.802-803). This option is facilitated by the fact that a large number of elderly people own their homes in Spain. In 1993, 69% of the elderly lived in dwellings which they owned (INSERSO, 1995a, p.39), although many of the places where old people live are not adequately equip-

---

Assistential pensions for people aged 66 or over existed from the 1960s but were abolished in 1992, except for those already receiving the benefit. The amount is fixed yearly and is the same for all people who receive it. Afterwards, many of these people have applied for non-contributory old age pensions, because the amount of the latter is higher.

22 The state rewards relatives who live with the elderly by granting these relatives personal income tax relief. IRPF tax payers can benefit from tax relief if they live with one or more parents, grandparents, and so on, whose income is lower than the minimum wage. In 1997 the amount of the exemption was: 16,500 pesetas (868 Swedish crowns) if the relative is 65-75 years old; 32,900 (1,731 Swedish crowns) if the relative is aged 75 or over. In the fiscal year 1993, 446,817 IRPF tax payers were the beneficiaries of the first tax exemption (for living with a relative aged 65-75 years) and 441,991 of the second tax exemption (for living with a relative aged 75 or over (MEH, 1995: 108).

ped to meet their needs.[23] Nevertheless, it is important to understand that, in general, members of Spanish families do not need to live together in order to feel that they belong to a moral community whose members should share economic resources and provide care when required (CES, 1995, p.286; Pérez-Díaz and Rodríguez, 1994, p.35).

When the elderly are in need of care or of any other type of help, they are helped by relatives in the majority of cases. For instance, when an old person is ill, she or he is taken care for by relatives in 90% of the cases (Rodríguez, 1994, p.56). These relatives are usually (although no exclusively) women, mainly spouses or daughters and, to a lesser extent, daughters-in-law and other female relatives (INSERSO, 1995b). The majority of the elderly who declare that they need help are helped by others. In 1993, the opposite was the case to less than 4% of old people who declared that they needed help but did not receive it (INSERSO, 1995a, p.63).

The preceding paragraphs should not lead the reader to the conclusion that the elderly in Spain are simply dependent people. Help and care are provided reciprocally by the elderly and their relatives. For instance, in 1993, 35% of the elderly with children confirmed that they helped them with domestic work or in caring for their grand-children (INSERSO, 1995a, p.79).

When the elderly need the help of others, they (and their relatives) get very little help from the state. Social services provided by the authorities for the elderly are very scarce in Spain in comparison with other countries. Personal social services appeared above all in the late 1980s, in contrast with other EU member states where they have been developed since the 1960s and 1970s. The main social services for the elderly are home helps, day care centres, holiday programmes, stays in places with thermal baths and subsidies to non-profit non-governmental organisations working with the elderly, and to the elderly associations (CES, 1994a). To exemplify the lack of social services in Spain, it may be mentioned that the number of beneficiaries of the main social service, home helps, was 25,214 old people in 1993 (CES, 1994a, p.242).[24]

To summarise, public provision of social services is very scarce in the Spanish welfare state. This circumstance hinders the participation of some women in the labour market in equal terms with men, since women perform most (unpaid) care work. There is still another dimension in which continental welfare states have not enhanced women's capacity to gain economic independence via labour market participation. The importance of the state as an employer of women has already been stressed (Meyer, 1994). Because the continental welfare state provides very few social services, it employs less women than if the welfare state were less transfer-oriented and provided more services. The reason is that care is in

---

23 In 1993, 66% of the dwellings where the elderly lived had no heating, 18% had no telephone, and 7% had no hot water (INSERSO, 1995a, p.41).

24 This number refers to beneficiaries in the territories administered at that time by the central state in this policy area, that is, all regions except Andalusia, the Basque country, the Canary Islands, Catalonia, Galicia, Navarre and Valencia (Spain is composed of 17 regions).

all countries mainly provided by women, whether on an unpaid basis or in exchange for wages (if the wages are paid by the state, this provision of care is called 'social services'). In Spain, 29% of female wage-earners and 21% of male wage-earners were employed by the state (calculated by the author from data contained in INE, 1996, p.223, p.225; second quarter of 1996 data). It has been argued that the comparatively better situation of women in Scandinavia has been achieved in part through an 'alliance' between women and the welfare state (if I am allowed to use this personalising metaphor). Social policy has not only diminished women's responsibility for providing unpaid care work in the family sphere, but has also employed women in the sector of public provision of services (Langan and Ostner, 1991, p.135).

III. Equal employment policies

As has been observed, Spanish women face obstacles if they attempt to gain economic independence by performing paid work. The labour market is segmented and women are overrepresented in the worst segments, that is, those who are unemployed, employed in the underground economy or temporarily employed in the formal sector of the economy. The welfare state provides few social services which help women to combine family and work responsibilities. These obstacles still exist in spite of the development of equal employment policies (EEP)[25] at the central state level during the last twenty years. As we shall see, the main EEP in relation to gender have been the revision of discriminatory legislation, the extension of paid maternity leave and non-paid parental leaves (see the preceding section for a description of these leaves), and the promotion of research on labour matters with an analytical focus on gender. In this section I argue that the impact of EEP has been limited, because EEP have not tackled either the segmented structure of the labour market or the continental characteristics of the Spanish welfare state.

With respect to the revision of discriminatory legislation inherited from former times, the 1978 Constitution included the prohibition of gender discrimination before the law (art.14), in the labour market (art.35.1) and in the civil service (art.35.1). Former legislation has been revised, in order to abolish its discriminatory aspects. In practice, this process of revision meant that women were allowed to perform some types of work which were prohibited to them in the past, such as night work, or to perform various jobs also previously closed to them, for instance, in the police, in the army, or the mining sector (Valiente, 1994, pp.301-311).

---

25 According to Mazur (1992, p.54), 'equal employment policy means any policy (legislation, decree, program, etc.) which targets direct or indirect discrimination based on gender, race, religion or age in hiring, firing, professional training and promotion'. In this paper I concentrate on the study of EEP in relation to gender at the central state level (and not at the regional or local level), because the right to legislate in labour matters belongs to the central state (MTSS, 1995, p.32).

Nowadays the principle of equality of all citizens before the law informs general legislation. The discriminatory clauses that exist are contained in collective agreements negotiated between representatives of employers and workers. Wage discrimination is one of the most common forms of gender discrimination. It occurs with the creation of labour categories that include only or mainly women. These female workers are paid less than workers included in mixed, or male categories. Many job offers are also discriminatory, because they are directed to only one sex. This is common, as can be seen from the job offer pages of newspapers (De la Fuente and Crespán, 1995; Sáez, 1994, p.139).

The revision of discriminatory legislation and the subsequent approval of gender-neutral new legislation has been an important reform. Legislators have sent a clear message to society that overt gender discrimination is no longer tolerated (at least in general legislation). Women may now use the law to fight for or defend a better position in the labour market. Nevertheless, the importance of the reform cannot be overstated, since very few women have initiated a legal process in matters of gender discrimination (De la Fuente and Crespán, 1995, p.1; Sáez, 1994, p.29).

Another significant EEP has been the promotion of research on issues related to women and the labour market by the main state feminist institution at the central state level, the Institute of the Woman (Instituto de la Mujer, IM).[26] One objective put forward in the founding documents of the Institute was to study all aspects of women's situation in Spain. This is an important task, because when the IM was founded in 1983, little research of this type existed, particularly compared with the level of research on the status of women in other advanced industrialised democracies. The IM has published books, given grants to researchers, established awards and prizes for the best books and articles, commissioned pieces of research, and established a documentation centre in Madrid.

The aforementioned EEP have led a very small number women to fight in court for equal treatment in the work place, have provided an important number of working women with a paid-maternity leave (but have not helped them to combine professional and caring responsibilities after the end of this leave), and have contributed to increase the knowledge about gender issues in the labour market. Nevertheless, EEP have not tackled the segmentation of the labour market in the four spaces differently populated by women and men, nor have they modified (even slightly) the continental characteristics of the welfare state. As a result, EEP have been of limited help in demolishing the obstacles that women face for the achievement of equal status in the labour market.

---

26 Since the 1960s, institutions with the concrete purpose of promoting gender equality have been set up, developed (and sometimes even dismantled) in most industrial countries. In social science literature such institutions have been called 'state feminist' institutions, bureaucracies or machineries. The people who work in them are described as 'femocrats' or 'state feminists' (Stetson and Mazur, 1995).

IV. Stratification among women

The labour market and the welfare state foster stratification along class lines (Esping-Andersen, 1990; 1995) but also along gender lines (Langan and Ostner, 1991; Lewis, 1992; Orloff, 1993; Sainsbury, 1994). In this section I argue that the labour market and the welfare state might also produce stratification within sexes, as is the case of different age groups of women in Spain. As I shall explain, a very different set of professional opportunities and constraints has been given to women under or over approximately 45. Although very different situations within both age groups can be found, it is possible to generalise about the differences between the two. Generally speaking, women over 45 came of age empowered with less education than men of their cohorts and social class. Women over 45 came of age at a time when housewifery was the prevalent option for women. As a result, most of them abandoned the labour market (if ever present there) and never returned. Women under 45 are empowered with the same education as men of their cohorts and social class, and many attempt to participate in the labour market at a time when housewifery is a socially discredited option.

With regards to women over 45, the majority of them do not participate in the labour market, as can be seen in Table 10.1. It was often the case that these women had not attained the same educational level as men of their generation and social class (as is shown in Table 10.3), since they grew up in a period when more importance was attached by families and the state to the education of men than to that of women. Women over 45 came of age during the authoritarian regime, when housewifery was the option for married women encouraged by public policies and by the official discourse and propaganda. Moreover, housewifery was broadly seen as the most socially accepted choice. Therefore, while it was not that uncommon for single young women to work for wages, most women left the labour market after marriage (if they were ever present there). Since then, they have been almost entirely in charge of domestic tasks, and have also cared for any relative in need of care.[27]

What makes these women over 45 different from other women of that age in other countries is that most of them left the labour market forever and not only for a limited period of time. Housewifery was seen in the past as a long-term status, and not as a temporary situation mandated by the requirements of rearing children. After having been out of the labour force for so long (two or more decades), it is not feasible for most of them to return to the formal labour market (spaces 1 and 2) although their chances in space 3 are slightly higher.

---

27 Class differences are, of course, important among these women who are older than 45. Upper-class women could hire domestic workers to perform household tasks and care, while low-class women not only perform most household and caring tasks in their households, but, in some cases, also in the household of others as domestic workers in order to supplement the family income. In any case, women of all social classes have had in common the responsibility for organising (and/or providing themselves) the performance of household duties and of caring. In the past, they have also had to face a social stigma, if they wished to engage in paid work outside the home after being married or having children.

Table 10.3
Educational attainment (university level) by age group and gender, Spain, 1991

Years old	20-24	25-29	30-34	35-44	45-54	55-64
Men	8.0	15.6	14.2	12.5	8.5	5.7
Women	13.9	19.8	15.7	10.0	4.6	2.8

Source: OECD (1994, p.67).

A common situation for women aged 45 or over is to live in a household where a relative (usually the husband) is employed as a 'core' worker. Given the high rate of unemployment and temporary employment, and the low activity rates in Spain,[28] many 'core' workers provide for other relatives. In families with one 'core' worker and dependent relatives it is beneficial for the family as a whole that the 'core' worker maintains the status of a fixed-termed employee. This usually implies the maintenance of a gendered division of labour within the households (he provides and she performs domestic and caring work). The problem is that situations which can be beneficial from the family point of view might be detrimental for individual members of the family, if they try to achieve independence from each other but end up choosing options that erode their potential to be economically independent.

As for women under 45 (named 'younger' women in what follows), they have come (or are coming of age) after a hidden revolution has taken place in Spanish families, as many parents have decided that they should give their daughters and sons the same education. A number of studies have demonstrated the existence of this attitude (Aguinaga and Comas, 1991, pp.181-183; Escario, Alberdi and Berlín, 1987, p.49), which contrasts with the traditional idea that boys needed an education to prepare them for work outside the home, whilst girls should be trained to be home-makers. This traditional idea has also been revealed by research (De Pablo, 1976, p.378). Moreover, and more importantly, parents have been acting in accordance with these egalitarian ideas regarding their offspring's education. In addition, educational policies have increasingly promoted the enrolment of girls and women in education. As a result, many young women are now as qualified as the men of their generation and social class (or even more qualified) to participate in the labour market). This can be seen in Table 10.3, which shows that educational attainment at university level in 1991 was higher for women than for men under 35. Thus, in comparison with older women, younger women have the advantage of being more educated.

---

28 The activity rate is the proportion of active people (the employed and the registered unemployed) in the population of working age. The Spanish activity rate (48%) is the second lowest in the EU after Italy (47%), and it is seven points below the EU average (55%) (Eurostat, 1996b; 1995 data).

Younger women are encouraged to perform paid work outside the home, since performing a paid job after marriage or the first delivery is no longer a socially and politically stigmatised option. Quite the contrary, housewifery is now a socially discredited status, to the amazement of some women over 45 who consider that either they had been cheated when they were encouraged or forced to be housewives or that younger women are nevertheless choosing the wrong option of being workers and mothers at the same time.

In Spain, a large proportion of young adults live in their parents home until their mid-or late-twenties. In Spring 1995, 77% of people aged 15-29 lived in their parents' home. Moreover, this was the case for 52% of people aged 25-29 (Martín Serrano, 1996a, p.5; 1996b, p.2). Most young women and men leave their parents' home to marry and form a new household. From this moment, younger and older women have in common the fact that they are both in charge of the organisation (and in many cases also the actual performance) of household and caring duties. Both women live in a country where the welfare state is transfer-oriented and offers very limited social services. Most younger women are not 'core' workers and are married to men who are not 'core' workers either. This circumstance pushes younger women to participate in the labour market (Adam, 1996). It is in this context that we have to understand why Spain (together with Italy) has the lowest fertility rates in the world (synthetic index of fertility: 1,22 in 1994 – Eurostat, 1996a, p.116) (Esping-Andersen, 1995). Women are 'choosing' to have fewer children and to delay their pregnancies, after having postponed marriage (the number of children born out of wedlock is in Spain very low in comparative terms) while attempting to participate in a segmented labour market, and finding little or no help from the state to combine professional and family responsibilities.

It is again important to remember that most women who perform paid jobs do so on a full-time basis, in contrast to other countries where part-time work is very prevalent. Nevertheless, the regulation of part-time work has changed in recent years, and it is now an attractive option for employers. As a result, the number of part-time jobs is increasing. As in other countries, these jobs are mainly performed by women. Most new part-time jobs performed by women are for very low skilled workers. In contrast, an important number of part-time jobs performed by men are for very skilled workers (CES, 1996, pp.158-162).

V. Conclusion

In Spain in the last three or four decades the number of women participating in the labour market has increased significantly. Nevertheless, women are entering a segmented labour market, in which, in comparison to men, they are underrepresented in the core (composed of those with indefinite-duration contracts), and overrepresented among those temporarily employed or employed in the informal economy, and especially among the registered unemployed. In fact, in Spain a significant number of women begin to participate in the labour market by registering as unemployed instead of starting to work for wages. Given the very high rate of female unemployment and the still high number of women who do not perform paid work and are not registered as unemployed, a crucial division in the Spanish female population of working age is still between those who perform paid work and those who do not. This is different from other countries where the majority or a significant number of women are wage-earners, and where there is a fundamental division of the labour force into 'good jobs' and 'bad jobs' (O'Connor, 1993). In addition, given the high rate of temporary contracts in Spain, a central division within the group of women (and men) who work for wages is between those who have an indefinite contract and those who do not.

In their attempts to be among those who perform paid work, women in Spain (and in other continental welfare states) find little support from a welfare state which is heavily transfer-oriented and provides very few personal social services. Although it cannot be argued that women have a subordinate position in the Spanish labour market mainly because the welfare state is of a continental type, it is true that care is provided in most cases by women and that in some cases care-giving is conflictual or incompatible with the performance of paid work.

In Spain, a segmented labour market and a continental welfare state are the main (or two of the main) barriers against the equal status of women in the economic sphere. These obstacles have not been tackled by the introduction and development of equal employment policies over the last twenty years. These policies have consisted of the revision of discriminatory legislation inherited from former times and the subsequent approval of gender-neutral new legislation; the extension of paid maternity leave and non-paid parental leave from paid employment to care for small children (and the inclusion of fathers among their potential beneficiaries); and the promotion of research on issues related to women and the labour market. These policies are important because they have allowed women to fight in court for equal treatment in the work place, although very few have initiated a legal process with regard to gender discrimination. Equal employment policies have allowed women and men to stop working in connection with child birth while still receiving their salaries, although the overwhelming majority of men have decided not to 'benefit' from maternity leave. Finally, in part as a result of equal employment policies, information and knowledge about gender issues in the labour market is broader than it was two decades ago. Nevertheless, equal employment policies have been of very little help in demolishing the main obstacles that women face to achieving equal status in the economic sphere: segmentation in labour market and the continental characteristics of the welfare state.

Finally, the labour market and the welfare state (among others) have provided a very different set of opportunities and constraints for women who are either over or under 45. The former have been given many incentives to leave the labour market (if they were even present there) after marriage or the first delivery, while the latter have been given some incentives to try to participate in the labour market.

A future paper could explore three related questions. First, it would be interesting to research further what incentives women younger than 45 years old have been given in their attempts to be wage-earners. Given the lack of personal social services provided by the state, it might be the case that the majority of these younger women are given incentives to participate in the labour market not on equal terms with men, but rather as another category of workers: less committed to their jobs, because these have to be compatible with the performance of household and caring duties.

Second, it would be important to study intra-family solidarity. Many younger women are now as educated as the men of their cohort and social class. This might be the outcome of gender equality policies in the area of education, but it is more the result of family strategies of empowering not only sons but also daughters. It is not clear if families later support or not (and how) adult women once they are participating in the labour market.

Third, the development of part-time work will have to be followed carefully. A peculiarity of the Spanish labour market is that many women remain in employment after marriage and child rearing, performing full-time jobs although there is a lack social services (child care, for instance). As we said, in recent years, part-time work has been increasing. Two future scenarios seem now possible: the maintenance of the *status quo;* or the further increase in part-time jobs to reach the same level as in other countries. This would mean the appearance of another gender division in the Spanish labour market, between full-time workers (mainly men), and part-time workers (mainly women, and possibly the young too).

References

Adam, P. (1996), 'Mothers in an Insider-Outsider Economy: the Puzzle of Spain', European University Institute, Department of Economics, January (mimeo).

Aguinaga, J. and Comas, D. (1991), *Infancia y adolescencia: la mirada de los adultos*, Madrid: Ministerio de Asuntos Sociales.

Bentolila, S. and Blanchard, O.J. (1990), 'Spanish Unemployment', *Economic Policy* No.10:233-281.

Bentolila, S. and Dolado, J.J. (1993), 'La contratación temporal y sus efectos sobre la competitividad', *Papeles de Economía Española*, No.56:112-130.

Bentolila, S. and Dolado, J.J. (1994), 'Labor Flexibility and Wages: Lessons from Spain', *Economic Policy* No.18:54-99.

Bentolila, S., Segura, J. and Toharia, L. (1991), 'La contratación temporal en España', *Moneda y Crédito* No.193:225-265.

Bradshaw, J., Ditch, J., Holmes, H. and Whiteford, P. (1993), *Support for Children: A Comparison of Arrangements in Fifteen Countries*. London: HMSO.

CES [Consejo Económico y Social] (1994a), *España 1993. Economía, trabajo y sociedad: memoria sobre la situación socioeconómica y laboral.* Madrid: CES.

CES (1994b), *La situación de la mujer en la realidad socio laboral española.* Madrid: CES.

CES (1995), *España 1994. Economía, trabajo y sociedad: memoria sobre la situación socioeconómica y laboral.* Madrid: CES.

CES (1996), *España 1995. Economía, trabajo y sociedad: memoria sobre la situación socioeconómica y laboral.* Madrid: CES.
Cousins, C. (1994), 'A Comparison of the Labor Market Position of Women in Spain and the UK with Reference to the 'Flexible' Labor Debate', *Work, Employment & Society* Vol.8, No.1 (March): 45-67.
Cousins, C. (1995), 'Women and Social Policy in Spain: the Development of a Gendered Welfare Regime', *Journal of European Social Policy* Vol.5:175-197.
De la Fuente, D. and Crespán, J. (1995), 'La problemática de la aplicación del principio de igualdad en el ámbito laboral', Paper presented at the *Jornadas sobre legislación y jurisprudencia en el marco de la igualdad de oportunidades de las mujeres*, Madrid, Instituto de la Mujer, 13-15 December.
De Miguel, A. (ed) (1994), *La sociedad española, 1994-95*, Madrid: Complutense.
De Pablo, A. (1976), 'La familia española en cambio', in *Estudios sociológicos sobre la situación social de España,* ed. by Fundación Foessa, 345-405. Madrid: Euramérica.
Dex, S. (1991) [1985], *La división sexual del trabajo: revoluciones conceptuales en las ciencias sociales*, Madrid: MTSS.
Doeringer, P.B. and Piore, M.J. (1971), *Internal Labor Markets and Manpower Analysis*, Lexington, Massachusetts: D.C. Heath.
Dolado, J.J. and Bentolila, S. (1992), 'Who Are the Insiders? Wage Setting in Spanish Manufacturing Firms', *Banco de España, Documento de Trabajo* No.9229.
Dolado, J.J. and Jimeno, J.F. (1996), 'The Causes of Spanish Unemployment: a Structural Var Approach', Madrid, FEDEA, Documento de Trabajo 96-19.
Durán, A. (1995), 'Política de pensiones: situación y perspectivas', in *Las actividades económicas de los mayores*, ed. by SECOT [Seniors Españoles para la Cooperación Técnica], 465-481. Madrid: SECOT.
El País 24 February 1997:65.
Escario, P., Alberdi, I. and Berlín, B. (1987), 'Actitudes de los varones ante el cambio familiar: informe de investigación',(mimeo).
Esping-Andersen, G. (1990), *The Three Worlds of Welfare Capitalism*, Princeton (New Jersey): Princeton University Press.
Esping-Andersen, G. (1995), 'Welfare States Without Work: the Impasse of Labor Shedding and Familialism in Continental European Social Policy', *Centro de Estudios Avanzados en Ciencias Sociales, Instituto Juan March de Estudios e Investigaciones Estudio/ Working Paper* No.71.
Eurostat (1996a), *Demographic Statistics 1996*. Luxembourg: Office for Official Publications of the European Communities.
Eurostat (1996b), *Statistiques en bref: population et conditions sociales,* No.3, Luxembourg: Office for Official Publications of the European Communities.
Guillén, A.M. (1992), 'Social Policy in Spain: From Dictatorship to Democracy (1939-1982)', in Ferge, Z. and Kolberg, J.E. (eds), *Social Policy in a Changing Europe*, Frankfurt am Main and Boulder (Colorado): Campus Verlag and Westview Press.

Guillén, A.M. (1996), 'Citizenship and Social Policy in Democratic Spain: the Reformulation of the Francoist Welfare State', *South European Society and Politics* Vol.1:253-271.
Guillén, A.M. (forthcoming), 'Regímenes de bienestar y roles familiares: un análisis del caso español', *Papers: Revista de Sociología.*
INE [Instituto Nacional de Estadística] (1994), *Censos de Población y Viviendas 1991, características generales de la población, tomo I, resultados nacionales*, Madrid, INE.
INE (1995), *Movimiento natural de la población española 1992, tomo I, resultados a nivel nacional y su distribución por provincias y capitales*, Madrid: INE.
INE (1996), *Encuesta de Población Activa: Resultados detallados, segundo semestre 1996*, Madrid: INE.
INSERSO (1995a) *Cuidados en la vejez: el apoyo informal*, Madrid: Ministerio de Asuntos Sociales.
INSERSO (1995b), *Las personas mayores en España: perfiles, reciprocidad familiar*, Madrid: Ministerio de Asuntos Sociales.
Jimeno, J.F. (1993), 'La reforma del mercado de trabajo: caminando (lentamente) en la dirección adecuada', *Cuadernos de Información Económica* No.80-81:31-39.
Langan, M. and Ostner, I. (1991), 'Gender and Welfare: Towards a Comparative Framework', in Room, G. (ed), *Towards a European Welfare State?* Bristol: School for Advanced Urban Studies, University of Bristol.
Lewis, J. (1992), 'Gender and the Development of Welfare Regimes', *Journal of European Social Policy* Vol.2:159-173.
Martín Serrano, M. (1996a), *Informe Juventud en España 1996: avance de resultados (septiembre 1996)*, Madrid: Instituto de la Juventud.
Martín Serrano, M. (1996b), *Informe Juventud en España 1996: primer avance de resultados*, Madrid: Instituto de la Juventud.
Mazur, A.G. (1992), 'Symbolic Reform in France: Egalité Professionnelle during the Mitterrand Years', *West European Politics* Vol.15:39-56.
MEC [Ministerio de Educación y Ciencia] (1995), *Estadística de la enseñanza en España 1992/1993: educación infantil/preescolar, General Básica/primaria y enseñanzas medias/enseñanza secundaria*, Madrid: MEC.
MEH [Ministerio de Economía y Hacienda] (1995), *Memoria de la Administración Tributaria 1994*, Madrid: MEH.
Meyer, T. (1994), 'The German and British Welfare States as Employers: Patriarchal or Emancipatory', in Sainsbury, G. (ed), *Gendering Welfare States*, 62-81. London: Sage.
Missé, A. (1997), 'El espejismo de la reforma laboral', *El País* 10 febrero:64-65.
MTAS [Ministerio de Trabajo y Asuntos Sociales] (1996), *Anuario de Estadísticas Laborales y de Asuntos Sociales 1995*, Madrid: MTAS.
MTAS (1997), *Boletín de Estadísticas Laborales* No.140 (January).

MTSS [Ministerio de Trabajo y Seguridad Social] (1995), *La política de empleo en España: informe de base sobre instituciones, procedimientos y medidas de política de empleo*, Madrid: MTSS.

O'Connor, J.S. (1993) 'Labor Market Participation in Liberal Welfare State Regimes: Dual Breadwinning without Dual Breadwinner Social Policy Frameworks.' Paper presented at the International Sociological Association Research Committee 19 Workshop on Comparative Research on Welfare States in Transition, University of Oxford, 9-12 September.

OECD [Organization for Economic Cooperation and Development] (1994), *Employment Outlook*, July 1994, Paris: OECD.

Orloff, A.S. (1993), 'Gender and the Social Rights of Citizenship: the Comparative Analysis of Gender and Welfare States', *American Sociological Review* Vol.58:303-328.

Pérez-Díaz, V. and Rodríguez, J.C. (1994), 'Inertial Choices: Spanish Human Resources Policies and Practices (1959-1993)', *Analistas Socio-Políticos/Research Paper* No.2(b).

Piore, M.J. (1971) 'The Dual Labor Market: Theory and Implications', in Gordon, D.M. (ed), *Problems in Political Economy: an Urban Prospective*, Lexington, Massachusetts: D.C. Heath.

Rodríguez, J.A. (1994), *Envejecimiento y familia*, Madrid: Centro de Investigaciones Sociológicas and Siglo XXI.

Ruesga, S.M. (1991), 'Las otras trabajadoras: un análisis de la participación femenina no registrada en la actividad económica', *Revista de Economía y Sociología del Trabajo*, No.13-14:114-128.

Ruggie, M. (1984), *The State and Working Women: A Comparative Study of Britain and Sweden*, Princeton, New Jersey: Princeton University Press.

Saéz, C. (1994), *Mujeres y mercado de trabajo: las discriminaciones directas e indirectas*, Madrid: CES.

Sainsbury, D. (ed.) (1994), *Gendering Welfare Regimes*, London: Sage.

Stetson, D.M. and Mazur, A.G. (eds) (1995), *Comparative State Feminism*, Thousand Oaks (California): Sage.

Valiente, C. (1994), *Políticas públicas para la mujer trabajadora en Italia y España, 1900-1991*, Madrid: Centro de Estudios Avanzados en Ciencias Sociales, Instituto Juan March de Estudios e Investigaciones.

Valiente, C. (1995) 'Children First: Central Government Child Care Policies in Post-Authoritarian Spain (1975-1994)', in Brannen, J. and O'Brian, M., *Childhood and Parenthood: Proceedings of ISA Committee for Family Research Conference on Children and Families, 1994*, London: Institute of Education.

Wilkinson, F. (ed) (1981), *The Dynamics of Labor Market Segmentation*, London: Academic Press.

11 Changing patterns and practices of (un)employment and the Swedish welfare state

Johanna Esseveld

Introduction

There seems to be agreement amongst social scientists and lay people alike that patterns of work and working life are changing so radically that we need to rethink (and reconceptualise) our ideas about work, employment and unemployment.[1] There also seems to be some agreement that levels of unemployment will remain high and that less permanent, more 'flexible' work practices are gaining ground. However, there is no agreement on what other outcomes of these processes of change there will be. Whereas some have suggested that changes in patterns of work and employment practices will lead to more horizontal and vertical integration at the workplace, and thereby, to greater equality between workers and salaried employees, others have suggested that there will be further polarisation between different categories of workers and between the employed and unemployed. Formal education, work qualifications and work experience (particularly as they relate to technical know-how) have been suggested as important sources of social division in the future, separating those who will belong to the core workforce and those on the periphery. I tend to agree with the latter point of view and would add to this stratification list that women and men will be affected differently by any such changes, since political and economic power structures are always gendered. The same can be said for recent immigrants. From this I conclude that social relations of gender and ethnicity need to be considered as an integral part of an analysis of emerging employment patterns and possible processes of polarisation and marginalisation.

In this paper I examine (un)employment patterns in Sweden on the basis of the results from a number of different research projects carried out by myself and Karen Davies, a colleague at Lund university between 1982 and 1994.[2] Our

1 See, for example, Allen et al, 1986, Brown, 1984, Purcell, 1985, Purcell et al, 1986, Pollert, 1990 and recent issues of the journals *Arbetsmarknad och arbetsliv*, *Scandinavian Journal of Social Welfare*.

2 The projects referred to are respectively 'Unemployment and Identity. A study of women outside the labour market during the 1980s' (funded by the Council for the Humanities and the Social Sciences and the Delegation for Social Research), 'Women, unemployment and the grey area of the labour market' (funded by the Department of Labour) and 'Temporary Employment and its Relation to Flexibility' (received funding

earlier research centred on women's experiences of unemployment and movement in the labour market. Later work focused on forms of temporary employment and their relation to (un)employment. The results of these studies are presented in different sections of this paper. Much of this presentation remains descriptive, but I believe that the framework which I present here can further an understanding of contemporary changes in patterns of work and working life.

Instead of focusing on *unemployment per se* and its effects on individuals or juxtaposing unemployment and employment, I suggest a framework where the *complex* – and continuously changing – *interrelation* between permanent employment, temporary forms of employment and unemployment are given a central position. Such a framework allows us to follow changes in patterns of work and working life, changes in patterns of (un)employment as well as processes of differentiation and polarisation. Implicit in this framework is an assumption that such patterns and processes are embedded in contexts. Such contexts are global, national and local in nature. Important here are the general changes in economic growth and the economic crisis that characterise most Western countries. Also important is the more specific context of Swedish social practices and the particular form and content given to social policies in the Swedish welfare state. Thus, where some of the changes in (un)employment patterns can be seen as the result of economic and industrial restructuring (as part of global economic and political change) others are closely linked to the particular form(s) the relation between the welfare state and the labour market has taken in Sweden. The welfare state, in its dual role of employer and provider and implementer of social welfare, in fact hastens or cushions – and possibly even counters – the effects of the changes referred to.

Unemployment and identity

The project 'Unemployment and Identity' was carried out in the early and mid 1980s and occurred in a period marked by – in international comparison – relatively low unemployment in Sweden. The unemployment rate remained under 3% partly as a result of the extensive use of publicly funded programmes. Unemployment levels among women, and in particular among the relatively less-educated and immigrant women, however, were higher than among men in absolute as well as relative numbers.[3] Women's unemployment, however was little discussed in the social science literature of the time. Swedish research centred on the consequences of plant closures, youth unemployment and the psychological and physical consequences of unemployment.[4] Women's unemployment was made

from the Work Environment Fund). The research projects were carried out from 1982 through 1994.

3 See Davies & Esseveld, 1985, for statistical comparisons between unemployment levels by sex, age, branch of industry.

4 Three areas have elicited particular attention in Swedish studies on structural change: changes in employment patterns and the mobility of the work force (See e.g. Gonäs,

invisible in these studies in different ways; women were either not included in the study population, or were a small – invisible – minority in analyses of male-dominated workplaces. When these studies included women, their special situation was not problematised and it was often analysed according to 'traditional' models, where paid work is seen as the opposite of unpaid work and given a particular content.

In the few cases that women were specifically mentioned the assumption was made that unemployment did not affect them in the same way as it did men, as their roles as housewife, mother and homemaker were said to offer sufficient satisfaction. In one book, concerning the psychological consequences of unemployment, the suggestion was made that 'Women in general experience a weaker effect than men, probably because work outside the home isn't part of their traditional gender role in the same way as for men. They can always maintain respect from their environment through their (unpaid) work in the home'. (Oveson, 1978, p.55). We argued that such a statement may have reflected women's experience in more traditional societies where few women worked for pay, but could not go unquestioned (or at least should be made the basis for further study) in Sweden where more than 80% of women between the ages of 20 and 64 worked for pay.

In the research project, we used a particular perspective which combines the individuals' experiences with an analysis of social relations. This perspective was inspired by the Canadian sociologist Dorothy Smith. Smith takes her starting point in the everyday world of women and then moves to the social relations that structure the everyday world.[5] This choice of perspective meant presuming women to be agents, i.e., subjects who actively reflect on their lives, but also that their reflections, decisions and actions are not made 'freely'. Rather, they are structured by constraints such as prior life experience, prevailing ideologies, actual life situations, as well as social relations of gender, class and ethnicity. In our research then, we wished to describe and analyse women's experiences as well as unravel the social relations which influenced these experiences.

As a first step in our study on unemployment we went out in the field and tried to understand the meaning of unemployment at the individual level, i.e., as it was experienced by the women themselves. We centred on experiences of employment, loss of job and unemployment and the attempt to (re)find work. In our analysis we combined the women's descriptions with an analysis of the con-

1988, Lundmark & Malmberg, 1988, Nilsson, 1988); the relation between structural change and unemployment as well as the individual consequences of unemployment, (see e.g. Angelöw, 1988, Berglind, 1988, Davies & Esseveld, 1988a) and the relation between changes in production and technology and the altered demand for a more skilled and more highly trained and educated labour force (see e.g. Björkman & Lundquist, 1986, Nilsson, 1988).

5 This theoretical perspective is inspired by Dorothy Smith's writings, but it was given its specific content as developed through research and our own reflections on questions of theory and method.

straints on their attempts to find work.[6] We also studied their movement in the labour market and processes of marginalisation (and placement outside of the formal labour market and dependency on welfare state benefits) that followed longer periods of unemployment.

Our assumption that experience is embedded in a web of social relations meant that we included different structural contexts and how these (may have) influenced the women's experiences. One such context included family, community and the local labour market, another was national and included changes in the Swedish labour market and welfare state policy. Global changes were not explicitly discussed in our analyses.

The study was qualitative and longitudinal in nature. The methods used were participant observation and in-depth interviewing. We re-interviewed the same women at least three times over a period of about three years following redundancy and/or unemployment. We also carried out a sub-study in a food processing plant, where we followed decisions on redundancy and the complicated web of principles used in making these decisions. In a book entitled *Playing Hopscotch in the Swedish Labour Market (Att hoppa hage på den svenska arbetsmarknaden*, 1988) we showed that social relations of gender and ethnicity were implicitly included in these decisions – even if this was not the explicit intention.[7] The result of these negotiations was that of the fourth of the workforce that was made redundant, nearly all were women and most of them immigrant women, many with young children.

In the book, as well as the larger study, we not only examined the processes leading up to redundancy and its implementation, we also followed closely (for a period of nearly three years) the family and work histories of the women workers who lost their jobs.[8] The majority of women we studied were unsuccessful in gaining a permanent footing in the labour market and a few eventually left the formal labour market all together. Most of the women were in some form of

6 While we concentrated on the women, the analysis included a number of different levels: interactional aspects, local and national labour markets as well as the limits and opportunities provided by welfare state policies. One barrier we paid special attention to was in the women's interaction with unemployment officers and employers.

7 According to the Employment Protection Act (1974, 1982) an employer may not freely choose whom he wishes to make redundant when there is not sufficient work. Rather, he is obliged to follow the principle of seniority so that those workers who have joined the work place last should be the first to lose their jobs. However, this principle may be by-passed if a collective agreement is made at the local level permitting a different ranking concerning who is to be laid off. This latter clause was utilised at the factory. Management and unions agreed first on the group of older workers – which by necessity meant by-passing the rule of 'last in-first out' as most had worked at the factory for many years – and then negotiated about the other group of workers. In these negotiations the following principles were used: length of employment, level of skill, short-term leave (for illness and sick children) long-term leave (i.e. leave for study, long-term sickness but also parental leave) as well as 'how a worker gets along with other workers'.

8 See Davies & Esseveld, 1984, 1985, 1988, 1989, 1990 for analyses of the women's experiences of unemployment and temporary forms of employment, as well as their strategies to find work.

temporary employment or unemployed at the end of the three year period. Independently of whether they had re-found permanent employment, were unemployed, in governmental training programmes or temporarily employed at the end of this three-year period, all moved between different forms of temporary employment, governmental programmes and unemployment during the three-year period in which our study took place.

I illustrate below one such pattern of movement through a brief presentation of the work (and family) history of one of the women made redundant from the food-processing factory, Nevia.

Nevia's story

Nevia moved to Sweden from Southern Europe with her family when she was ten. She left school before the official leaving age and at fifteen she began working in a clothing factory. A few years later the factory shut down and she became unemployed. Shortly afterwards she gave birth to her first child. After a year's parental leave Nevia started looking for work. This was in 1978 and she had no difficulty finding work. Factory jobs were available and Nevia chose to start at a local food processing factory, since it allowed her to work evenings and solved her child-care problems. She was in her early twenties when she was laid off from the food factory in a period of economic downturn.

Following redundancy, Nevia spent the first months going to the employment exchange and unsuccessfully looking for work. After a few months of unemployment she was re-employed – but now on a temporary basis – at the food processing factory (from which she had earlier been laid off). The company needed temporary workers as the installation of some new machinery had been delayed. Prior to being offered temporary work, Nevia had become pregnant and at the end of a three-month period of work, she was not offered new employment. This contrasted with the situation of other workers taken on at the same time, who were subsequently offered different temporary jobs over a longer period of time.[9] Nevia became unemployed until the birth of her second child and took *parental leave from her unemployment* insurance.

Towards the end of her parental leave and with the threat of renewed unemployment on the horizon, Nevia contacted a number of clothing factories and landed a *temporary* job. This job was made possible by a labour market scheme

9 For example, Marica, another woman who had also been made redundant from the factory earlier, continued to work there on a temporary basis, accepting whatever work came up for a period of approximately two years. This meant that she was ensured work for shorter period of time, e.g. two or three months at a time and that during these two years, she constantly switched jobs. She also switched between day-time and evening, between working in the factory itself and the warehouse on the edge of the town, between working full-time and part-time, between working on the line and doing cleaning. In other words, she showed a great amount of flexibility and accommodation during this period (in the hope of getting renewed employment).

set up to help the unemployed to find employment. For a period of time (six months) a large part of her wage would be paid by the labour market authorities – after this period it was hoped that she would be employed on a regular basis. At first the job went well, indeed on several occasions during earlier interviews, Nevia expressed her wish to work in a clothing factory again (she had much preferred her first job to the job at the food factory). But after a while Nevia began experiencing problems at work and after further 'warnings' she was psychologically unable to continue working.

Nevia asked to be given another job at the factory but management answered that there were no openings. She therefore felt forced to leave the job. Nevia thus returned to the employment exchange. At the end of a three-year period she was unemployed and contemplating becoming a child-minder but had not yet contacted the local authorities about possible employment. Nevia thus moved from a permanent job to a continuous wandering between unemployment and different types of temporary jobs – one of them provided through state policy – during the three years.

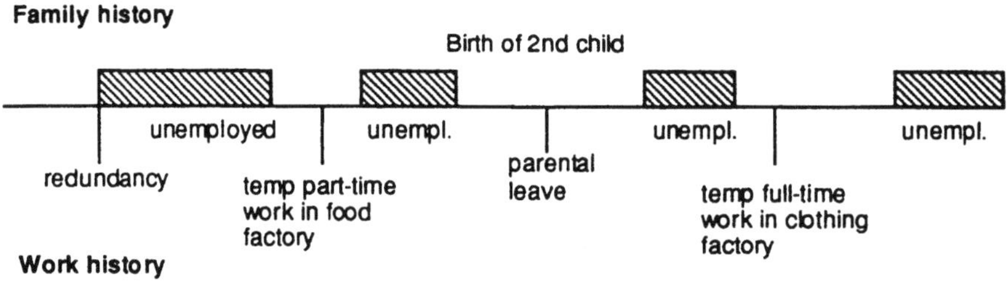

Figure 11.1: Nevia's experience of unemployment and subsequent movement in the labour market[10]

Nevia's experience pivots upon the ways in which gender, class and ethnicity combined to influence her past choices in terms of education, training and jobs. As is well documented, in a sex- segregated labour market women are pushed into a small number of occupations. Not surprisingly, Nevia chose both the clothing industry and the food processing industry which depend heavily on unskilled female labour and where economic restructuring has left its mark. The loss of her first job was due to the near eradication of the textile and clothing industry in Sweden. The loss of her job at the food processing factory was also due to the effects of structural change, but that just she was selected for redundancy was the result of a complicated web of processes.

Nevia had been among the last to be employed. But she also had been on sick leave both for herself and for her child, which was a contributory factor. And, lastly, she was an immigrant. After working for a while at the factory, she had

10 Nevia's family and work history is not on scale and is to be used as illustration only.

asked to change jobs, feeling unaccepted by the other workers on the line (cf. Cavendish, 1982). Nevia asked to be transferred to the cleaning section, where she could work alongside other women from her home country. While she was pleased with this move, it also ensured her 'invisibility' in an immigrant group. When the redundancies were enforced, her cleaning job was not rationalised away but she was replaced by a Swedish women who had been at the factory for a shorter period than she had, but whose 'contact with all the foremen was very good and they saw to it that she stayed', as Nevia put it.

In her periods of unemployment, she made considerable effort to find work. Two factors made her unattractive labour at a time when employers had a large pool of workers from whom they could choose those they wished to employ. On the one hand, she had two young children by this time. Liberal Swedish legislation as regards care of sick children makes employers wary of employing women with young children. On the other hand, Nevia gave several examples where employers had made it clear that they were uninterested in employing immigrants. A quotation from a personnel manager at the food processing factory, who was re-interviewed three years after the redundancies and just after a period of extensive re-hiring, will illustrate this particular company's view of the matter:

> ... of those applicants I give a job to, I require that they can speak and make themselves understood in Swedish relatively well ... for their own sake. Otherwise, they are jeered or called names. Those who we've taken on now fit in perfectly in the work-groups, and not just here, but in Sweden as a whole. They've adapted to the Swedish culture.

The first requirement that a worker should speak Swedish relatively well is perhaps justified, although it is interesting to put this in an historical perspective and note that it was unimportant in the 1970s, when there was a shortage of labour. It seems justified to conclude that the language requirement is used to keep out certain workers in times of economic downturn. The second requirement is more subtle. It is not *language per se* but the acceptance of certain cultural values that influences one's chance of finding work. To be hired, a worker has to fit the expectations of other, namely Swedish, workers, and accept 'Swedish' culture, whatever that may be.

While Nevia's experience of unemployment and short-term employment is, of course, specific to her situation, the pattern that emerges was found again and again among other working class – and immigrant – women in our study.[11] For all the women made redundant at the factory we studied, lower levels of education and formal training, the lack of language proficiency for some of the immigrant women, and a continued search for work in a very limited area of the labour market, made it difficult to find work. The type of jobs they had held during the 1970s were no longer available in the 1980s. Jobs in the manufacturing industry

11 This pattern was also found among women with higher education and in jobs with relatively high levels of unemployment such as journalists, social workers.

were disappearing in the local labour market, at the same time as there were fewer job opportunities in the care sector. The jobs offered were often not permanent or did not provide the sufficient number of hours they required. During this period, the number of people looking for work within traditional women's jobs rose drastically. Similar developments characterised the national labour market. In this type of labour market minority/immigrant women in particular experienced difficulties in finding work. During the mid-1980s for example, unemployment levels among this group of women were more than two and a half times as high as that of Swedish women in the region where we carried out our study. This was a situation that was to continue and to weaken their position even further over the next decade.

While most of the women in our study made considerable efforts to find work, they experienced difficulty in securing *permanent employment*. This did not mean, however, that they were unemployed for the period of our study, rather redundancy/unemployment was followed by a complex patchwork of short periods of temporary employment, substitute work, relief work, labour market training programmes, intermittent unemployment and other moments, such as re-education, parental leave and sick leave. Many of the women who had earlier worked in private sector industry found temporary employment in the public sector and were thus living under the continuous threat of renewed unemployment. A few eventually left the labour market altogether.

At the time we carried out our first study in the early 1980s, few had studied the relation between different forms of employment and unemployment and even fewer had studied the movement of individuals in the labour market. Since then however, some studies have followed the results of these qualitative projects and carried out similar analyses on a larger scale. Lena Gonäs' (1988) analysis of the extensive data from the STOP project at the Swedish Centre for Working Life provides evidence of similar patterns of movement and suggests important implications for gender relations. In this study, approx. 3,400 individuals (made redundant from 17 companies when closures or cut-backs were implemented) were followed over a two-year period. Gonäs reports that, at the end of the study, only 47% had found *permanent* employment. The remainder experienced what Gonäs calls 'permanent temporariness'. In breaking down these figures according to sex, she found that 60% of the men had found permanent employment, while the figure for the women was only 35%.

Below I will present some statistics on temporary employment. After this I will continue by suggesting how we should reconceptualise patterns of (un)-employment.

Temporary employment

The term temporary employment covers a wide variety of different categories: employment for a trial period, substituting for others, hourly employment, youth placement, seasonal work, project employment, government-created work schemes and relief work. It can consist of work that is the result of a labour market programme and employment that is provided by 'regular employers' (including the state and local authorities).

Temporary employment is often defined in contrast to work of 'indefinite' duration (Nätti, 1993) and varies considerably in how casual or permanent it is. It may consist of working one day per month at a hospital (belonging to a pool of casual workers from which an organisation chooses workers as required) or of working for many years at the same workplace in a string of different temporary positions – as a social worker or teacher, for example. In practical terms, the former is more closely linked to (repeated) periods of unemployment over time and to weakened social insurance rights and benefits. The latter may approximate a permanent job – at least in the sense of job continuity – but other disadvantages may be attached, which should not be overlooked. Long term sickness or injury on the job for those hired under any of the forms of temporary employment will often lead to the termination of such temporary employment, when a contract runs out instead of being renewed.

In 1987, the Swedish labour market statistics (AKU) added, for the first time, data concerning the degree of attachment to the labour market.[12] These statistics give a clear indication that gender plays a role in considerations of temporary employment. A higher percentage of women than men are temporarily employed and women made up around 60% of those temporarily employed since 1987.[13]

A comparison of the extent of temporary employment by sex and age shows that, for all ages, temporary work is higher among women than men. As expected, temporary employment is particularly prevalent among *young people* who have not, as yet, established themselves in the labour market. In 1987 the figure was 63% for young women between 16 and 24 while the figure for young men was 45%. For 1991, the figures had dropped to 56% for girls and 44% for boys, to rise again for 1995. In 1987, 26% of young women between 20 and 24 held temporary jobs; the equivalent figure for young men was 20%. In 1991, these had changed to 26,5% and 16% respectively. In Table 11.1 (in Appendix) the percentage of those temporarily employed is calculated in relation to those permanently employed for the years 1987, 1991 and 1995. This table shows not only that temporary employment is high for the age group between 16 and 24, but that for 1995 more young women are in temporary employment than in permanent employment. The table also shows a steady rise in temporary employment for all age groups and that the statistics are higher for women than men in all age groups.

Even if the figures show that temporary work is a phenomenon that is particularly characteristic of young people's lives, it is also important to draw

12 In the Swedish labour force surveys a broad definition of the concept of temporary workers is used. It includes wage and salary earners who are substitutes (replacing an absent worker), on trial, on 'stand by' or in seasonal work, in special youth programmes, in apprenticeship, in project work or in other kinds of casual work but excludes the self-employed.

13 There are some slight fluctuations: i.e., women made up 60% of all temporary workers in 1987; 63% in 1991 and 58% in 1995.

attention to the fact that approx. one in ten women on the Swedish labour market work in temporary jobs. As is well known, Sweden's labour market is highly sex-segregated (Jonung, 1989). In 1985, 56% of working women between 16 and 64 were employed in the public sector, mainly by local and county authorities. A large percentage of those employed in the public sector are temporary workers and many work part-time and under uncertain conditions. Related to occupation, temporary work is common in skilled public sector occupations, where temporary workers are often substitutes (teaching, health care and social service) or replace others in less-skilled, private service-occupations (catering, housekeeping and cleaning) or in male-dominated agricultural and forestry work. The figures for temporary employment in all occupations dominated by women are above the average for temporary employment. The exception is secretarial/office work where only 9% of women were employed on a short-term basis in 1987 and 7% for 1991. In some occupations, such as workers in care occupations, hotel and restaurant workers, as well as child-care workers the percentages are alarmingly high. Nearly one in four women working in some of the care held a temporary position in 1987 and slightly over one in five in 1991. The AKU-figures in relation to occupation and area of work, indicate differences regarding sex, but differences with regard to ethnicity and class cannot be deduced from these statistics. As indicated above, our previous research would lead us to expect particularly high figures of temporary employment among immigrants. An examination of the 'degree of attachment' statistics by occupation would also suggest this. The degree of temporary work is lower in secretarial/office work, which is the most common occupation among Swedish women. Immigrant women are found most predominantly in the cleaning trade (Leiniö, 1988), where temporary work is higher. The statistics on employment status by sex, ethnicity and age also support this suggestion. These statistics indicate that temporary employment is higher for immigrant women in all age groups.

A comparison of figures on temporary employment between 1987 and 1995 shows that there was a shift in the percentage of those temporarily employed between these years. (Table 11.2 in Appendix.) Again there are differences by sex. For women the shifts are from 13% of the total labour force for 1987, down to 11,5 % for 1991 and up again, to 14% for 1995. For men, the figures are 9%, 7% and 10% for 1987, 1991 and 1995 respectively. Temporary forms of employment initiated through public funds were not included in these statistics, however. Even these vary. During the late 1970s and early 1980s, for example, labour market policy programmes were expanded in order to prevent an increase in registered unemployment. While unemployment levels rose only slightly during this period, they remained at a low level compared to other countries, like Great Britain. During the same period, adults in government sponsored programmes of relief work, temporary employment and vocational training more than doubled and surpassed the official statistics on unemployment. In 1989, when unemployment was extremely low in Sweden, the percentage of people in government programmes of the total labour force reached a low of 1%. By 1995 the percentage of people in such programmes had risen to 7% of the total labour force.

Adding the rates of unemployment to the rates of temporary employment and government programmes provides us with an even more interesting picture.[14]

Table 11.3
Percentage of those permanently employed, temporarily employed, unemployed and those in government programmes for 1987, 1989, 1991, 1993 and 1995

Year	Permanently employed	Temporarily employed	In government progr.	Unemployed	In sum
1987	84%	10%	4%	2%	4 147
1989	88%	10%	1%	1%	4 193
1991	84%	8%	4%	4%	4 265
1993	75%	10%	7%	8%	4 106
1995	74%	11%	7%	8%	4 089

Sources: AKU-statistics for dec 1987, 1989, 1991, 1993 and 1995

This table reveals a number of changes which took place between 1987 and 1995. One such change is the radical reduction of the number of persons in permanent employment (from 88% for 1989 to 74% for 1995); another is the rise in levels of unemployment (from 2% in 1989 to a record low of 1% in 1989 and up again to reach 8% for 1995). The percentage of persons in government programmes rose from 1% in 1989 to 7% in 1995. The table also shows that the rate of those temporarily employed remained relatively stable during these years at 10% of the total labour force, with the exception of 1991 where the percentage of those temporarily employed was 8%.

But while the table gives us some insight into changes over time, it is also important to point out that it provides a *static* picture – i.e., it is impossible to estimate just how many persons moved between unemployment, temporary employment and permanent employment for these years. It is also impossible to estimate whether there are those who can be called *core-temporary workers* – i.e., rotating from temporary job to temporary job or whether there is a flow from temporary employment to unemployment (or permanent employment) and vice versa. But results from the qualitative research projects mentioned above seem to indicate that movement between (and within) these categories is quite common.

There are other aspects that are missing in my presentation so far. The discussion only relates to forms of (un)employment in the *formal labour market*, thus other forms of work, in e.g. the informal sector and unpaid work, while important,

14 As statistics on persons in government programmes are not available by sex I cannot present the statistics where those permanently employed, temporarily employed, unemployed and persons in government programmes are compared by sex.

have been left aside. In relation to the informal economy, it is difficult to offer firm conclusions on the basis of these figures; still the slight decrease in the total number of persons in the labour force over this almost ten-year period seems to indicate that more adults are *outside of the labour market* and either permanently relieved from having to seek employment, not anchored in any of the insurance benefit schemes and/or participating in the *informal economy* for example by *working on the side, exchanging services* and *scavenging* (Wallace and Pahl, 1986). It is possible, of course, to be both permanently employed, temporarily employed and working in the informal economy or to be both unemployed and participating in the informal economy at the same time.

So far, I have limited myself to a presentation of statistics on permanent employment, temporary forms of employment and unemployment. Statistics for part-time work were not included, nor are education and government-sponsored training programmes or sick leave and parental leave. Their inclusion would make for even more intricate patterns, as well as help clarify movements of individuals and groups – inside and outside the labour market.[15]

In what follows, I will take up the thread presented in the introduction and suggest that if we wish to make these intricate patterns and relations visible, we need to move beyond more traditional ways of conceptualising patterns of (un)employment.

Toward a reconceptualisation of employment/unemployment

In the introduction to this paper I suggested that there is agreement among social scientists that patterns of employment/unemployment are changing and that much attention has been given to more flexible forms of employment. The movement in the labour market of particular groups of people and the difficulties that some have to (re)gain more permanent positions are also fairly well accepted today. Interestingly enough however, much of the research in this area still makes use of rather traditional conceptualisations. In these frameworks, unemployment and employment are considered as clearly defined and dichotomous categories; in

15 Of the factory women made redundant, many were not unemployed on the first day after finishing at the factory. Some were on sick-leave prior to redundancy and this continued for a period after they were laid off. On their 'first day of unemployment' then, they collected sickness benefit rather than unemployment benefit. Some were on study leave at the time of the redundancies and were living on study grants. They became registered as unemployed temporarily during the holidays and on completing their education. One woman was, for example, eight months pregnant and was collecting pregnancy leave money on her 'first day of unemployment'. Furthermore, another woman who was made redundant had not been at the factory for a year and a half prior to the redundancies. She had been on parental leave and should have returned before the lay-offs. However, difficulties in obtaining local government child care had delayed her return – by which time the redundancies had been implemented.

addition, the content and type of employment (i.e., type of contract, full-time/part-time) are not problematised.[16]

Employment and unemployment, in other words, are used as defining concepts and the array of their meaning and content is not explored. In studies of unemployment, individuals are asked (after a period of time) whether they have found new employment or not. It is not specified whether such work is temporary in nature or whether it covers the number of hours they sought. Less permanent types of employment, as well as part-time employment, are lost in these studies. By not problematising the nature of employment, these studies have difficulty in visualising a possible movement in the labour market that may follow unemployment, as well as the fact that a particular period of unemployment may not have been the first one. Most of the women in our study of unemployment and identity had been unemployed before, even though, for some of them, a long period of time had passed between their last period of unemployment and their present one. Some of the women had never held a permanent position in their years in the labour market and had moved from one short-term temporary position to another, with intermittent periods of unemployment.

Some further reflections on the changing relations of (un)employment

In the introduction I suggested that changes in (un)employment patterns need to be contextualised. By this I mean that the forms these changes take in different countries depend on the particular type of welfare state, as well as the functioning of the labour market and the particular relationship between market and state. I also suggested that due to the gendered nature of the labour market and the welfare state, attachment to the labour market and patterns of movement between temporary employment, permanent employment and unemployment as well as movement from one form of temporary employment to another, differ for men and women and for Swedes and immigrants. This, in turn, influences the experience of unemployment and labour market movement.

Whereas there seems to be a trend towards higher levels of unemployment and more atypical forms of employment[17] in all Western societies, patterns and types of employment differ due, among other things, to differences in welfare state policies and intervention. Until the late 1980s, the breadth of Swedish welfare state policies has helped make it possible – despite changes in international capital – to keep unemployment levels relatively low. However, one side-effect has been the higher levels of non-permanent forms of employment and also that

16 This position is found in an otherwise excellent article on unemployment. (See Therborn, 1995).

17 See 'Temporary Work in Britain' (1985) with reference to catering, cleaning, manual occupations and office work, Bernstein (1986) for the casualisation of labour, Coyle (1985) for the sub-contracting of labour, Allen & Wilkowitz (1986) for work in the home and Huws (1984) for other forms of 'outwork' and Caire (1982) for a presentation of the situation in France.

part-time work and different forms of work sponsored by public funds have been more widespread in Sweden than in other countries. During the early 1990s – and until 1995 – active labour market intervention expanded even more.

In addition to policies that are aimed at bringing down unemployment levels, some of the labour and family policies mentioned earlier are of relevance to this discussion about Swedish patterns. Liberal policies in Sweden allow the individual various forms of leave of absence from (*permanent*) employment. This includes parental leave for up to one and a half years after child birth, study leave for longer periods of time, leave to take another job, and so on. Furthermore, parents with children under eight years of age are entitled to reduce their workday to six hours (and be able to return to full-time when desired). Such leave creates job vacancies, which are obviously temporary in nature. Liberal legislation, together with 'market-inspired' employment patterns, thus provides the soil for an elaborate system of temporary work. One could say that a special Swedish form of temporary employment has developed with the aid of labour market policies.

Conclusion

Against the background of the particular context of the Swedish labour market and welfare state, I have attempted to provide a conceptual framework which might help us understand the changing face(s) of employment and unemployment in contemporary Swedish society. In this framework, unemployment and employment are not considered as clearly defined and dichotomous categories, but as situated on a continuum where different forms of employment are included. This framework evolved out of a number of qualitative studies on unemployment carried out during the 1980s in the southern part of Sweden. In the second part of the paper, I presented some statistics about the changing relation between different forms of employment and unemployment at a national level. I do think that this particular way of conceptualising (un)employment patterns can be used to analyse these patterns in other countries. Because of the specific nature of the Swedish context, I earlier emphasised the question of temporary employment, in terms of both 'ordinary' jobs and government-created schemes. The prevalence of more temporary forms of employment is not restricted to Sweden however. Let me end by pointing out some more general trends which may make the 'Swedish example' more generally applicable.

Studies from Great Britain (e.g. *Temporary Work in Britain,* 1985) suggest that temporary work is on the increase, especially in such jobs as catering, cleaning and office work; the types of jobs that are most frequently filled by women. Traditionally, temporary workers have been used to cover holidays, sickness and seasonal work but it would appear that their use is expanding in order to reduce costs and help provide employers with increased flexibility.

Another change in the labour market is the move towards 'privatisation': work that earlier performed by the public or state sector is now being sub-contracted out to private firms. A well-known attempt at privatisation in Britain is the NHS putting hospital cleaning, catering and laundry services out to tender (see Coyle, 1985). Colin Gill (1988) links privatisation to the ability of small specialist groups in the service sector to 'run themselves more tightly'. While privatisation may not necessarily result in 'movement' in the labour market, as I presented it above, it raises questions concerning positions in the labour market. The privatisation of cleaning in many Swedish cities has led to a deterioration in pay and working conditions for the (mainly women and immigrant) workers and has meant that the workers lost many of the benefits associated with being a state employee.

A further international trend, linked to the above, is the 'casualisation' of labour. This term refers to the fact that certain types of labour are made casual so that workers/employees lose a degree of security in income and employment. This may involve sub-contracting as in the examples above but it takes place in the private sector as well as in the public sector. Deborah Bernstein (1986) has looked at the transition to sub-contracting in the case of cleaning work as it took place in Israel. For employers, it cut costs and was a way of finding new sources of labour. For the cleaners, it meant an intensification of labour and affected their wages and benefits.

Lastly, another trend is a professionalisation of jobs and occupations. While there has been considerable debate on reskilling and deskilling, little attention has been paid to women's 'ordinary' jobs. One example illustrates what I mean. The job of 'nursing auxiliary' (vårdbiträde) disappeared from the care sector in Sweden and the lowest position in the hospital hierarchy is now that of staff nurse (undersköterska). This profession requires two-years' training, while the former required only a twenty-week course, and jobs could often be found in this field without any training at all. This development has implications for women workers such as those presented on these pages, i.e. those who are less qualified and looking for unskilled work. There was considerable resistance among the women interviewed to formal education and training, especially if it was long-term. Thus, while these auxiliary jobs in the care sector earlier absorbed some of the women made redundant from the manufacturing industry, changing educational demands for such work will, in effect, exclude certain workers and reduce their choice of work areas – which is already limited by the sex (and ethnic) segregated labour market.

If there is now a general trend towards an expansion of temporary work and increased professionalisation, it is reasonable to assume that women with little formal education and vocational training will continue to move within and between various forms of temporary employment and unemployment on tomorrow's labour market. It is also reasonable to assume that similar patterns of movement will apply to other groups with a more marginal position in the labour market, such as recent immigrants. For some, these patterns of movement can be expected to lead to marginalisation and to positions outside of the formal labour market.

References

Acker, J. (1993), 'Reformer och kvinnor i den framtida välfärdsstaten', in Acker, J. et al. (eds), *Kvinnors och mäns liv och arbete*, Stockholm.

AKU (Arbetskraftsundersökningen) råtabeller, årsmedeltal, Statistiska Centralbyrån, 1987, 1991, 1993, 1995.

Allen, S. and Wilkowitz C. (1986), 'The Control of Women's Labour: The Case of Homeworking', *Feminist Review*, No 2.

Angelöw, B. (1989), *Att berövas sitt arbete – en företagsnedläggning och dess konsekvenser för de anställda*, Stockholm: Symposion.

Beechey, V. and Perkins, T. (1987), *A Matter of Hours. Women, Parttime Work and the Labour Market*, Cambridge: Polity Press.

Bernstein, D. (1986), 'The Sub-Contracting of Cleaning Work: a Case in the Casualisation of Labour', *The Sociological Review*, Vol. 34, No 2.

Björkman, T. & Lundqvist, K. (1986), *Yrkeskunnande och datorisering*, Statskontorets småskrifter 13, Stockholm.

Caire, G. (1982), 'The Increase in Temporary Work and the Regulation of the Labour Market', *Sociologie du Travail*, Vol. 24, No 2.

Coyle, A. (1985), 'Going Private: the Implications of Privatization for Women's Work', *Feminist Review*, No. 21.

Davies, K. and Esseveld, J. (1984), 'Arbetslösa kvinnor och det grå fältet", *Sociologisk forskning*, No. 1.

Davies, K. and Esseveld, J. (1985a), 'Women and Unemployment: A Qualitative Analysis or Playing Hopscotch in the Swedish Labour Market', *Women's Studies International Forum*, Vol. 8, No 4.

Davies, K. and Esseveld, J. (1985b), 'Kvinnoarbetslöshet i dagens Sverige – ett hot mot jämställdheten', *Jämställdhet i arbetsliv och samhälle*, Stockholm: TCO.

Davies, K. and Esseveld, J. (1989), 'Factory Women, Redundancy and the Search for Work: Toward a Reconceptualisation of Employment and Unemployment', *Sociological Review*, May.

Davies, K. and Esseveld, J. (1987), *Reflections on Research Practices in Qualitative Research*, Department of Sociology, Lund University, Lund.

Davies, K. and Esseveld, J. (1988), *Att hoppa hage i den svenska arbetsmarknaden. En studie av arbetslösa fabrikskvinnor*, Stockholm: Rabén & Sjögren.

Davies, K. and Esseveld, J. (1990), 'Spänningar i välfärdsstaten – exemplet tidsbegränsad anställning', *Kvinnovetenskaplig tidskrift*, No. 2.

Gill, C. (1988), 'New Technology and Industrial Relations', paper prepared for the ALC conference 'Structural Change and Labour Market Policy', Saltsjöbaden.

Gonäs, L. (1988), 'Structural Change – its Consequences for the Individual and Community', paper prepared for the ALC conference Structural Change and Labour Market Polity, Saltsjöbaden.

Huws, U. (1984), 'The New Homeworkers: New Technology and the Changing Location of White Collar Work', Low Pay Unit Pamphlet, No 28.
Jonung, C. (1989), *Occupational Segregation by Sex in Sweden*, Department of Economics, University of Lund.
Lindgren, G. (1983), 'Anpassning och protest. Om deltidsarbete i det kapitalistiska patriarkatet', *Kvinnovetenskaplig Tidskrift*, No. 3.
Nilsson, T. (1988), *Arbetare eller tjänstemän*, Lund: Arkiv.
Nätti, J. (1993), 'Temporary Employment in the Nordic Countries: A "Trap" or a "Bridge"', paper presented at the Nordic Sociology Congress, Gävle.
Olsson, S.E. (1990), *Social Policy and Welfare State in Sweden*,Lund: Arkiv.
Oveson, E. (1978), *Arbetslöshetens psykiska följdverkningar*, Stockholm: Rabén & Sjögren.
Piore, M.J. (1974), 'Notes for a Theory of Labour Marke Stratification' in Edwards et al. (eds), *Labour Market Segmentation*, Lexington, Mass.: Heath & Co.
Pollert, A. (1991), *Farwell to Flexibility*, Oxford: Blackwell.
Purcell, K. (1985), 'Work, employment and unemployment', in Burgess, R.G. (ed), *Key Variables in Social Investigation*, London: Routledge & Kegan Paul.
Smith, D. (1987), *The Everday World as Problematic*, Boston: Northwestern University Press.
Standing, G. (1986), *Labour Flexibility and Work Feminization*, Women at Work, No 2, ILO, Geneva.
Sundström, M. (1987), *A Study in the Growth of Part-time Work in Sweden*, Stockholm: Arbetslivscentrum.
Therborn, G. (1995), 'Patterns and meaning of unemployment', *Scandinavian Journal of Social Welfare*, Vol. 4:122-130.
Temporary Work in Britain: its Growth and Changing Rationales, IMS reports no 106, University of Sussex, 1985.
Wallace, C. and Pahl, R. (1986), 'Polarisation, unemployment and all forms of work', in Allen, S. et al. (eds), *The Experience of Unemployment*, Basingtoke: Macmillan.

Appendix

Table 11.1
Those temporarily employed by age as a percentage of those permanently employed for both sexes and for women for the years 1987, 1991 and 1995

	Both sexes			Women		
Age	1987	1991	1995	1987	1991	1995
16-24	47%	43%	77%	65%	57%	117%
25-44	9%	8%	15%	3%	10%	17%
44-59	4%	3%	5%	5%	5%	6%
60-	5%	4%	6%	6%	5%	8%

Table 11.2
Those permanently employed, temporarily employed and unemployed as a percentage of the total labour force by sex for 1987, 1989, 1991, 1993 and 1995

		Employed		Unemployed	Total work-force (1000)
		Permanent	Temporarily		
1987	women	85%	13%	2%	2 002
	men	89%	9%	2%	1 979
1989	women	86%	12%	1%	2 059
	men	92%	7%	1%	2 080
1991	women	86%	11,5%	2,5%	2 063
	men	89,5%	7%	3,5%	2 044
1993	women	81%	12%	7%	1 922
	men	80%	9%	11%	1 896
1995	women	78%	14%	8%	1 909
	men	80%	10%	10%	1 919

12 Equality in education and work: The limitations of liberal policies

Kathleen Lynch

Liberal equal opportunities policies have dominated public policy-making especially in the field of education (Arnot, 1991). While critical theorists, Neo-Marxists, feminists and post-modernists have challenged the liberal agenda in education, and public policy generally, they have not succeeded in breaking the stranglehold of liberalism on policy-making.

The clearest evidence of the power and influence of liberalism is in the European Union directives and decisions relating to equality and social exclusion. For example, the aim of the Third Poverty Programme which commenced in 1989 was 'the integration of the economically and socially less privileged groups in the Community' (EC Council Decision 18 July, 1989; 89/457/EEC). The aim was not to eliminate poverty but to manage it by integration. The fact that integration between unequal partners will only produce further inequality is self evident, but ignored. Within the field of education, a resolution was passed by the Council of Ministers and the Ministers of Education in 1985 promoting an action research programme on equal opportunities for girls and boys. This resolution was also couched in liberal language and no directive was passed requiring member countries to implement the recommendations emanating from the findings. And to say this is not to deny that there have been no gains from liberal policies, there have been gains, but the gains have been made primarily by the relatively disadvantaged within any given disadvantaged group.

A central thesis in this paper therefore is that the pursuit of liberal policies promoting equality of opportunity can be a mere distraction from the business of equality in a more substantive sense (Baker, 1987). To understand why this is the case, one has to examine its intellectual origins in liberal political philosophy.

The philosophical origins of liberalism and its failure to address economic inequalities

In terms of the balance between the values of equality and liberty, liberals occupy a midline position between conservatives and radicals. While they place a higher value on equality than conservatives, who prioritise general prosperity or even security above other goods, they value the freedom of the individual over and beyond the general realisation of equality objectives (Dworkin, 1984). Justice as fairness is a central tenet of contemporary liberalism, and within this perspective 'Justice denies that the loss of freedom for some is made right by a greater good shared by others' (Rawls, 1971, p.28).

Because of the prioritisation of freedom over equality, the focus of interest within liberalism has been on promoting equality of opportunity for individuals rather than equality of condition. And the model of justice which underpins liberalism is basically individualistic. It is concerned with removing irrelevant considerations or barriers affecting individuals. The individualistic position of this model is blind to the discrimination which lies within institutions themselves, the discrimination which is structured within them. It focuses on individuals *qua* individuals rather than on individuals as group members, or individuals as relational actors in institutional systems structured around inequality.

Liberalism, like all political philosophies, is of its time and place, and is profoundly shaped by the historical context of its existence (Hall, 1986, p.47). Although liberalism is a fractured philosophy with both conservative and radical tendencies (with Adam Smyth and John Locke on one side and Thomas Paine on the other) in the analysis of equality, liberals have always weighed in on the conservative side. The reasons why this happens arises from the sociological roots of liberalism. It emerged in the seventeenth and eighteenth century *in opposition* to the old feudal order and *aligned with* the emerging bourgeois order (ibid. p.39). The antagonism which led to the emergence of liberalism was essentially one *within* the elites of society; an antagonism between the old feudal lords and the champions of free trade, the merchant classes. Up to the eighteenth century, privileges and powers had been legally defined in the interests of the feudal estates.

> The *roturier* was not merely a social inferior, but the victim of economic disabilities imposed by law. The noble by inheritance or purchase did not merely possess a title; he was the owner of profitable immunities. The special characteristic of the class system in France and Germany had been, in fact, that inequality was not primarily economic, but juristic, and that, in spite of gross disparities of wealth, it rested on difference, not merely of income, but of legal status. (Tawney, 1964, pp.92-93)

Since the major inequalities which the bourgeoisie experienced were legal rather than economic the focus of their interest was juristic rather than economic.

> A distinction was drawn between *egalite de droit* and *egalite de fait,* between formal or legal equality and practical or economic equality. The primary aim of reformers was the achievement of the first, since, once the first was established, the second, in so far as it was desirable, would, it was thought, establish itself. (ibid. p.94-95)

And the logic of liberalism was correct. If legal barriers were removed between those elites in society who had similar resources in terms of wealth and power, then equal opportunities was realisable for the disadvantaged group (the new bourgeoisie). Both groups could then compete equally as they had access to equal resources. The problem is however, that the conditions which operated for the bourgeoisie vis-a-vis the feudal lords do not operate in the relations between most dominant and subordinate groups in contemporary European society. Juristic inequalities are generally of far less significance than economic inequalities or power inequalities. While recognising that there are groups for whom formal equality before the law is still a problem, groups such as the unemployed, women or disabled people are often more disadvantaged in Western European societies by their lack of resources rather than by the legal barriers to their advancement.

Liberal reformers have been centrally concerned therefore, with ensuring that people are equal in both legal and quasi-legal terms. The interest is in formal, legalistic equality rather than substantive, economic equality. Liberalism is primarily concerned with protecting equal formal rights and ensuring equality of access: 'once the rules governing admissions to places of education, appointments to jobs and promotions are fair, a society is an equal opportunity society', (O'Neill, 1977, p.179). Unequal results are justified if everyone has an equal opportunity to succeed.

Liberals also believe that equal opportunity is to be achieved by maximising the economic and political liberty of the citizen. They have espoused the cause of an open meritocratic society where those with intelligence and ambition (IQ+Effort) can rise to the top. Liberty is defined therefore in a negative way – it is defined as freedom from constraint so that one can be free to compete. The law is there to regulate between competing contenders 'without questioning or interfering with the basic dispositions of wealth and power in society' (Hall, 1986, p.42). The primary *focus is on ensuring equal formal rights and equality of access* to basic goods and services in education by removing all formal and informal barriers to entry and participation.

Liberal educationalists have, however, moved beyond a simple preoccupation with equality of access and equal formal rights (with increasing pressure from marginalised groups such as women, disabled people and ethnic and racial minorities) and supported fair equal opportunities policies as opposed to just formal equal opportunities. The principle of fair equality of opportunity refers to when 'positions are to be not only open in a formal sense, but that all should have a fair chance to attain them' (Rawls, 1971, p.73). Thus liberal educationalists have supported policies which *enable* and *encourage equal participation* in education for marginalised groups. With equal participation, the aim is to ensure that marginalised groups will be able to participate on equal terms with other groups once they enter the system. However, while this facilitates success it does not guarantee it. *Equality of outcome*, which would *ensure* equal rates of success for marginalised groups within the different systems of education, via such procedures as quotas or preferential appointments is not part of the liberal agenda, and neither is *equality of condition* which would be concerned with ensuring that there was equality in the living conditions of all members of society.

Both the weak and the strong versions of liberal equal opportunities policies fit in comfortably with the interests of the dominant educational, economic and social order. In many respects they legitimate existing structured inequality while offering selective mobility into elite positions for those who are selected out. The fact remains that in a highly unequal society, someone has to occupy the subordinate positions even if the identity of those occupying them may change from white to black, from male to female or from citizen to migrant worker.

Limitations of the liberal equal opportunities approach to equality in education

Those who have been involved in teaching, research and/or policy initiatives relating to the elimination of social class inequalities in education, are familiar with the outcome of policies devoted to the promotion of formal equality of educational opportunity; it has resulted in a trickle of social mobility between social classes but it has had no real impact on the class structure. There are a number of reasons why policies designed to promote both formal and fair equality of opportunity in a highly stratified society will not promote equality in any substantive sense.

First, the concepts of both formal and fair equality of opportunity are premised on the assumption that the social hierarchies remain; all that differs between this and a system in which there is no emphasis on equality of opportunity is who ends up on top. The whole point of equality of opportunity is to 'regulate the competition for advantage: this does not alter the inequalities themselves' (Baker, 1987, p.46). It does not propose 'the absence of violent contrasts of income and condition but equal opportunities of becoming unequal' (Tawney, 1964:103). Indeed policies of equal opportunity are lauded from public platforms often on the understanding that this very limited notion of equality which they propose will be:

> content with ceremonial honours. It retains its throne, on condition that it refrains from meddling with the profitable business of the factory and the market place. Its credit is good, so long as it does not try to cash its cheques. Like other respectable principles it is encouraged to reign, provided that it does not attempt to rule. (ibid.)

The problem stems from the fact that:

> From its inception classical liberalism was identified with the 'free market' and opposed any intervention by the state to remedy the unequal consequences of market competition or to distribute goods, resources and opportunities more equitably between the competing classes. (Hall, 1986, p.41)

Classical liberalism has never opposed hierarchies or gradations in society except where these rested on legal privilege (Tawney, 1964, p.102). In fact, in many respects, the inequalities emerging from the meritocratic order are regarded as legitimate, inevitable and indeed, even desirable. They are seen as desirable in so far as they offer an incentive to work and compete; they are seen as inevitable and legitimate in so far as they reflect the so-called 'natural' differences in talent (Davis and Moore, 1970).

Within the liberal model, personal character and individual attributes, rather than public institutions or structures, become accountable for success or failure. Factors such as gender, social class, ethnicity, religion, race, disability or sexual orientation, are examined, not in relational terms for their equality impact, but rather in individualist, what Bourdieu (1973) called, 'atomistic terms'. The causes of inequality are sought within the attributes themselves rather than within the structures and institutions which order the relations within and between these attribute-bearing individuals. While there is a growing body of research and theory, especially in the feminist field, which challenges this orientation, it is still standard practice in educational theory and practice to locate the problem of inequality within the dominated rather than the dominant, within women rather than men, within black rather than white, within migrant workers rather than the host society, etc. (Mac an Ghaill, 1994).

Consequently when policies are introduced to promote equality in education, we tend to focus on ways in which the dominated rather than the dominant are problematic: the focus is on how women need to change in order to succeed in a male-dominated world, rather than how men and the education institutions they have constructed must be adapted and changed; it is on how working class people must adapt rather than how middle class values in education are to be challenged; it is on how 'to cope' with disability or cultural difference rather than invent non-disablist and truly inter-cultural systems.

Selective mobility for those who succeed at adapting to the dominant order is the goal. Liberal equal opportunities policies in education (in practice if not in theory) are very much about selecting out members of marginalised or disadvantaged groups to become socially mobile within the existing system. And the measure of success is to achieve equality of access and, perhaps participation, by marginalised groups within the dominant systems. Thus equality for many groups has been measured in terms of upward social mobility. If the proportion of working class students who enter higher education rises, or if there is a rise in the proportion of women taking engineering then it is assumed that equality objectives are being realised. The focus is not on the ways in which feminist forms of knowledge are structurally excluded from education itself. Neither is there a focus on how the ordering of economic and labour relations creates a stratified labour market which makes inequality in social class terms inevitable, and which thereby devalues the forms of knowledge associated with lowly paid occupations including knowledge relating to caring and personal relationships. As there is an individualist rather than a relational approach to the explanation of inequalities, then it is not surprising that moral approbation frequently follows educational success, while its opposite follows failure, for disadvantaged groups. And those who are structurally excluded find that they are held personally accountable for their own exclusion.

While social mobility is a laudable goal from the perspective of those who are successful, it does not radically alter the pattern of inequality which exists. Logically, it is not possible to enable all those who are disadvantaged to succeed, both because there are not sufficient places at the top of the privilege pyramid for all who might be technically eligible to occupy them, and because those who currently occupy elite positions will resist substantial displacement. Also, selective mobility from within any marginalised group will inevitably favour the most advantaged within that group (e.g. middle class women over working class women, white women over black women, able-bodied over disabled) as such groups are best positioned to avail of opportunities in a competitive situation. This both reinforces inequalities within the marginalised group and weakens the group through selective out-migration.

Meritocracy

Within the liberal tradition, equality of educational opportunity is normally defined in meritocratic terms. And within this frame of reference, equality is an issue principally for those who are deemed talented (Young's [1961] famous dictum, IQ+Effort=Merit). Yet to develop talent (ability+effort), access to privileged resources is essential. In a hierarchically and patriarchically stratified society, one cannot draw a clear dichotomy between ascribed and achieved qualities. Students who have prior access (via their homes/habitus) to the cultural talents that schools value are the most likely to be labelled intelligent, and those who know that they have most to gain from the education system are the most likely to work hard and be ambitious. Lack of developed talent is a function, in many ways, of the hierarchical orderings of society itself, while lack of effort is a function of the lack of visibility and availability of opportunity (Tumin, 1970).

The net outcome of equal opportunities policies based on meritocratic principles therefore, is the sponsoring of the 'talented' into elite positions; and given the structure of opportunity in society, the talented and the privileged are closely related. It is those who have the resources to develop talent who gain most, both within a given group and in a comparative group context.

Because policies based on the principles of equalising opportunities presuppose the existence of social hierarchies, they do not pose a serious threat to patriarchal, disablist, ethnocentric or capitalist values. The identity of those who compete for privilege may change, but the individualistic competition and the anti-community values which this entails remain the same (Baker, 1987). Thus, a culture based on meritocratic principles is basically anti-communitarian as each person is rewarded constantly for maximising self interest. Divisions between the successful and the unsuccessful, between the haves and have nots are merely exaggerated in a system guided by the principle of equal opportunity as it is now assumed that those who get to the top 'deserve to'; they owe no debt to their inferiors. This is one of the most divisive features of meritocratic systems, and of equal opportunities policies premised on such principles within societies without equality of condition.

Another problem with a liberal equal opportunities approach to equality issues is that it assumes wrongly that the successes and failures of one generation can be separated from the life chances of the next without altering the structural conditions under which success and failure are created. This may be a logical possibility but it is not generally a social possibility. One cannot give equal opportunities to children whose parents own vastly different resources; when governments try to do this, all that happens is that those parents who have extra resources use these to offset the effects of equal opportunities policies designed to help the disadvantaged. Financial, power and other differentials operating outside of education maintain educational differentials within the system. We will only have equality in education and in society at large when we have what Tawney has termed practical or economic equality. 'In the absence... of a large measure of equality of circumstances, opportunities to rise must necessarily be illusory' (Tawney, 1964, p.107).

There is a wealth of educational evidence showing how liberal equal opportunities policies as applied in relation to social class have not altered the patterns of class participation in higher education in particular (Cobalti, 1990; Halsey, 1991; Breen et al., 1990). Basically, Raftery and Hout's (1992) thesis of maximally maintained inequality (MMI) is true, and that is that working class people have only succeeded in entering privileged sectors of education when middle class demand for those sectors have been satisfied. (If the same principle were applied to women, then it is obvious that women will only get the types of positions men now occupy when all men's ambitions for those positions are satisfied!). Effectively this is as good as saying that liberal equal opportunities policies have failed. Access to superior power, wealth, and other resource differentials outside of education have enabled the middle classes to maintain their differentials within education. The impact of superior financial resources on educational attainment is direct in its reproductive effects on inequality. Those who own or can buy superior access to cultural resources required for high levels of educational attainment tend to do so. Superior economic capital becomes translated in to superior credentialised cultural capital, in the form of grinds, fee-paying tuition, extracurricular development and educationally supportive social networks and alliances (Bourdieu and Passeron, 1977).

Furthermore, the fact the middle and upper classes of society (especially men within these classes) are closely integrated into the educational decision-making machinery of most States, both directly through their own representative bodies (such as political parties) and indirectly through the mediating bodies which manage and control the day-to-day running of educational services (such as managerial bodies, curriculum and assessment bodies, trade unions, local authorities, etc.) means that they can order the pattern of educational relations in their own class (and/or gender or racial interest) (Lynch, 1990). There is no hidden hand guiding the educational system as the bodies which seek to influence and define the educational agenda are usually overt and direct in their interventions (Department of Education, 1994).

What is being suggested therefore is that most equality policies in education are framed in terms of liberal notions of equality of opportunity. The focus of attention is on promoting equality of opportunity between the dominated and dominant groups. The aim is not to eliminate hierarchies of knowledge, power, wealth and privilege which create unequal structures and positions, but rather to enable people to compete more equally for the unequal positions.

This is not to suggest here that there is no gain for anyone in promoting liberal equal opportunities policies. There is gain for the relatively advantaged within the marginalised or excluded group who are selected out into more privileged positions. And these select view may become role models or activists on behalf of their group of origin. However, the myth of liberalism is that the selection or success of the few will become the pattern for the many.

Locating liberalism within an equality studies framework

This section of the paper will attempt to locate liberal educational thought within the context of the equality framework devised at the Equality Studies Centre in University College Dublin (1995). The framework we have devised for setting equality objectives has been developed in a national policy context. While we do not claim it to be the only way in which to formulate thinking about equality objectives, it does provide a framework for policy development which has proved effective in promoting and developing thinking about equality objectives in a wide range of public policy contexts. The framework has been used to analyse the position of a wide range of groups including women, disabled people, working class groups and ethnic minorities such as Travellers.

Equality objectives can, in some respects, be regarded as operating along a continuum. At one end of the continuum is the minimalist conception of equality which defines equality in terms of *equal formal rights and opportunities* and is a central component of equality of access. *Equality of participation* represents a stage beyond this where the focus is on enabling and encouraging members of different social groups to be equally able to participate in society, while *equality of success or outcome* is concerned with ensuring equal rates of success for these groups. At the opposite end of the continuum is the concept of *equality of condition* which aims at creating equality in the living conditions of all members of society. This refers to an ideal state where all goods, privileges and resources are distributed equally according to need. And it is important to note the emphasis here on equality in the living conditions of all members of society rather than citizens. Frequently rights are only accorded to citizens with attendant negative consequences for those who are defined as non-citizens.

Equality objective no. 1: Equal formal rights and opportunities, and equality of access

The minimalist conception of equality is that which defines equality in terms of the provision of equal rights to participate in economic, social, political, and cultural, (including educational) life, where such rights are construed as the absence of legal and institutionalised barriers to entry and participation in a given institution or system. This view is linked to the idea of formal equality of opportunity, i.e. the idea that no one should be prevented from entry to education, employment, politics, etc., or in advancing from one level of participation to another, on the grounds of gender, sexual orientation, ethnicity, disability, or any other irrelevant characteristic, and that access to, and advancement within these institutions should be based on merit.

In terms of providing equal access to a given institution or system, the removal of legal or quasi-legal barriers does not address the problem of non-formal barriers to entry. To have equality of access, not only must formal legal and quasi-legal barriers be removed, non-formal barriers must also be eliminated. To a large extent, formal and quasi-legal barriers to equal access and participation in education have been removed in Europe, although there are exceptions such as the requirement for entry to primary teaching in Ireland, where disabled people have experienced direct discrimination which is not yet outlawed under law.[1]

Also non-formal barriers often operate which effectively exclude disabled people. An example of a non-formal barrier would be the fact that schools and colleges have no facilities to cater for deaf or blind students and no provisions in their budget to address their needs (for example for an interpreter or a brailling service). Ethnic minorities can experience similar indirect discrimination when schools fail to take any account of their culture and lifestyle; they are refused entry with the excuse that the school 'has no resources for coping with children who are different'.

Scope and limitations of equal formal rights and opportunities and equality of access

The vindication of formal rights and opportunities through legislation, and the removal of legal and quasi-legal barriers to access in fields such as education, employment and goods and services for particular target groups, both guarantees their rights and eliminates forms of discrimination against them. However, the outlawing of discrimination[2] does not, in and of itself, guarantee any more substantive form of equality for the target group, such as equality of participation.

Moreover, there are quite significant difficulties in outlawing indirect discrimination against target groups owing to its relative invisibility and indetermina-

1 Rule 155 (4) (a) of the Rules for National Schools formally excludes a person from entering primary teacher education colleges unless she/he 'is of sound and healthy constitution and free from any physical or mental defect likely to impair his (her) usefulness as a teacher'.

2 Direct discrimination occurs when someone is treated differently when they should be treated the same and when as a result they experience a disadvantage. *Indirect discrimination* refers to the differential impact of the same treatment where the differential is not justified. It occurs when a condition or requirement is set such that a considerably smaller proportion of one than of another groups can comply with it, which is to the detriment of the person(s) concerned and where the person using the condition or requirement cannot show it to be justified.

cy. For example, the selection mechanisms used by schools can, in fact, indirectly discriminate against working class students, even though discrimination is not intended. An example of this is the way selection for certain second-level schools operates in Ireland. What happens is as follows. A large number of second level schools hold tests in the spring preceding the autumn enrolment in order to group classes at entry. While this is a reasonable arrangement from the schools' viewpoint, in terms of planning for the autumn, it impacts differentially and unfairly on working class students, as they are often less likely to know about the tests and their importance, this lack of knowledge being a function of their relative exclusion from education itself. The same problem arises with the 'first come first served' entry requirement which is widely used for selection in both primary and second-level schools. Lack of information means that parents do not apply in time and therefore their children are excluded by default. As there is evidence that working class parents are less knowledgeable about the operation of selection mechanisms and other procedures in relation to schooling, there is an onus on the schools to make information about selection widely known especially in working class areas so that working class students are not excluded indirectly from access to particular schools. The same type of problem occurs for other groups which are educational outsiders in a given society such as migrant workers.

Equality objective no. 2: Equality of participation

It is now widely recognised that equality of formal rights and opportunities has little impact on the promotion of equality in any substantive sense. Substantive equality depends not simply on having the formal right to participate but on having the actual ability and resources to exercise that right, that is by being able to participate.

The second way in which equality can be conceptualised therefore is in terms of equality of participation. This involves both *enabling* a designated disadvantaged or minority group, or an individual member of the group, to participate and *encouraging* them to participate.

Enabling participation means ensuring that the basic material needs and the basic psychological, educational and other needs of the target group are met so that they are in a position to participate on equal terms. For example, if working class children are to participate on equal terms with middle class children in public examinations, they must have access to the same quality and level of resources. If women who have worked full-time in the home as carers and domestic workers for many years are to return to the paid labour market and participate equally with others, they need to be prepared educationally and psychologically for such a return.

To have equal participation, it is also necessary to encourage participation. *Encouraging participation* means ensuring that the members of the target group are motivated to participate and are accepted by others as full participants. This means going beyond provision for basic or other needs. It could mean the development of a proactive policy in a given school such as equality training for teachers and equality work with students which would create a climate encouraging practices promoting equal participation. Or it could mean affirmative action through direct advertising for marginalised groups to enter a given programme, or devising special support services so that they will be able to participate fully and effectively if they do enter.

Scope and limitations of equal participation

Equal participation assumes the pre-existence of equal formal rights and opportunities and equality of access. Policies based on the equal participation principle go beyond the protection of formal rights and the prevention of discrimination as they actively intervene to enable and encourage equal participation. However, enabling and encouraging equal participation does not guarantee or ensure it: while interventions such as improved education and training about equality issues within a given school may make the environment for women or disabled people more favourable, or while developing access programmes for various types of disadvantaged students to enable them to enter higher education will undoubtedly improve their rates of participation, such policies do not guarantee equal participation as the interventions work on the principles of facilitating equality rather than ensuring it. Voluntarism and selectivity are at the heart of the equal participation objective. The agency or body that sets out to promote equal participation is required to enable or encourage participation, it does not have to ensure it. Schools and colleges can effectively lay claim to promoting the equal participation objective by engaging in a selective range of activities although the scope and level of the interventions may be far from comprehensive. They can have public legitimacy although their interventions have limited impact. Moreover, as noted above already, policies promoting equal participation will favour the relatively advantaged among the disadvantaged as they will be in the strongest position to avail of whatever services and supports are offered.

Also, addressing inequalities in participation varies according to the nature and scope of the group/person's marginalisation and according to context. Policies which enable a particular group, such as disabled people, to participate in education will generally do little to foster the participation of racial or ethnic minorities except for those minority group members who are disabled. Indeed, even within a group such as disabled people, it is clear that many of the strategies adopted to improve the participation of people with one type of impairment (e.g. mobility impairments) will not assist people with unrelated (non-mobility) impairments such as deafness, mental illness or learning difficulties. Heterogeneity within and between marginalised groups has to be recognised in the development of any policies to promote equal participation. Yet many equality policies fail to take account of this.

In addition, the heterogeneity of contexts must be recognised, as the policies required to promote equal participation in areas such as employment, the media, education or recreational activities will vary considerably.

Equality objective no. 3: Equality of outcome or success

Equality of outcome represents a stage beyond the objective of equal participation and refers to policies which promote equality in the outcome of social processes. In particular, equality of outcome between marginalised or excluded groups and those not marginalised means achieving overall equality between these groups in terms of access to, and the distribution of, educational, economic, cultural, political and other benefits.

The degree of success people experience in the course of their participation in a given context, is the primary determinant of status in contemporary society. If society was not hierarchically stratified in terms of wealth, power and privilege, then the question of equality of success or outcome would not be so significant. However since society is so stratified, then it follows that achieving equal rates of success or outcomes for particular groups is one way in which to define equality. If women, for example, are to be equal to men in terms of success, this means that they must be ensured success at the same rates as men; they should have proportionate representation in all privileged positions.

International experience shows that there is no easy proofing mechanism for realising equal success for different social groups and no given structure which will guarantee it in the absence of equality of condition (equality objective, no. 4 below). However, it is clear that any serious attempt to redress the problem involves policies commonly referred to as 'affirmative action', 'preferential treatment' or 'reverse discrimination', and 'quotas'. It should be noted moreover, that a number of these strategies could also be employed to achieve equality of participation. For example, affirmative action could include the running of a special third-level access programme for disabled students to enable them to participate on equal terms with able-bodied students when in the third-level education system.

Scope and limitations of equality of outcome

Equality of outcome is the strongest of the three equality objectives cited so far, as it aims to ensure equal rates of success or outcome by direct intervention to overcome disadvantage. In addition, equality of outcome assumes that equality of access and equal participation exist.

There are, however, a number of difficulties associated with the realisation of this objective. The most obvious one is the fact that groups which are dominant in the present system, and/or who are already beneficiaries, will resist any strategy for their displacement. And equality of outcome policies would effectively demand displacement, for example, in sensitive areas such as entry to higher education.

Another difficulty is the complexity of managing quota systems for example, especially with groups where definitional problems arise in relation to their identification, such as with disabled people. Also, positive discrimination or quota systems are likely to be most effective for easily identifiable large groups such as women, and where the quota set is at a substantial level. Given the fact that women represent more than half the population, the promotion of policies of equality of success or outcome would clearly have a considerable advantage for them. The principle would also have a positive and visible effect on large groups such as working class people, while its impact on smaller groups, albeit significant, would be less visible. Their low representation in the population (e.g. less than 1% of the population in Ireland belong to the Traveller ethnic minority group) would mean that the quota could be met by appointing or selecting very small numbers of people. Furthermore, even if equality of outcome policies are successful, and equal rates of success for marginalised groups are achieved, the mobility out of these marginalised groups by the successful minority, can indirectly weaken the marginalised group further as the most advantaged are selected out.

Notwithstanding these difficulties, equality of outcome, represents a radical challenge to existing policies, like equality objectives 1 and 2, it operates by comparing particular disadvantaged or marginalised groups with their counterparts as groups i.e. the disabled and able bodied, men and women, etc. If operated singly for one group, without being simultaneously implemented for all other groups, the principle of equality of outcome would result in substantial inequalities within the group itself. For example, if equality of outcome was pursued as an objective for women but not for disabled people or working class people, it would not address inequalities among women arising from race, social class or disability. If equality of outcome is to be fully effective therefore, it needs to be operationalised for all groups simultaneously.

Although equality of outcome would represent a major advance in the promotion of equality in society, it does not address the fundamental problems of hierarchies of power, wealth and other privileges. What it does is to replace or supplement the existing elites within the economic, political, educational and other hierarchies with new elites from hitherto disadvantaged groups. While this would represent a significant shift in the balance of power and privilege, it must be noted that privileged positions are by definition scarce and only a small number of any given group will ever enter these positions.

Also, regardless of which disadvantaged group is in question, it is likely to be the relatively advantaged from within that group which will become upwardly socially mobile in any system which promotes equality of success or outcome. (The same issue arises with equal participation policies.) It is the relatively privileged who will be best positioned to take advantage of the new opportunities for participation or success.

Equality objective no. 4: Equality of condition

If equality of condition were adopted as an objective, it would involve the development of an egalitarian society which would be committed to equality in the living conditions of all its members (both citizens and non-citizens) taking due account of their heterogeneity be it arising from gender, ethnicity, race, disability, religion, age, sexual orientation or any other relevant attribute. It would not simply be concerned with equalising the position (access, participation and outcome) of marginalised groups at each level within the hierarchies of wealth, power and privilege. Rather, it would involve the equalisation of wealth, power and privilege. It would mean having substantial equality in working conditions, job satisfaction and income across different occupations; an educational system devoted to developing equally the potential of every member of society; a radically democratic politics which aimed at the equal participation and influence of all citizens; and a restructuring of family and personal life for the sake of enriching the personal relationships of every individual. Policies based on the second and third criteria of equal status could clearly contribute substantially to satisfying this fourth criterion, although they would continue to fall short of it.

The structures and mechanisms required to promote equality of condition would involve widespread changes in constitutional and legislative frameworks, as well as in the political, economic, social and cultural infrastructures of the society. Taxation, legislation and education would be among the many mechanisms required to bring about change.

Limitations of policies bases on objectives 1, 2 and 3

The principles of equality of access, participation and outcome are essentially focused on the concept of *distribution*. Privileges (and education is defined as one of these) are defined as goods which are unevenly distributed and which should and could be distributed more equitably.

The limitations of each of these three approaches to equality is that they are based, in part, on the assumption that education itself is an implicitly unproblematic good. The content, process and structures of education are only subjected to critique or required to change for secondary reasons, namely in order to promote an exterior objective such as equal access, participation or outcome. Even equality of outcome, which is clearly the strongest of the three objectives, only requires that schools are changed *in order to* promote equality in rates of success for particular groups. The hierarchies of cultural practice which are institutionalised in the curricula of schools, and the hierarchies of power which are institutionalised in the modes of assessment and in organisational and pedagogical practice, are not required to change except and in so far as change is necessary to achieve equal access, participation or outcome for a particular target group. The issue of equality however, is not just a distributional one, it is also an issue of ensuring *equal respect* for all groups and individuals. This demands that the culture, lifestyle and values of minority and other groups are given full and equal recognition within a given education system and that systems for equalising the distribution of power are also introduced. The issue of equality is not just about getting disadvantaged groups and individuals 'in and out of the system' successfully, it is about changing the nature of education itself in both its curricular substance and its organisation.

Education and equality of condition: Equal respect

Issues internal to the education system: Organisation and management

The practices and procedures which govern the organisation of the school as a social system, and which determine the nature of pedagogical relations in classrooms, are crucial in determining the outcomes of equality policies. Schools are remarkably similar both in the structure of their power relations and in the nature of their pedagogical practice to what they were in the 19th century. The banking concept of education with its implicit belief in the superior knowledge and authority of the teacher and its passive view of the learner is still highly pervasive. Such hierarchical relations are antithetical to the development of an egalitarian perspective as they habituate both pupil/student and staff consciousness to a mode of educational and organisational relations in which dominance and subordinancy are naturalised. And as the length of time spent in schools rises throughout Europe, the potential formative influence of schooling also increases. If schools are not participatory democracies in their organisation, and dialogical in their pedagogical practice, then it is likely that equality goals pursued through the curricula (e.g. about democracy and rights) will be self-defeating as the hidden curriculum of schooling will contradict the message of the formal curriculum. And students are subjected must more systematically and consistently to the equality message (or the inequality message) of the former rather than the latter. Equality of condition would require a deconstructing of the hierarchies of organisational and pedagogical practice in schools and colleges. It would require changes in styles of management, discipline and organisation to make schools and colleges truly democratic and accountable to children and young people, and not only to so-called educational partners, be these teacher bodies, parents, or whoever, all of whom are adults. More open and democratically structured pedagogical, organisational and management styles, taking account of the basic dialogical pedagogical principles developed by Freire (1972a, 1972b, 1973) would therefore be a pre-requisite for equality of condition. For it is amazing how children and young people are so rarely consulted in matters and decisions that directly affect their lives. They are not defined as legitimate partners in education. Yet there are very few adult interest groups that one would dare to speak about without consulting directly with them. Would men hold a conference on women without consultation? Would disabled people be ignored in developing policies relating to themselves? Even if such events happened, it is not politically acceptable to act in this way. We have not yet begun to take young people and children seriously as legitimate partners in their own education. Yet the UN convention on the Rights of the Child (ratified by many European countries) states that:

> The States Parties shall assure to the child who is capable of forming his or her own views the right to express those views freely in all matters affecting the child, the views of the child being given due weight in accordance with the age and the maturity of the child. (Article 12.1)

Issues internal to the education system: Curricula and assessment

Schools and colleges are the principal institutions in our society for transmitting and legitimating cultural forms. Most of what is incorporated in the formal curricula of schools and colleges does not take full account of the life world of working class people, ethnic minorities, disabled people, Travellers, women or groups such as linguistic minorities. At present, only two forms of human intelligence are given full recognition in most formal Western educational systems: linguistic and logical-mathematical. All the other intelligences, including spatial, musical, the personal intelligences (intrapersonal and interpersonal) and bodily-kinesthetic intelligence have a relatively lowly place in education (Gardner, 1983, 1993). Yet much service work, such as teaching, nursing, marketing etc., and all caring work, requires personal intelligence while bodily kinesthetic intelligence is required in fields as diverse as sport, drama, mime and dance. An egalitarian policy would mean devising a new curriculum; one in which all types of human intelligence were given equal recognition. This would mean bringing about changes in the nature of what is taught within syllabi, introducing new subject matter and altering modes of assessment.

The pre-occupation of so much of formal education with credentialising those forms of knowledge and human understanding which can be assessed and measured through the medium of written language and mathematics is, in fact, a factor creating inequality and disability in education. For example, many people have insights, competencies, skills and abilities which cannot be measured through the linguistic medium, yet such people are heavily penalised and often labelled disabled or failures in schools; examples include people whose primary interests is in the visual/spatial sphere, those who work through the oral rather than the written medium, those who are primarily oriented to the bodily-kinesthetic sphere, and those whose principal competencies are in the inter-personal and intra-personal areas. The problem is not that such people are unwilling to learn or are educationally disabled, but that the education system does not allow them the means of expression or the opportunity to develop the fields of competence and interest which they have (ibid.). Neither the curricula nor the modes of assessment allow for the differences in intelligences between pupils. Not only do certain forms of knowledge predominate in education, so also do the modes of assessment associated traditionally with these forms of knowledge; namely pencil and paper tests of linguistic and mathematical capabilities. In effect, equality of condition would mean changing the school, the curricula and modes of assessment, not just making minorities or other marginalised groups fit the system as it stands. To do this would require considerable research investment as there has been very little research on how to develop musical, personal or visual-spatial intelligences on a truly universal scale.

Equality of condition would require not just that such groups were enabled to access, participate and succeed on equal terms with others, but that the organisation of school life (what is referred to in educational circles as the hidden curriculum of schooling) and the formal curriculum took account of their life style and culture and included it fully in the school/college. It would mean mainstreaming differences into the curriculum, organisation, culture and life of the school.

Scope and limitations of objective 4

As equality of condition represents the maximal type of equality objective, it overcomes the limitations which hold for the other objectives. Most importantly, it is the only effective means of overcoming the types of limitations arising from equality of outcome, namely the problems posed by the hierarchical structures of institutions and systems, and the threat to equality posed by selective social, economic and political mobility out of marginalised groups.

What equality of condition recognises is that the solution to the problem of inequality does not rest with changing the attributes and attitudes of particular individuals. Inequalities do not arise from the intrinsic nature or characteristics of marginalised or excluded groups but from the way in which their unique characteristics are handled. Moreover, they persist because positions are differentially rewarded or resourced in terms of wealth, power and privilege, not because of the character of the people who occupy these positions. Yet most policies treat the marginalised or excluded group as the problem when the problem lies with the structures of the institutions and systems which people occupy and the attitudes of those who control them.

While the limitations of objectives 1 to 3 in promoting equality (equality of access, participation and outcome) are intrinsic to the objectives themselves, the limitations of equality of condition are extrinsic to the objective. The difficulties are primarily political and institutional, namely the difficulty of realising equality of condition in a society which is already structured around income, power and wealth inequalities, and where such differentials are protected by a variety of legal, institutional and other political and social supports. Within education, the dilemma arises in relation to credentialising forms of cultural capital (namely knowledge and understanding) and utilising modes of assessment, which are not the forms of capital and modes of assessment legitimated by those who control the cultural markets both within and without education. The reality of educational power relations is that the status, power and income differentials of those who manage and mediate educational services (be these civil servants, teachers or whoever) are contingent on maintaining the existing hierarchies of cultural relations. And while the identity of these mediators changes from country to country[3], in all countries these proximate decision-makers within the machinery of the state exercise considerable power to direct policy and determine the forms of knowledge which will or will not be credentialised and how they are assessed. In particular, university professors, teachers, educational managers, researchers and related professionals, have all benefited substantially from the ideology which proclaims the superiority of so-called mental labour over manual labour – their pay differentials are tied to it. And as the educational currency in which they deal has placed a high value on linguistic and mathematical coinage, any devaluation of these intelligences and related modes of assessment pose a threat to their professional and career interests.

While there is no readily available solution to this dilemma, what can be recognised and made more visible to existing elites and power holders in society is that the cost of inequality, politically, socially and economically is high. That is to say, while it may be unrealistic to expect privileged groups or individuals to support egalitarian aims, on the grounds of principle or on the grounds of compassion, what is possible is that they may come to support it on the basis of enlightened self-interest. Wastage of educational ability, poverty, unemployment, ethnic tensions, gender tensions, and other by-products of inequality create political and social instabilities and conflicts in a given society. These instabilities result in both direct costs and opportunity costs which are considerable. Such costs if enumerated and publicised could contribute to developing a commitment to equality even among those whose immediate self-interest may not be visibly served by equality of condition.

Even if a given society does not adhere to the principle of equality of condition, a recognition of its importance does influence the way in which objectives are framed and targeted. For example, a move to promote greater equality in the distribution of income and wealth through the promotion of greater equality in taxation structures, would move society towards this objective; the introduction of systems and structures which promoted participatory democracy in decision-making would also help in the realisation of equality of condition.

The failure to recognise the importance of equality of condition, on the other hand, means that powerful interest groups who own and control disproportionately large resources of wealth, power and income in society, will always be in a position to use their extra resources to circumvent or challenge equality policies set out under objectives 1, 2 and 3, and to undermine their effectiveness as they see fit. This, in turn, will put considerable expense and onus on the State and its agents to defend the policies it has enacted.

---

3 Within Ireland, the teacher unions, the Catholic Church, civil servants, higher educational institutions, especially universities, and, increasingly, parent associations are the major mediators of educational services. No doubt the identity of these mediators would be different in other countries.

Summary: Equality objectives

Four equality objectives have been outlined here: Equal formal rights and opportunities and equality of access; Equality of participation; Equality of outcome or success, and Equality of condition. These four objectives can be construed as being on a continuum with the objective of equal formal rights and opportunities representing the minimal level of equality and equality of condition the maximal level of equality. The notion of a continuum of equality helps illustrate how the various stages are inter-related and interdependent – equal participation cannot operate without equal formal rights while both equality of access and equal participation are prerequisites for equality of outcome etc. Viewing the stages of equality as a continuum also clarifies the scope and limitations of the different equality objectives.

The first three objectives are concerned with ensuring that the members of disadvantaged groups, as defined by particular characteristics such as gender, disability or ethnicity, have, on average, the same rights and opportunities, ability to participate or success rates as other groups. By contrast, equality of condition is fundamentally concerned with eliminating hierarchies of wealth, power and privilege not just with ensuring that all groups access, participate or succeed at equal rates within an accepted hierarchy.

Conclusion: Equality in education and equality of condition

Equality of condition: Economic issues

To have equality of condition *within education,* it would be essential to have equality of condition in the economic and political spheres as well. As education is, in a number of respects, 'a cultural commodity' which can be bought, the pre-existence of large income and wealth differentials allows relatively privileged classes and groups to gain differential access to education in its credentialised form, both in terms of the nature of the award (degrees, diplomas, certificates etc.) and the level at which these are attained. Economic capital can be translated directly into cultural capital. Without an equalisation of income and wealth differentials, those with superior resources can always use them to improve their rates of achievement above and beyond that of less privileged groups.

Moreover, a dialectical relationship exists between economic value and cultural value. The low economic value placed on activities such as caring for others (which is badly paid and of low status especially within the home) feeds back into the cultural market and education and reinforces the low status of the knowledge base on which caring is based – notably interpersonal and intrapersonal intelligence. Thus knowledge about how to develop satisfying, emotionally rewarding and supportive personal relationships is not a subject for analysis in most schools (or if it is, it is part of the secondary rather than the primary knowledge system). The gendered nature of this exclusion is self evident.

Although it is often argued by liberals that the state can intervene to make up the differentials between groups through intervening to subvent and support marginalised groups in education to the level that they will be able to compete equally with more privileged groups, this is untenable. The reason being that the state will never have sufficient resources to distribute to make up the differentials; even if it were to collect sufficient resources in terms of taxes (which in itself is unlikely) the reality is that the state must spend a considerable proportion of these in the business of collecting and redistributing monies, so the amount available for direct interventions is reduced accordingly. The scale of the intervention required is not commensurate with the resources available; and the resources could not be made available without eliminating the very differentials which make the redistribution necessary in the first place.

Also, to argue that the state can effectively (as opposed to ineffectively or partially) offset the effects of economic and political inequalities in society by just intervening in the education site is not plausible. To act exclusively on the education site without acting simultaneously on other sites, such as in the law, in taxation and in the media, means that the egalitarian effects of state interventions in education will be counteracted in other spheres by those with access to superior resources.

Furthermore, in an economically and politically stratified society, such as that which operates in most of the welfare capitalist states in Europe, the state itself is seriously constrained in its ability to act against powerful and political economic interests not least because its own survival is dependent on taxation and returns on accumulated capital from such interests (Offe, 1984). In addition, the mediators and managers of educational (and other) services have career, status, power and income-related interests vested in the status quo (Lynch, 1990). Liberal reformers frequently ignore these contradictions at the heart of state action. The response is not just to ask teachers to become transformative intellectuals as Giroux (1981, 1983), McLaren (1989) and other critical theorists suggest, but rather to develop a counterforce of political action by mobilising the marginalised and excluded groups both inside and outside education. Only though organised and systematic democratic action, based on principles of participatory democracy, will change occur. I will return to this question in the next section.

However, before doing so, it is important to note the other ways in which the economic sub-system interfaces with education on a daily basis and thereby influences the context in which schooling operates.

Because of the direct link which exists increasingly in society between level of education and employment (OECD, 1995), educators and students are keenly aware of the forms of knowledge which matter and which types of values matter when it comes to utilising this knowledge. The mediation of the values of the economy takes place through a variety of channels and contexts. Most importantly, the school itself is a porous institution (McDonnell, 1995). The boundaries between it and other major institutions such as the media and the family are open and permeable. As students and teachers are themselves participants in a variety of institutions such as the media, the family, and indeed the economy, outside of school, they are made aware of which parts of education have market relevance in the economy. They constantly experience the nature of popular values through media advertising and through direct or indirect experience of the economy. The interactive relationships between the participants in education, educators themselves, and other powerful opinion and value formation institutions, such as the media and the economic sub-system means that inegalitarian values emanating in other sites inevitably pervade the ethos of schools even in schools where the official ideology of the school is anti-materialist and anti-capitalist (Lynch, 1989). Furthermore, at the level of management and decision-making, educational bodies are generally publicly controlled and accountable. The forms of knowledge which they credentialise have to be validated and approved by public boards and bodies. And in certain countries the interest groups which have an increasingly powerful influence on the development and approval of curricula in education are industrialists and representatives of the business sector (Arnot, 1992). What is at play here is not economic determinism in some crude sense in which the economy directly determines the character and nature of education. While the heavy hand of capital is wielded at times (as in the provision of the 1988 Education Act in Britain granting a special place to industrialists in the management of schools), the way in which the values of the market pervade the ethos of the school is more subtle and pervasive. It comes through the daily transportation of values and ideologies within and between the nexus of school, home, family, work and the media. The daily encounters involving dialogue, action and interchange make schools themselves sites where the values from other public domains are channelled, as well as challenged and developed. And given the sites from which values are transposed in to education, especially the economy and the media (both of which are intrinsically linked to capital via profit maximisation) schools have to confront the daily infusion of values which at best are indifferent to equality values, but which are, more likely, opposed to them. Schools first task therefore is to challenge sets of values and beliefs which are anti-egalitarian. This disestablishment of negative anti-egalitarian values and practices will not only take place within curricula and pedagogical practice but also in terms of school organisation and management and in terms of external relations. Equality in education needs to pervade the organisation of the school including pedagogical practice, school organisation, management, curricula and modes of assessment.

What is being suggested here is that schools and formal education are intrinsically linked to the economic subsystems of society. No matter how microscopically focused our individual interest in teacher education may be, it is impossible to understand and change the way education operates without addressing the way in which the demands of the economy interface with educational practice. To many this may read as a return to some type of outmoded economic determinism. However, as there is considerable evidence across Europe that educational credentials are being utilised increasingly to select candidates for jobs, and as this is, in part at least, related to the growth of knowledge-based industries, especially in the services sector of the economy, the influence of the economic sub-system on education cannot be underestimated especially by those who are interested in equality.

Equality of condition: Power and decision-making – working with not for

Some of the most innovatory and imaginative work in the field of education, in terms of both pedagogy and organisation is in the field of adult education. Basing their work on the Freirean principles of dialogue, emancipation and empowerment, the adult educationalists, working often in the poorest sector of education, have developed models for management, teaching and consultation which radically challenges the efficacy of methodologies and practices in the more formal education sectors. While there is much written about the difficulties of translating Freirean principles of pedagogy into schools and classrooms, in the long run, the move in that direction is as inevitable as it is desirable, the reason being because of the change in the nature of authority relations in most Western countries from traditional authority to rational authority.

Within domestic households, and in public life, authority is not longer accepted simply because the person holds a position; authority has legitimacy when there is a reason for accepting it, when it is rational in the Weberian sense. While recognising that there is great cultural variation in the ways in which schools and classrooms are managed, the organisation of many schools (both in the relations between staff and students, and between management and staff) is often based on the supposition that traditional authority is still acceptable. The result is sometimes a confrontation between student and teacher, silent resistance, or, more often, ritual obedience and withdrawal, with the inevitable poverty of learning that ensues. There is a need to invest money in research to develop more dialogical methods in teaching and more democratic and participatory methods of management.

Dialogical relationships are not only crucial for the promotion of equality within schools and classrooms (Freire, 1972a), they are also crucial for the development of effective equality policies at regional, national or international level. And the development of effective equality policies in education means that professional educators and researchers must be working *with* rather than for marginalised groups in the development of equality policies in education. There are two considerations at issue here. On the one hand, a dialogical relationship is essential because of the dangers inherent in any equality process that the target group becomes the object of charitable desire or professional career interest; in either case, the danger is that the interest of the professional or the philanthropist will take precedence over the interest of the target group. In other words, a form of colonisation takes place whereby the goal of equality becomes the project of a 'disinterested group', and ultimately the group's own self preservation will take precedence over equality considerations for the target group. The net outcome of this process is often the enactment of liberal reforms which give legitimacy to the work of the professionals but which have only marginal impact in terms of equality outcomes. Without powersharing between the target equality group, policy makers and professionals, colonisation of the marginalised is often the unforeseen by-product of policy action. Thus liberal equality policies have come to predominate, not simply because these are the politics which are most politically palatable to the existing powerbrokers in education, but also because the marginalised peoples and groups at which these policies are supposedly directed are not an integral part of the decision-making process. Their voices, if represented at all, are mediated by professionals (such as teachers, psychologists, doctors, social workers, health care workers etc.) and other service agencies outside their control. And mediated voices are not, by definition, organic voices. To move beyond the liberal agenda, it is essential that the oppressed groups, which have been marginalised in educational decision-making, are brought into the policy-making process at all stages as equal partners with full and adequate rights of self-representation which are resourced and supported – by these women, children, racial, or other minorities.

Moreover, all institutions and systems, including education, are structured around institutional lethargy. And bureaucratic lethargy is in the interests of the existing elites. Even where resistance is not organised, the prevailing elites can rely on the lethargy of the educational decision-making processes to forestall change, or to introduce minimalist changes at a given time. To ensure that egalitarian policies are promoted in education within a reasonable timeframe, the inertia of bureaucracy and vested interests must be confronted. Only the marginalised and oppressed groups themselves will have the energy, insight and commitment to demand this, although they may, of course, benefit from alliances and support .

Also, if equality policies in education are developed without the direct and immediate involvement of the target group (for example, disabled people, working class people, migrant workers, gay or lesbian groups) then there is a strong likelihood that the types of issues which are addressed, or the way in which they are addressed will not be in line with the real needs of the group. In addition, the question of politics and alliances come in to play. If 'resistance for equality' only takes place within the education site, and, within this context, the principal actors are professional educators, then the scope and the nature of the equality impact will be very limited. The promotion of equality in education must be linked in strategically with interventions by the primary actors for equality, namely community and other grassroots groups representing the oppressed and marginalised at local, regional and international level. It must also link in with work in other sites (such as in the taxation area, the media and the law) and with other states.

Those who work in a given sphere of interest, such as education, can be rather naive in the belief that change enacted within the site will have indirect impact on other sites. This is not necessarily the case; and the best example of this is the case of women whose superior performance in education bears no relationship to their lowly position within the household or the paid labour market. We are naive in our understanding of the forces which are reigned against equality. The beneficiaries of inequality such as global patriarchal capitalists do not confine their action to one site. In Britain, industrialists and other capitalist interests got their rights to influence education policy written in to the Education Act (1988). A similar attempt was made in Ireland in the early 1990s (Department of Education,

1992). Indeed, the election of Berlusconi to power in Italy in the early 1990s shows how organised capital can not only control the media but can use it effectively to ensure particular 'democratic' outcomes. The virtual monopoly of such a powerful opinion formation institution as the media means that the democratic process itself can be put in jeopardy as hegemonic control over opinion formation is concentrated in a very small number of hands. Similar developments are occurring within other countries and in other fields of action. If there is an interest in an equality project in Europe, then work must take place across sites (the media, the labour markets, the law, the family etc.) as well as education, and the only way to ensure that this happens is through liaising with those groups which are activists in these different arenas. This may seem to be an unrealistic project to some, but it has as much to do with orientation as with action. There is a need for a global movement to promote equality as those who oppose equality are also organised on a global scale.

Part of the problem in promoting change lies within the systems of liberal representative democracy which have been built up in Europe. The structures of participation and decision-making are such that change requires a radical conversion, not only of the public, but also of the mediators and managers of the institutions of education themselves. The parallelogram of forces which reign in on the formal education system means that a whole array of vested interests must be satisfied if change is to occur (Archer, 1982). As radical change will threaten existing interests, compromises are reached which appear to be highly democratic, but which inevitably protect those interests which are dominant. The problem lies in the weakness of representative systems of democracy and the political culture emanating from the. The system of representative decision-making which has built up around education, means that those with the best resources and organisation are most effective in having their voices heard. (We can see this happening now at a grand scale within the European Union where large companies and interest groups hire full-time lobbyists to try to influence decisions of the European Commission and, eventually of the European Parliament). Marginalised and vulnerable groups often have no formal channels to engage in an effective and ongoing way in decision-making; women's groups, ethnic minorities, migrant workers, Travellers and Gypsies, refugees or disabled people are frequently without a direct voice in education decision-making. Professionals or voluntary workers frequently speak on their behalf. Others claim their voice and mediate their message. This results in the build up of an array of professionals or voluntary agencies which provide second-hand information on inequalities but which cannot be a direct voice, by definition. Moreover, their own professional interests can often cut across the interests of the group. We have direct evidence of this for many years in deaf education and in fields of education dealing with learning disabilities.

Institutionalising a spirit of revolution (and by this I mean 'a new spirit and the spirit of something new', Arendt, 1984, p.59) rather than of liberal reform is at the heart of the equality agenda. And to be effective any revolutionary change must involve the subjects of the revolutionary change as key participants and decision-makers. If there has been any lesson learned from the work of the South

American educationalist, Paulo Freire, it is that the process is part of the outcome in any educational endeavour; the medium is part of the message. If the process for realising change or promoting equality is fundamentally inegalitarian, then the outcomes achieved will also be inegalitarian. Freire links political outcomes with pedagogical form in particular. He highlights the way in which educational practice is infused with political objectives; therefore in an hierarchically organised society which is fundamentally inegalitarian, the resulting social, cultural, economic and political relations of oppression and exploitation are reproduced in schools. The job of education in this context is to develop a dialogical pedagogy 'in which learners and teacher engage in active interaction with knowledge in conditions of mutuality and respect' (Silva, and McLaren, 1993, p.39). This is the position adopted by a host of critical theorists especially in the US including Aronowitz and Giroux (1991), McLaren (1989) and Apple (1982, 1986). While not assenting to the position of many contemporary critical theorists in regard to the claims they make about the power of liberatory educational practice to create radical change (such as the claims made by Aronowitz and Giroux, 1991), the Freirean insight that the medium is a large part of the message is a fundamental principle which would re-orient educational practice. Moreover, the medium includes the nature of organisational practice in schools as well as the pure pedagogical practice.

If equality in education is only addressed as an issue internal to classrooms and schools, two problems will arise. First, it will lead to ignorance about how education is linked to other subsystems which help frame its content and intentions, and which thereby have a direct bearing on what, when and how equality-oriented change will take place within it. And there is a danger of only changing aspects of educational experience which have an equality impact simply within the internal market of the educational system itself but little else outside of it. The question which is central for those who want radical change in equality terms in education (as opposed to liberal changes which only impact on the peripheries and have marginal impact) is how to operationalise and institutionalise a revolutionary equality spirit in education; that is how to ensure that an equality-promoting spirit become part of the raison d'etre of the education institution.

Liberalism consigns us to a narrow reformist view of educational change – one which, at best, will bring limited gain for the relatively advantaged among the disadvantaged. Moreover, the internal logic of liberal policies does not allow for anything more radical. It treats education as an autonomous site with an ability to promote equality internally irrespective of external forces. Such is not the case however. In a global context of structured inequality, the promise of liberal equal opportunities policies is realisable for only a small minority of relatively advantaged people within a given disadvantaged group. Egalitarians need to confront this inevitability and work for substantive equality objectives both within and without education. And this means confronting realistically the anti-egalitarian forces which are evident across Europe. There is a need for strategic organisation, planning and alliances working not only with other professionals but with activists themselves.

Liberal equal opportunities policies represent a mere distraction from the real issues of equality. Principles of equal opportunity make systems of inequality seem reasonable and acceptable; they move the debate away from inequalities of wealth, power and prestige to the question of how to distribute inequalities more fairly (Baker, 1987, p.46).

References

Apple, M. (ed), (1982), *Cultural and Economic Reproduction in Education*, London: Routledge and Kegan Paul.

Apple, M. (1986), *Teachers and Texts: A Political Economy of Class and Gender Relations in Education*, London: Routledge and Kegan Paul.

Archer, M.S. (1982), *The Sociology of Educational Expansion*, Beverly Hills: Sage.

Arendt, H. (1984), 'The Revolutionary Tradition and its Lost Treasure', from *On Revolution* (1963), London: Viking Penguin, in Sandel, M. (ed), *Liberalism and Its Critics*, New York: New York University Press.

Arnot, M. (1991), 'Equality and Democracy: A Decade of Struggle over Education', *British Journal of Sociology of Education*, Vol. 12:447-466.

Arnot, M. (1992), 'Feminism, Education and the New Right', in Arnot. M. and Barton, L. (eds), *Voicing Concerns: Sociological Perspectives on Contemporary Education Reforms*, Oxfordshire: Triangle Books.

Aronowitz, S. and Giroux, H. (1991), *Post-Modern Education: Politics, Culture and Social Criticism*, Minneapolis: University of Minnesota Press.

Baker, J. (1987), *Arguing For Equality*, New York: Verso.

Bourdieu, P. (1973), 'Cultural Reproduction and Social Reproduction', in Brown, R. (ed), *Knowledge, Education and Cultural Change*, London: Tavistock.

Bourdieu, P. and Passeron, J-C. (1977), *Reproduction in Education, Society and Culture*, London: Sage.

Breen, R. et al. (1990), *Understanding Contemporary Ireland*, Dublin: Gill and Macmillan.

Cobalti, A. (1990), 'Schooling Inequalities in Italy: Trends over Time', *European Sociological Review*, Vol. 6:199-214.

Davis, K. and Moore, W.E. (1970), 'Some Principles of Stratification', in Tumin, M., *Readings on Social Stratification*, New Jersey: Prentice Hall.

Department of Education (1992), *The Green Paper on Education*, Dublin: Government Publications.

Department of Education (1994), *Report of the National Education Convention*, Dublin: Government Publications.

Dworkin, R. (1984), 'Liberalism', in Sandel, M. (ed), *Liberalism and Its Critics*, New York: New York University Press.

Equality Studies Centre (1995), 'Equality Proofing Issues', Paper presented to the *National Economic and Social Forum (NESF)*, January 25th, Dublin Castle, Department of the Taoiseach (NESF), Dublin.

Freire, P. (1972a), *Pedagogy of the Oppressed*, New York: Penguin.
Freire, P. (1972b), *Cultural Action for Freedom*, New York: Penguin.
Freire, P. (1973), *Education for Critical Consciousness*, New York: Continuum.
Gardner, H. (1983), *Frames of Mind: The Theory of Multiple Intelligences*, London: Penguin.
Gardner, H. (1993), *Multiple Intelligences: The Theory in Practice*, New York: Basic Books.
Giroux, H. (1981), *Ideology, Culture and the Process of Schooling*, Philadelphia: Temple University Press.
Giroux, H. (1983), *Theory and Resistance in Education*, London: Heinemann.
Hall, S. (1986), 'Variants of Liberalism', in Donald, J. and Hall, S. (eds), *Politics and Ideology*, Milton Keynes: Open University Press.
Halsey, A.H. (1991), 'Educational Systems and the Economy', *Current Sociology*, Vol. 38:79-101.
Lynch, K. (1989), *The Hidden Curriculum*, London: Falmer Press.
Lynch, K. (1990), 'Reproduction: The Role of Cultural Factors and Educational Mediators', *British Journal of Sociology of Education*, Vol. 11:3-20.
Mac an Ghaill, M. (1994), *The Making of Men: Masculinities, Sexualities and Schooling*, Milton Keynes: Open University Press.
McDonnell, A. (1995), 'The Ethos of Catholic Voluntary Schools', Unpublished Ph.D. Education Department, University College Dublin.
McLaren, P. (1989), 'On Ideology and Education: Critical Pedagogy and the Cultural Pedagogy of Resistance', in Giroux, H. and McLaren, P. (eds), *Critical Pedagogy, the State and Cultural Struggle*, Albany: SUNNY Press.
Offe, C. (1984), *Contradictions of the Welfare State*, London: Hutchinson.
O'Neill, O. 'How do we know when Opportunities are Equal?', in Veterling-Braggin, M. et al. (eds), *Feminism and Philosophy*, Littlefield, N.J.: Adam and Co.
Organisation for Economic Co-operation and Development (OECD) (1995), *Education at a Glance*, Paris: OECD.
Raftery, A. and Hout, M. (1993), 'Maximally Maintained Inequality: Expansion, Reform, Opportunity in Irish Education, 1921-1975', *Sociology of Education*, Vol. 33:41-62.
Rawls, J. (1971), *A Theory of Justice*, Oxford: Oxford University Press.
Silva, T.T. da and McLaren, P. (1993), 'Knowledge Under Siege: The Brazilian Debate', in McLaren P. and Leonard, P. (eds), *Paulo Freire: A Critical Encounter*, London: Routledge.
Tawney, A.H. (1964), *Equality*, New York: Allen and Unwin.
Tumin, M. (1970), 'Some Principles of Stratification: A Critical Analysis', in Tumin, M. (ed), *Readings on Stratification*, New Jersey: Prentice Hall.
Young, M., *The Rise of the Meritocracy, 1870-2033*, London: Pelican.

13 Women's creativity and the Swedish study circles

Louise Waldén

Each year between one and two million Swedes take part in evening classes organised by adult educational associations. Every weekday evening in autumn and spring, people go out to spend three hours learning something, along with five to ten others, in groups known as study circles. This important feature of Swedish culture is easily ignored when Sweden is viewed from outside or from above (compared with university education, for example). Yet, when one sees Sweden from inside and from below, the culture of study circles forms a finely meshed net covering the whole country.

Study circles devoted to handicrafts – classified as practical-aesthetic circles – are a meeting place for traditions from various origins: pre-industrial society, the cultural heritage of different regions, the educational aspirations of popular and political movements, craft professions, and domestic handicraft. Three images from 1991 may serve as examples.

Image one

November 30, the anniversary of the death of King Charles XII, has become a day for unofficial celebration in the form of nationalistic demonstrations. In recent years, there has been an increasing element of hostility toward immigrants, with the result that the day has also become an occasion for protest against racism. People from the suburbs converge on the centre of Stockholm to take part in anti-racist counter-demonstrations.

I am travelling in the opposite direction, out to Tensta, one of the suburbs with the highest density of immigrants. The Workers' Educational Association is organising a special 'Study-Circle Day'. The hall in Tensta is packed with stalls, where study circles display their works: Turkish embroidery and Persian glass painting; Chilean handwork and Syrian dressmaking; mushroom picking and bee-keeping; and studies of literature. There is an extensive programme of events on the stage – music from Uruguay and the Andes; from Iran and Kurdistan; children's dances from Brazil and Bangladesh – presented between information about study circles. Many of the women are wearing Muslim veils; native Swedes are in a minority.

Image two

A few weeks previously, I was in Leksand to take part in a knitting symposium at the Folk High School for Handicraft, which specialises in vocational training in old crafts. Leksand is in the heart of Dalarna, the archetypal Swedish province.

On the way to the high school, I visit the museum to study *kurbits* paintings and folk costumes. Right next door is one of the oldest craft shops in Sweden, owned by the Handicraft Association. The window is decorated with 'Dala Horses', woven ribbons, embroidered folk head-dresses. The neighbouring building houses the premises of the Adult Educational Association, an organisation with its roots in both the farmers' and liberal movements in Sweden. Here, some of Sweden's foremost knitting artists are holding a group exhibition of their work. A short distance away is the oldest café in Leksand, its walls adorned with quilts illustrating a variety of techniques: knitting, crocheting, sewing.

The throng in the town centre looks no different from that seen in any small town in Sweden, with people rushing around in jeans and tights, in miniskirts and grey slacks, in anoraks and leather jackets. Just a few decades ago, however, you could still see women in Leksand wearing folk costumes any day of the year. To-day, it is still the usual thing to wear folk dresses on ceremonial occasions such as weddings, christenings, confirmations, and funerals.

When I get to the Hantverkets Folkhögskola (the Folk High School for Handicraft) in Leksand, someone shows me the way to another crafts school, Sätergläntan, which is run by the National Association of Swedish Handicraft Societies. People can come here for short courses in craft techniques. Study-circle leaders often take part in order to learn more and improve their knowledge and skill.

I observe how many threads appear to converge in Leksand: the folk culture of Dalarna, the province that has become a symbol of Sweden; the craft professions; the Folk High School; the traditions of domestic handicrafts, handed down in the courses of Sätergläntan; the decorative artists, represented by the exhibition of knitting art; and the everyday art of the home, illustrated by the quilt on the wall of the café. Through the study circles, all these traditions are passed on by and to 'the folk'. The folk are no longer the people born and bred in an agrarian society, but those who have been disinherited by industrial society. In study circles these people are now reclaiming old knowledge and passing it on through living hands. Sometimes, they rescue techniques that would otherwise die out, like the technique of knitting with two ends I learned at the symposium – a method with medieval traditions that has now been preserved by the study circles.

Image three

Late one evening, I am on the subway train from the southernmost suburbs of Stockholm to the northern outskirts. On my knee I have my Saami bag with pewter-thread embroidery. The man in the seat opposite wonders if I know what the embroidered symbols mean. When I shake my head, he asks me if I come from the north. When I shake my head again, he gestures as if he were going to snatch the bag from me and then he upbraids me in a threatening voice: only Saamis are entitled to carry Saami bags; people like us from the south, who know nothing of the traditions and symbols, have no right to carry them.

Three images from Sweden in 1990s – a triptych giving different perspectives on arts and crafts and on the practical-aesthetic study circles.

In Tensta, I experience the way the language of the hands – like that of music, painting, and dance – unites people who speak different languages and bear different cultures. It is both national and international: Turkish embroidery, Persian glass painting, and music from Latin America tell us something about the cultures in which they have arisen. This is something I can grasp without understanding the Turkish, Persian, or Spanish languages.

In Leksand, I encounter the many traditions that converge in practical-aesthetic study circles: cultural preservation as practised by the museums; the craft traditions of peasant society as cherished and guarded by the Handicraft Association; the craft skills that require special schools and training; the personal creative territory of the professional decorative artists. In the study circles, these traditions meet people's creative needs – an important force that drives so many Swedes to devote so much of their spare time to arts and crafts.

In the subway, finally, I encounter the defence of ethnic distinctiveness, an assertion of separateness that was unexpected. Such confrontations regarding who has the right to ethnic arts are not uncommon in Sweden today and may in fact be explosive. Yet, in the little group of the study circle, shared interest often becomes more important than provocations and different points of departure.

Education and schooling

The characteristics of the study circle are the small group and the principle of self-education. The first circles were formed at the start of this century, when education was communicated from the top down. The idea of the study circle was that people should learn from one another.

The labour movement was the first to form an organisation for this purpose, Arbetarnas Bildningsförbund (The Workers' Educational Association), which was started in 1912. This was soon followed by others. Today, there are eleven educational associations that organise study circles in Sweden. They represent a wide variety of political opinions, religious faiths, and interest groups. A typical feature of the educational associations is that they are based on particular ideologies which they convey in their study activities. They all share the ideal of making education available to everyone, outside the sphere of regular state education. The study circle is the smallest cell in this adult education drive, the offshoot that reaches deepest into society. Study circles can be found everywhere, in the biggest cities, the smallest villages, and the most sparsely populated part of Sweden. Study circles give schooling in democracy in practice: self-government, cooperation, exchange of opinions on equal terms. Study circles in Sweden attract between two-and-a-half and three million participants each year. This figure includes some who take part in more than one circle at a time, but it is still estimated that more than a million people annually educate themselves in almost three hundred fifty thousand study circles.

About half of these circles deal with the study of literature, history, languages, civics, political and union issues, mathematics, computers, and so on. These theoretical and intellectual circles continue the original aim of the education associations, offering people the book learning that was once the sole privilege of the upper classes. Yet, this is precisely the kind of knowledge that has become all the more accessible to everyone with the expansion of schools and state education. On the other hand, everyday skills in handicraft, which were widespread in the childhood of the popular educational associations, are receding rapidly. They are no longer automatically handed down within the family and the time devoted to them in school is constantly being reduced.

The culture of manual skills

Handicrafts are creative activities. Manual knowledge is not just practical, it is also aesthetic. Thus the educational associations classify study circles in handicrafts as aesthetic, and this section accounts for almost half of all study circles. It also includes circles in the 'fine arts' – drama, dance, music, the visual arts – but the practical-aesthetic circles predominate. The majority of participants are women. There are circles for most crafts: weaving, woodwork, lace making, knife making, basketry, embroidery, quilting, making folk costumes, vegetable dyeing, blacksmithing, bookbinding, knitting. By the far most common, however, are the textile arts, including needlework.

Despite their large number, these textile circles have an obscure, not to say invisible, place in the educational associations. They are rarely mentioned in the annual reports, and they are described in condescending terms as 'occupational therapy' or 'hobbies'. This is how they are evaluated from the outside. But I wondered what they look like from the inside. To find out, I spent an autumn and a spring as a member of study circles in dressmaking, quilting, weaving, and lace making.

What I found was a culture of manual skills that appears to have its roots in pre-industrial society, before machines and technology took over most human work. This is a culture where achievement – in both quantitative and qualitative terms – depends on human ability. The learning process more often goes by way of the body and the hand than by reading books. My old school skills had to be revived, since they proved to be necessary in order to learn the various crafts.

To learn how to weave, I had to calculate volume and dimensions, to divide, multiply, and count using X's. In patchwork quilting, I saw geometry in concrete shapes: squares, triangles, circles, rectangles, rhombi, hexagons, the size of an angle in degrees; all this became useful in different patterns. When I heard that lace making required the same talents as maths, chess, and computer science, I realised how hard it would be for me to learn. Designing a pattern for a garment calls for the architect's ability to translate three-dimensional models into two-dimensional plans. I had expected crafts to be practical, but not to be so technical. In the culture of manual skills, I found the kind of talent that is usually termed 'scientific' – a talent considered rare among women.

I already knew that handicraft satisfied the need to create, and the yearning for beauty. But I did not expect it to involve a heightening of one's aesthetic perception. I became aware of this when the paintings at Moderna Museet (Museum of Modern Art) in Stockholm suddenly had more to say to me than before. I realised then that I had become more aware of the harmony of colours and the effect of contrasts, of the relation of forms to one another, of how sense impressions and thoughts can be transferred to structures and nuances of colours.

I was prepared to find differences between the theoretical and the practical culture, but I was surprised by the similarities, by the fact that I found things that I had previously encountered in my book learning. At the same time, the knowledge became more real, more concrete, when put to practical use in the work of my hands. Perhaps this is one reason people continue to do things with their hands that can be done much faster – and often with greater perfection – by machine. Another reason may be the need to pass on the cultural heritage that is inherent in the traditional manual crafts.

Every craft, moreover, has its own cultural heritage. Those who are willing to listen can converse with earlier generations, learning about the availability of raw material and conditions of production in the past, which, in turn, raises questions about environmental changes, the consumption of resources, the conditions of working life. Traditional patterns tell us about a bygone conceptual world, about status symbols and ways of marking boundaries, and about religious edicts. They can reveal their models, which can be lilies from the court of the French king, sailors' presents from foreign lands, or details observed in the homes of the Swedish upper class. These models were then interpreted, changed, and simplified, reappearing in a folk tradition.

When old techniques are handed down, the cultural heritage is preserved. But it is preserved by living hands, which means that it is subject to change. Old traditions live on, new ones arise. The rag rug can serve as an example. It testifies to the way things used to be saved for reuse. But it was also a souvenir album. The rug was woven from old, worn-out clothes and textiles, but it was also woven from the memories of the people who had worn the clothes, from occasions when the textiles had been used. It became a subjective souvenir album, decipherable only by those who could identify the origin of the rags.

The rag rug I wove is made of old jeans from the last two decades, jeans that became too small for my children and jeans that I had worn out. The rug reminds me of a time when boundaries appeared to be erased, boundaries between classes, between genders, between generations. Everyone could wear jeans and use their time for something other than thinking out a personal dress style, for instance, human relations and social issues.

Yet, jeans also encapsulate a longer collective memory. Jeans were the first mass-produced garments. The characteristic double seams were made possible by the first mass-produced technical apparatus, the sewing machine. Both were born in the United States, which was to be a pioneer in the process of industrialisation. In the mid-nineteenth century, however, it was still a sparsely populated agrarian country, where labour was expensive. This stimulated innovations which could replace manual work with machines. The mass production of commodities had a market in all the immigrants who were able to cross the Atlantic, bringing with them only the barest essentials.

Just as much as the old peasant textiles, then, my rag rug made of old jeans is suffused with collective and subjective memories.

A cultural heritage in women's hands

The participants in my four study circles were all women, and typically Swedish women, to boot. Almost all of them had families and full-time jobs. Most of them had an education and qualified professions. The participants in the one pensioners' circle that I joined had similar backgrounds; they had been in gainful employment for most of their lives, while also shouldering responsibility for the children and the household. These women are scarcely in need of 'occupational therapy'. Their time is actually at a premium.

Of their own free will, they sacrifice some of their spare time – and quite a lot of money – on coming once a week to learn a textile craft. This new knowledge does not give them higher status or a better chance of a rise in salary and promotion. On the contrary, wasting time on handicraft is in the eyes of many people a dubious pursuit. Some of the women are therefore anxious to conceal their interest in handicraft. This culture has a breadth and depth seldom suspected by outsiders, but visible in certain contexts, as when tens of thousands of women invade textile exhibitions, or in the number of study circles on textiles.

Handicraft is also the basis for the sewing bee, a widespread female form of gathering which in Sweden is called *syjunta*. Under the cover of needlework, women get together, converse, and create community, in roughly the same way that men can legitimately leave the family to mix under the cover of sports. This special female form of gathering can be found in the study circles. While hands are busy doing useful things, tongues are discussing matters great and small. Major issues such as politics, society, the conditions of human existence are brought to a concrete everyday level. There is a constant exchange of information: where to shop at the lowest prises, how to deal with authorities, doctors, unemployment offices. Recipes and household hints are swapped. Talk about children and grandchildren reflect the past, the present, and speculation about the future. New items gleaned from the mass media are analysed in terms of personal experience. The flow of information in modern society is thus transformed into everyday knowledge of practical use. In this way, modern-day women pass on a female culture in the study circle.

The reality of the textile circles reveals the values hidden in condescending labels such as 'occupational therapy' or 'women's hobbies'. This value-system puts book learning before dexterity, theoretical knowledge before practical skills, and male spheres of interest before female ones. Yet, their priorities show that the women in the circles have a different value system. To them, creativity, togetherness, and concrete knowledge are central. In addition, for many of them it is a great source of satisfaction to know that they are also the stewards of a textile heritage and a female tradition.

PART III.
TECHNOLOGY AND ORGANISATION

14 Cultures, languages, technologies

Manfred E.A. Schmutzer

> ... *technology is at the same time a cause and a consequence of the values and norms of the society in which it develops; technology is a social force as well as a product of society.* (O. Mayr, 1986)

Introduction

The object of this paper is twofold: in the first place we want to contribute to bridging the deplorable gap between the engineering and the social sciences. There is a need for a 'new technical paradigm', to use H. Böhme's words, i.e. for a frame of mind which takes the social implications of technical activities and innovations into account. Secondly we intend to contribute to the development of the methods of technology assessment and technology evaluation.

Basic to our approach is the anthropological interpretation of culture as a way of life or lifestyle which is shared by a group and establishes the necessary preconditions for consensus, cooperation and living together.[1]

Let us start out by explaining what we mean by a way of life. In his work on the process of civilisation Elias (1969) points out some of the phenomena that make up the concept. But certainly there is more to it than handkerchief and cutlery. A way of life manifests itself, above al. in the perception of time, in the way the affects are controlled, in value judgements and norms, in the forms of social intercourse and interaction. In his work, Elias mentions affect- and self-control, individualisation and the way a single person is made and sees these as the characteristic traits of modern Western man.[2] In his view, modern man and his hallmark – scientific-technical civilisation – is characterised by the cult of individualism carried to extremes. This theme is forcefully presented, above all, in his historical studies, where he shows the preponderance of an egocentric picture of man, of the

1 Lifestyles may be refined – cultivated – in varying degrees. The beautiful people usually possess the necessary means to present their refinements as the most perfect. Despite such variations they remain part of a continuum, a topology. They are interrelated through certain basic operations which are possible between them and only between them.

2 Snow e.g. characterises modern man by quoting Trilling: ... I dare maintain, that the idea, to give oneself over to experience up to the point of self-destruction without concern for ones own person or for morality, to free oneself totally from the bonds of society, that this idea is an element which is present somewhere in the mind of every modern person ... (Snow, 1963).

ideal of the homo clausus for whom society is purely external. Other historians and anthropologists have voiced similar diagnoses.[3]

The opposite of the above ideal is embodied by an attitude which represses the ego as far as possible: the 'we-feeling' is predominant, creating whole groups as the smallest social units.[4] To show how this is expressed in the Anglo-Saxon tradition we quote R. Williams (1958):

> ... a culture is not only a body of intellectual and imaginative work; it is also and essentially a whole way of life... The crucial element in English life since the Industrial Revolution is ... between alternative ideas of the nature of social relationship. ... (Williams 1958, p.325)

Williams sees these alternative cultures realised in 'working class culture' and 'bourgeois culture'. A cautionary word may be in order at this point for the German reader, because here we all too often perceive the above dichotomy as an ideological construct. It seems important therefore to add a further quote:

> ... what is properly meant by working class culture. It is not proletarian art, or council houses, or a particular use of language; it is rather, the basic collective idea, and the institutions, manners, habits of thought and intentions which proceed from this. Bourgeois culture, similarly, is the basic individualistic idea and the institutions, manners, habits of thought and intentions which proceed from that. (ibid., p.327)

Let us keep in mind that the essential category here is the form of social relationships, which may be one of two types: collectivism on the one hand, individualism on the other. The concept of 'forms of interaction' covers a number of important behavioural patterns, or styles of thought and perception, as described by psychologists and anthropologists (e.g. Levi-Strauss, 1962). To wit, forms of communication, language, ways of defining and solving problems, attitudes towards risk, and above all how socialisation is achieved in the respective culture. All these factors make up a way of life, which is defined by their totality.[5]

The two mutually exclusive types of social relationships each practise their specific form of socialisation. Obviously they remind one of the distinction between 'society' (Gesellschaft) and 'community' (Gemeinschaft) introduced by Tönnies more than hundred years ago. With Tönnies the conflict lay between city and country, between metropolis and village. We wished to put this traditional

---

3 For instance Dumont (1966, 1967), Sahlins (1976), Macpherson (1962), Polanyi (1944), Elias (1939).

4 For examples see Borst (1979), Dumont (1966) etc.

5 Besides pointing out the existence of two fundamentally different patterns of socialisation, Elias also shows how these predispositions enter into theories of social science – for instance in the case of Parsons or Weber – (Dumont gives the analogue for French sociology, 1967), which thus themselves become corresponding agents of socialisation.

background in perspective by quoting R. Williams above. The working-class is city-bound, it is an essential constituent of industrialisation, yet its basic tenets are collectivity, solidarity, communality. The other side, the individualistic bourgeois, entrepreneur, capitalist, is fully aware of this state of things. It is a matter of political-tactical predispositions, but also of ideological-cognitive ones.

It will therefore not come as a surprise that specific methods and social techniques have been developed to ensure the production of individualistic members of society psycho- and sociogenetically. As carriers of these methods and techniques we might mention the modern school (Durkheim 1902, 1903), the army (Foucault 1975), and a high mobility which is generated by marked geographical disparities and specific technologies of transport. This, of course, does not exhaust the repertoire of techniques, but others, such as the development and cultivation of specific modes of language may also be found on the other side, which has its strategies of education and socialisation as well.[6]

Once it is agreed that the form of social relationships constitutes the difference between cultures and that the genesis of these relationships is anything but random, but is supported by refined social techniques, we may use Max Weber's (1922) terminology for the characterisation of cultures. Weber discerns processes of association (Vergesellschaftung) and processes of community-building (Vergemeinschaftung). These concepts will prove useful for our further descriptions.

The above-mentioned processes could also be described by making use of Georgescu-Roegen's concepts of the 'arithmomorphic' and the 'dialectic' continuum. Association (Vergesellschaftung) aims at establishing an arithmomorphic continuum in the mind as well as in the practical life of society. Community-building (Vergemeinschaftung), on the other hand, realises a dialectic continuum in which contradictions are integrated, not banished. Banished, though, is everything which cannot be discussed in this universe of discourse: strangers, aliens and the alien. Cultures based on solidarity have a tendency to be xenophobic.[7]

Let us stress that either individualism or collectivism are the constitutive traits of cultures, but that these basic forms may be further differentiated. Starting from a 2x2 contingency table the British anthropologist Mary Douglas developed

---

6 Mannheim (1929/1936) mentions the educational method of the workshop, which he considers typical for the formation of mutual relationships – we call them heterarchical – between master and apprentice. Additionally he points out the lack of systematic procedures, and the preoccupation with concrete situations instead of abstract language-centred explanation. It will not then come as a surprise that the product of such cooperation is seen as a collective one. The design of communal meeting-places, the arrangement of seats – in a circle, in confrontation as in the English Parliament, or oriented towards the front as in the case of the fourth-wall-stage, are everyday examples of the handling of social situations by means of technical devices.

7 The result of the discussion up to this point might be the impression that associative cultures are solely a product of post-medieval Europe. This would be just as false as to understand science as the unique product of the same period and region. Recurrent tendencies towards associativity may be found in diverse historical periods. There is not only the Periclean epoch: Goody (1983) points, in this context, to a tendency in the Christian religion in the third century, and Weber (1922) calls the monk the first individualist.

'group-grid-analysis', which one of her collaborators, M. Thompson, renamed 'cultural theory'. Here we find four distinct types of forms of interaction and thus of lifestyles. Like Williams – or E. Durkheim – the proponents of Cultural Theory understand 'culture' as a way of life which is above all determined by the 'nature of social relationships'. A differentiation results from taking into account two variables which Douglas regards as constitutive for the self-perception of a group. There is, on the one hand, the way in which the 'internal-external relationship' of the group is defined and, on the other, the group's internal structure. Douglas takes these variables as continuous, which means that categories may be defined only approximately by considering extreme values, e.g. in the following way:

- internal/external relationship: closed versus open,
- internal structure: vertically structured versus egalitarian (i.e. no vertical structure but a horizontal network).

Accordingly, the following patterns are possible:

- closed, egalitarian
- closed, non-egalitarian
- open, egalitarian
- open, non-egalitarian

This attempt at categorisation may be interesting or not, but by itself it may not claim to be better than any other. However, by using a formal mathematical model, I have been able to show that it really is a system of categories, i.e. that it can be used to classify all possible types. It follows that the above cases are clear-cut, mutually exclusive types, with no continuum of intermediary possibilities.

My argument was roughly as follows. Interaction patterns may be represented in matrix form, where a matrix element, properly normalised, describes the intensity of interaction between two group-members. Obviously, the matrix may also be regarded as defining a linear transformation which maps a vector-space into an image-vector-space. If we let the interaction matrix operate on vectors which are interpreted as resources of the interaction partners, the image vector may be seen as the resulting resource distribution achieved by the process of interaction. Thus, we have a system of non-homogeneous linear equations, which, if a solution exists, enables us to compute the initial resource distribution leading to a given final distribution via the process of interaction. The existence or non-existence of a solution depends upon the properties of the interaction matrix. If, for instance, the rows of the matrix are linearly dependent, i.e. if the interaction pattern is closed or cyclical, no solution will exist.

Now, a system of equations either has a solution or it does not, that is we have two distinct, mutually exclusive alternatives. This furnishes us with two categories, the interpretation of which is that a closed system will not produce individually discernible results while an open system will. We have thus established a connection between open and individualistic systems on the one hand, and closed and collectivistic systems on the other. The model represents the above mentioned four types in a unique way. The correspondence with the concepts of cultural theory is perfect, since interior structure may be represented in the model in an analogous manner. Likewise, the two concepts, community (Gemeinschaft) and association (Gesellschaft), are now given precise meanings by referring them to distinct interaction structures. Two of the types have the character of communities, the other two that of associations. The closed, egalitarian and the open, non-egalitarian type, represented in the model by systems of equations with no solution or only a trivial solution, stand for community; the open, egalitarian type and the closed, non-egalitarian type model individualistic associations or societies. They in turn are characterised by systems of equations which possess non-trivial solutions, the second type showing a clear hierarchical structure.

Since our categorisation, derived as it is from the Cultural Theory approach, is complete and disjoint, and thus formally perfect, we give it preference over all other attempts at classification. Henceforth we shall therefore make use of the following terminology: Zeromatrix (waiting-room) and Clan for the community types; Market and Bureaucracy or Hierarchy for the two association types.

Social change

In contrast to the usually accepted idea of social change, which is heavily indebted to the Darwinist concept of differentiation of species, I shall not be concerned with differentiation of existing systems, but rather with their breakdown and possible rebuilding; breakdown is perhaps too strong a term and is better replaced by mobility. Our attention will thus not be directed towards established social systems proper, but rather towards their marginal groups, or rather towards individuals which have already moved beyond the borders of the systems. If this kind of exclusion goes on for a longer stretch of time or in appreciable numbers, the excluded, uprooted or alienated individuals must needs search for or rebuild new interaction structures. Since closed, established groups are usually quite unapproachable, these structures will predominantly incorporate other aliens.

During this process there is no behavioural homomorphism between the interacting organisms and, although individually they operate strictly as structure-determined systems, everything that takes place through their interactions is novel, anticommunicative, in the systems that they then constitute together, even if they otherwise participate in other consensual domains. If this process leads to a consensual domain, it is in the strict sense, a conversation, a turning around together in such manner that all participants undergo nontrivial changes until a behavioural homomorphism is established and communication takes place. These precommunicative or anticommunicative interactions that take place during a conversation, then, are creative interactions that lead to novel behaviour. The condition under which a conversation takes place (common interest, spatial confinement, friendship, love, or whatever keeps the organisms together), and which determine that the organisms should continue to interact until a consensual domain is established, constitute the domain in which selection for the ontogenetic structural coupling takes place. Without them, a consensual domain could never be established, and communication, as the coordination of non-creative ontogenetically acquired modes of behaviour would never take place (Maturana, 1978, p.54).

To translate the situation which has been described in the above paragraph into the terminology of Cultural Theory, it may be said that a certain number of people from different groups are excluded. Those excluded at first represent the type of the zeromatrix because, being still caught up in the ideas and action patterns of their former cultures, they are unable to interact and are outer-directed. They constitute an open system devoid of interactions. The point of interest is that at which conversation begins, where creative interactions start to develop, which in turn create novel behaviour, including new patterns and forms of interaction. For this to happen these people must learn to perceive themselves as individuals and no longer only as parts of a culture. The discovery of the ego occurs, the ego is idealised and romanticised. But still interaction cannot take place, all the necessary preconditions are not yet established. As Maturana puts it:

> Linguistic communication always takes place after the establishment of an ontogenetic structural coupling, and in that sense is trivial because it shows only that the engineer's situation has been established. What is not trivial however, is what takes place in the process of attaining communication through the establishment of ontogenetic structural coupling and the shaping of consensual domain. (ibid.)

In this process new languages, new patterns of activity, new forms of consensus must be developed in order for – last but not least – new interaction patterns to evolve. These patterns may not be freely chosen, but are subject to diverse boundary conditions, of prime importance being the length of the required socialisation period. Clans will require very long socialisation times, the times for markets are much shorter, hierarchies may be found somewhere in between, since their disciplinary structures must be seen as restricted – and not only as restrictive – socialisation.

Obviously cooperation structures also differ in efficiency. W.G. Ouchi (1980), who, independently of Cultural Theory, developed a similar system of categories, has suggested a useful point of view for the judgement of efficiency. Markets are characterised by short-livedness, strongly conflicting interests and simplicity of interaction. If more complex forms of cooperation are required, markets are no longer suitable organisational patterns and are replaced by hierarchies and bureaucracies. These work with clearly defined objectives and are capable of reducing interior conflicts by means of suitable sanctions. They in turn break down if problem complexity increases still further and if patterns of activity can no longer be clearly defined. In situations of this kind clans will be successful where consensus may still be established and upheld, even in very unclear and complex situations, on account of the close intimacy of the members. This intimacy is the result of very long socialisation times and will only be possible if the number of group members is not too large. Ouchi mentions also a fourth type of structure, into which he puts schools; this fourth type is very similar to what we called zeromatrix.

Looking at these differing ways in which cooperation can be organised, it is easy to see that they will also evolve specific forms of communication or language games. Language, after all, must not only meet the different requirements mentioned above, but it must also adapt to differing boundary conditions.

Languages

It is very likely not by chance that M. Douglas developed her group-grid-theory on the basis of a socio-linguistic model of B. Bernstein (1971). Let us briefly sketch this model. Bernstein discerns two language types which he relates to Durkheim's distinction between mechanical and organic solidarity. The first type is cultivated in an environment in which all speakers have access to the same fundamental assumptions and share them. This form of language he calls public language: it is non-individualistic, avoids statements in the first person singular, delights in circular forms of argument, and uses a very restricted vocabulary. It supports tradition and authority. The second form of language, which Bernstein terms formal language, develops where consensus is scarce. In contrast to the first type it is individualistic, logical, precise and object-oriented. The relation of these language types to our categories of Gesellschaft (associative groups) and Gemeinschaft (communal groups) should be obvious. Bernstein further distinguishes between two types of code, elaborated and restricted. Codes are the products of a superimposed social matrix. A restricted code should not only convey information but is also meant to express relationships of dominance and subordination. Elaborated codes are not encumbered by aims of this kind, they are more egalitarian and free. Their environment though is less well ordered and regulated. It must be possible to use them innovatively, to describe and explain novel situations. Theirs is an individualistic orientation, their meanings, in Maturana's words, have to be negotiated. To avoid misunderstandings, to achieve the aims of negotiations, an extreme refinement of the vocabulary becomes a necessity. This is the classical situation, which Mead refers to as the communication process between ego and alter. The ability to master a code is imparted during socialisation, it is specific to a culture or must be evolved in a process of conversation, as mentioned above.

We repeat, language types and code types are culture-specific, they are imparted via characteristic programmes of socialisation.

> *Language is not* an organisation of natural stimuli, as is for instance a packet of photons which we experience as light-stimulus. It is a man-made organisation of stimuli, *an artefact*, in the same way as a work of art is an artefact; ... As linguists are well aware, language is not one means of communication among others; it is that which is the basis of all communication; better still language is the true basis of culture. Relative to language all other systems of symbols are accessory or derived.
>
> (Eco, 1962, my translation and italics)

Why this is the case was formulated as early as 1936 by the well known linguist B. L. Whorf in his description of the function of language:

> *Language produces an organisation of experience.* We are inclined to think of language simply as a technique of expression, and not to realise that language first of all is a classification and arrangement of the stream of sensory experience which *results in a certain world order*, a certain segment of the world that is easily expressible by the type of symbolic means that language employs. In other words, language does in a cruder but also in a broader and more versatile way the same thing that science does.
>
> (Whorf, 1936, p.55, my italics)

Under these circumstances it is hardly surprising that this world order is in accordance with the prevalent social structure or organisation, or rather that it has been generated or modelled with this accordance as the objective. Maturana draws the following conclusions, 'The logic of the description is isomorphic to the logic of the operation of the describing system.' (Maturana, 1978, p.60). '... the emitter and receiver must be operationally congruent for the phenomenon of communication to occur...'. (Maturana, 1978, p. 54).

Combining these statements by Eco, Whorf and Maturana, we may say that the world order which is established by language corresponds to the logic of the social system.[8]

After this digression, let us return to our main topic. If there really is an isomorphism between the type of description and the organisational pattern of the descriptive system, we should, according to cultural theory, not only be able to discover types of language corresponding to types of social structure but in general, types of artefacts showing the same correspondence. As regards languages, Bernstein's typology of languages and codes furnishes a basis. Restricted and elaborated public languages may be contrasted with restricted and elaborated formal languages. Bernstein himself has established a correspondence between language types, individualistic associations and collectivistic communities. To do the same for codes will not be difficult. Bureaucracies by necessity employ a restricted code, primarily for disciplinary reasons. Markets, where discipline is a secondary concern, rely on elaborated codes. Clans are also dependent on restricted codes for a variety of reasons, as Bernstein points out in

---

8 This is also true for science, which must conform to this internal logic. If this line of thought is pursued further one soon arrives at theories like those of Duhem or Fleck. On the other hand, one could argue that the following becomes necessary whenever this world order through a common language is not given: the development of proof-oriented science as a new integrative form of language to generate a new world order. A precondition for this is the existence of a highly elaborated code which minimises misunderstandings, stemming from the diverse old orders still present in the mind. Precision of expression and congruence relative to a given world order are quasi inversely proportional: the better the congruence the less precision and vice versa. Indeed, we often find a multitude of highly articulate sophists as the forerunners of new sciences.

his characterisation of public language. This leaves an elaborated code of a public language for our category of the zeromatrix. This should at least be plausible when the social situation of isolated, not yet resocialised individuals is taken into account, where private languages arise, with an interest in differentiated expression. but not yet socially negotiated. Maturana's turning around in a conversation has not yet come to an end.

Technologies

We shall now consider technology, the third concept in the title of this paper. It might be asked where the connection between technology and languages or codes is to be found. The question is not new; Rammert (1988, 1989), Hörning (1988) and others have tried for quite some time to interpret technology as a form of communication, a medium or a system of symbols. Perspectives still diverge, with Luhmann's concept of medium and a semiological approach in the tradition of R. Barthes indicating the extremes of the field. Our position as developed in the following, might, we hope, integrate the diverging perspectives.

First let me point out that the approaches mentioned above do not contain irreconcilable contradictions. In art, which, for instance in architecture, has close ties with technology, we find a variety of different styles, not all of the same kind, as say the difference between Romanesque or Gothic cathedrals. L. White (1962) has pointed out that in the 13th and 14th centuries interest in general shifted from the building of cathedrals to the making of clocks. There is a change not only in the style of building but in the whole direction of technological interest. This cannot be explained simply by progress in the means of production – neither clocks nor cathedrals are such means – but solely by changes in the initial social conditions. In this context White says:

> Suddenly, towards the middle of the fourteenth century, the mechanical clock seized the imagination of our ancestors. Something of the civic pride which earlier had expended itself in cathedral-building now was diverted to the construction of astronomical clocks of astounding intricacy and elaboration. No European community felt able to hold up its head unless in its midst the planets heeled in cycles and epicycles, while angels trumpeted, cocks crew, and apostles, kings, and prophets marched and countermarched at the booming of the hours. (White, 1962, p.124)

The processions of angels, prophets and planets illustrate the change that had occurred; the dynamism of the high middle ages, which we shall further discuss below, could no longer be represented by the static order of the habitat, of the house of God. New models of the world were about to replace the old order, and clocks were first of all such world models[9], models of a cosmic order of changing

[9] White (op. cit.) also shows that, since antiquity, clocks have originated from such world models.

qualities of hours and months. Time in the sense of timing complex processes (Elias, 1984) required the quality of time to gain public presentation. Gradually quality disappeared and with it the above processions, a consequence of further change in the social needs being reflected in the technologies of a period or a culture.

The work of O. Mayr (1986) enlarges on these ideas. Mayr shows the diversity of the basic concerns which are represented by pointing out the culture-specific differences in technological interest and progress. Thus in authoritarian Germany fascination with clock-work remained unabated while England, on its way to democracy, shifted its interest to regulating mechanisms and feedback devices. In this we see not so much Zeitgeist at work, but rather the spirit of the underlying social relationships which we have been talking about. It is not only the style or styling of technical objects, be it automobiles, steam-engines, or sacred buildings, which constitutes their symbolic meaning, but the very fact that cathedrals, steam-engines, diesel-motors, telephones or robots are built expresses a cultural bias, which we have to investigate.[10]

We can supplement the metaphoric narratives (Ricoeur, 1975) of the last paragraph with microstudies which set out to analyse and decode at the semantic or syntactic level. Here we are mainly concerned with those approaches which regard modern technology predominantly as a collection of steering and controlling procedures, i.e. the discussion is about actions and rules for actions and their integration into a larger framework. This point of view becomes increasingly important, as technology is no longer perceived exclusively as hardware but is understood as regulated procedures in accordance with the original etymology of the word. Grimms German Dictionary, for instance, has the following definition:

> Technik, f., aufgenommen aus franz. technique, vom griech. lat. technica (nämlich ars), die Kunst und Gewerbstätigkeit und der Inbegriff der Erfahrungen, Regeln, Grundsätze und Handgriffe, nach denen bei der Ausübung einer Kunst oder eines Gewerbes verfahren wird.
> (... the art and craft and the totality of the experiences, rules, principles and manipulations used in the exercise of an art or craft.)

As v. Gottl-Ottlilienfeld or A. Paulinyi (1987) point out, technology must be seen as Realtechnik, that is as the conglomerate of human activities and organisational rules which is necessary for the production and application of artefacts. Mechanisation (Technisierung), accordingly, is the process which increasingly introduces artefacts or devices into given activity patterns or operational procedures, thereby substituting human activity instead of achieving cooperation via a

10 The following quotation from Freyer (1929) seems pertinent: 'The societal activity of a human group together with the techniques used, is, just like any other activity, a whole and must be seen as such... the technical means follow from this fundamental decision, they are generated by it, it establishes their context. They are found, because they are sought.'

process of conversation. B. Joergens already expressed these views ten years ago when he wrote:

> ... that things are in a certain way crystallisations from systems of activities, that the form of these crystallisations must be seen as a function of need and perception, of target values and information, and that these crystallisations stabilise systems of activities, that they are, using A. Gehlen's phrase, external anchors of experience and action.
>
> (Joergens, 1979, p.129, my translation)

and when he drew the following conclusion:

> This, on the other hand, means that the engineering sciences must be understood as sciences concerned with a certain type of behavioural system (Verhaltenssysteme). (Joergens, 1979, p.127)

Viewed from this perspective Maturana's enigmatic statement '... linguistic communication ... is trivial because it shows only that the engineer's situation has been established' (ibid., p.54), appears in a new light. What is taking place here is the building of a consensual and cooperative set of interactions, which is first established at the factual level, i.e. at the level of artefacts, and which later on is also represented at the language level. If this is the deeper meaning of Technisierung (mechanisation), then we must have an isomorphism not only between language and cooperation structure, but also between the structure of language and the structure of technology, which must be understood as the expression of a situation that already exists at the social level. The image theory of language also acquires a new meaning under these circumstances: language is to be seen as part of a construction process, which generates reality and therefore must be the result of social activity and negotiation. What Maturana calls turning around is in the same way relevant for technical constructions and for their representation by language. At this point it becomes obvious that we shall not be able to avoid the vexing question of why this detour is necessary. But before we take it up we shall give a resumé of our line of argument.

Eco thinks of language as an artefact, as a thing created, and maintains that in relation to language all other systems of symbols are accessory and derived.[11] Whorf points out that this artefact in turn creates a certain organisation of experience, i.e. a world order.[12] Maturana explains that the logic of description must be isomorphic to the logic of the operations[13] of the descriptive system and that there must be congruence between the partners of an interaction. This permits us to see the production of artefacts as the central point in the discussion, and to state that the establishment of a world order is not only a question of language, but also the

11 This is still in keeping with an image theory.

12 Both Whorf and Eco create order in a world as found, not as constructed.

13 Only Maturana sees the creative activity as primary and does not take the world as given.

result of a mixed strategy which entails the production of diverse artefacts, among which we find language as well as physical things.

Maturana's isomorphism postulate entitles us to apply categories of social organisation to all systems of artefacts, be they languages or things. The immediate consequence of this is that we may answer the old vexing question about the social compatibility of technologies or physical systems. The answer is that they are socially compatible if they are isomorphic to the given cooperation structure. The concept of social compatibility has thus been given a definite meaning, which we may use in future work, and which no longer necessitates recourse to empirical snapshots with their irritating dependence on unique and concrete situations. Our approach thus permits not only the classification of the infinite variety of cultures as interaction patterns into four characteristic types but it also enables us to talk about culture-specific artefacts, which include languages and technologies.

The genesis of socio-technical systems

We shall now set out to integrate our modified version of Cultural Theory with the above sketches of social change and our remarks concerning the socio-genetic identity of things and languages. As a point of departure we take the situation of the zeromatrix introduced above, i.e. a situation where a number of excluded persons of differing cultural background must, for a variety of reasons (Maturana mentions spatial proximity, common interests, love etc.) enter into relationships of cooperation.

This abstract description immediately gains in vividness if we refer to concrete historical situations. Impressive examples of such situations come from periods of European history which are notable for their innovative zest, i.e. Greek and Hellenistic Antiquity (Finley, 1963), the Middle Ages between 1000 and 1300 (Gimpel, 1976), and the beginning of the modern period (Hill, 1972).[14] All these periods have the following features in common: high social mobility, the development of a markedly individualistic self-image – characterised by rationality, entrepreneurship, scientific attitude – and noteworthy technical innovations. Having written about these periods at length in earlier work, I will here confine myself to quoting J. Gimpel (1976), partly with the intention of dispersing doubts which, it seems, will most easily arise in connection with the Middle Ages.

> Some of the features that accompanied this first (i.e. medieval, M.S.) revolution seem strangely familiar.
>
> There was a great increase in population, which led to massive movements of people. They emigrated; they opened up and colonised new lands; they founded and built new towns. Conditions favoured free enterprise, and this led to the rise of self-made men. Capitalist companies were formed and their shares bought and sold. Entrepreneurs were fully prepared to use

14 The references are to be understood as examples, standing for a huge volume of literature.

ruthless business methods to stifle competition. They introduced extensive division of labour to increase efficiency and their enterprises called into being a proletariat whom they could exploit. The workers retaliated with wage claims, absenteeism, and strikes.

Energy consumption increased considerably. Technological innovations brought about improvements in the efficiency of existing methods and also led to a successful search for new sources of energy. Many of the tasks formerly done by hand were now done by machines. (p. viii/ix)

The period was characterised by a sense of optimism, a rationalist attitude, and a firm belief in progress (ibid).[15]

This concise description of a specific period of the Middle Ages could also serve, without any major changes, for corresponding periods of antiquity or of the beginning of the modern period. High mobility brings about a situation – that of the zeromatrix in our terminology – which forces people to search for and develop new patterns of cooperation. This is accompanied by efforts to create a new form of rationality as a basis for new language games and new patterns of consensus; it also entails the creation of new proof procedures, to settle doubtful cases, and the use of technical innovations in cooperation structures. In other words, the engineer's situation is established. But during this process the formerly pliable social material hardens and a reverse movement sets in.

At a certain point, the dynamism of the Middle Ages began to fail and symptoms of decline became evident. The population ceased to grow, differences between the classes hardened, and there was less social mobility (Gimpel, 1976, p. ix).

There was a decline in old moral values. People became less public-spirited, and with this went a growth of permissiveness. There was a growing awareness of aesthetic values. Many people turned away from traditional religion to embrace new esoteric cults. Rationalism gave way to mysticism (ibid. p. ix/x).

Despite all the similarities shown above one should be wary of stretching the analogies to far. There are many areas in which the periods in question differ from each other. Antiquity for instance is unique insofar as consensus was almost exclusively established on the basis of language games. By language games in this context we mean also scientific methods such as taxonomy or logic, legal innovations such as the codification of law, or political innovations such as the development of the procedures of democratic government.

The Middle Ages supplemented language games by integrating things into activity patterns, e.g. by the use of machines in the medieval factories, the Cistercian monasteries (Duby, 1979). Consensus was still mainly achieved by dialectic procedures, on the basis of methods of proof accepted once and for all.

The modern period proceeds quite differently. In his arguments, Descartes relies on the power of proof of the doctrine of artefacts: the fact that something can be manufactured is sufficient proof of its correctness (Loeck, 1986). In principle,

15 At this point I would like to remind the reader of what was said at the beginning of the section Technologies.

this kind of proof is held to be applicable to any kind of discourse. For Leibniz the mechanical produce-ability of a scientific statement becomes the criterion of its truth (Krämer, 1988). At the same time, we find a novelty in technological development; first in the military, but only a short time later also in the area of technical production, personal expertise and craftsmanship are replaced by mechanisation. Guilmartin (1974) shows how the shortage of trained archers and artillery men in the 16th century was compensated by the building of cheap guns which permitted faster loading and thus offset the inferior marksmanship of the gunners by a higher rate of fire. While huge losses on the battlefield give a plausible motive for military innovation, the parallel civilian development is not as easily explained. In a Venetian print of 1636 the Italian Abbe Lancelotti reports that 50 years before a certain Anton Müller had observed a machine in Danzig simultaneously weaving 4 to 6 pieces of fabric. The machines inventor was said to have been murdered on the instigation of the city council. This obviously did not kill the invention, because 50 years after the Lancelotti print the German Emperor was petitioned by the guild of braidmakers and ribbon weavers to forbid the use of such ribbon mills, which consequently must have been quite frequent by the end of the 17th century. As we know, even the Emperor's prohibition could not stem the tide of progress, which rolled on in its diverse forms and finally turned into what is now commonly called the industrial revolution.

The essential feature of this development is the reduction or elimination of such practices of social integration as professional training or socialisation. Their place is taken by devices which communicate by means of another language and whose ability to convince is neither founded on logic as in antiquity, nor due to a dialectic integrating all contradictions as in the Middle Ages, but lies in a syntax or formal calculus which precludes misunderstandings or misconceptions *ab initio*.

The leading role of language, so dear to Eco the linguist, is tacitly abolished and preference is given to the category of artefacts. Its resistance to misunderstanding turns out to be sufficient to ensure cooperation without socialisation[16], this all the more so when artefacts are made into whole systems by coupling them via power engines. The work machine forms the basis of the socio-technical system, that is of a method and its implementation, which replaces the social component and permits cooperation without interaction. Socialisation with regard to a certain cooperation is made unnecessary by mechanising the latter. We fully agree with Linde (1972), when he says that social institutions or organisations are now realised by means of equipment, their basic principles concerning the form and kind of cooperation being kept insofar as they are incorporated into the devices as grammar or syntax. This provides us with an instance of Leibniz' criterion at work.

Adam Smith had already foreseen the full extent of this development (Wieland, 1992). Division of labour is based on the principle of division and

16 It should be pointed out that devices or equipment can deal out sanctions. Misuse or abuse of a device, in other words the refusal to accept the proper code, meets with various sanctions (see also Linde, 1972). The spectrum of these sanctions extends from simple malfunction, via destruction of the device, to physical punishment of the misuser through accident or even death.

combination, whereby a network of operationally connected elements is constructed. This will also entail the adaptation of the human factor, which may now be achieved, as far as it still is necessary, via the short-cut of drill and disciplinary methods. Smith explicitly calls this construction a system, and regards it as a machine.

'A system is an imaginary machine invented *to connect together* (italics mine) in the fancy those different movements and effects which are already in reality performed' (quoted by Wieland, p.369).

Thus for Smith a machine is a device which not only performs certain processes but which above all links them together. In other words,: division of labour means the design of a machine which links work machines together. In his theory of moral sentiments Smith states quite clearly that this system comprises the whole of human society, which is a socio-technical system.[17]

A development of this kind presupposes pronounced phases of individualisation. That this has precisely been the case in the period indicated (17th/18th century) all over Europe and that individualism indeed became the leading idea in influential circles need not be demonstrated in detail; it will suffice to refer to the testimony of N. Elias (1939, 1969, 1970, 1987).

These phases of individualisation are accompanied by the development of democratic aspirations and of rational procedures and by an attitude which Ellul (1954) has called technical intention, meaning a frame of mind which favours technical inventions. Other attentive observers, for instance S. Giedion (1948) and T. Hughes (1989), have also remarked on this. The result of technical intention is not only a surprising number of successful technical inventions (a study of the unsuccessful ones might also be highly rewarding) but also that society and the world in toto are seen in the image of a machine, specifically as clockwork. And it perfectly fits this rationalist world-machine to see language as an image of the world and not as the result of societal negotiations and socialisation (Winograd and Flores, 1986). This view postulates very specific characteristics of language and in turn does not fail to discover them empirically. And as we shall see, this leads to the development of characteristic forms of technology. But before we proceed, let us repeat what was said at the beginning of the section on technology.

There we mentioned the great narratives which find expression in the innovative development of new technologies, as for instance clocks. It turns out that these narratives, which are recounted by implementing and maintaining such technologies, are myths, that they have a quasi-religious character. They are cosmologies and as such represent social realities, just as Durkheim and Douglas have said. This representation is carried out on many levels simultaneously, not only the content, but also the form, the choice of the means of expression and of the representing artefact are adequate and isomorphic. Thus not only the large-scale features of the narrative but also its microstructure, the sentences, words and grammar, like a hologram, contain the same message: the desired and the experienced form of living together, the form of social interaction.

17 Human society appears ... as a huge machine, whose regular and harmonic working produces thousand pleasant effects. (According to Dreßen, 1982).

H. Zemanek (1981) has pointed out that the basis for all attempts at language-processing is to be found in the philosophical position of L. Wittgenstein's Tractatus Logico-Philosophicus (1921/22). There Wittgenstein expounds his theory that reality is mapped (abgebildet) onto language and that relations in reality and in language are not only in agreement but necessarily obey the same logical laws. The atoms of information (bits) obtained by digitalisation are aggregated in accordance with syntactical rules, which themselves are constituents of a logical structure. Thus we find here a perfect analogy to the methods used for organising the work of a number of semi-skilled workers, which we have referred to above. The theoretical framework is supplied by C. E. Shannon's conception of information as a sequence in time of yes/no decisions and N. Wieners theory of control and transmission of information.

Although Wittgenstein himself thoroughly revised his ideas on language in his later years and came to see it as the complex result of human interaction, his earlier view has continued to be of influence in computer science and has led to the development of Artificial Intelligence from the late fifties onward. In the roughly thirty years of its existence this field of research has had some astounding successes in so-called Microworlds[18], but of late has been increasingly subject to criticism (Dreyfus, 1972; Winograd and Flores, 1986). By regarding Wittgenstein's Tractatus as the seminal work of A.I., it becomes clear that the whole branch of research is not fundamentally dependent on computer technology but is rather the adequate contemporary implementation of an older philosophical programme, called the rationalist tradition by Winograd and Flores (op. cit.). The opposite of this is the hermeneutic conception as represented by M. Heidegger, E. Husserl, or M. Gadamer. They understand language as a social product and as the essential factor of socialisation, as does G.H. Mead (Schaff, 1964; Bernstein, 1971).

In the rationalist world language is the mirror of an absolutised reality, words are simply names. It follows that one language may be translated into another by the application of a certain algorithm, which is the basic tenet of machine translation. In contrast, the hermeneutic approach, where language is the result of complex negotiations and subject to continuous re-interpretation, negates the possibility of ever formalising and mechanising natural human language.

---

18 These are clearly demarcated areas of technical or scientific disciplines, having defined concepts and sets of formalised behavioural rules, which are unique and therefore not in need of interpretation.

According to S. Krämer (1988) formalisation makes the following three characteristic premises. The subject of normalisation must

- be given in written form, i.e. as an ordered sequence of well-defined symbols,
- be reducible to a scheme, i.e. to a reproducible procedure which is not content-dependent,
- not be dependent on semantic interpretation for operations to be performed on it.

S. Krämer (1988) sees computers '... as machines, who help us to build up symbolic worlds by forming and transforming strings of symbols' (Krämer, 1988, p.4, my translation).

Such worlds have no history and are, at least from the hermeneutic point of view, the results of wishful thinking, quite unrelated to reality. This appraisal may be correct as regards wishful thinking, but if this kind of thinking is applied to constructive engineering, its ties to reality may be much closer than the hermeneutic school imagines. In this case the socialising power of language is greatly reduced.

In short, we must not only think of computers as symbol-processing machines but must also take into account the fact that they are the result of a rationalistic and individualistic philosophical tradition, as exemplified by the concept of the information atom, i.e. the bit. It is not only that digital computers function according to the laws of a specific internal order (Boolean Algebra), they also represent this order externally. Their background is provided by a picture of man, which is atomistic and asocial insofar as it reduces to insignificance the social context into which language communication is embedded. The concept of symbol-processing machines can thus also be understood as the reproduction of a situation in which humans meet as individualised strangers with mutually unknown personal histories and can therefore only cooperate on the basis of intermediary devices.

What we said in the last paragraph only applies to digital computers. It has almost been forgotten that in the beginning of computerisation other options existed, as for instance analogue or hybrid computers, and that analogue computers are not at all built on the rationalistic, individualistic principles of the digital machines. Although common lore has it that the success of the digital machines is due to economic causes, we would like to register some doubts, which arise in particular when one looks at the motives behind some other decisions along the path of computer development.

S. Turkle (1990), for instance, points out that the personal computer (PC) not only works for us but also on us. This is what she calls the inner computer revolution, while we would prefer to call it behaviour-shaping personality formation. Turkle's extensive studies have demonstrated how behavioural patterns and personality structures are changed by working with computers. In the interviews she conducted there are indications that interacting with a machine enforces personality structures which differ from those originally given. This is one example of many where a technology becomes an agent of socialisation.

This kind of re-socialisation can frequently be observed in people who are gifted with a certain kind of creative thinking, which Turkle calls artistic. Referring to Lévi-Strauss' The Savage Mind (1962) she speaks of bricolage, that is pottering in a positive sense. People who prefer this style of work usually find working with conventional computer programs difficult, because these are not suited to their needs. Projects such as MITs ATHENA, which attempt to computerise university education, tend to discipline students with this kind of working-style. The (possibly ideological) aim of these projects seems to be to form certain personality structures by championing structured methods in contrast to less planned styles of work.

Bricolage is a form of science in its own right which Lévi-Strauss finds in non-western cultures. This kind of science proceeds atheoretically, using as points of departure small functional models, which, through pottering, are changed, adapted and made suitable for practical needs. According to Turkle, personalities with a leaning towards this kind of science often have difficulty in using hierarchically structured program-systems. Such systems are very abstract insofar as they are designed on the principle of black-boxing (i.e. a method which at the start plans sub-programs only by specifying their input and output and not their internal working, thus only making sure that the subprogram can be integrated into the main system). Such people prefer programming methods where all the details are given at any time and may be assembled by pottering. Turkle shows that this kind of working-style is mainly associated with Apple's Macintosh products in contrast to IBMs top-down approach, which Turkle sees as the prototype of hierarchically structured programming methods. This demonstrates how different philosophies influence the implementation of technologies, once again underscoring our thesis that the organising principles of apparatus mirror preferences in social organisation. There is no such thing as a neutral tool; in the background we always find social institutions intent on moulding personalities and integrating them into a preferred social structure.

Dijkstra's paradigm of Structured Programming is an example of a programming method which by banning unconditional branches (GOTO statements) and providing other suitable language constructs aims at developing individualised and easily controllable program structures. The so-called GOTO controversy (Dijkstra, 1968) once again illustrates how technologies are modelled on social structures. The GOTO statement of certain programming languages permits jumps to any other statement within the program, we might say it permits unrestricted contacts. Clearly this implies an egalitarian organisational concept. At the start of the industrial production of software in the late sixties when hierarchies of programmers started to work on large projects, egalitarian ideas of software-organisation quickly seemed out of place. One may give any number of rational reasons for this, as does Dijkstra, the foremost being efficiency-motivated layered division of labour and the necessity for of controlling it; the fact remains that once again technology and social organisation have been put into correspondence, an isomorphism has been established.

Artistically generated programs mark the opposite position. Turkle recalls the following episode at MIT: after a lecture by Dijkstra the well-known chess-programmer Greenblatt is said to have declared Structured Programming as unsuitable for writing chess-programs, an opinion which Dijkstra apparently did not contradict. Greenblatt, an expert in the A.I. domain of chess-programming, has developed a special tool, which enables him when playing complex games to access elements of his program and to change them on the spot. This procedure is not based on a deductive theory, it is obviously more similar to the way an artist works than is Structured Programming. Like Linné's botanical classification, Greenblatt's method aims at analysing specific cases and at assigning them a place within a complex overall structure. Thus it is a descriptive, not an imperative instrument.

Turkle's approach identifies, as does our own, two different kinds of science, two kinds of personality structure, two forms of knowledge, corresponding to which we find forms of language, methods and apparatus. In the section on the genesis of socio-technical systems yet another type of science, the dialogic-dialectic science of scholasticism was mentioned. Turkle also mentions a third kind of computing machine, which she terms the romantic machine, but which is better known under the name of perceptron. The perceptron is based on a radically different kind of architecture, that of neural networks. Machines of this type are self-programming, they present closed entities whose internal functioning is not interfered with. By assigning values to the outputs associated with certain inputs, the machine may be made to behave sensibly. This does not quite meet H.A. Simon's (1979) definition of intelligent behaviour as the reproducible result of rational procedures. Since the precise micro-details of the function of the perceptron's functioning are not prescribed, we are entitled to say that we find here a different kind of intelligence (Dreyfus, 1988).

The meaning of neural networks from the sociogenetic point of view may also be seen in Turkle's work. She gives a list of names for neural machines in which we find society of mind, biological machine and similar expressions. A name like emergent artificial intelligence implies that results are obtained through the interaction of unspecified agents within the machine. Here intelligence is not the result of the computer following rules but that of discursive interaction.[19] Turkle has very aptly called the perceptron the romantic machine. Romantic it is insofar as it reminds us of a social structure which we called clan and which we only find in rudimentary form in Western civilisation. If, however, we look back five or six centuries into European history we find clans as the dominant form of social organisation and it is this retrospect which justifies the term romantic.

19 This possibility, long denied and fought by the orthodox A.I. community, again shows the impressive plasticity of technology. As a result of preferred social structures and their associated patterns of thought, not all possibilities are exploited, as is exemplified by the vehement, twenty-year-long refusal of the hard-liners of strong A.I. to take the perceptron seriously. Dreyfus and Dreyfus (1988) give the history in detail. In this context it may also be of interest that Winograd, after interesting initial successes in A.I., has left the field, becoming an adherent of the hermeneutic approach to language. He now is engaged in producing software to support negotiation processes and the clearing up of misunderstandings.

Examples of a similar nature may also be found outside the field of computing. In his study of the rise of mass-production in the U.S., Roe Smith (1985) has shown how a problem of logistics (keeping armies supplied) has generated a characteristic form of organisation (hierarchical, because extended dispositions are involved, as Ouchi would point out), how this in turn created a suitable technology in the armaments sector (standardised mass-production), and how this technology finally caused the whole production process to be restructured. Work which was organised in workshops on the basis of a clan-like group of skilled craftsmen, changed into a standardised, mechanised process in modern factories, which by extensive division of labour can do without skilled labour.

But there are still other instructive examples. It is quite in line with the ideas we have developed so far to interpret writing as a technology. The work of Goody, Watt (1963) or Ong (1982) also takes this position. These authors show that the invention of the alphabet in ancient Greece is the characteristic feat of an individualised, open and egalitarian society. In contrast to earlier systems Greek writing was easy to learn and to use. Markets with their special conditions of socialisation demand user-friendly technologies, something which the earlier systems of writing, like Chinese or Egyptian, certainly could not claim to be. These systems were typically restricted codes and, having arisen in the context of administration by bureaucrats and experts, were certainly not egalitarian. It fits into the picture that proponents and defenders of archaic forms of society such as Plato preferred orality to written communication as a matter of principle, and it shows the negative attitude of clans to technical innovation.

Our theme is also illustrated by a number of studies of contemporary topics by other scientists. We mention T.P. Hughes' (1983) papers on power-grid systems and his American Genesis and the study by Weltz and Lullies (1983) of the introduction of text-processing systems, which they called Menschenbilder der Betriebsorganisatoren (Man as pictured by organisation experts). We shall give a brief resumé of this work, because its results are very close to our own approach.

This long-term study collected organisation experts' attitudes and images of man relating to the substitution of human work by mechanical work.

The study identifies three types of expert which fit easily into the framework of Cultural Theory. The authors label them technology-oriented, organisation-oriented and work-oriented. The first type simply sees the substitution of human work as the objective of introducing text-processing. Organisation-oriented individuals tend to see this technical innovation as a means of improving central leadership and control. For the third type the technical aspect is a side-issue, he mainly believes in improving the work situation and puts his hopes in the workers' ability to learn. The intentions of this type seem to be rather pragmatic and undogmatic, he tends to have a negative attitude towards standardisation and mechanisation.

In the terminology of Cultural Theory this last type of person is a representative of community-oriented clan-thinking. He relies on extensive socialisation, on willingness to cooperate and on the readiness to identify oneself with a group. Substitution of human work is not his aim, nor is centralist control. The second of the above types is the classic representative of hierarchical thinking; he expects considerably less of the staff (their socialisation being less thorough), which means he has to enforce cooperation by control measures. The technology oriented type of person has the least expectations and thus has to replace human cooperation by reliable equipment, which by its design is better socialised, more user-friendly than human partners. We have already met this type as a representative of short-lived market organisations. Pictures of man are the result of experiences during socialisation, which in turn rest on ideas concerning the quality and desirability of forms of human cooperation. It does not come as a surprise that several other empirical studies arrive at similar results, although it seems that examples of community-orientation are not infrequently overlooked, being remote from the current individualistic paradigm, and confused with the market or hierarchical type.

Yet another remark may be in order. Our argument so far has mainly dealt with the genesis of interaction structures. Cultures, though, are long-lived phenomena which are passed on through socialisation; that is, congruence of action is achieved through congruent socialisation. But, because of their immanent logic, individualistic cultures are characterised by only weak efforts at socialisation, which endangers the very existence of their structure of interaction structure. This lack of socialisation has to be compensated by perpetuated mechanisation.[20] The technophilia of such systems is thus a result of their internal logic, just as systems based on solidarity, with a high degree of socialisation, tend to be technophobic and averse to innovation. J. Gimpel's historical observations underline these statements. It follows that the intentions which are implicit in a technology should also be analysed, differentiated and ordered in types.

Since the offers implicit in a technology must be accepted nolens volens, an analysis of the wishes and needs engendered by societal facts is in order. But this kind of background study has only rarely been undertaken. One exception is M. Giesecke's (1991) study of the development of book-printing in Europe. He writes:

> Only the printing-press is able to resurrect the dead and to render immortal thoughts and authors. The dream of life eternal becomes reality for many Greek and Latin authors and, of course, for those of the 15th and 16th centuries: the printing-press has saved them for all time from the peril of oblivion. (Giesecke, 1991, p.152, my translation)

In order to understand the victory of book-printing in Europe in the 15th century it is necessary to seriously study the projections of the time as they are expressed in many quotations. What in the modern view seems to be effusive, exaggerated praise, is precisely the kind of argumentation needed at the time to transform an assembly of tools into the unspeakable. Without this unrestrained enthusiasm for the new invention, which at the same time made people blind to so many other

20 Berger , Berger and Kellner (1973) write: 'Technological production leads to anonymous social relationships' (p.33, my translation). I agree but would like to stress that the cause is not technology but the preferred culture, which produces the technology.

contemporaneous things, Gutenberg's machine would have taken the same leisurely development as so many similar inventions in Asia. Technical instruments must attract societal projections in order to become catalysts of social change. The bigger the claim – one might also say the megalomania – the bigger the catalytic effects to be expected on social evolution (ibid. p.156).

Rammert (1988) takes the case of photography in the rural environment as an example of a technical offering in decline. It seems to me that this negative attitude should be contrasted with the high acceptance of photography in other cultural surroundings. R. Williams (1974) explains this high acceptance by the high mobility and the migrations which separate families, circumstances in which photography made a sort of spiritual bond possible. In our terminology this is exactly the spiritual bond and sense of belonging that exists between zeromatrix and clan. In this context, Van Genep (908) speaks of the rite of leave-taking and that of place-holding. If place-holding is seen to be an important task of photography, its non-acceptance becomes understandable up to the time when the depopulation of the rural regions first entered the farmers' conscience; until then there was no need for place-holding. Photography of course also had other functions, one of which was to generate a static feeling in a world that was moving ever faster (Williams, 1974). This demonstrates once more the importance of social mobility for technical innovations and it establishes the role of the camera as a ritual device par excellence, which has to satisfy socially determined wishes. We are not exaggerating when we say that the great feasts in the life-cycle, the rites of passage, could no longer be celebrated without it.

What we miss in many studies is thus a consideration of the genesis of needs, and the explanation why, when and in which context these needs are satisfied by technical equipment rather than by other means. As Williams puts it, '... a technological response to a need, is less a question about the need itself than about its place in an existing social formation' (Williams, 1974, p.19).

In order to understand the strange preference for technological responses, we must study the changes in the relationships (organisations, transactions, cooperation) between humans and things. These changes can hardly be described by means of the pale concepts of a differentiation of the world into a system world and a world of everyday life (Lebenswelt). In any case it must be taken into account that changes in relationships will also change personality traits, because 'the macrocosmos of the group and the microcosmos of the single individual depend upon each other in their structure and are more or less adapted to each other' (Schröter, 1984, p.14).

The analogue is also true for the connection between organisational structures and overall societal characteristics, as Ouchi (1977) and Ouchi/Johnson (1978) have shown. This holographic view of the relationship between the individual and its society has been one of the guiding principles of our work from its beginning and the reason why questions of socialisation have been treated rather broadly. The efforts to integrate language into the picture also stem from this position; language is not only an instrument that makes cooperation possible; apart from this practical aspect, it is also an important instrument of socialisation, a technology to shape minds.

Things and languages both provide possible responses to problems, both generate and support social order. An order once chosen is exclusive, there cannot be several different orders at the same time. That is the reason why both artefacts, things and languages must be consistently structured and represent the same code. Although Hörning (1988) points out that certain technologies are applied in very different work-organisational environments, which he interprets as a lack of interdependence between technologies and organisational forms, we do not see this as contradicting our position. Some technologies are adaptable and can be made to fit given requirements through a process of cultural criticism (Baark/Jamison, 1986). To give an example, a computer will remain a computer, but hardware and software may assume a wide variety of forms and realise very different qualities.

This plasticity is, however, not shared by all technologies, as Dankbaar (1988) has demonstrated. Industrial production of steel by the puddling procedure seems extremely unlikely, for instance, and industry already created more suitable methods in the 19th century. Not every technology fits every organisational form and its specific techno-structures. T.P. Hughes (1989) has coined the term 'reverse salient' for this.

Resumé

At the beginning of this paper I declared that one of its aims was to bridge the deplorable gap between the social and the engineering sciences. Studies like the present one may contribute to the discussion depending on a variety of circumstances which determine the acceptance they gain and the influence they exert. But when it comes to bridging gaps, what is needed is a perspective which enables us to identify the common ideas, which up to now have only rarely been described and not very thoroughly at that.

The present approach treats things and languages on an equal basis. Both are agents for the genesis and formation of cooperation, both language and technical mechanisation act as powerful instruments for the establishment of order. Language however relies on socialisation, which mechanisation has a tendency to replace. This tendency is due to the ideology of individualism and its cultivation, which proclaims self-sufficiency, self-realisation and other ego-centred ideals as central values. Mechanisation as the substitution of social relationships follows from this as a more or less direct consequence and thus the sociogenetic aim of the engineer's activity is formulated. But this means in other words that the socio-politically naive attitude of the past with which technical innovation was approached should not be practised any longer. Engineers should be just as knowledgeable in social matters as in scientific and technical matters. To this end social science needs a language culture, its means of socialising being language and not mechanisation, which is understood and does not present itself in the guise of an exotic idiom and which must not be too remote from the technical habits of thought and expression. The present paper, which is indebted to Cultural Theory, makes an attempt to contribute to the development of such a style of language, since, as the history of science repeatedly shows, a consensus at the language level is a precondition for scientific progress (Kuhn, 1961).

If the social relevance of engineers is taken seriously enough to ask more of them than merely developing appropriate technologies, it becomes imperative to furnish them with tools which help assess to this appropriateness. The debate on the topic of social compatibility suffers not only from a shortage of methods but also from conceptual chaos and a lack of theoretical foundation. Post-hoc studies are of little use, they always come too late. What is needed is an instrument with predictive capability, i.e. a theory-guided understanding of the consequences of technical innovation and its motivating intentionality. M. Dierkes (1988) makes the following comment:

> *The analysis of consequences (of technical innovation) is complicated, as recent studies show, by the fact that the perception and evaluation of such consequences depend on the institutional and organisational context* of the development and the application of a technology. *The same technologies have different consequences when organisation differs, and different organisational structures develop different technologies,* perceive the risk and utility of technologies in different ways and evaluate them differently. The organisational context of a technology is thus very important for the type and intensity of its consequences. During the last few years therefore technological research in the social sciences has centred on the *problem of determining the influence of organi-sational and institutional factors on the development-process of technologies.* Here it has been found that *differing organisational cultures* play an important role in shaping and directing technologies in their developmental phases.
>
> (Dierkes, 1988, p.2, translation and italics mine)

But these organisational cultures are the carriers of values, norms and intentions of great diversity; and this brings us back to the quotation of O. Mayr (1986) which we have used as a motto at the beginning of this paper:

> ... technology is at the same time a cause and a consequence of the values and norms of the society in which it develops; technology is a social force as well as a product of society. (O. Mayr, 1986, p.15, my translation)

The approach developed in the present paper leads to a categorisation of different organisational cultures and, by taking into account their specific sets of values and norms, makes the determination and prediction of the genesis and acceptance of technologies possible. By adopting it, technology assessment might finally be able to achieve what engineers – and society – expect it to achieve.

References

Baark, E. and Jamison, A. (1986), 'The Technology and Culture Problematique', in Baark, E. and Jamison, A. (eds), *Technological Development in China, India and Japan – Cross Cultural Perspectives*, London: Macmillan.

Berger, P.L., Berger, B. and H. Kellner H. (1973, 1975), *Das Unbehagen in der Modernität*, Frankfurt am Main: Campus.

Bernstein, B. (1971), *Class, Codes and Control, Vol. I., Theoretical Studies towards a Sociology of Language*, London: Routledge & Kegan.

Borst, A. (1979), *Lebensformen im Mittelalter*, Frankfurt am Main: Ulstein.

Dankbaar, B. (1988), 'New Production Concepts, Management, Strategies and the Quality of Work', *Work, Employment & Society*, Vol. 2:25-50.

Dierkes, M. (1988), 'Leitbilder der Technikentwicklung und Gestaltung von Technikfolgen – ein neuer Ansatz in der sozialwissftl. Technikforschung', Thesenpapier für d. Konf. Perspektiven wirtschafts- u. sozialwissenschaftl. Technikforschung: Institution – Organisation – Alltag, Bonn, Nov. 1988.

Dijkstra, E.W. (1968), 'Go-To-Statement Considered Harmful', *Communications of Assoc. Computing Machines*, Vol. 11:147-148.

Douglas, M. (1970, 1973), *Natural Symbols*, Middlesex: Penguin.

Douglas, M. (1982) (ed), *Essays in the Sociology of Perception*, London: Routledge and Kegan.

Dreyfus, H.L. (1972, 1979), *What Computers Can't Do, The Limits of Artificial Intelligence*, New York: Harper and Row.

Dreyfus, H.L. and Dreyfus, St.E. (1988), 'Making a Mind versus Modeling the Brain: Artificial Intelligence Back at a Branchpoint', *Daedalus*, Winter.

Dreßen, W. (1982), *Die pädagogische Maschine: Zur Geschichte des industrialisierten Bewußtseins in Preußen/Deutschland*, Frankfurt am Main: Ullstein.

Duby, G. (1979, 1981), *Der hl. Bernhard und die Kunst der Zisterzienser*, Stuttgart: Klett-Cotta.

Dumont, L. (1967), 'The Individual as an Impediment to Sociological Comparison and Indian History', in Singh, B. and Singh, V.B. (eds), *Social and Economic Change*, Bombay: Allied Publ.,

Dumont, L. (1966, 1972), *Homo Hierarchicus*, London: Paladin.

Durkheim, E. (1902, 1903, 1984), *Erziehung, Moral und Gesellschaft*, Frankfurt am Main: Suhrkamp.

Eco, U. (1962, 1973), *Das offene Kunstwerk*, Frankfurt am Main: Suhrkamp.

Elias, N. (1939, 1987), *Die Gesellschaft der Individuen*, Frankfurt am Main: Suhrkamp..

Elias, N. (1969, 1976), *Der Prozeß der Zivilisation*, 2 Bde., Frankfurt am Main: Suhrkamp.

Elias, N. (1970, 1971), *Was ist Soziologie*, München: Juventa.

Elias, N. (1984), *Über die Zeit*, Frankfurt am Main: Suhrkamp.

Elias, N. (1987), 'Wandlungen der Wir-Ich-Balance', in Schröter, M. (ed), *Die Gesellschaft der Individuen*, Frankfurt am Main: Suhrkamp.

Ellul, J. (1954, 1964), *The Technological Society*, New York: A.A. Knopf.

Finley, M.I. (1963, 1975), *The Ancient Greeks*, Middlesex: Penguin.
Foucault, M. (1975, 1977), *Überwachen und Strafen – Die Geburt des Gefängnisses*, Frankfurt am Main: Suhrkamp.
Freyer, H. (1929), 'Zur Philosophie der Technik', in (1987), *Herrschaft, Planung und Technik*, VCH, Acta Humaniora, Weinheim.
Gennep, A. van (1908, 1960), *Les Rîtes de Passage*, London: Routledge & Kegan.
Giedion, S. (1948, 1982), *Die Herrschaft der Mechanisierung*, Frankfurt am Main: Europ. Verlagsanstalt.
Giesecke, M. (1991), *Der Buchdruck in der frühen Neuzeit – Eine histor. Fallstudie über die Durchsetzung neuer Informations- und Kommunikationstechnologien*, Frankfurt am Main: Suhrkamp.
Gimpel, J. (1976, 1977), *The Medieval Machine – The Industrial Revolution of the Middle Ages*, London: V. Gollancz Ltd.
Goody, J. and Watt, I. (1963), 'Entstehung und Folgen der Schriftkultur', in Gough, K. (1986, 1991), *Entstehung und Folgen der Schriftkultur*, Frankfurt am Main: Suhrkamp.
Goody, J. (1983, 1989), *Die Entwicklung von Ehe und Familie in Europa*, Frankfurt am Main: Suhrkamp.
Gottl-Ottlilienfeld, F. von (1923), *Wirtschaft und Technik*, Tübingen.
Grimm, J.u.W. (1935), *Deutsches Wörterbuch*, Bd. XI, SI. Abtlg. I. Tl. (T-TrettigS); bearb. v. Lexer, M., Kralik, D.
Guilmartin, jr. J.F. (1974, 1980), *Gunpowder and Galleys – Changing Technology and Mediterranean Warfare at Sea in the 16th Century*, Cambridge: Cambridge University Press.
Hill, C.H. (1972), *The World Turned Upside Down*, Middlesex: Penguin Books.
Hughes, T.P. (1983), *Networks of Power: Electrification in Western Society, 1880-1930*, Baltimore: John Hopkins, University Press.
Hughes, T.P. (1989), *American Genesis – A Century of Invention and Technological Enthusiasms, 1870-1970*, New York: Viking Press.
Hörning, K. (1988), 'Technik im Alltag und die Widersprüche des Alltäglichen', in Jörges, B. (ed) (1988), *Technik im Alltag*, Frankfurt am Main: Suhrkamp.
Jörges, B. (1979), 'Überlegungen zu einer Soziologie der Sachverhältnisse', *Leviathan*, Vol. 7:129-137.
Knie A. (1991), *Diesel – Karriere einer Technik: Genese und Formierungsprozesse im Motorenbau*, Berlin: Sigma Bohn.
Krämer, S. (1988), *Symbolische Maschinen – Die Idee der Formalisierung in geschichtlichem Abriß*, Darmstadt: Wissenschaftliche Buchgesellschaft.
Kuhn, T.S. (1961), 'The Function of Measurement in Modern Physical Science', in Woolf, H. (ed) (1961), *Quantification, A History of the Meaning of Measurement in the Natural and Social Sciences*, Indianapolis: Bobbs-Merrill.
Lévi-Strauss, C. (1962, 1966), *The Savage Mind*, London: Weidenfels.
Linde, H. (1972), *Sachdominanz in Sozialstrukturen*, Tübingen: Mohr.
Loeck, G. (1986), *Der cartesianische Materialismus und Maschine, Gesetz und Simulation*, Frankfurt am Main: P. Lang Verlag.

Macpherson, C.B. (1962, 1970), *The Political Theory of Possessive Individualism (Hobbes to Locke)*, London: Oxford University Press.
Mannheim, K. (1929, 1936), *Ideology and Utopia – An Introduction to the Sociology of Knowledge*, New York: Harcourt, Brace & World.
Maturana, H.R. (1970), 'Biology of Cognition', in Maturana, H.R. and Varela, F. (eds) (1980), *Autopoiesis and Cognition – The Realization of the Living*, Dordrecht: Reidel Publ. Company.
Maturana, H.R. (1978), 'Biology of Language: The Epistemology of Reality', in Miller, G.A. and Lenneberg E. (eds) (1978), *Psychology and Biology of Language and Thought*, New York: Academic Press.
Mayr, O. (1986, 1987), *Uhrwerk und Waage: Autorität, Freiheit und technische Systeme in der frühen Neuzeit*, München: Beck.
Ong, W.J. (1982), *Oralität und Literalität – Die Technologisierung des Wortes*, Opladen: Westdeutscher Verlag.
Ouchi, W.G. (1977), 'The Relationship between Organisational Structure and Organisational Control', *Adm. Science Quarterly*, Vol. 22:95-113.
Ouchi, W.G. (1980), 'Markets, Bureaucracies and Clans', *Adm. Science Quarterly*, Vol. 25:129-141.
Ouchi, W.G and Johnson, J.B. (1978), 'Types of Organisational Control and Their Relationship to Emotional Wellbeing', *Adm. Science Quarterly*, Vol. 23:293-316.
Paulinyi, A. (1987), 'Das Wesen der technischen Neuerungen in der Industriellen Revolution. Der Marxsche Ansatz im Lichte einer technologischen Analyse', in Pirker, Th., Müller, H-P. and Winkelmann, R. (eds.) (1987), T*echnik und industrielle Revolution*, Opladen: Westdeutscher Verlag.
Polanyi, K. (1944, 1957), *The Great Transformation – The Political and Economic Origins of Our Time*, Boston: Beacon Press.
Rammert, W. (1988), 'Technisierung im Alltag – Theoriestücke für eine spezielle soziologische Perspektive', in: Joerges, B. (ed) (1988), *Technik im Alltag*, Frankfurt am Main: Suhrkamp.
Rammert, W. (1989), 'Technisierung & Medien in Sozialsystemen – Annäherung an eine Soziolog. Theorie d. Technik', in Weingart, P. (ed) (1989), *Technik als sozialer Prozeß*, Frankfurt am Main: Suhrkamp.
Ricoeur, P. (1975, 1986), *Die lebende Metapher*, München: W. Fink.
Sahlins, M. (1976), *Culture and Practical Reason*, London: University of Chicago Press.
Schaff, A. (1964, 1983), *Sprache und Erkenntnis*, Wien: Europa Verlag.
Schaff, A. (ed) (1976), *Soziolinguistik*, Wien: Europa Verlag.
Schröter, M. (1984), Vorwort zu Elias, N. (1984), *Über die Zeit*, Frankfurt am Main, Suhrkamp.
Simon, H.A. (1979), *From Substantive to Procedural Rationality*, Oxford: Oxford University Press.
Smith, M.R. (1985), 'Army Ordnance and the "American System" of Manufacturing 1815-1861', in *Military Enterprise and Technological Change – Perspectives on the American Enterprise*, Cambridge, Mass: MIT Press.

Tönnies, F. (1887, 1991), *Gemeinschaft und Gesellschaft – Grundbegriffe der reinen Soziologie*, Darmstadt: Wissenschaftl. Buchgesellft.
Turkle, S. (1990), 'Revolutions in Mind: Computers are Changing the Way we Think', *Journal of Computing and Society*, Vol. 1:83-106.
Weber, M. (1922, 1985), *Wirtschaft und Gesellschaft*, Tübingen: J.C.B. Mohr.
Weltz, F. and Lullies, V. (1983), *Menschenbilder der Betriebsorganisatoren, Technik und Gesellschaft,* Frankfurt am Main: Campus.
White, L., Jr. (1962), *Medieval Technology and Social Change*, Oxford, Clarendon Press.
Whorf, B.E. (1936), 'The Punctual and Segmentative Aspects of Verbs in Hopi', in Chase, St. (ed) (1970), *Language, Thought and Reality*, Cambridge, Mass: MIT Press.
Wieland, J. (1992), 'Adam Smith' System der politischen Ökonomie', in Krohn, W. and Küppers, G. (eds) (1992), *Emergenz: Die Entstehung von Ordnung, Organisation und Bedeutung*, Frankfurt am Main: Suhrkamp.
Williams, R. (1958, 1987), *Culture and Society*, London: Hogarth Press.
Williams, R. (1974, 1979), *Television – Technology and Cultural Form*, London: Fontana, Collins.
Winograd, T. and Flores, F. (1986), *Understanding Computers & Cognition*, Ablex Pub.
Wittgenstein, L. (1921/22, 1960), 'Tractatus Logico-Philosophicus', in *Schriften von L. Wittgenstein*, Frankfurt am Main: Suhrkamp.
Zemanek, H. (1981), 'Was ist Informatik?' in *Informatik – Aspekte und Studienmodelle, Schriftenreihe der TU-Wien*, Wien: Springer.

15 New technology and new organisation – or – just new rhetoric?

Elisabeth Sundin

Working life, like the whole of society, is in an intense period of transformation. One of the main driving forces behind this is often said to be the so-called new technology. This refers to the variations of the 'new information technology' which can take many different forms of expression, some of which have a revolutionising potential. With the new technology it is assumed that distance in time and space can be suspended. The time of cyberspace is here! The virtual organisation will replace the old business structures with their roots in the industrial breakthrough at the end of the 1800s. Although we read and hear of this new world more or less daily, it is more often a question of utopia – or dystopia (depending on how one sees it) – than the result of empirically established observations of reality. In this article, I shall leave both utopia and dystopia open and limit myself to what is, or has been, a reality – this is exciting and difficult enough. If we forget that what occurs becomes what becomes, because it is what it is, also that it is what it is because it has been what it has been, we may land easily but completely wrongly in both research and debate.

The visionary discussions about work, technology and organisation continue to spin a thread which has been socially and scientifically important for a long time – perhaps always. The relation between technology and organisation in working life is, then, not a new discussion topic. It has long been on the agenda within research which focuses on the problems and conditions of working life. The tenacity of the discussion – it never seems to reach an end – can have several reasons. The foremost is probably that the content touches on the fundamental questions of business and leadership: how should the work be organised, and with the help of which technologies? These questions must be answered if production is to flow. And this in turn poses a practical problem which constantly needs attention. It is obvious that social sciences should focus on this problem. Another reason for the large and seemingly never ceasing interest is that it is on these decisions and designs that the central negotiations between employer and employees take place and at an organisational level between management and employed.

The above questions focus on how organisations should be designed and who should decide this, which technology should be used and who should control and use this technology etc. Here the large corporate organisations provide a special arena for discussion and legitimacy. Even the character of the questions is a subject for debate and discussion. From one perspective such questions concern power and control, class struggle, to use an ideological term which was the focus of much of the 1960s working life research. From another perspective it is solely a question of rationality.

There is greater agreement concerning a third reason for this great interest. Adequate modern technology and modern organisation are seen as prerequisites for a welfare society which can give all inhabitants an economically acceptable life. Even between people/organisations who express differences of opinion as far as method is concerned, it is possible to find agreement about the goal of achieving a balance. A fourth reason for this focus on technology in the organisational context is that technology has come to have a symbolic meaning which embraces gender identity, competence, and power. Technology is here something more than technique.

The practical significance, ideological attribute and theoretical interest of topic area have spurred extensive writing on these questions which has filled many shelves. It is not meaningful to attempt to repeat what others have written or try to assemble a review of the state of the knowledge. (Some comprehensive works are, however, referred to below). I shall henceforth pay more attention to technology and organisation than to work inasmuch as my own research interests circle around these two concepts. Moreover, organisation embraces work, that is, the human and material capital which, through organisation, is combined in a productive manner. Technology is also closely linked to work; how work is carried out is determined by the technologies available.

The discussion I pursue and the presentation I give of my own work and that of others have some features which can constitute my contribution to this lively research and policy field:

- the problematic character of the relation between technology, organisation and work with regard to possible prediction and generalisation, and therewith the need for detailed empirical studies;
- the contradictory mixture of modern and obsolete, of radical and conservative, in contexts assumed to be economically rational;
- the annexation by the economy of technology and organisation;
- the importance of gender relations for an understanding of the connection between technology and organisation;
- the new entrepreneurship operates under new assumptions and conditions.

The fifth item emanates explicitly from the new streams of thought concerning technology and organisation; the others seem to be more 'eternal' in character.

As far as the structure of the article is concerned, I shall begin with a discussion of the relation between technology, organisation, and economy. This is conducted mainly with the help of other researchers' work, which forms the foundation for the presentation of my own studies of the introduction of CAD at some Swedish workplaces. A further discussion concentrates on the latest organisational changes that have been especially aggressively launched within the public sector. Perceptions and practice with regard to new organisational forms is also included in this second part of the paper. In the final section the first and second items above, my main conclusions, are motivated and substantiated.

Technology, organisation and economy – an inseparable unit

Technology and organisation can only with difficulty be discussed without involving economy. This fact is the key to an understanding of the connection between technology and organisation in working life. The simple model below illustrates how technology, organisation, and economy stand in exchange relationships to one another, a topic which is discussed in the first part of my paper. Such mutually dependent relations are eternal and independent of the technology and organisation here under consideration.

Figure 15.1

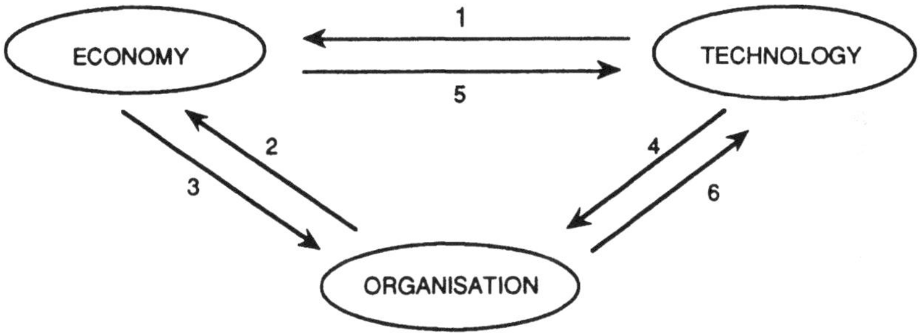

The terms technology, organisation and economy are in many ways of a different character. In this connection, I shall treat them as variables which can be issues for decisions regarding form and direction are concerned. The illustration is based upon what was for a period the usual way of describing companies and organisations as consisting of different systems. One can, then, see and study companies as a technical system, as a decision system, as an economic system, etc. (Bruzelius and Skärvad, 1989). The advocates of the system perspective argue that it has great advantages because the dynamic and potentially mutually contrasting aspects are emphasised. According to the model, to the system perspective and also to empirical reality, technology, organisation, and economy influence each other. Changes within one lead unconditionally to changes in the others. This applies to all hierarchical levels, the international, the national, and the organisational, within all social sectors. After this, I limit myself to the organisational level and the public sphere. That is, I do not include households in spite of their many similarities with other organisations as far as the relation between technology, organisation and work is concerned, for example with regard to the gender division of labour.

It is important to carry out empirical studies at the organisational level. This is emphasised strongly by many researchers interested in the theory of technology (Latour, 1991; Webster, 1991). It is at this level that reality is enacted. What is happening in the workplace is what we learn from statistics and debate as being the development of the labour market. But we never go to the labour market in the morning, we go to a job, to a certain workplace. In order to comprehend the labour market we must comprehend the situation at the workplace.

Let us take the above model as our starting point for a review of how the three components, technology, organisation and economy, influence each other. We see here an internal organic system where the three subsystems are initially in balance. The incentives to, and/or demands for change – this applies to technology as well as to everything else – almost always come from outside, seen from the viewpoint of the individual organisation (Håkansson, 1987; Sundin, 1995). Individual companies and organisations cannot be regarded as closed systems inasmuch as they are not. They always have contacts with the surrounding world, for example in the form of links with the market via customers or contractors. In order not to be subjected to all too frequent demands for changes from outside, whether it be technology or the organisation, companies/organisations often try to establish long-term, stable relationships. For some sectors this is so successful that it is more adequate to describe companies/organisations as components in a network rather than as individual players. At worst the drive for stability also leads to the necessary changes being blocked, at best to the coordination of the efforts of many (Axelsson, 1987; Håkansson, 1987). In spite of this drive for stability and continuity, demands for change constantly seep into the organisation and propagate there.

A brief survey using the numbers in the above model shows how change in one part of the organisation also influences the others:

1) *Technological changes influence the economy*
   That technological changes influence the economy is often itself the argument for them even if, as many studies show, this is not always the case, at least not in the intended manner. This situation is also further discussed below.

2) *Changes in organisation which influence the economy*
   Organisational changes occur frequently. Certain advocates of organisation claim that only constant change prevents stagnation. Sometimes the motives are economic but sometimes they are of a more diffuse origin. There are even researchers who claim that organisational design has more to do with modes than with rationality (Borgert, 1992). However that may be, organisational changes always have economic consequences. From this it is clear also that situation 3 below is common.

3) *Economic reasons to change the organisation*
   Technology and organisation are closely related. How, In which way, as well as What is cause and What is effect, have been and are the subject of a lively discussion between both researchers and practitioners. Parts of this discussion are presented in the next section. It is, however, not too daring to claim situation 4 here.

4) *Technological changes influence the design of the organisation*
No matter what the reasons are which trigger off technical change, it has both organisational and social consequences. The content of these varies, not only in strict empirical terms but also the interpretation of these terms. This is dealt with to some extent below, in connection with the presentation of earlier research.

5) *Economic incentives for a change in technology*
Economic incentives for a change in existing technology are very common. They can be manifested partly as plans to save labour expenses with the help of technology but also through changes in a more productive direction of the work itself (see e.g. Kraut, 1987). Both potentials are often put forward as sales arguments from possible suppliers. On the whole, even if it succeeds, this does not necessarily lead to an absolute reduction of labour needs inasmuch as it may result in increased demand.

6) *Organisational changes influence technology*
The design of the organisation is seen by many as steering the choice of technology; consequently changes in the former also lead to changes in the choice of technology and/or of technical applications. Examples of this are given below with the help of other researchers. Here the influence lies at different levels: the organisational set-up in reality steers by determining which technology is current but also mentally, by determining which technology is conceived as relevant. In connection with organisational changes, changes also often occur with regard to technology, for example to whom the technology is conceived to belong.

What determines what?

The correlations presented above have been the focus of lively discussions, some of which I wish to report here because this also has relevance for today's and tomorrow's situation. The new technology is not new in all respects. By studying earlier experiences we can sometimes find clues for assessing what is genuinely new. While I limit myself to the debate which focused on the relationship between technology and organisation, the great importance of the economy forms a natural background and restriction. The technology/organisation debate has engaged many researchers. There are therefore many variations in the chain of reasoning, and many eminent researchers have attempted to summarise these variations (see e.g. Grint, 1991; Webster, 1991). Here I refer to Wanda Orlikowski's presentation (1992); she claims that there are three different ways of looking at the technology/organisation relationship:

- the technological imperative
- the strategic choice model
- technology as a trigger to the perspective of structural effects.

The technological imperative

The foremost, or at least most often referred to, defender of the technological imperative is Joan Woodward (1965), who through her research argues that she has shown that a specific production adjustment demands a specific technology and that this, in turn, steers the organisation. This is predictable and measurable. It is today difficult to find any convinced technology-determinists, or perhaps more correctly, it is difficult to find individuals who present themselves as such. On the other hand, it is not difficult to find reports which make a technology-deterministic impression on the reader, of either a pessimistic or optimistic nature. The former, the pessimistic, include Braverman (1974) and many of his followers. Like many other Marxist researchers, Braverman asserts that technology is used throughout to control the labour force and fragment the workers' competence (Löwstedt, 1985). Technology-determinism also appears among certain technology enthusiasts. It is, for example, not at all unusual to hear claims that the organisation must acquire new technology in order to keep up with its competitors. Their proposals are often adopted relatively uncritically and in disregard of economic arguments (Scarbrough and Corbett, 1992).

Non-deterministic standpoint

With the help of other researchers, I shall now give some examples of how the non-technology-deterministic variants are presented and argued for. One such researcher is Robert Kraut (1987), who in his book on the transformation of work in the service sector, emphasises that the outcome is determined by social factors, not by technology per se. He bases this partly on his own empirical observations, partly on that of others. Orlikowski's second and third variant above are also of this type. She claims that technology can condition but never determine; the outcome is dependent on the players. In the second model, strategic-choice, technology is a dependent variable which is steered by people's actions. However, the social context in general is not always emphasised, nor is the structure-creating effect of the existing technology. The social context is in focus in the third variant. As has been observed, we are here concerned with the old player/structure discussion. Orlikowski makes visible the difference in terms of time and space which not infrequently exists between technical construction and its usage. This also gives a certain leeway for the users' design. 'The ongoing interaction of technology with organisations must be understood dialectically, as involving reciprocal causation, where the specific institutional context and the actions of knowledgeable, reflexive humans always mediate the relationship' (Orlikowski, 1992, p. 423).

In this connection I would also like to report what researchers who are more or less loosely affiliated to the so-called SCOT School have affirmed and contributed. Some of them have adopted the concept of 'the seamless web' to illustrate how closely woven technology and society, technology and politics, are (Elliot,

1988). Many of them have a strong preference for studying technology in its different phases, that is, subject areas which were earlier dominated by historians specialising in the history of technology or technicians with a special interest in history. Among others, Thomas Hughes (1988) is of the opinion that both groups became all too technically internalised in their approach. One must realise that technology is socially constructed. An effective way to achieve this is to use the network approach as a method.

The network approach in the SCOT-version in contrast to that which Håkan Håkansson et al argue for, has the disadvantage of not being sufficiently historical. There is a risk that the conditions which exist at the time of introduction and during the studies are not adequately considered (Saetnan, 1991). SCOT researchers are nondeterminists in that they do not believe that there are any clear-cut technologies. Its applications always contain a compromise. The solution could always have been different. In order to understand, we must simultaneously think about the social and the technical. Technologies are born out of conflict and do not stabilise until the relations in which the conflict developed are stabilised. This means that the actual consequences can be quite different from what is anticipated inasmuch as the stability situation is a compromise. According to this approach then, technology is a part of a social process and in itself a social construction. A variant on this main stream of thought abolishes the difference between artefacts and individuals and sees all as players (Bijker et al., 1992).

An intermediate position is taken by those who call attention to the fact that the organisational consequences of technical changes are mediated through existing social networks and role groupings (Barley, 1990). Representatives of this position often direct criticism, of both material and nonmaterial nature, at their research colleagues for paying too little attention to the possibilities and behaviour of the players and for all too strictly keeping to one hierarchical level. Among other things, this leads to terminological problems with regard to such central concepts as structure, technology, organisation and institution.

In this connection, it is necessary to deal with the qualification discussion, or the question whether new technology has negative or positive consequences for the labour force. This discussion is often pursued from the viewpoint of the hierarchically lowest-placed labourers (at least as long as they are men) but has relevance also for other categories, to which I shall return to in the presentation of my own studies. Studies and discussions concerning skilling and deskilling are based on Harry Braverman's now more than 20-year-old study. It argues for the deskilling hypothesis in which deskilling is seen as a strategic tool in the employers' attempts at total control. Later empirical studies have, however, been full of contradictions (Kraut, 1987; Grint, 1992).

My own studies can be said to contribute to these contradictions. I myself find it difficult to be deterministic with regard to the role of technology in working life. The inconsistency appears when one does not make it clear to oneself from whose viewpoint the discussion is being pursued and analysis made (cf. Mirvis et al., 1991). The conclusions that are drawn in these matters are, in other words, largely based on values.

The aim of the overview given above was to put today's new technology, new organisations, and discussions concerning them, into a context. We have not reached the end of history, nor are we at the beginning of history. Nor is all technology new. At the same time as the nurse looks at the monitor, she can place her hand on the patient's forehead, both to determine body temperature. As the home help orders goods with the help of a terminal she or he can put on the coffee maker. I leave internet communication to speak directly with some students. Each period seems, however, to have its own new technology – and in a somewhat shorter time perspective its own favourite organisational model. Today the different applications of information technology are in fashion. What is it that is genuinely new about this technology? And what is it that is genuinely new about the organisational models which are now being launched? I shall illustrate these discussions with examples from my own research: with regard to technology, the introduction of CAD in map production; with regard to organisation, the new entrepreneurship made possible through the loosening up of the public sectors as well as the distance-bridging potential of new information technology in both the public and private sectors.

New technology and new organisation

Case 1 and 2. The introduction of CAD

In this section I shall refer to my own empirical studies to illustrate the interaction between technology, organisation, and economy (Sundin, 1993, 1995a and b). The topic in two studies was the purchase of CAD (Computer Aided Design) for the production of maps. This is a question of technology being introduced into an office setting even though, in a way, it is a question of production. The first two cases concern events which are presented by those involved as the introduction of new technology. In both cases the origin of the chain of activities could just as well be described as economic inasmuch as it was the demands of the market which necessitated the purchase of the new technology. In one case, a town-planning office, the workplace carries out a task, the compilation of detailed plans, which is an integral part of a long chain from plans to construction. The builders and contractors send their documents and maps to the office, the office complements with more material collected from other interested parties and sends it all on for further treatment or for use as a steering instrument. The town-planning office is then a link in a production chain which produces planning documents. If anyone in the chain changes the technology, then all must do so, or put differently, all must change at the same time. If some refuse, they must be replaced. In this case, a technology-deterministic expression would be appropriate. This truth applies in part also to the other organisation studied, the topographic-map unit of the Surveyors' Office. They also produce maps but even other so-called information on position, for sale to the public as well as for organisations. If an aeroplane manufacturer is not interested in maps but in other CAD products, then these must be delivered. I have found these cases to be enlightening; they reveal clearly the new enforced way of working. Sometimes researchers and their studies convey doubt in this matter. There is, say for instance Scarbrough and Corbett, from the viewpoint of the labour force no greater difference between so-called flexible production systems and Tayloristic systems.

Economic circumstances can be said to underpin the course of events. As regards the organisational changes following technological changes, technology was, however, first; we have a relation-4 case. The two workplaces were different in size: the town-planning office had about ten employees and the map unit of the Surveyors' Office just over 80. The active professional categories were, however, from the beginning. Farthest down in the organisation were the female map drawers, in the middle, a group of mainly male engineers, and at the top, academic surveyors and architects. In short, professionally, the result can be presented as follows. The big winners were the middle group, the male engineers, at the planning office and the female drawers at the topographic-map unit. The latter now enjoy their organisational existence as engineers, after further education in mainly field work, which was the male engineers' most distinct task. The map drawers at the town-planning office, in contrast, lost the 'struggle for CAD'. All except one lost their jobs when manual drafting disappeared. CAD was taken over by the male engineers.

This contradictory results show, if nothing else, that the negative determinist's expectation, that women are always the losers in connection with the introduction of new technology, is not correct. The outcome is, however, not randomised and the explanation lies, all the same, in gender-relation stability. The course of events at the town-planning office seems to correspond to the negative expectations and that at the Surveyors' Office appears to be the surprise. In the latter case, it became clear that the room's gender label was stronger than that of technology. On the introduction of CAD there was, as was mentioned earlier, a clear professional division of labour. which was at the same time a gender division of work – but there was also a spatial division of work. The latter division proved to be very important since it supported parts of the gender work-division identity. Included in the male engineers' work was field work, that is, going out into the Swedish countryside to collect basic data for compiling the maps. Sometimes this field work involved living away during parts of the year, great freedom in action, and an ample expense allowance. The rhetoric surrounding the field work emphasised the hardships. When CAD was introduced, it was placed squarely in the women's office area. It was a typical indoor technology. Everything contributed to it being assumed to be a female tool; in spite of it being the newest technology, it was female. The women learned to use it and achieved such a high rate of production that the male engineers with their more or less unchanged work methods could not provide them with data at the necessary pace. The management chose to solve this imbalance in production by training the women in field-work methods. This meant a break with the gender work division and took place under considerable protest.

This case clearly shows how the effects of new technology can never be understood outside their organisational contexts in which gender work division and gender stigmatism are important ingredients (see also Petterson, 1996). Further it shows that there is always an opportunity for strategic players to influence the way the technology is integrated with the organisation. Modifications are possible (see also Webster, 1991). In this case, it was management who drove through their plans. That this was effected with the help of economic arguments augmented their stand. Another important point in this connection is the need to take into account how tasks which were earlier divided were brought together by means of the new technology. This has an enriching potential as the case of the surveyors' office showed. However, the political question is always for whom. Everything is dependent upon how this is carried out. In the cases presented, examples were given of how a previously clearly subordinate group had their work content extended and their competence increased, not only in their own eyes but also in the eyes of the other members of the organisation. Nonetheless, they cannot take command of the power over technology. In the other case, although it was the same technology and the same production, the new technology ended up with another group of employees: the male engineers. It is noteworthy that the clear-cut professional group, the architects at the town-planning office, lost their position. This indicates that the new technology has clear revolutionary potential in that it can deal with information, the basis of knowledge production. Therein lies the risk, or chance, depending on how one sees it, to really change the position of the professions in organisations and thereby in society at large. If this is actually realised or not is a political question. Opportunities always exist and technology can be an instrument in the hands of the predominant profession.

The related cases, together with the experiences of other researchers, indicate that, in spite of everything, the real organisational consequences are relatively limited. The major changes at the town-planning office can be explained by the decrease in building, not by the new technology. The organisational practice seems relatively stable. The virtual organisations seem to be more discussed than implemented, so to say. I shall nevertheless not leave the organisational aspects completely but deal with them with the help of the new entrepreneurship which seems to be emerging in the wake of the new technology and the new organisational ideology. Here it is mainly the latter which is debated and primarily with regard to the transformation of the public sector.

Case 3: The reorganisation of the public sector

Also in connection with the ongoing reorganisation in the public sector it is possible to see economic reasons as the trigger. In hard economic times decision-makers are forced to seek to reorganise in order to run operations with unchanged or diminished resources. There are, however, others, both debaters and researchers, who claim that the incentives are ideological. In my model this could be applied so that the starting point for a changed organisation is not economic but ideological, that the starting point lies in ideas about organisation per se.

I shall now take up the extent and content of the so-called privatisation from the perspective of the new entrepreneurs and, to some extent, of their employees again, with the help of my own experiences. Linköping county, where I have carried out my studies, has made itself known for, and prides itself on, being in the front line of privatisation, so to speak. On different occasions, the county has encouraged its employees to start their own businesses, to submit tenders covering operations carried out by their workplace. The buyer/producer concept that has been adopted facilitates such transitions.

The ideal picture of the advocates of privatisation is one where an employee who is full of ideas about how the operations should be made more effective and more pleasant has earlier been hindered by the public monopoly and now through the new laws and deregulation is freed from society's fetters. She (for municipal employees are most often women) submits and receives tenders, becomes a businesswoman, employs previous work associates, and perhaps some others, is happier, and gives the community more for its money. Is this what happened? Well yes, there are such examples but before I present one such, I would like to point out that the underlying notion of a frustrated, unsatisfied civil servant is not entirely accurate. A survey of the extent to which the community's operations were carried out after the reforms by so-called alternative suppliers, that is alternative to the county's own operations, showed that it was rather limited (Hammar and Sundin). Most of those which did exist emanated from the time prior to the changes, mainly child care, which was carried out in close connection with idealistic and ideological movements, or certain services which the county always purchased, for example, care of children and young people with problems, taxis for the handicapped and technical services. The fact that they were relatively few was mainly explained in terms of the fact that no one wanted to operate as a entrepreneur; it was, then, not because of many alternative tenders being turned down. We can only speculate over the reasons. Poor compensation may be one.

But there are, in fact, new entrepreneurs who correspond to the view which the advocates of privatisation have. One such is the librarian who placed an offer for 'her' district library (Sundin to be published) and was accepted. She now operates the library as her own. She works innovatively in many ways and seeking collaboration with schools, with child-care and elderly-care services, with the local bathhouse, etc. She does the cleaning herself and manages the purchase of books and other material in a new way. Is she then one of the modern entrepreneurs? Perhaps so, for she is definitely not a old time entrepreneur. In the notions, both theoretical and practical, it is presumed that one of the foremost attributes of entrepreneurship is the freedom of the individual, the will to steer one's own life manifested in not having a boss (see e.g. Chell, 1991). While 'our' entrepreneur has no boss, it is a great exaggeration to claim that she has gained great self-determination. The conditions laid down by the community for accepting her tender stipulated that operations may not be changed in any essential respects. She cannot raise new funds by expanding her market to video consumers or her assortment to include pornographic literature, nor can she cut down on opening hours in order to reduce expenses. Consequently, she works within very tight economic and organisational limits. The differences between her and the librarians still working within the municipal setting seems little, seen from their own viewpoint. For the municipality's part there may, however, be a greater difference. Control is, in fact, increased by demands for specifications in the tender. It also seems as though the power in the hands of the politicians and civil servants involved is increased in comparison to that of the new entrepreneurs. The former want a short tender period; the first ran for only 1.5 years. The main motive is to imitate the players on the market, who are expected to work under strict economic conditions. This may certainly be so but more often means long-term stable relations rather than tenders and price comparisons at short intervals.

Such constraints on emerging entrepreneurs seem to also exist in connection with business ventures emanating from within private sector organisations. In the path of the new unemployment, an entrepreneurship has developed which springs from the unwillingness of large organisations to take their responsibility as employers rather than from the desire of entrepreneur to stand on her own two feet. Sometimes this move is related to new technology; thanks to the new information technology, certain jobs can be carried out by self-employed people in their own homes. In this connection I also want to point out that the demand for the technological changes described above as triggering off the purchase of CAD machines came from customers and suppliers. Such demands for the adaptation of technology have become much more common and are usually directed from the large organisations towards the small. Each chain-store proprietor must, for example, be electronically linked to the distributor's data and information network. The skilled craftsman must nowadays have a mobile telephone so as to be easily reachable. This gives him an advantage; he does not risk missing a job because he cannot be reached. At the same time this changes the relations with the customer: it is no longer necessary to pester the workmen (so much); I can always reach them and demand an explanation when they do not come as agreed. This means, then, less freedom for the craftsmen.

In summary, it seems to me that the new technological and organisational solutions influence small-business conditions in a negative direction. The incentive structure of entrepreneurship has, presumably, changed. The power relations have shifted from the small businessmen to the large, and to the consumers. This is an important consequence of the new technology.

In summary

Through the studies of empirical reality, both my own and those of others, evidence has been found for the relations which were specified in the model presented. Economic incentives for the introduction of new technology are very common. They were used in 'my' cases too. However, the outcome is not always as expected. The constructors of technology have, for example, often not been able to foresee the areas of application, not even for the artefacts which they develop. A well-known historical example is the telephone: those who introduced it never imagined it would spread to individual households. Research is full of such examples also with regard to the organisational level (see e.g. Orlikowski, 1992). It is just as common that the potential of technology is far from fully utilised, for example by personnel at all hierarchical levels. This applies perhaps in an especially high degree to the new information technology (Scarbrough and Corbett, 1992). The many 'faults' which have been acknowledged and analysed show that the rationale is more a matter of rhetoric than of practice also in industry and working life. Although this is perhaps to be expected, it should be pointed out since rationality as a norm is very strong.

With regard to the economy as trigger for both technical and organisational changes (relations number 5 and 3 in Figure 15.1) it may be noted that the economy is not only important in itself but also as argument. Economic reasons have the status of being the highest rationality. The rationale is positive (Brunsson, 1990). It may then be tempting for those who absolutely want to have the new technology to use the long-term economic rationale as argument. It is so much more tempting since cost insensitivity has shown itself to be especially strong when it comes to technical investments. (Tijdens, 1991). Old technology can even be presented as a threat to the company's entire existence, something which there certainly are examples of in history. In the related cases concerning the purchase of CAD, this can be seen as an absolutely necessary technical change. As far as the reorganisation of a privatising character is concerned, the economic argument is less convincing.

Whether or not technology steers the organisation (relations 4 and 6 in Figure 15.1) has long been the topic of a lively and amusing debate. In the cases presented, it seems as though the technology really triggered off organisational changes. That the outcomes were different cannot, however, be explained in technical terms; the causes must be sought in the organisational structure and culture which prevailed at the time of introduction. In the cultural context gender work division played a decisive role for both outcomes. This seems to be true also in other contexts. Gender seems to play a major role in organisational practice in general and perhaps especially with regard to technical applications. This fact has been considered to a surprisingly small degree in the popular discussion or in scientific reporting. In this respect, the so-called new technology is not new. Like the old new technologies, it may, however, trigger off changes in the gender division of labour. It may, then, be claimed that new technology always seems to influence the organisational design. However, it is not possible to determine how without a thorough analysis of the organisation in question.

The fact that technical changes are always mediated in their organisational contexts means that the consequences become less radical than they might be in unaffected surroundings. The social and organisational answers to radical new technology seem to be predominantly conservative. As stated above, organisations are spontaneously conservative for reasons of self-preservation, and this applies also to technology. The immediate reaction is to meet the new element in a proven reliable manner and attempt to adapt it to the existing structures. From the management's point of view this may be difficult to handle, given that they want to bring about a real change. The evidence says that contradictory assessments are many. The question here is whether the new technology in this respect means something new. Until someone produces proof of the opposite, I do not believe that this is so.

Finally we must comment on relations number 2 and 1 in Figure 15.1, those showing that the technical and organisational changes influence the economy. In part, this is self-evident. New technology means an investment; investments cost money. If the organisational sluggishness is all too great, things may stop here. The same danger lies in the organisational changes. There may be considerable discrepancy between the normative level of the formal rules, the level of practice, and the players' experiences of what happens at the cognitive level (Löwstedt, 1992). These discrepancies can be everywhere, from assessments of what is new, what is profitable, to what is natural (cf. Akrich 1992 and Akrich 1995). In these respects the new information technology may mean something new, something ever more difficult, and ever more discrepancy-creating in that tangible data are converted into partially abstract data, etc.

This discussion reminds us that, for all the relations studied, the assessments of whether they are positive or negative depends upon the viewpoint from which they are seen. The case studies are clear examples of this: what was favourable for the map drawers at the surveyors' office was not good for the engineers at the same workplace. What may seem to be successful organisational changes for the municipal representatives may seem to be a minor catastrophe from the standpoint of the previous employees. The picture is even more complicated if we extend the interest group by, for example in the last-named case, including the clients and inhabitants in the assessment. In one of the cases it appeared as though one profession would lose their position by failing to adopt the new technology as their own. Should this be manifested on a large scale, we shall truly have before us something new, something which can transform the entire working and industrial life, and perhaps in the long run also the education system.

The conclusions from earlier studies state, among other things, that it is difficult to generalise as far as the design and effects of technology and organisation are concerned. These are very difficult to separate from each other. They must be seen as completely intertwined processes, say for instance Scarbrough and Corbett (1992), and I am inclined to agree with them. The trends are extremely contradictory. This applies in particular to the so-called new technology. Sometimes it is said that the new technology is new in that it permeates everywhere. Although it is, in this sense, of the same sweeping character as electricity, it does not affect all core areas. Some production is still carried out as before even after the new technology is applied to associated tasks. In order to go further in the assessment we must carry out thorough studies. Thus far we can only say that what is definitely new is the rhetoric.

References

Akrich, M. (1992), 'The De-Scription of Technical Objects', in Bijker and Law (1992).

Akrich, M. and Pasveer, B. (1995) 'Technologies of giving birth. Comparing women's bodies and competences during "normal" birth in France and The Netherlands'. Paper presented at the International Workshop The Mutual Shaping of Gender and Technology, University of Twente, The Netherlands 6-8 October 1995.

Axelsson, B. (1987), 'Supplier Management and Technological Development', in Håkansson, H. (ed), *Industrial Technological Development. A Network Approach*, New Hampshire: Croom Helm Ltd.

Barley, S.R. (1990), 'The Alignment of Technology and Structure Through Roles and Networks'. *Administrative Science Quarterly*, Vol. 35:61-103.

Besselaar, P., van den et al. (eds.) (1991), *Information System, Work and Organisation Design*, Amsterdam: North-Holland.

Bijker, W.E. and Law, J. (1992), *Shaping Technology/Building Society. Studies in Sociotechnical Change*, Cambridge, Mass.: The MIT-press.

Borgert, L. (1992), *Organisation som mode. Kontrasterande bilder av svensk hälso- och sjukvård*, Stockholm: Stockholms universitet.

Braverman, H. (1974), *Labor and Monopoly Capital*, New York: Monthly Review Press.

Brunsson, N. (1990), 'Individualitet och rationalitet som reforminnehåll', in Brunsson and Olsson (1990).

Brunsson, N., Olsson, J.P. (1990), *Makten att reformera*, Stockholm: Carlsson.

Bruzelius, L.H., Skärvad, P-H. (1989), *Integrerad organisationslära*, Lund: Studentlitteratur.

Chell, E. (1991), *The Entrepreneurial Personality. Concepts, Cases and Categories*, London: Routledge.

Elliot, B. (1988), *Technology and Social Process*, Edinburgh: Edinburgh University Press.

Grint, K. (1991), *The Sociology of Work. An Introduction*, Cambridge: Polity Press.

Hammar Chiriac, E. and Sundin, E. (1995), *Den offentliga sektorns omvandling och kvinnors företagande*, Arbetsnotat nr 147, Tema Teknik och social förändring, Linköpings universitet.

Hughes, T.P. (1988), 'The Seamless Web: Technology, Science et cetera, et cetera', in Elliot (1988).

Håkansson, H. (1987), *Industrial Technological Development. A Network Approach*, New Hampshire: Croom Helm Ltd.

Håkansson, H. (1987), 'Product Development in Networks' in Håkansson (1987).

Kraut, R.E. (ed) (1987), *Technology and the Transformation of White-collar Work*, Hillsdale, N.J.: Erlbaum.

Law, J. (ed.), *A Sociology of Monsters. Essays on Power, Technology and Domination*, London: Routledge.

Löwstedt, J. (1985), 'Contingencies or Cognitions? Two Paths for Research on Organisation and Technology', *Scandinavian Journal of Management Studies*, Vol. 1:207-225.
Löwstedt, J. (1992), 'Organizing Frameworks in Emerging Organizations: A Cognitive Approach to Analysis of Change', *Human Relations*, Vol. 46:501-526.
Mirvis, P.H., Sales, A.L. and Hackett, E.J. (1991), 'The Implementation and Adoption of New Technology in Organizations: The Impact on Work, People, and Culture', *Human Resource Management*, Vol. 30:113-139.
Orlikowski, W.J. (1992), 'The Duality of Technology: Rethinking the Concept of Technology in Organizations', *Organisation Science*, Vol. 3:398-425.
Pettersson, L. (1996), *Ny teknik, ny oganisation – nya genusrelationer?*, Tema Teknik och social förändring, Linköpings universitet.
Scarbrough, H. and Corbett, M.J. (1992), *Technology and Organisation. Power, Meaning and Design*, London: Routledge.
Soetnan, A.R. (1991), 'Rigid Politics and Technological Flexibility. The Anatomy of a Failed Hospital Innovation', *Science, Technology and Human Values*, Vol. 16:419-447.
Sundin, E. (1993), *Ny teknik i gamla strukturer*, Stockholm: Nerenius and Santérus Förlag AB.
Sundin, E. (1995), *Teknik och organisation i teori och praktik*, Stockholm: Nerenius and Santérus Förlag AB.
Sundin, E. (1995), 'The Social Construction of Gender and Technology', *The European Journal of Women Studies* Vol. 2:335-353.
Tijdens, K. (1991), 'Decentralized Office Technology and Women's Work', in Besselaar, P. (1991).
Webster, J. (1991), 'Advanced manufacturing technologies. Work organization and social relations crystallised', in Law, J. (1991). Woodward, J. (1965), *Industrial Organisation: Theory and Practice*, Oxford: Oxford University Press.

16 Social precarisation and controlled autonomy. Contradictions within the changing production systems

Béatrice Appay

Flexibility and democracy: The magical roots of the consensus

'Economic growth is good for workers'. The World Bank asserts its belief and faith in these few words.[1] It also claims that the fear that growth will primarily benefit capital, create few jobs, and fail to raise wages is unfounded. However, the Bank recognises that workers often feel the pain as real wages fall, unemployment rises, and employment shifts into informal activities.[2] The report concludes that the problems of low incomes, poor working conditions, and insecurity affecting many of the world's workers can be effectively tackled in ways that reduce poverty and regional inequality. It explains in detail how this can be achieved by increasing labour market flexibility which is essential in all regions of the world undergoing major reform. According to the World Bank, the most important reforms involve lifting constraints on labour mobility and wage flexibility, as well as breaking the ties between social services and labour contracts.[3] Measures to increase flexibility can influence the overall trajectory and speed of recovery. If properly implemented, the 'shock' is short-lived... if it is not, this is probably due to changes not having been implemented fast enough and more of the 'shock therapy' is recommended.

Support for such plans of action comes not only from the United States but from all over the world; from governments, academic and corporate elites, and other major international bodies such as the OECD and the EU.[4]

---

1 World Bank (1995).

2 Op.cit. p.6.

3 Op.cit. p.110.

4 OECD (1995a and 1995b). The main message of the OECD report is that a declining capacity on the part of OECD countries to adapt to change and to innovate is the principal reason for the emergence of structural labour market problems and that institutional reforms and policy actions over a wide range of areas are required to remedy the situation. Adapting to change requires more flexibility, in particular flexibility of working-time, making wage and labour costs more flexible, and reforming employment security provision, reforming unemployment and related benefits in ways that impinge less on the efficient functioning of labour markets. In other words, *according to the OECD report, mass unemployment is not due to the flexibilisation of production, but to a lack of flexibility and so forth, more flexibility is required.* See as well EC (1994).

In this paper we will see how the French consensus and the post-fordist debate relate to this international way of thinking. It will address the question: are we confronted with the belief that the search for greater flexibility leads towards economic growth and consequently towards greater democracy? In focusing on the paradox between the atomisation of the labour force and a continued economic concentration, this paper will demonstrate that the process of externalisation as well as the development of cascading subcontracting contradict such a belief. Through the concept of controlled autonomy, it will contribute to an understanding of how and why the actual trends of economic restructuring do not lead towards greater democracy but towards greater social precarisation[5], hypercompetition and survival.

The French consensus

The French consensus on economic restructuring shows that the search for greater flexibility is widely recognised as a necessary step towards economic recovery and economic growth. It finds its legitimacy in the belief that economic growth leads towards greater wealth for the nation as a whole and consequently creates the means to redistribute this new wealth through social welfare systems and new employment opportunities. Redundancies and mass unemployment are seen as temporary sacrifices for a better future.[6] This consensus is based on a postulate and a belief: the postulate is that the flexibility of labour is a necessary means for economic survival and expansion in a period of intense international competition; the belief is that economic growth and democracy are tied together and evolve in the same direction: 'economic growth generally benefits the majority of a country's population'.[7] Those who do not follow these ideas of 'la pensée unique'[8], are accused of being unrealistic.

I do not consider that democracy and capitalism are linked in such simplistic terms, which state that 'economic growth' leads to 'wealth for all'. If capitalism and democracy are linked together then it is as a result of conflictual tendencies. The history of the labour movement is there to remind us that democracy has been built over the years through deep social conflicts. Those who are suffering from the actual economic and social restructuring, and they are many, know that there is no obvious link between economic growth and wealth for all and that their sacrifice for a better future is more than hypothetical. It is probably for this reason

5 This analysis is based on results from a CNRS-INSERM programme of research on social precarisation. See IRESCO (1995:9-12).

6 Coriat and Taddéi (1993); Minc (1994), and more recently Boissonnat (1995), which favours a wider openness to international competition, encourages partnership between the larger firms and their subcontractors, flexible links between employment and self-employment, working-time flexibility. For a more critical approach of the French current debate on working-time flexibility see Hirata and Senotier (eds) (1996).

7 World Bank (1995:41).

8 Ramonet (1995).

that in December 1995, the majority of the French population supported or accepted the long strike in France which paralysed the public transport sector throughout the country for several weeks.

Democracy is the result of different 'rapports de force' but the process of flexibilisation undermines them. Consequently, it is not surprising to find that flexibility leads not so much to economic recovery and democracy, but to the precarisation of labour and social welfare systems, and to the rise of exclusion and inequalities.

The post-fordist debate and the concept of lean production

In the international academic debate on economic restructuring, the question of the flexibilisation of production is more central than ever but this has not always been the case.[9] In the mid-70s the analysis of wage-earning relations and the crisis of industrial relations were the key issues. A consensus emerged on the diagnosis that existing 'rigidities' within the 'fordist model of production' were a major hindrance to economic growth and competitiveness. Later in the mid-80s, the debate focused on the search for greater flexibility. This led to international academic interest being drawn to the new role played by smaller firms. Industrial districts were put into perspective by Piore and Sabel, who believed that there were new possibilities for democracy and for industrial relations at the local level. In their optimistic view of the new paths for democracy and competitiveness, they proposed the concept of flexible specialisation,[10] which was then debated all over the world.

In this phase of the debate, scientific interest focused on the growing importance of smaller specialised firms in the search for more flexible productive systems. Mass production, in relation to concentration and rationalisation, was no longer considered the only path forward. Concepts such as deconcentration, co-operation and partnership[11] were developed in relation to specialisation, competence and autonomy. In this context, smaller firms and networks represented the basis from which new trends in capitalism were developing.

However, the analysis of mass production has continued to follow the century-long trend of focusing mainly on what is happening within the larger firms. It is in this context that the 'new concepts of production'[12] emerged in the

---

9 Boyer (1987)

10 Piore and Sabel (1984).

11 In the same period of time, through the 80s and the beginning of the 90s, subcontracting had been mainly analysed in terms of cooperation and partnership, partly under the influence of the 'Japanese model' and the way it has been pictured: see Altersohn, C. (1992). The 'partnership model' refers to the relationships between contractors and suppliers in terms of trust, excellence and involvement.

12 In a recent conference (Stockholm: Arbetslivsinstitutet, 14 September 1995) M. Schumann clearly highlighted the fact that the 'new concepts of production' have emerged in the 80's as concepts of rationalisation to raise productivity in direct relation to pilot projects in large firms. See Kern H. and Schumann M. (1984).

80s. In this perspective, smaller firms continue to be ignored in the analysis.[13] Very few studies in fact attempt to analyse the internal restructuring of larger firms in relation to the growing importance of smaller firms and to the atomisation of the labour force.

A lot has been said and written about current changes in productive systems and the future for industrial societies. Although the facts show an intense social crisis, revealed by unemployment figures, the tone of the debate is resolutely optimistic and the 'Japanese model' has played an important role. 'The machine that changed the world'[14] is another example of this strong emphasis on a bright future, which seems to be a recurrent characteristic of MIT's studies. It explains how to become lean, fit and flexible, and how to implement organisational changes to reach world class levels. Although it focuses on the automobile industry in reference to the 'best' Japanese firms, the authors consider that the principles of lean production can be applied equally to every industry across the globe. 'The conversion to lean production will have a profound effect on human society – it will truly change the world'.[15] The book aims to facilitate the transition from mass production to leanness, 'how to spread these changes to all corners of the globe in everyone's mutual benefit'.[16] From this angle the authors are convinced of the advantages of what they call lean production[17], not only for the firms which are successful in implementing this new mode of production but for everybody. The world class automobile firms refer to IMVP[18] studies and 'The machine that changed the world' to orientate corporate strategies. Most academics concerned with changes in production also refer to this book. Such an impact both at industrial and academic levels is quite rare. It could make one wonder if the book itself is not 'the machine to change the world', a machine which legitimises what is called 'the one best way', a machine to demonstrate that there is only one way to go forward and that the only way to survive is to conform. The means behind the book were not mean, nor lean: five million dollars[19] were invested.

In those books and reports which contribute to implementing the faith in 'the one best way', competitiveness, growth, flexibility and democracy are tied together, and the manner in which they are linked contributes to the creation of the legitimacy of such orientations. A recent book[20] has developed a critical approach to lean production and has explored the Swedish alternative in analysing the fate of Uddevalla as a symbol of human centred production, contrary to the idea of the 'one best way'. To contribute to alternative lines of thought, this paper proposes a

---

13 From this perspective, Schumacher has been highly criticised.

14 Womak, Jones and Roos (1990).

15 Op.cit. p.8.

16 Op.cit. p.11.

17 A term proposed by John Krafcik, in reference to the 'best' Japanese firms in the automobile sector.

18 International Motor Vehicle Program.

19 As is proudly announced on the front page cover, the book is based on a 5 million dollar five-year study on the future of the automobile.

20 Sandberg, A. (1995).

framework of interpretation which highlights complex and contradictory processes. It explores the idea that concentration and deconcentration are not in fact contradictory processes but are the two roots of a paradox. The concept of controlled autonomy is used here to put into perspective emerging forms of social and productive systems linking the large to the small and the global to the local. It focuses on the emergence of new types of strategic firms, the externalisation of labour and cascading subcontracting in relation to changes within and amongst large and small firms. This paper takes examples from previous empirical research and recent studies in different industries.

How to shrink and expand at the same time: The externalisation process

The analysis of the English and French production systems[21] revealed the emergence of 'brain firms' during a period of intense economic crisis. Over a period of five years these large firms were rapidly downsizing whilst at the same time increasing their turnover, their capacity and scope of action as well as their strategic power at local, national *and* international levels.

These transformations were carried out to implement highly adaptable means of production to respond rapidly to market fluctuations while reducing risks, social and financial, liability and costs to a minimum. The survey confirmed that there was a clear trend towards: 1) a drastic reduction of labour in larger firms previously involved in production; 2) restructuring through cascading subcontracting and other forms of direct/indirect control. This phenomenon was particularly strong in Britain during the Thatcher period.

The main reason given at the time for reducing the labour force within the larger firms was the prevailing economic crisis and recession. This interpretation was based upon the hypothesis that the firms were experiencing economic difficulties. However, apart from this phenomenon, the study revealed another: the drastic reduction of the labour force was not necessarily linked to recession but to strategic growth. It highlighted how economic recession and expansion can be combined; a process based on internal/external restructuring during a period of intense economic uncertainty. The analysis of subcontracting firms provided further information showing that it was not a mere reduction of the labour force but a wider restructuring of the production systems led by the double strategy of Minimising costs, risks and responsibilities and Maximising quality, efficiency, and profits, the two 'Ms' strategy.

In France, such drastic changes were not observed until later, although in both countries large firms were active in capturing small markets previously left to the smaller firms. Economic concentration followed a more traditional route particularly by means of take-overs. It is now clear that expansion through absorption was soon to be followed by internal/external restructuring into more autonomous units of production to penetrate local markets or to achieve specific targets or func-

---

[21] Appay, B. (1988).

tions. With a ten year difference economic restructuring in both countries finally followed a similar route in which economic concentration combined control with autonomy and concentration with atomisation.

Atomisation, subcontracting and expansion are part of a wider process of restructuring, in which strategic firms strive to be competitive at all levels whilst reducing risks and costs. It provides a different view to the post-fordist debate, in which the main track of lean production is presented as the desirable model to follow. In fact, the concept of lean production, exemplified by the 'Japanese model', hides a major structural tendency: the externalisation of labour.

'Employment for Life' is widely recognised as being one of the three major traits of the 'Japanese model'.[22] This well established link between the Japanese model and Employment for Life helps to *legitimise* the attraction exerted on other economies which are struggling with mass unemployment and where casual labour is developing rapidly. Industrial countries are pushing for an even greater casualisation of labour, in the name of a model which is claimed to be characterised by the famous 'Employment for Life'.

But in fact, the figures[23] show that the vast majority of the labour force is employed by subcontractors. Hypercompetition, strong hierarchies between subcontractors, precarious employment and sometimes poor working conditions are hidden behind the Japanese model. The main counterpart to job security offered by the 'best' companies is precarious work or bad employment status for others, women in particular. H. Hirata[24] highlighted the very deep gender division of labour from which the 'Japanese mode' suffers. Behind employment for life there is a high level of competition and division within the labour force which is socially accepted and start at school level. It also means strong demarcation lines between men and women, inequalities and exclusions.

The major traits of the Japanese model, such as employment for life, salary based on seniority and company unions, relate to the 'best' companies. This angle of analysis, which focuses on what is happening *within* the major firms, tends to give a distorted representation of restructuring and the way the labour process is changing. To develop a wider understanding it is necessary to broaden the scope of analysis within the firms themselves, large or small, and their relationships from local to global levels. With the intensification of world competition it becomes even more important to understand the dynamics of the 'rapports de force' between firms. The externalisation process can then be observed from different angles: the restructuring of major firms; the rising importance of small and medium-sized enterprises; employment ratios within SMEs and self-employment; or the emergence of mass unemployment. The analysis of cascading subcontracting provides an approach to understanding the relationships between these phenomena from the formal sector to the informal one, from 'best practices' to unemployment.

---

22 See Auer (1995). The other two major traits are: 1) salary based on seniority; 2) company unions.

23 Op.cit. p.445.

24 Hirata (1992).

The web and the pyramid

The increase in subcontracting in different industries and countries has been analysed in a recent CNRS-INSERM research programme.[25] Kurumi Sugita[26] focused on the system of cascading subcontracting which lies behind 'partnership' in Japan. As an example she studied a Japanese subcontractor producing up to 30% of the total number of television sets produced by a well known television brand. The inquiry was extended to the network of firms behind this supplier. The 'network' was made up of 15 independent medium sized and small firms which together employ up to 600 people. There are at least three subcontracting levels and clear lines of subordination between the firms; the lower the level in the subcontracting network, the poorer are the employment and working conditions. This hierarchical and precarious organisation of employment is far from being an exception in Japan; in fact it is so generally accepted that it is even not discussed. Although already criticised by some authors[27], this subject is, on the whole, rarely mentioned or even analysed. Cascading subcontracting is hidden behind the supplier who is the only one to have direct contact with the manufacturer. At the end of the subcontracting chain, the firms are all very small, each with only 10 to 30 employees.

Cascading subcontracting is a concept which puts the relationships between companies into perspective: their hierarchies and autonomy, their independence, co-operation and lines of subordination. It profoundly differs from 'outsourcing' which also refers to new forms of co-operation between the firms through subcontracting but which provides a horizontal perspective to their relations. 'Cascading subcontracting' is a three dimensional concept. As a metaphor one can visualise a combination of the web and of the pyramid structures. However, quite often only the tip is visible: the relationships between the main contractor and the first tier of subcontractors. Cascading subcontracting is based on one major rule and principle: the externalisation of financial, social and environmental risks and costs as well as their related responsibilities. However, it is not simply the result of reducing costs, risks and liability but of the logics of the two 'Ms'. It explains how control and autonomy are interrelated, how partner–ship, cooperation and subordination are combined in shaping new forms of social relations.

Other case studies[28] show that the same phenomenon has expanded rapidly elsewhere in the last decade. The automobile industry used to concentrate large units of production in which trade-unions developed their strength. In France, and

---

25 Appay and Thébaud-Mony (eds) (1995).

26 Op.cit. p.62.

27 In this more critical perspective, see in particular Hénoret (1993); see as well Altmann (1995). As pointed out by N. Altmann, only recently is massive criticism emerging, under the pressure of increasingly intensive forms of work, decreasing corporate profits and trade conflicts, in particular within the Japanese Automobile Workers' Union.

28 In particular, for example, in the French nuclear industry, in which cascading subcontrating has rapidly expanded in the maintenance sector over the last few years. See, Lallier (1995); Doniol-Shaw (1995); STED (1995).

again referring to the 'Japanese model', subcontracting has been mainly interpreted in terms of partnership.[29] However, A. Gorgeu et R. Mathieu moved away from this type of interpretation when confronted with the recent reorganisation of labour among the suppliers to the Renault and PSA plants.[30] Their study concerns new factories built by the suppliers close to the main assembly plants, to take over the activities previously carried out in the manufacturer's own plants. Between 1988 and 1994, 34 factories were created as a direct result of this externalisation process. The new plants are totally independent, but are dedicated to the manufacturer's assembly plant and work to Just In Time delivery obligations. If they fail to meet the required objectives (e.g. delays in delivery or the supply of faulty products), future co-operation is reviewed with the risk of their being downgraded on the suppliers' list. This reorganisation of work follows the basic principles of controlled autonomy. For the subcontractors room for manoeuvre is very limited but responsibilities are great in the sense that, if they fail to meet the objectives, their future is at stake. Within these new plants, workers are recruited from the local labour-market. It is a younger workforce with no trade-union tradition. The number of full-time workers is reduced to a minimum, topped-up by part-timers and temporary workers as and when required. Unions are rarely represented.

Here one can very clearly see a major difference between Before and After the restructuring process: the unions have disappeared.

Economic concentration and atomisation: The roots of a new paradox

A major consequence of the externalisation process is a shift of employment towards smaller firms. An analysis of national statistics shows that the number of small firms has increased whilst the number of large firms has decreased. The rise of smallness means that now, in France for example, more than half of the total labour force is working within these small firms whilst in the eighties nearly two thirds of the total employment was provided by large firms. The small firms' dominant trait is a high level of adaptability in order to survive. They also have an important characteristic: when they disappear they disappear quietly and quickly with no social conflicts or front page news.

The atomisation process represents the rise of a far more precarious system of employment. It is the result of the externalisation of social risks and responsibilities towards more flexible and unstable structures down to the individuals themselves. I would like to illustrate how autonomy and external control, indirect or direct, interrelate within production itself and how this is becoming one of the major principles of the new socio-technical system which is emerging.

In the changing organisational forms, the large and the small refer now to different company structures. For example the core firms, which have developed a

29 See in particular Lecler (1993).

30 Gorgeu and Mathieu (1995).

particular expertise together with *lean, fit and flexible* (LFF) structures can be small, but they can also be very large in terms of:

- the scope of their strategic power;
- their power to control and organise the productive network with or without direct involvement;
- and their influence at local and global levels.

This represents a major shift in the history of economic concentration which used to be defined by two major indicators: labour concentration and economic turnover. Small firms have been regarded as a declining form in the process of expansion and concentration into large units of production. Economic concentration has been considered as a dominant trend for industrial societies and assimilated with labour concentration in relation to mass production and the rationalisation of production. The core firm example shows how concentration and deconcentration are not opposing trends but are perhaps the two sides of the same process. In this context, atomisation does not mean the end of economic concentration, it progresses along other lines such as turnover, market shares, financial strength and strategic power. The concept of controlled autonomy[31] has been created to put this double and paradoxical tendency into perspective. In this perspective, strategic concentration highlights emerging structures in which concentration and atomisation are strategically organised. This applies to the core firms as they develop their capacity to introduce and organise flexible forms of production, stimulated and controlled from a distance.

Contemporary analyses should explore these two interrelated tendencies of concentration and atomisation. Instead, the analyses either demonstrate the acceleration of economic concentration in terms of strategic and financial power or they focus on deconcentration. In the latter case they tend to emphasise the move towards autonomy and local responsibility, the development of networks, cooperation and partnership, a new role for smallness in a more democratic world. These lines of interpretation overlook a major trend, that of an emerging world where these two tendencies are deeply interrelated in terms of power, domination and precariousness, autonomy and innovation... Compared with the MIT views[32] in the search for emerging patterns of industrial practices, this analysis is less optimistic. It interprets the consequences of such dominant trends in terms of greater social precarisation, which means the rise of precariousness within the organisation of work in relation to the undermining of social welfare systems, and the rise of hypercompetition sustained now by national and international policies considered world-wide as legitimate and justified.

---

31 Appay (1994).

32 See Piore and Sabel (1990), *The Second Industrial Divide*, Basic Books, 1984; Dertouzos, Lester and Solow (1989) and Womack, Jones and Roos (1990).

References

Altersohn, C. (1992), *De la sous-traitance au partenariat industriel*, Paris: L'Harmattan.

Altmann, N. (1995), 'Japanese Work Policy: Opportunity, Challange or Threat', in Sandberg (ed), pp.329-365.

Appay, B. (1988), 'Quelle main d'œvre pour demain? Une étude comparative France/Grande Bretagne', *Revue Française de Sociologie*, Vol. 29:81-115.

Appay, B. (1994), 'Concentration and atomisation of productive systems: the paradox of controlled autonomy', Paper presented at XIIIth World Congress of Sociology, Bielefeld.

Appay, B. and Thébaud-Mony, A. (eds) (1995), *L'organisation du travail, ses processus d'exclusion et ses effets sur la santé*, Paris: IRESCO.

Auer, P. (1995), 'Lean Production. The Micro-macro Dimension, Employment and the Welfare State', in Sandberg (ed), pp.437-459.

Boissonat, J. (1995), *Le travail dans 20 ans*. Paris: La Documentation Française.

Boyer, R. (1987), *La flexibilité du travail en Europe*, Paris: La découverte.

Coriat, B. and Taddéi, D. (1993), *Entreprise France made in France*, Paris: Librairie Générale Française.

Dertouzos, M.L., Lester, R.K. and Solow, R.M. (1989), *Made in America. Regaining the Productive Edge*, Boston: MIT Press.

Doniol-Shaw, G. (1995), *Sûreté et organisation de travail en centre nucléaire*. Chinon: CGT-CNPE.

EC (1994), *European Community White Paper – Croissance, compétitivité, emploi*, Bruxelles: EC.

Gorgeu, A. and Mathieu, R. (1995), 'Relations de sous-traitance et organisation du travail: le cas des équipmentiers automobiles en France', in Appay, B. and Thébaud-Mony, A. (eds) (1995).

Hénoret, A.L. (1993), *Le clou qui dépasse. Récit du Japon d'en bas*, Paris: La d'ecouverte.

Hirata, H.S. (1992), *Autour du "modèle" japonais, automatisation, nouvelles formes d'organisations et de relations de travail*, Paris: L'Harmattan.

Hirata, H.S. and Senotier, D. (eds) (1996), *Les femmes et le partage du travail*, Paris: Syros.

IRESCO (1995), *Action scientifique-fédérative. La travail et la santé comme révélateurs des processus de précarisation sociale*, Paris: IRESCO.

Kern, H. and Schumann, M. (1984), *Das Ende der Arbeitsteilung?*, München: C.H. Beck.

Lallier, M. (1995), *Sous-traitance. Le cas du nucléaire*, Chinon: CGT-CNPE.

Lecler, Y. (1993), in GERPISA *Trajectories of automobile firms*, Paris.

Minc, A. (1994), *La France de l'an 2000*. Paris: La Documentation Française.

OECD (1995a), *The Annual Report of the OECD 1994*, Paris: OECD.

OECD (1995b), *Job Studies: Facts, Analysis, Strategies*, Paris: OECD.

Piore, M.J. and Sabel, C.F. (1984), *The Second Industrial Divide*, New York: Basic Books.

Ramonet, I. (1995), 'La pensée unique.' *Le Monde diplomatique*, January.
Sandberg, Å. (ed) (1995), *Enriching Production. Perspectives on Volvo's Uddevalla Plant as an Alternative to Lean Production,* Aldershot: Avebury.
Sugita, K. (1995), 'Cascades de sous-traitants au Japon', in Appay and Thébaud-Many (eds), pp.61-77.
Womak, J.P., Jones, D.T. and Roos, D. (1990), *The Machine that Changed the World*, New York: Ranson.
World Bank (1995), *Workers in an Integrating World. World Bank Development Report 1995*, New York: Oxford University Press.

17 General qualification as a societal and an individual need

Knud Illeris

During the last 20 years the development of adult education in western capitalist countries has been dominated by continuous expansion and an ever-increasing emphasis on the importance of the so-called general or soft qualifications. These types of qualification are seen not only as a crucial parameter for competition on the labour market, but also as individual necessities for the management of daily life in modern society, which is complex and rapidly changing.

However, it has never been quite clear what is actually meant by 'general' or 'soft' qualifications or how to develop or support such qualifications in (adult) education or what sort of behaviour and qualification this requires on the part of teachers.

These were the three key questions behind the 'General Qualification Project', a three-year research project initiated in 1992 by the Adult Education Research Group at Roskilde University. The project involved six (part-time) researchers with different professional backgrounds, and was financed by the Ministry of Labour, the Labour Market Authority, the Danish Research Academy, and Roskilde University.

The construction of the project was unique in at least two ways.

Firstly, it is quite unusual for commissioned research projects to be basic research. Very briefly, the whole discussion about commissioned research at universities concerns clients buying the utility value of the universities' competence without contributing to the basic research that is the necessary precondition. However, in this case the clients considered that it would be in their interest to contribute to establishing a basic understanding of the area.

Secondly, the construction implies that before and during the project, the researchers conducted practical development work in Danish adult vocational training. This has ensured concrete, intimate knowledge of, and interaction with, the area of practice to which it is primarily related. While this naturally was of decisive importance to the clients in connection with the first point, in my opinion it has also served to enhance the basic research perspective.

I shall here try to sum up some of the most important results of the project and some of the understanding we have achieved on the basis of the three key questions mentioned above.

What is general qualification?

As to the first question, about the meaning of 'general' or 'soft' qualification; it sounds rather simple and easy to give a precise definition of this with some elaborations and explanations. However, the lion's share of the project time was spent in clarifying this concept and the basic understanding of the nature of general qualification, even though one theoretically-oriented and five practice-oriented sub-projects have been implemented within the framework of the project.

In fact there already exist a great number of partly contradictory and mutually competing understandings of what general qualification is. Therefore reasonably goal-oriented practice presupposes clarification that goes beyond these immediate understandings and offers a point of departure common to different fields of practice.

After some introductory explorations we started by reviewing the most important (German and Danish in particular) contributions to qualification theory, the development in the understanding and design of qualification analyses and existing qualification models. In this way we gradually reached a central theme in the development which later became essential to our understanding.

With regard to theories, analyses and models we observed how the earlier contributions regarded qualifications as having an objective existence that could be isolated, defined and categorised as a basis for an attempt to describe exactly the qualification content of various jobs and education programmes for individuals and groups. It could also be seen how, on the basis of the acknowledgement of the insufficiency of these approaches, the theories and models have increasingly respected the fact that qualifications simultaneously have a subjective character, i.e. that they are linked to living human beings and cannot be fully understood without this link to the individual's life course, actual situation, ideas about the future, experience, attitudes, interests, patterns of action, preferences, aversions, inhibitions and the like.

Parallel with this development in understanding, the objective qualification demand in companies and in society has shifted from more specific qualifications towards more general areas of understanding, attitudes and personality. Moreover, the two developments are obviously connected because as personality-oriented qualification demands manifest themselves, the subjective factor is increasingly more directly involved.

The unavoidable conclusion – which may be the most central result of the General Qualification Project – is that *qualifications must be understood in their duality between the objective demands that determine them and the subjective embedding that constitutes their conditions of existence.*

However, when this double perspective is applied to the concept of *general qualification*, a further complication arises: what is general differs according to whether one is working with the objective or the subjective side of qualification.

When qualification demands are viewed objectively, general qualifications are those that apply in many contexts: for instance being able to read, write and do arithmetic; being able to use broadly applicable implements and machines such as knives, forks, bicycles, cars or PCs; knowing and understanding a great number of general conditions at work and in the community, being independent, flexible, responsible, creative, good at cooperating and the like.

But seen subjectively, from the point of view of the individual person, the general is the personal touch, the way one is and becomes involved in things, one's interest in and perspective of understanding, one's conscious and unconscious goals and urges, the potential for life scope and resistance which individuals have developed on the basis of their conditions of existence and experience and which enter into every single qualification from the most concrete to the most abstract as a personal fingerprint.

If general qualification is to have any significance as a practical concept which can be used in, for example, educational planning, we must insist on this whole complicated duality. If not, we will merely prolong misunderstandings and impair communication with the ensuing lack of confidence and the inappropriateness which has characterised both the discussions and practice that have developed in the name of qualification.

So, in fact, one implication of the General Qualification Project might be that the concept of general qualification when fully elaborated is so complicated and unwieldy that its appropriateness as a practical concept for guiding action is questionable.

At the same time, it is crucial to insist that no qualifications can be developed or used, or even exist, independently of living human beings who will always set their imprint on them and associate their personal circumstances with them. For, irrespective of one's choice of words this implies that today an educational or vocational initiative cannot be imposed on the participants. The demand expressed in the concept of general qualification reflects the need for quality and flexibility in the processes that cannot be developed apart from the people who perform them. At the same time modern people are increasingly demanding such qualities of labour. Recent research in Germany and Denmark has indicated that the young generation tends to prefer unemployment if they cannot get jobs which can give them a subjectively reasonable degree of personal satisfaction (Baethge, 1990; Simonsen, 1994).

In continuation of this understanding we have developed a search model which is suited to maintaining the double subjective and objective perspective as the basis for understanding qualification processes as they take place in education programmes, at work and in other life contexts.

The model deals with 'subjectivity viewed in the perspective of qualification'. Thus in our construction the point of departure was taken in (materialistically based) theories of subjectivity to identify essential areas of subjectivity of importance in connection with qualification.

By subjectivity we understand here the individual's active, selecting interaction with the physical and societal environment. This interaction always takes place in one of two basically different areas. First there is the area of working life, the basic feature of which is the demand for increase in value. Second there is the rest of existence, which we call the field of social life, where the requirement for increase of value does not have this structuring function. The area of social life could also be further divided, for example, into a private sphere and a public sphere. However, we have not done this in order to avoid making the model too complicated. The most important thing is to distinguish between where the requirement for an increase in value has a structural force and where it does not.

On the other hand we have introduced a third, somewhat different, area: the personal. It is the case that in interaction with the environment there will always be something that is 'relevant to the case', relating to something that the interaction is dealing with. But to a greater or lesser degree there will also be something that affects the individual as a person. This may be a more or less profound, direct challenge to the person's identity, or is perhaps 'merely' an appeal to such personal qualities as responsibility, creativity or the like. For this reason, one might say somewhat schematically that even though we are only operating with two synchronic spaces for interaction, there are three spaces of experience in subjectivity. We have tried to illustrate this in the figure of 'The Tulip':

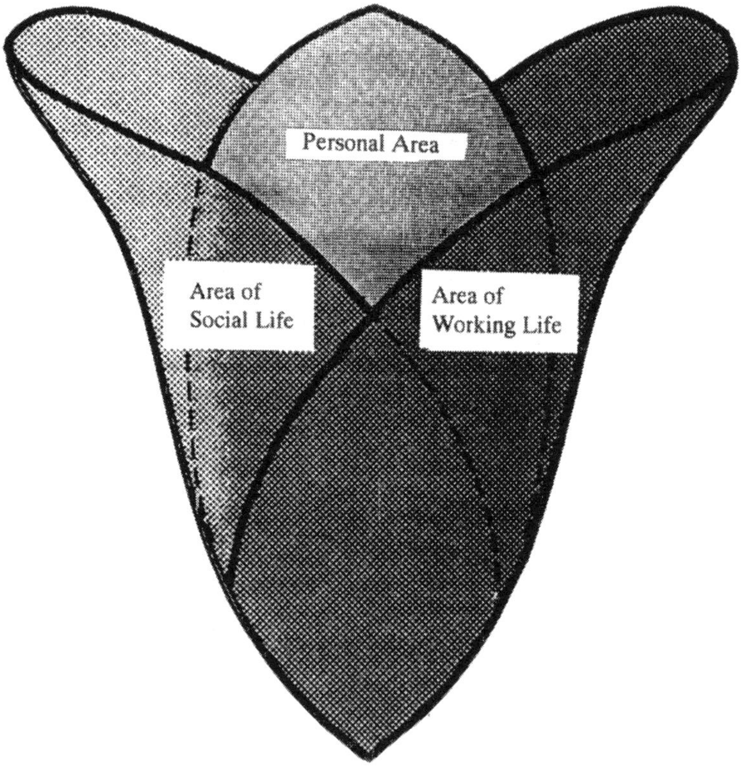

Subjectivity viewed in the perspective of qualification.
I: 'The Tulip'

The other dimension that is part of our search model has to do with different levels of subjectivity which in the personal area may be characterised as 'depths'. Whilst our personal identity is a profound part of us and does not change easily, a situation can make a more immediate appeal to, for instance, responsibility. Elsewhere the levels have more to do with specificity, learning processes and transferability: learning a certain technique or a word in a foreign language is something rather limited; learning to understand the principles of the periodic system in chemistry, although more complicated, is useful in many connections; making up your mind about foreign workers is complicated in quite a different manner that has to do with the basic societal attitudes of the individual.

As mentioned before, we work in the search model with three spaces of experience in subjectivity. In accordance with the considerations above, we have defined three levels for each of them: the basic, the comprehensive and the specific. In this way the search model has nine fields to which processes of qualification can be related and within which qualifications can be developed. The borders between the nine are not sharp and the criteria for delimitation are based on different kinds of dimension. The model is illustrated by the figure of 'The Map':

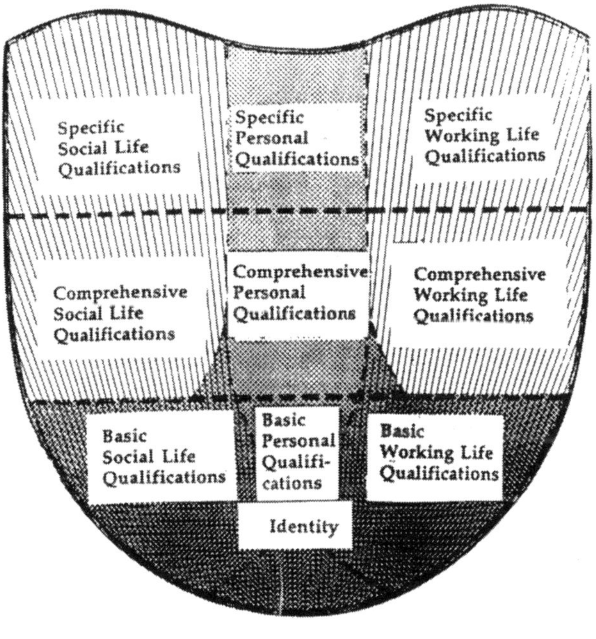

Subjectivity viewed in the perspective of qualification.
II. 'The Map'

The search model makes no attempt to postulate that subjectivity in fact looks like this: it should be understood far more pragmatically. In our opinion, it provides some appropriate classifications for understanding and discussing qualification processes – a model and some categories that show the great breadth, and some important contexts that maintain that qualifications are attributes not only of labour but also of living people. This should suggest how complex the problems are rather than providing the basis for quick solutions.

How can general qualification be taught?

The answer to the project's first question is too complex to lead directly into a consideration of how the process of general qualification can be organised. To advance at this level we must return to the objective basis in qualification demands, and rather than asking about the nature of general qualification, we must ask more directly about the content of the new demands that has caused the discussion about general qualification to flourish.

Our answer is by no means a definition of the content of general qualification; it is rather a description of the important features of present demands regarding general qualification. Against the background of the rest of the project work, we have summarised these central features of qualification as follows:

- *general skills in communication, abstraction and symbol analysis;*
- *an active, structural understanding of social and working conditions;*
- *personal engagement and agreement in identity in relation to relevant activities;*
- *active individual and collective potential for development and resistance.*

It goes without saying that this summary could have been formulated in many ways and that it must be understood as what we, on the basis of our work, currently perceive as the most important fields of content for general qualification which one must take into account at the practical level.

The decisive characteristic of all these fields is that they involve personality and identity quite differently from the mere isolated acquisition of knowledge and skills. This sets some conditions for the learning process that first and foremost have to do with *motivation.*

Of course, motivation also plays an important role in the acquisition of knowledge and skills; it is of importance for the speed, quality and possibility of using what is learned. But in matters of personality and identity, when learning also encompasses what we usually call personal development – active motivation, positive and personal commitment take on the character of a necessary condition. The lack of such commitment means that the mental potential for transcending the individual's former limitations and barriers simply does not exist. On the contrary, encouraging such development will usually cause defence reactions that contribute to cementing the barriers.

It is, however, important to understand here that active motivation is not just a matter of what one would immediately like to do. Not least one may also talk about adults' motivation of necessity, comprising material necessity, what individual adults may experience as morally or ideologically conditioned necessity, or a personal, psychologically conditioned inner necessity. The strongest motivation is probably found when it has the nature of personal objectives which usually consist of a mixture of elements linked to desire, necessity and personality that can be both conscious and unconscious in nature. (This appeared clearly in two subprojects dealing with analyses of participants and working places respectively.)

It is, however, implicit in these formulations that motivation is also linked to content, that one would like to achieve *something* different from and more than general personal development. And this something is very important in an educational context as it is this that turns the motivation into an educational motivation. If motivation only concerns general life scope and personal development, it can be used in all possible and varying activities and perhaps persuade in a more goal-oriented way through therapy and the like. But in the educational context, it is more directional and encompasses an element of content that one would like to cultivate or develop.

Thus general qualification educationally demands the presence of at least a minimum of motivation, related to the education in question, and the practice of the education must be able to activate this motivation.

On this basis, it is possible to list some central conditions that generally qualifying education programmes should meet.

In the first place, there must be some guidance or supervision in connection with admission to the programmes to ensure that participants realise what they want to get out of them. This requires quite radical innovative re-thinking of the types and general procedures of guidance and supervision offered to or imposed on applicants. To put it bluntly, it should be a matter of counselling people rather than guiding them towards an education. It should primarily have to do with clarifying the motivation of the individual, with the choice of education programme coming in second place.

Secondly, education programmes should give priority to and be designed to meet participants' needs before those of the current labour market. This kind of priority is also in accord with the recruitment and personnel policy of most modern enterprises, it being more important to attract motivated staff than people with a qualification profile that is absolutely right. If the motivation is there it is rarely a problem to provide the practical upgrading of qualifications or any re-training that might be necessary.

Thirdly, the framework and practice of the education programmes should be flexible enough for participants to feel they have some connection with their motivational starting point. This latter is a pedagogical goal that many adult education teachers strive to attain. However, it presupposes flexibility, i.e. that individual teachers have enough freedom to adapt content and method to the needs of the participants with many different types of educational motivation.

Fourthly, it is important that the environment at the places of education is such that the participants are able to experience them as a framework for and invitation to both professional and personal development. Our school culture sub-project has shown that all this is extremely important for general qualification and that there is a tendency in adult education in Denmark for the strong sides of the education programmes to dominate while their less strong sides are further weakened through the physical and mental environment of the places and their self-conception. For instance, the strength of adult vocational training programmes derives especially from their close association with and orientation towards the labour market, while participant orientation is weaker, being at best something that individual teachers establish.

On the more general level of educational planning this points towards a broad range of different adult-education programmes which would appeal to people with very different motivation and interests, even though they might be difficult to administer. It is also important to establish roughly equal conditions for the different types of adult education, for instance the financial basis, the conditions of appointment for the teachers and the situation of participants with regard to financial and other support. Equal status respecting the differences in the content of the study programmes would also ease cooperation between different programmes of adult vocational training, which is sorely needed at present.

At the practical pedagogical level the importance of the motivational factor must lead to a consideration of how participants' interests and preferences can be employed and how they can influence the educational activities. To support the impact of this important feature on the daily activity patterns we have developed another search model in the project:

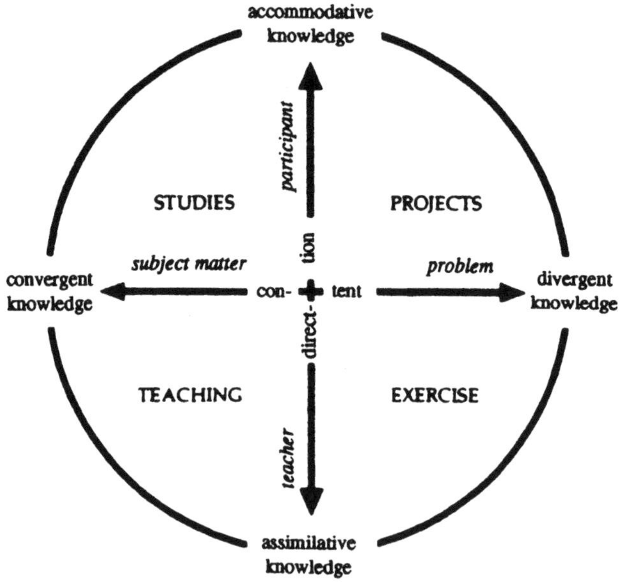

A didactic search model

The assumption behind this model is that the two basic didactic dimensions concern the choice of educational content and the direction of activity patterns. The content dimension extends from traditional subject-matter orientation to problem orientation, where practical and societal problems of relevance to the participants steer the choice of content. Similarly, the direction dimension extends from the traditional teacher direction to what we call the participant direction, indicating that process decisions are made by the participants with the teachers acting as consultants.

With reference to the model of experiential learning developed by the American psychologist David A. Kolb (1984), we assume that subject orientation favours the acquisition of convergent knowledge, whereas problem orientation favours divergent knowledge, the teacher direction favours assimilative knowledge, and the participant direction favours accommodative knowledge.

By crossing the two didactic dimensions in the same way as Kolb crosses the dimensions of learning, four main types of educational activities occur: *teaching* as dominated by teacher direction and subject orientation; *exercise* as dominated by teacher direction and problem orientation; *studies* as dominated by participant direction and subject orientation; and *projects* as dominated by participant direction and problem orientation.

As the motivation of the participants is directly engaged in participant direction and problem orientation, the model indicates that activity patterns other than teaching should be implemented in order to support the acquisition of divergent and accommodative learning processes, and thereby also the sort of personal development that is the core of general qualification.

Thus this search model implies that there are fundamentally different types of educational activity that support fundamentally different types of learning process and thereby also support the development of fundamentally different types of qualification. Depending on the educational aims in question, a corresponding balance of educational activities should be practised.

How should teachers be qualified?

The third area of the General Qualification project concerning teachers' qualifications has been partly dealt with above. In practice, teachers should, first and foremost, be able to create a connection between the content and activities of the education programmes and the motivation and qualifications of the participants.

This requires that the professional competence which teachers usually have is used as a decisive basis for their appointment. At the same time it requires that this competence is linked to an overview and flexibility that allows the individual teacher to approach the content of the teaching in as many ways as match the different participants' needs and prior qualifications.

And this brings us to the central point, namely that above and beyond professional competence, general qualification primarily makes demands on the teachers in the personal area, or to put it in another way, their own general qualifications.

Today an adult education teacher must be fully professionally qualified and, at the same time, not be bound by this professionalism; he/she must also be so personally confident as to be able to function as an intermediary between the individual participant and the educational goals, between the subjective and the objective sides of general qualification.

Although this is a stringent requirement, it can be met in so many ways that it is hard to define it more closely, let alone establish exact criteria for it. It can be said that it partly has to do with developing a teacher identity without losing one's professional identity, of making the two identities converge and converting them into a practice where, while becoming involved with one's participants, one is still able to keep the professional distance required to be able to do the job.

Perspectives for general qualification

It is my hope that the presentation above has shown how an inner necessity has led from the issue that started with new demands for qualifications on the labour market into a much broader and deeper relation concerning necessities in personal development in present-day society. It may also be understood in the following way, that the demand for general qualification is but one of many approaches to the individual's situation in relation to actual societal development.

It is a matter of what has been termed the service society, the information society, the post-modern era and much besides. In relation to earlier epochs, this society is characterised by the cultural liberation of the individual (Ziehe and Stubenrauch, 1982), a liberation from old norms and traditions, and simultaneously a liberation and a compulsion to choose personal norms, lifestyle, even identity, from among apparently endless possibilities and offers.

Common national culture and the sub-cultures of individual social groups – working-class, rural, upper middle class and petty-bourgeois – are becoming weaker and disappearing. Instead we are liberated individuals related to markets for labour, education, culture, consumption, partners and much else. We must constantly make choices because the old ties that regulated life no longer exist, and we always know that we can change our minds if our first choice no longer satisfies us or if we should like to do something else.

What manifests itself here as a demand for general qualifications, manifests itself in other areas of life as the understanding, overview, independence, and flexibility by which personal lives navigate through many situations of choice where anything seems to be possible but where, on examination, the actual choices are fewer than they seem.

When the education programmes are considered in a broader perspective, general qualification is about personal development, professional and human, in order to be able to manage in this post-modern market society. At the same time, this is increasingly a precondition for managing on the labour market and thus for supplying companies with the labour they need.

Thus the demand for qualification is, at least to some extent, identical with a demand for the development of whole, mature individuals who can manage their choices and their lives both at and outside work. It has become more difficult to establish the borderline between vocational and non-vocational orientation in education and in everyday life. Each of the two areas of life, however, is still basically structured by its own logic. In the final analysis, the vocationally oriented is about what can pay, and the non-vocationally oriented about what is needed. The more these two kinds of logic become intertwined, the more difficult it will be for the individual to administer the duality.

Reports

The General Qualification Project includes two reports in English (as well as a number of reports written in Danish):
Qualifications and living people, 1994.
General qualification, 1996.

The project reports are available from the Adult Education Group, Roskilde University, Box 260, DK-4000 Roskilde. Phone: +46 75 77 11, ext. 2708. Fax: +46 75 40 26.

Other references

Baethge, M. (1990), 'Arbeit und Identität bei Jugendlichen', *Psychosozial*, 43.
David A. and Kolb, D.A. (1984), *Experiential Learning*, Englewood Cliffs: Prentice-Hall.
Simonsen, B. (1994), 'Young People and their Relation to the Labour Market', in *Adult Education and the Labour Market*, Ljubljana: Slovene Adult Education Centre.
Ziehe, T. and Stubenrauch, H. (1982), *Plädoyer für ungewöhnliches Lernen*, Hamburg: Rowohlt.

Notes on the contributors

Sheila Allen
is Professor of Sociology at the University of Bradford, where she is also Adviser on Equal Opportunities. Her research on work has over several years been particularly related to gender and ethnicity. She is currently writing a book for Oxford University Press on Feminist Contributions to Sociology.

Béatrice Appay
is chargé de recherche at CNRS, Centre National de la Recherche Scientifique, Paris. She holds a doctorate in sociology and has carried out extensive international comparative research on contemporary changes in the labour process, both in France and the U.K. Her latest co-edited book 'La précarisation sociale, travail et santé' is the result of a CNRS-INSERM research programme on economic restructuring and its social consequences.

Ulla Björnberg
is Professor at the Department of Sociology, Göteborg University. At present she is leading a research programme on the theoretical and methodological development of gender and family sociology. Ulla Björnberg has been engaged in several international projects on family policy, on reconciliation of employment and family life and on single mothers, in Eastern and Western Europe. Member of the European Observatory on national family policies.

Johanna Esseveld
is employed at the Department of Sociology, Lund University. She has written a number of articles and a book on women's unemployment and is currently leading two research projects: one on women's participation and leadership in Swedish unions and another on political and economic leadership. The latter project is part of a large international, comparative study. Among her recent publications are Kvinnopolitiska Nyckeltexter (1996) and "Objectivity and Truth: Problems in Feminist Research" (1996).

Knut Halvorsen
is Professor in social policy at the Faculty of Economics, Local Public Administration and Social Work at Oslo College. He has a Bachelor's Degree in Business Administration and a Master's Degree in Sociology. He is currently Head of the Research Unit at the Faculty. He has written several books on unemployment and marginalization and on the interplay between the labour market and social policy.

Jan Holmer
is Professor at the Department of Working Life Science, University of Karlstad. He has studied changes in working life, their significance for various groups of employees and the conditions for the active participation of employees in the

process of change. His particular interest is in education as a means of support in ongoing change and learning processes. He has published textbooks on qualification and on participation-oriented research.

Knud Illeris
is Professor of educational research with special attention to adult and vocal education at Roskilde University. Research and developmental work in project education, experiential learning, and learning and motivational psychology.

Jan Ch. Karlsson
is Professor at the Department of Working Life Science, University of Karlstad. He has written extensively in the field of work, for example on the concept of work, the position of work in everyday life, and the development and consequences of modern work organisation.

Gunnar Adler-Karlsson
has DrL and PhD in economics; prof. V.I; author of some fifteen books on economic warfare, evolution of social systems, and work (mainly on how to get rid of wage slavery). In 1974-1987 he was Professor of international economics, Roskilde, Denmark. Since 1979 director of the Capri Institute for International Social Philosophy.

Anna-Karin Kollind
is researcher and lecturer at the Department of Sociology, Göteborg University. She wrote her doctoral thesis on Freud's early works, and has studied stepfamilies and the history of family counselling in Sweden. At present, she is conducting a study on transactions of time and money within families.

Kathleen Lynch
is a founder member of the Equality Studies Centre in University College Dublin. The Centre undertakes research and teaching (both graduate and outreach non-graduate) on all types of equality issues, including poverty and economic inequality, development issues, women's issues, and minorities. Kathleen is a sociologist whose principal research interests are in equality issues generally, and education.

Ray E. Pahl
is graduated from the University of Cambridge and the London School of Economics. He is Emeritus Professor of Sociology at the University of Kent at Canterbury and Visiting Professor at the ESRC Research Centre on Micro-Social Change at the University of Essex. His research interests focus on work, family, households and community. Among his many publications are "Divisions of Labour", "On Work" and, most recently, "After Success" (Polity Press).

Andrew Sayer
is Professor at the Department of Sociology, Lancaster University, UK. First degree in Geography, moved subsequently into urban and regional studies and then into "postdisciplinary studies", working mainly on industry and uneven development, philosophy and methodology of the social sciences, and more recently, political economy and social theory.

Manfred E.A. Schmutzer
is Head of the Institute of Technology and Society at the Technical University, Vienna. He has a degree in Mechanical Engineering from that university and a PhD from the School of Social Science, University of Essex, UK. He is also the founder and editor of the journal Technik Kontrovers. His most recent book: Ingenium and Individuum. Eine sozialwissenschaftliche Theorie von Wissenschaft und Technik (Springer).

Adrian Sinfield
is Professor Emeritus of Social Policy at the University of Edinburgh. He has carried out primary and secondary research into the social impact of unemployment in the United Kingdom and the United States and has acted as adviser to government and independent studies of unemployment. In 1981 he was co-founder of the Unemployment Unit, a research and intelligence organisation, which he chaired for its first ten years.

Elisabeth Sundin
has a PhD in Business Administration from Umeå University. She is now Assistant Professor at the Department of Technology and Social Change, Linköping University, Sweden. Her main research interest is the connection between gender-technology-organisation-economy. Among her recent works are "Teknik och organisation i teori och praktik" (Technology and organization in theory and practice). (Nerenius & Santérus), and "The Social Construction of Gender and Technology" in The European Journal of Women's Studies, Vol. 2, No. 3, August 1995.

Stephen Toulmin
is Henry R. Luce Professor at the University of Southern California. He has written on the methods of the sciences ever since the 1950s, most recently on "practical reason" in medicine and elsewhere. He also works with Swedish colleagues on Participatory Action Research.

Celia Valiente
is Associate Professor (Profesora Asociada) of Sociology at the Autonomous University of Madrid. Her major area of research is comparative public policy with an analytical focus on gender. She received an undergraduate degree in history and a PhD in Sociology from the Autonomous University of Madrid, Spain, and a M.A. in Social Science at the Instituto Juan March de Estudios e Investigaciones, Madrid. She wrote a doctoral dissertation titled "Public Policies for Women Workers in Italy and Spain, 1900-1991" (in Spanish), under the supervision of Juan J. Linz.

Louise Waldén,
has a PhD and is senior lecturer in cultural studies at the University College Gävle-Sandviken. Her research field is cultural studies including gender, technology, voluntary adult education (i.e. study circles) in cultural fields (i.e. handicraft).